ARCHITECTURE EXAM REVIEW

BALLAST'S GUIDE TO THE A.R.E.

VOLUME I: STRUCTURAL TOPICS

THIRD EDITION

David Kent Ballast, A.I.A.

PROFESSIONAL PUBLICATIONS, INC.
Belmont, CA 94002

Architecture Exam Review
Ballast's Guide to the A.R.E.

Volume 1: Structural Topics
Third Edition

Printed in the United States of America

ISBN: 0-912045-44-2

Professional Publications, Inc.
1250 Fifth Avenue, Belmont, CA 94002
(415) 593-9119

Current printing of this edition: 3

Revised and reprinted in 1995.

TABLE OF CONTENTS

16 LONG SPAN STRUCTURES—TWO-WAY SYSTEMS

17 SOLUTIONS

BIBLIOGRAPHY

INDEX

LIST OF ILLUSTRATIONS

PROFESSIONAL PUBLICATIONS, INC. ● Belmont, CA

LIST OF TABLES

INTRODUCTION

1 THE ARCHITECT REGISTRATION EXAMINATION

The Architect Registration Examination is a uniform test given nationwide to candidates who wish to become licensed architects after they have served their required internship. Although the responsibility of professional licensing rests with each individual state, member boards of each state subscribe to the examination prepared by the National Council of Architectural Registration Boards (NCARB). One of the primary reasons for a uniform test is to facilitate reciprocity; that is, to enable an architect to more easily gain a license to practice in states other than the one he or she was originally licensed in.

The A.R.E. is prepared by committees of the NCARB with the assistance of Educational Testing Service (ETS). ETS helps with production, distribution, and scoring, as well as serving as a consultant for testing the format and writing of questions.

The examination is given in each state at the same time and graded uniformly. All parts except the site and building design divisions are machine-graded. The two design divisions are graded by trained jurors meeting shortly after the test. Although the design grading is somewhat subjective, the jurors follow uniform guidelines, assisted by master jurors, who offer guidance, maintain uniformity, and resolve borderline cases.

In the last several years, the California board has administered its own test. However, beginning in 1990 California will return to the use of the A.R.E., administering a supplemental examination to address the state's special concerns.

The A.R.E. has been developed to protect the health, safety, and welfare of the public by testing a candidate's entry-level competence to practice architecture. Its content relates as closely as possible to the situations encountered in practice. It tests for the kinds of knowledge, skills, and abilities required of an architect, with particular emphasis on those services that affect public health, safety, and welfare. In order to accomplish these objectives, the exam tests for (1) knowledge in specific subject areas, (2) the ability to make decisions, (3) the ability to consolidate and use information to solve a problem, and (4) the ability to coordinate the activities of others on the building team.

The examination is continually evolving. Currently, for example, the NCARB is developing and testing a computer-adaptive exam. The use of computers will allow the exam to be given more frequently, speed up reporting of grades, and improve reliability. One interesting feature of a computer-based exam is that it will allow ability and knowledge to be demonstrated progressively as the test is taken. The answer to one question will affect the difficulty of the next so that a more competent candidate will answer fewer difficult questions and probably finish earlier.

2 EXAMINATION FORMAT

The examination as it currently stands consists of nine divisions given over a period of four days. The divisions and their durations are as follows:

Division	
A: Pre-Design	3 hours
B: Site Design	$3\frac{1}{2}$ hours
C: Building Design	12 hours
D: Structural, General	$2\frac{1}{2}$ hours
E: Structural, Lateral Forces	$1\frac{1}{2}$ hours
F: Structural, Long Span	$1\frac{1}{2}$ hours
G: Mechanical/Plumbing/Electrical	$2\frac{1}{2}$ hours
H: Materials and Methods	$2\frac{1}{2}$ hours
I: Construction Documents and Services	$3\frac{1}{2}$ hours

The divisions are administered as follows:

> Day 1: Divisions D, E, F, and G
> Day 2: Divisions H and I
> Day 3: Divisions A and B
> Day 4: Division C

The exact format of the examination may be changed slightly from year to year, but a candidate still needs to have the basic knowledge and skills required to practice architecture. This book provides the essential outline of the subject matter the candidate should know in preparing for the test, whatever its format may be.

3   TYPES OF QUESTIONS ASKED

In previous exams, there has been a single building on which many of the questions in all divisions have been based. Samples of the building's construction drawings, specifications, and other data have been given in the test information package to help simulate an actual practice situation. Many questions are based on the information given about this sample building. Other questions are based on memory of facts and general knowledge of the subject matter. Other questions test the application of facts and general knowledge to specific situations given in the test.

The A.R.E. uses four types of questions and variations of each of these types. In all except the graphic presentation of the site planning and building design divisions, the form of the answer is multiple choice so the test can be machine-graded.

The first type of question is multiple choice. The candidate is asked to select from four possible answers to a problem that may be based on written, graphic, or photographic material. The problem may require that you perform a calculation to respond correctly, but in the simplest form, a multiple choice question simply gives four choices following the question.

In other multiple choice questions, there may be a list of five choices or statements following the initial written or graphic information, and the four possible answers will be various combination of the five statements. For example, from the five statements you may be asked to decide which ones are correct or which ones are incorrect. In some of these question types, you may be asked to select the answer that correctly ranks the five statements in some order. Others ask that you match words or phrases from two lists, selecting the answer that provides the proper match.

The second type of question is written identification. This uses a key list of words or phrases around which several questions are based. Written identification questions may simply be definition type questions, or they may use written or graphic evidence in presenting a problem. You are asked to look at a diagram or read about a situation and then use the list to select your answer. The list may contain two or more responses that are very similar or seem to be correct, but only one may be selected.

In the third type of question, a written simulation is presented, which is intended to put you in a situation that you might encounter in practice. The written part may be accompanied with drawings, tables, diagrams, forms, or photographs to supplement the question. The simulation is followed by a series of options—single words, phrases, or statements—from which you must select the best one in the context of the given situation.

The fourth type of question is the graphic presentation in which you are required to create a drawing or series of drawings to complete the problem. These are used for the 12-hour building design problem and the $3\frac{1}{2}$-hour site design problem.

Even though the first three types of questions are structured to allow for multiple choice, for machine grading, they often require that you do much more than simply select an answer from your memory. You must, for example, combine several facts, review data given in the test information package, perform a calculation, or review a drawing.

For the structural portions of the exam, extensive, complete calculations of a structural problem are usually not required. The time allowed for the structural portions simply does not allow for it. Instead, you should expect to do portions of a calculation in order to answer a question. In some cases, two or more questions may carry an example through several calculations related to the same situation. Other structural questions focus on your knowledge of structural concepts rather than straight calculations.

4   STUDY GUIDELINES

Your method of studying for the A.R.E. should be based both on the content and form of the exam, as well as your school and work experience. Because the exam covers such a broad range of subject matter, it cannot possibly include every detail of practice. Rather, it tends to focus on what is considered "entry-level" knowledge and knowledge that is important for the protection of public health, safety, and welfare. This is not to say that other types of questions are not asked, but it should help you direct your review.

Your recent work experience should also help you determine what areas to study the most. If you have been involved with construction documents for several years, you will probably require less work in that area than in others with which you have not had recent experience.

This review manual was prepared to help you focus on those topics that will most likely be included in the exam in one form or another. As you go through the manual, you will probably find some subjects familiar or that come back to you quickly. Others may seem like a completely foreign subject. These are the ones to give particular attention to when using this manual. You may even want to study additional sources on these subjects, take review seminars, or get special help from someone who knows the topic.

The following steps provide a useful structure for organizing your study for the examination.

step 1: Start early. You cannot review for a test like this by starting two weeks before the date. This is especially true if you are taking all portions of the exam for the first time.

step 2: Go through the review manuals quickly to get a feeling for the scope of the subject matter. Although this manual and the companion manual on the non-structural portions of the exam have been prepared based on the content covered, you may want to review the detailed list of tasks and considerations given in the NCARB study guides.

step 3: Based on this review and a realistic appraisal of your strong and weak areas, set priorities for your study. Determine what topics you need to spend more time with than others.

step 4: Divide the subjects you will review into manageable units and organize them into a sequence of study. Generally, you should start with those subjects least familiar to you. Based on the date of the examination and when you are starting to study, assign a time limit to each of the study units you identify. Again, your knowledge of a subject should determine the time importance you give it. For example, you may want to devote an entire week to earthquake design if you are unfamiliar with that and only one day to timber design if you know that well. In setting up a schedule, be realistic about other commitments in your life as well as your ability to concentrate on studying for a given amount of time.

step 5: Begin studying and stick with your schedule. This, of course, is the most difficult part of the process and the one that requires the

most self-discipline. The job should be easier if you have started early and set up a realistic schedule, allowing time for recreation and other personal commitments.

step 6: Stop studying a day or two before the exam to relax. If you do not know the material by this time, no amount of cramming will help.

Here are some additional tips:

Know concepts first, then learn the details. For example, it is much better to understand the basic ideas and theories of waterproofing than it is to attempt to memorize dozens of waterproofing products and details. Once you fully understand the concept, the details and application are much easier to learn and to apply during the exam.

Do not overstudy any one portion. You are generally better off reviewing the concepts of all the divisions of the test than becoming an overnight expert in one area. For example, the test may ask general questions about plate girders, but it will not ask that you perform a complete, detailed design of one.

Try to talk with people who took the test the year before. Although the exam questions change yearly, it is a good idea to get a general feeling for the types of questions asked, the general emphasis, and areas that previous candidates found particularly troublesome.

For the structural divisions of the exam, it is difficult to say precisely which formulas and constants should be committed to memory. Since no references are allowed, most of the factual data needed to solve the problems are given. This includes items like tables, complex formulas, etc.

The intent of the exam is more to test your ability to properly select what you need to solve a problem and correctly apply it than it is to test your powers of memorization. Because of this, you should be familiar with how to use the various tables found in the *Manual of Steel Construction*, open-web joist tables, structural wood tables, tables included in the UBC, and similar resources.

5   WHAT TO BRING TO THE EXAM

Reference materials are not allowed in the test, but there are some necessary "survival items" that you will need or that will make things a little easier. A partial list for the structural divisions includes:

- calculator
- extra batteries for calculator
- no. 2 pencils and paper

- pencil sharpener or lead pointer

- highlighter markers

- eraser

- watch

- tissue

- aspirin

- snacks

6 TIPS ON TAKING THE EXAMINATION

Even if you are completely familiar with the subject matter, taking the A.R.E. can be an arduous process simply because of its length and the concentration required to get through it. As with any activity requiring endurance, you should be rested when you start the exam. You should have stopped studying a day or two before the first test day in order to relax as much as possible. Get plenty of sleep the night before and every night between test days.

Allow yourself plenty of time to get to the exam site so you do not have to worry about getting lost, stuck in traffic jams or other transportation problems. An early arrival at the exam room also lets you select a seat with good lighting and as far away from distractions as possible. Once in the room, arrange your working materials and other supplies so you are ready to begin as soon as you are allowed.

The proctor will review the test instructions as well as general rules about breaks, smoking, and other "house-keeping" matters. You can ask any questions about the rules at this time.

Once the test begins, you should quickly review the material given to you in the information packet. For the structural divisions of the test, this will include such things as beam formulas, steel tables, excerpts from the building code, and similar items. You do not need to study this material. Simply make a mental or written note about what is included so you know it is available when a question requires that you use it.

Next, check the number of questions and set up a schedule for yourself. If you plan on tackling the questions one by one in sequence, you should have completed about half the questions when half of your allotted time is up. In your scheduling, leave some time at the end of the period to double-check some of the answers you are most unsure of and to see that you have not marked two responses for any question.

Finally, you are ready to start. For the multiple choice questions, there are two general ways to proceed. You should select the one you feel most comfortable with.

With the first approach, proceed from the first question to the last, trying to answer each one regardless of its difficulty. Divide the time allotted by the number of questions to give yourself an average time per question. Of course, some will take less than the average, some more. If you are not able to confidently answer a question in your allotted time or a little more, make a note of it and move on to the next one. If you have time at the end, you can go back to the most difficult questions.

With the second approach, go through the test three times. During the first pass, read each question and answer the ones you are sure of and that do not take any lengthy calculations or study of the information packet. Since you will be jumping around, always make sure you are marking the correct answer space. If a question does not fit into the "easy-to-answer" category, make a mark next to it indicating whether you can answer it with a little thinking or easy calculation or whether it seems impossible and may be a best-guess type of response.

During the second pass, answer the next easiest questions. These should be the ones that you can confidently respond to after some deductive reasoning or with a calculation with which you are familiar. Once again, make sure you are marking the correct numbered spaces on the answer sheet.

During the third pass, answer the questions that remain and that require extra effort or those for which you have to make the best guess between two of the most likely answers. In some cases, you may be making your best guess from among all four options.

Using the three-pass method allows you to get a feeling for the difficulty of the test during the first pass and helps you budget the remaining time for the unanswered questions. One of the tricks to making this method work is to not go back to reread or reanswer any completed question. In most cases, your first response (or guess) is the best response. No matter which approach you use, answer every question, even if it is a wild guess.

Here are some additional tips:

Make a notation of the answers you are most unsure of. If you have time at the end of the test, go back and recheck these if you really think it may help. Remember, your first response is usually the best.

Many times, one or two choices can be easily eliminated. This may still leave you with a guess, but at least your chances are better between two choices than among four.

Some questions may appear too simple. While a few very easy and obvious questions are included, more often the simplicity should alert you to rethink all aspects of the question to make sure you are not forgetting some exception to a rule or special circumstance that would make the obvious response an incorrect one.

Watch out for absolute words in a question like "always," "never," or "completely." These often indicate some little exception that can turn a seemingly true statement into a false statement or vice versa.

Be on the alert for words like "seldom," "usually," "best," or "most reasonable." These indicate that some judgment will be involved in answering the question, so look for two or more options that may be very similar.

Occasionally, there may be a defective question. This does not happen very often, but if you think you found one, make the best choice you can. The question is usually discovered, and either it is not counted in the test or credit is given for any one of the answers.

As a final thought: try to relax as much as possible during your study for the test and during the examination itself. Worrying too much is counterproductive. If you have worked diligently in school, obtained a wide range of experience during internship, and have started your exam review early, you will be in the best position possible to pass the A.R.E.

SELECTION OF STRUCTURAL SYSTEMS

1

This chapter provides a broad overview of many of the common structural systems and materials used in contemporary construction. Its purpose is to present some of the primary characteristics of structural systems and to review some of the most important criteria for their selection. For more detailed information on specific structural materials and calculation methods, refer to later chapters in this manual.

1 STANDARD STRUCTURAL SYSTEMS

A. Wood

Wood is one of the oldest and most common structural materials. It is plentiful, inexpensive, relatively strong in both compression and tension, and easy to work with and fasten. Wood is used primarily in *one-way structural systems*, where the load is transmitted through structural members in one direction at a time.

Joists are a common use of wood. They are light, closely spaced members that span between beams or bearing walls. Typical sizes are 2×6, 2×8, 2×10, and 2×12. Typical spacings are 12 inches, 16 inches, and 24 inches on center. The typical maximum normal span is about 20 feet, but spans up to 25 feet are often used.

The space between joists is usually spanned with plywood or particle board subflooring on which underlayment is placed in preparation for finish flooring. Sometimes, a single sheet of 3/4-inch subfloor/underlayment is used, although it is not as desirable. Because joists are slender, they must be laterally supported to avoid twisting or lateral displacement. The top edge is held in place by sheathing, but bridging must be used to support the bottom edge. Maximum intervals of no more than 8 feet are recommended. Either solid or cross bridging may be used. See Figure 1.1 (a).

Solid wood beams are still used to a limited degree but not in the sizes they once were. The availability of solid beams with large cross-sectional areas in suitable lengths is limited, especially in grades that provide the desired strength. Solid wood beams for longer spans have generally been replaced with glued laminated construction.

The most common use of solid wood beams is with plank-and-beam framing in which members of 4 inch or 6 inch nominal width span between girders or bearing walls at spacings of 4, 6, or 8 feet. Wood decking, either solid or laminated, is used to span between the beams with the underside of the decking being the finished ceiling. The normal maximum span for the beams in this system is about 10 to 20 feet. See Figure 1.1 (b).

Glued laminated construction is a popular method of wood construction. These structural members are made up of individual pieces of lumber 3/4-inch or 1 1/2-inch thick glued together in the factory. Standard widths are 3 1/8 inch, 5 1/8 inch, 6 3/4 inch, and 8 3/4 inch. Larger widths are available. Typical spans for glulam construction range from 15 feet to 60 feet.

One of the advantages of glulam construction is appearance. Structural members are usually left exposed as part of the architectural expression of the structure on the interior. In addition, glulam members can be manufactured in tapered beams, tapered and curved beams, and various styles of arches.

In an effort to employ the many structural advantages of wood and increase utilization of forest products while minimizing the problems of defects and limited strength in solid wood members, several manufactured products have been developed.

One is a *light-weight I-shaped joist* consisting of a top and bottom chord of solid or laminated construction separated by a plywood web. See Figure 1.1 (c). This type of joist is used in residential and light commercial

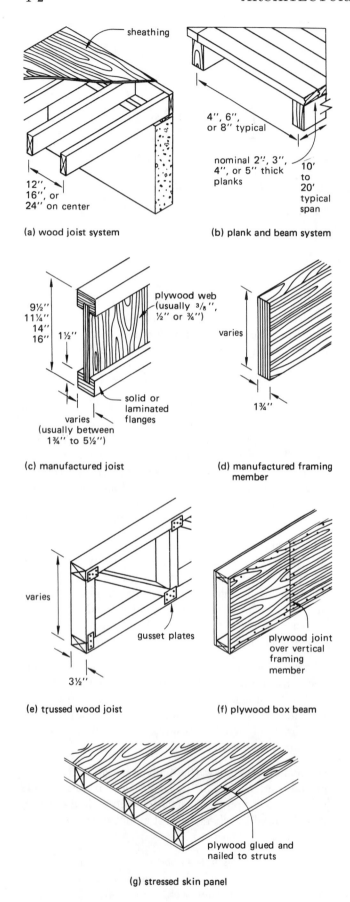

(a) wood joist system

(b) plank and beam system

(c) manufactured joist

(d) manufactured framing member

(e) trussed wood joist

(f) plywood box beam

(g) stressed skin panel

Figure 1.1 Wood Structural Systems

construction and allows longer spans than are possible with a joist system. It has a very efficient structural-shape, like a steel wide flange, and because it is manufactured in a factory, problems such as warping, splits, checks, and other common wood defects are eliminated. This type of product is stronger and stiffer than a standard wood joist.

Another manufactured product is a wood member manufactured with individual layers of thin veneer glued together. See Figure 1.1 (d). It is used primarily for headers over large openings, and singly or built-up for beams. It has a higher modulus of elasticity than a standard wood joist and its allowable stress in bending is about twice that of a douglas fir joist.

A third type of manufactured product is a *truss* made up of standard size wood members connected with metal plates. See Figure 1.1 (e). Typical spans range from about 24 feet to 40 feet and typical depths are from 12 inches to 36 inches. A common spacing is 24 inches on center. These types of trusses are useful for residential and light commercial construction and allow easy passage of mechanical ductwork through the truss.

Two other types of wood structural members are possible, but their use is infrequent because of other product availability and the difficulty in constructing them properly since they are usually site-fabricated. One is the *box beam* fabricated with plywood panels glued and nailed to solid wood members, usually 2 × 4 framing. See Figure 1.1 (f). Box beams are often used in locations where the depth of the member is not critical and where other types of manufactured beams cannot be brought to the building site. *Stressed skin panels* (see Figure 1.1 (g)) are the other type of built-up wood product. Like box beams, they are constructed of plywood glued and nailed to solid 2 inch nominal thickness lumber and are used for floor or roof structures.

B. Steel

Steel is one of the most commonly used structural materials because of its high strength, availability, and ability to adapt to a wide variety of structural conditions. It is also a ductile material which simply means that it can tolerate some deformation and return to its original shape and that it will bend before it breaks, giving warning before total collapse. Steel is particularly suited for multifloor construction because of its strength and structural continuity.

Two of the most common steel structural systems are the *beam-and-girder system* and the *open-web steel joist system*. See Figure 1.2 (a) and 1.2 (b). In the beam-and-girder system, large members span between vertical supports and smaller beams are framed into them.

The girders span the shorter distance while the beams span the longer distances. Typical spans for this system are from 25 feet to 40 feet with the beams being spaced about 8 to 10 feet on center. The steel framing is usually covered with steel decking which spans between the beams. A concrete topping is then poured over the decking to complete the floor slab.

Open-web steel joists span between beams or bearing walls as shown in Figure 1.2 (b). Standard open-web joists can span up to 60 feet with long-span joists spanning up to 96 feet, and deep long-span joists capable of spanning up to 144 feet. Depths of standard joists range from 8 inches to 30 inches in 2-inch increments. Long-span joist depth ranges from 18 inches to 72 inches. Floor joists are typically placed 2 to 4 feet on center while roof joists are usually placed 4 to 6 feet on center. Open-web steel joists used in floor construction are usually spanned with steel decking, over which a concrete topping is poured. Sometimes wood decking is used, but with closer joist spacings.

Open-web steel joists are efficient structural members and are well-suited for low-rise construction where overall depth of the floor/ceiling system is not critical. They can span long distances and are noncombustible. Because the webs are open, mechanical and electrical service pipes and ducts can easily be run between the web members.

C. Concrete

There are many variations of concrete structural systems, but the two primary types are *cast-in-place* and *precast*. Cast-in-place structures require formwork and generally take longer to build than precast buildings, but can conform to an almost unlimited variety of shapes, sizes, design intentions, and structural requirements. Precast components are usually formed in a plant under strictly controlled conditions so quality control is better and erection proceeds quickly, especially if the structure is composed of a limited number of repetitive members.

The majority of cast-in-place concrete systems utilize only mild steel reinforcing, but in some instances post-tensioning steel is used. Precast concrete systems, on the other hand, are usually prestressed, although sometimes only mild reinforcing steel is used.

Sometimes concrete is precast on the site, but this is usually limited to wall panels (normally refered to as tilt-up panels) of moderate size. Lift slab construction is still used as well. In this procedure, floor slabs of a multistory building are cast one on top of the next on

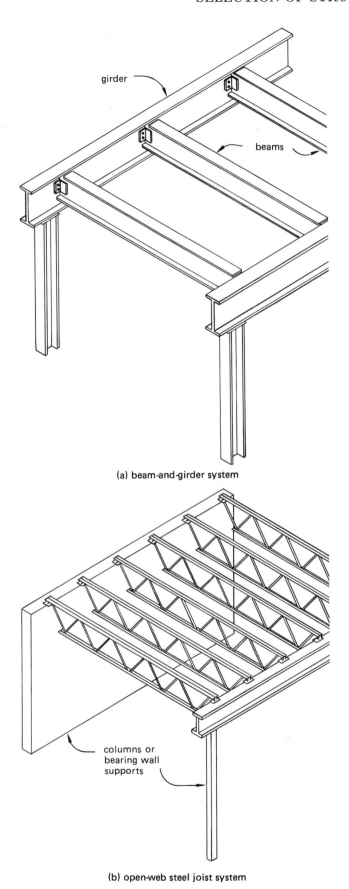

(a) beam-and-girder system

(b) open-web steel joist system

Figure 1.2 Common Steel Structural Systems

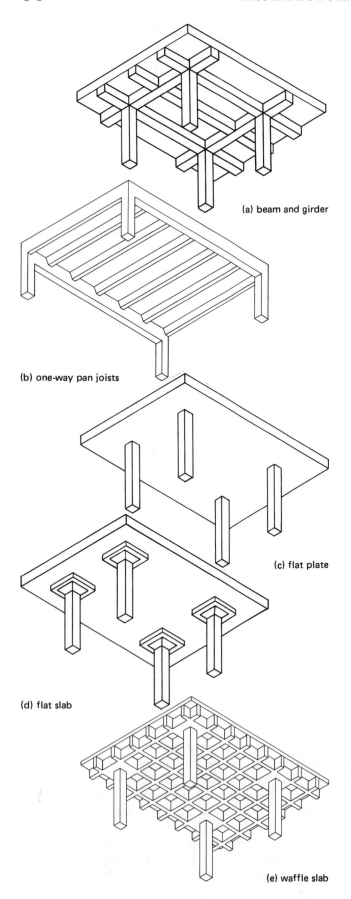

(a) beam and girder

(b) one-way pan joists

(c) flat plate

(d) flat slab

(e) waffle slab

Figure 1.3 Concrete Structural Systems

the ground around the columns and then jacked into place and attached to the columns.

Cast-in-place concrete structural systems can be classified into two general types, depending on how the floors are analyzed: *one-way systems* and *two-way systems*. In one-way systems the slabs and beams are designed to transfer loads in one direction only. For example, a slab will transfer floor loads to an intermediate beam which then transmits the load to a larger girder supported by columns.

One of the common types of one-way systems is the beam-and-girder system. See Figure 1.3 (a). This functions in a manner similar to a steel system in which the slab is supported by intermediate beams which are carried by larger girders. Typical spans are in the range of 15 feet to 30 feet. This system is economical for most applications, relatively easy to form, and allows penetrations and openings to be made in the slab.

A *concrete joist system*, Figure 1.3 (b), is comprised of concrete members usually spaced 26 or 36 inches apart, running in one direction, which frame into larger beams. Most spans range from 20 feet to 30 feet with joist depths ranging from 12 inches to 24 inches. A concrete joist system is easy to form since prefabricated metal pan forms are used. This system is good for light or medium loads where moderate distances must be spanned.

There are three principal two-way concrete systems: the *flat plate*, *flat slab*, and *waffle slab*. In most cases, all of these are designed for use in rectangular bays, where the distance between columns is the same, or close to the same, in both directions.

The flat plate is the simplest. See Figure 1.3 (c). Here, the slab is designed and reinforced to span in both directions directly into the columns. Because loads increase near the columns and there is no provision to increase the thickness of the concrete or the reinforcing at the columns, this system is limited to light loads and short spans, up to about 25 feet with slabs ranging from 6 inches to 12 inches. It is very useful in situations where the floor-to-floor height must be kept to a minimum or an uncluttered underfloor appearance is desired.

When the span of flat plates is large, or the live loads are heavier, flat plates require drop panels (increased slab thickness around the columns) to provide greater resistance against punching shear failures. Column capitals (truncated pyramids or cones) are sometimes also used to handle punching shear as well as large bending moments in the slab in the vicinity of the columns. This type of flat plate is usually referred to as a flat slab.

See Figure 1.3 (d). This system can accommodate fairly heavy loads with economical spans up to 30 feet.

The waffle slab system, Figure 1.3 (e), can provide support for heavier loads at slightly longer spans than the flat slab system. Spans up to 40 feet can be accomplished economically. Like the one-way joist system, waffle slabs are formed of prefabricated, reusable metal or fiberglass forms which allow construction to proceed faster than with custom wood forms. Waffle slabs are often left unexposed with lighting integrated into the coffers.

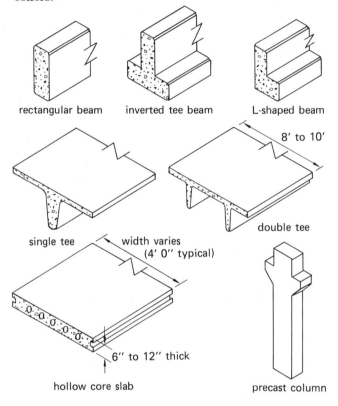

rectangular beam   inverted tee beam   L-shaped beam

single tee   width varies (4' 0" typical)

8' to 10'

double tee

6" to 12" thick

hollow core slab   precast column

Figure 1.4 Typical Precast Concrete Shapes

Precast structural members come in a variety of forms for different uses. Figure 1.4 illustrates some of the more common ones. They can either be used for structural members such as beams and columns, or for enclosing elements such as wall panels. Concrete for wall panels can be cast in an almost infinite variety of forms to provide the required size, shape, architectural finish, and opening configuration needed for the job. Precast concrete members are connected in the field using welding plates that are cast into the member at the plant.

When used for structure, precast concrete is typically prestressed; that is, high-strength steel cables are stretched in the precasting forms before the concrete is poured. After the concrete attains a certain minimum strength, the cables are released and they transfer compressive stresses to the concrete. When cured, the concrete member has a built-in compressive stress which resists the tension forces caused by the member's own weight plus the live loads acting on the member.

Single tee or *double tee* beams are a popular form of precast concrete construction because they can simultaneously serve as structural supports as well as floor or roof decking, and they are easy and fast to erect. A topping of concrete (usually about 2 inches thick) is placed over the tees to provide a uniform, smooth floor surface, and also to provide increased strength when the tees are designed to act as composite beams.

Because of the compressive stress in the concrete caused by the prestressing forces, unloaded beams from the prestressing plant have a camber built into them. This is the upward curvature of the structural member. The stressing in the cables is calculated to provide the correct camber and strength for the anticipated loading so that when the member is in place, and live and dead loads are placed on it, the camber disappears or is greatly reduced.

Post-tensioned concrete is yet another structural system that takes advantage of the qualities of concrete and steel. In this system, the post-tensioning steel (sometimes called *tendons*) is stressed after the concrete has been poured and cured. Post-tensioning tendons can be small high-strength wires, seven-wire strands, or solid bars. They are stressed with hydraulic jacks pulling on one or both ends of the tendon with pressures about 100 to 250 pounds per square inch of concrete area for slabs and 200 to 500 pounds per square inch for beams.

Post-tensioned structural systems are useful where high strength is required and where it may be too difficult to transport precast members to the job site.

D. Masonry

As a structural system in contemporary construction, masonry is generally limited to bearing walls. It has a high compressive strength but its unitized nature makes it inherently weak in tension and bending. There are three basic types of masonry bearing wall construction: *single wythe*, *double wythe*, and *cavity* (see Figure 1.5). Both of the layers in double wythe construction may be of the same material or different materials. Cavity walls and double wythe walls may be either grouted and reinforced or ungrouted. Single wythe walls have no provisions for reinforcing or grouting.

Unit masonry bearing walls offer the advantages of strength, design flexibility, appearance, resistance to weathering, fire resistance, and sound insulation. In addition, their mass makes them ideal for many passive solar energy applications.

The joints of masonry units must be reinforced horizontally at regular intervals. This not only strengthens the wall, but also controls shrinkage cracks, ties multi-wythe walls together, and provides a way to anchor veneer facing to a structural backup wall. Horizontal joint reinforcement comes in a variety of forms and is generally placed 16 inches on center.

Vertical reinforcement is accomplished with standard reinforcing bars sized and spaced in accordance with the structural requirements of the wall. Typically, horizontal bars are also used and tied to the vertical bars with the entire assembly being set in a grouted cavity space. In a single wythe concrete block wall, only vertical reinforcing is used with fully grouted wall cavities.

One important consideration in utilizing masonry walls is the thickness of the wall, which determines three important properties: the *slenderness ratio*, the *flexural strength*, and the *fire resistance*. The slenderness ratio is the ratio of the wall unsupported height to its thickness and is an indication of the ability of the wall to resist buckling when a compressive load is applied from above. The flexural strength is important when the wall is subjected to lateral forces such as from wind. Finally, the fire rating depends on both the material of the wall

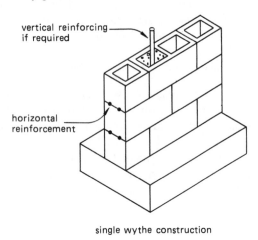

single wythe construction

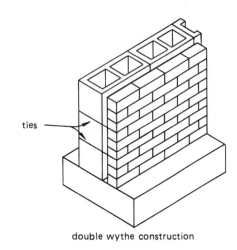

double wythe construction

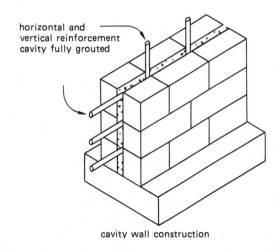

cavity wall construction

Figure 1.5 Types of Masonry Construction

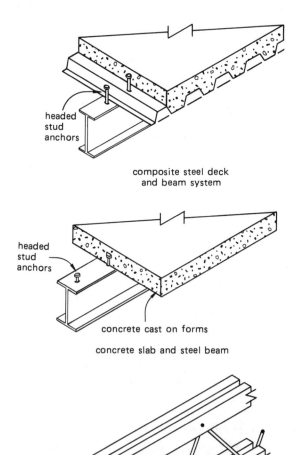

composite steel deck
and beam system

concrete slab and steel beam

open-web steel joists
with wood chords

Figure 1.6 Typical Composite Construction

and its thickness. These topics will be discussed in more detail in Chapter 12.

E. Composite Construction

Composite construction is any structural system consisting of two or more materials designed to act together to resist loads. Composite construction is employed to utilize the best characteristics of each of the individual materials.

Reinforced concrete construction is the most typical composite construction, but others include composite steel deck and concrete, concrete slab and steel beam systems, and open-web steel joists with wood chords. See Figure 1.6.

In composite construction with concrete and steel beams, headed stud anchors are used to transfer load between the concrete and steel, making them act as one unit. Composite steel deck is designed with deformations or wires welded to the deck to serve the same purpose. Composite open-web joists are used to provide a nailable surface for the floor and ceiling while using the high strength-to-weight ratio of steel for the web members.

There are many other types of composite constructions that are less frequently used. These include trusses with wood for compression members and steel rods for tension members, and concrete-filled steel tube sections.

F. Walls and the Building Envelope

Nonbearing walls are generally not considered part of the structural system of a building, but there are two important structural considerations when deciding how to attach the exterior, non-structural envelope to the structural frame. The first is how the *weight* of the envelope itself will be supported, and the *second is how exterior loads*, primarily wind, will be transferred to the structural frame without damaging the facing.

How an exterior facing is attached depends, of course, on the specific material and the type of structural frame. Panel and curtain wall systems are attached with clips on the mullions at the structural frame. The size and spacing of the clips is determined by the structural capabilities of the curtain wall or panel system.

Stone and masonry facings are attached with clip angles, continuous angles, or special fastenings to the structural frame at the floor lines. If additional attachment is required, a grid of secondary steel framing is attached to the primary structure and then serves as a framework for the facing. Lightweight facings such as wood siding, shingles, and stucco need to be applied over continuous sheathing firmly secured to the structural wall framing.

One of the most important considerations in attaching exterior facing to the structural frame is to allow for expansion and contraction due to temperature changes and slight movement of the structural frame. Materials with a high coefficient of thermal expansion, such as aluminum, require space for movement within each panel, at the connection with the structural frame, and sometimes at the perimeter of large sections of the facing. Movement can be provided for by using clip angles with slotted holes, slip joints, and flexible sealants.

Materials with a low coefficient of expansion, such as masonry, still require expansion joints at regular intervals and at changes in the plane of the wall. If these are not provided, the joints or masonry may crack or the facing itself may break away during extreme temperature changes.

Usually, steel-framed buildings do not present many problems with movement of the structural frame, but concrete and wood structures will move enough to present problems. Concrete structures are especially subject to creep, a slight deformation of the concrete over time under continuous dead load. This condition must be accounted for when designing and detailing connections. Wood structures also deform over time due to shrinkage of the wood and long-term deflection. Since most wood buildings are relatively small, this is not always a problem, but should be considered in attaching exterior facings.

2   COMPLEX STRUCTURAL SYSTEMS

A. Trusses

Trusses are structures comprised of straight members forming a number of triangles with the connections arranged so that the stresses in the members are either in tension or compression. Trusses can be used horizontally, vertically, or diagonally to support various types of loads when it would be impossible to fabricate a single structural member to span a large distance.

Although trusses are primarily *tension/compression structural systems*, some amount of bending is present in many of the members. This is due to loads applied between the connections and secondary bending and shear stresses at the connections themselves caused by minor eccentric loading.

Trusses can be field-fabricated or assembled in the factory as is the case with open-web steel joists and wood trussed rafters. The primary limiting factor is the ability to transport them from the factory to the job site.

Trusses are discussed in more detail in Chapter 5.

B. Arches

Arches may have hinged or fixed supports. A hinged arch is a structural shape which is primarily subjected to compressive forces. For a given set of loads the shape of an arch to resist the loads only in compression is its *funicular shape*. This shape can be found by suspending the anticipated loads from a flexible cable and then turning the shape upside down, as Antonio Gaudi did in many of his structural studies. For a hinged arch supporting a uniform load across its span this shape is a parabola. However, no arch is subjected to just one set of loads, so there is always a combination of compression and some bending stresses.

At the supports of a hinged arch there are two reactions: the *vertical reactions* and the *horizontal reactions*, or *thrust*, as shown in Figure 1.7. Since the loads on the arch tend to force it to spread out, the thrust must be resisted either with tie rods which hold the two lower portions of the arch together or with foundations which prevent the spread. For a given span, the thrust is inversely proportional to the rise, or height, of the arch; if the rise is reduced by one-half, the thrust doubles.

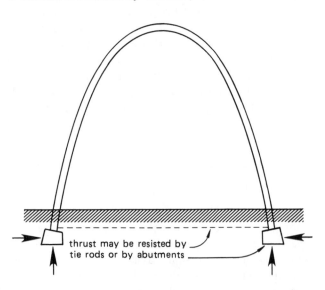

Figure 1.7 Reactions of a Hinged Arch

Arches can be constructed of any material: steel, concrete, wood, or stone, although each has its inherent limitations. Arches can also take a variety of shapes, from the classic half-round arch of the Romans, to the pointed Gothic arch, to the more decorate Arabic arches, to the functional parabolic shapes. Since the shape of a building arch is often selected for its aesthetic appeal, it is not always the ideal shape and must be designed for the variety of loads it must carry in addition to simple compression. Wood arches typically span from 50 to 240 feet, concrete arches from 20 to 320 feet, and steel arches from 50 to 500 feet.

Although arches may have fixed supports, they are usually hinged. This allows the arch to remain flexible and avoids developing high bending stresses under live loading and loading due to temperature changes and foundation settlement. Occasionally, an arch will have an additional hinge connection at the apex and is called a *three-hinged arch*. The addition of the third hinge makes the structure statically determinate whereas two hinged or fixed arches are statically indeterminate.

C. Rigid Frames

In contrast to a simple post-and-beam system, a rigid frame is constructed so that the vertical and horizontal members work as a single structural unit. This makes for a more efficient structure because all three members resist vertical and lateral loads together rather than singly. The beam portion is partially restrained by the columns and becomes more rigid to vertical bending forces, and both the columns can resist lateral forces

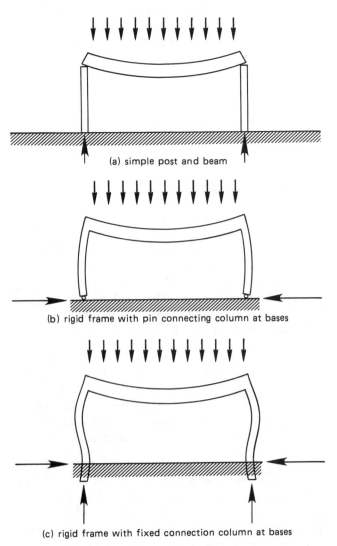

(a) simple post and beam

(b) rigid frame with pin connecting column at bases

(c) rigid frame with fixed connection column at bases

Figure 1.8 Post-and-Beam and Rigid Frames

because they are tied together by the beam. See Figure 1.8.

Because the three members are rigidly attached, there are forces and reactions in a rigid frame unlike those in a simple post-and-beam system. This is shown in Figure 1.8 (b and c) and results in the columns being subjected to both compressive and bending forces and a thrust, or outward force, induced by the action of the vertical loads on the beam transferred to the columns. As with an arch, this thrust must be resisted with tie rods or with appropriate foundations.

The attachment of the columns to the foundations may be rigid or hinged. This results in slightly different loads on the columns. The fixed frame as shown in Figure 1.8 (c) is stiffer than the hinged frame and the thrust in the fixed frame is also greater.

When a horizontal beam is not required, such as in a single-story structure, a rigid frame often takes on the appearance of a gabled frame as shown in Figure 1.9. This shape decreases the bending stresses in the two inclined members and increases the compression, making the configuration a more efficient structure. Because rigid frames develop a high moment (see Chapter 3) at the connections between horizontal and vertical members, the amount of material is often increased near these points as shown in the tapered columns and roof members in Figure 1.9.

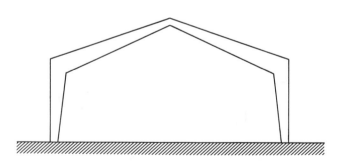

Figure 1.9 Gabled Rigid Frame

D. Space Frames

In simplest terms, a space frame is a structural system consisting of trusses in two directions rigidly connected at their intersections. With this definition it is possible to have a rectangular space frame where the top and bottom chords of the trusses are directly above and below one another. The bays created by the intersection of the two sets of trusses then form squares or rectangles. The more common type of space frame is a *triangulated space frame* where the bottom chord is offset from the

top chord by one half bay, and each is connected with inclined web members. See Figure 1.10.

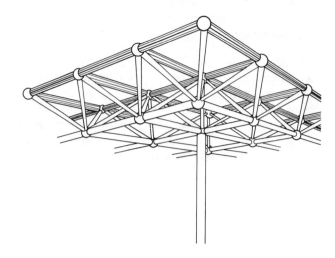

Figure 1.10 Typical Space Frame

Space frames are very efficient structures for enclosing large rectangular areas because of the two-way action of the components acting as a single unit. This results in a very stiff structure that may span up to 350 feet. Span-to-depth ratios of space frames may be from 20:1 to 30:1. Other advantages include light weight and the repetitive nature of connectors and struts so that fabrication and erection time is minimized.

The structural design of a space frame is complex because they are statically indeterminate structures with numerous intersections. A computer is needed for analysis and design.

E. Folded Plates

A folded plate structure is one in which the loads are carried in two directions, first in the transverse direction through each plate supported by adjacent plates and secondly in the longitudinal direction with each plate acting as a girder spanning between vertical supports. See Figure 1.11. Since the plates act as beams between supports, there are compressive stresses above the neutral axis and tensile stresses below.

Folded plates are usually constructed of reinforced concrete from 3 to 6 inches thick although structures made of wood or steel are possible. Typical longitudinal spans are 30 to 100 feet with longer spans possible using reinforced concrete.

F. Thin Shell Structures

A thin shell structure is one with a curved surface that resists loads through tension, compression, and shear in the plane of the shell only. Theoretically, there are no bending or moment stresses in a thin shell structure. These structures derive part of their name (thin) because of the method of resisting loads; a thick structure is not necessary since there are no bending stresses.

Since thin shells are composed of curved surfaces, the material is practically always reinforced concrete from about 3 to 6 inches thick. The forms can be domes, parabolas, barrel vaults, and the more complex shape of the saddle-shaped hyperbolic paraboloid. Thin shell domes can span from 40 feet to over 200 feet while hyperbolic paraboloids may span from 30 to 160 feet.

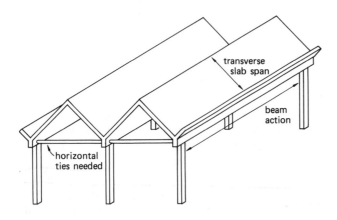

Figure 1.11   Folded Plate Construction

G. Stressed-Skin Structures

These structures comprise panels made of a sheathing material attached on one or both sides of intermediate web members in such a way that the panel acts as a series of I-beams with the sheathing being the flange and the intermediate members being the webs. Since the panel is constructed of two or more pieces, the connection between the skin and the interior web members must transfer all the horizontal stress developed. Stressed-skin panels are typically made of wood as shown in Figure 1.1 (g), but are also fabricated of steel and other composite materials. Although long-span steel stressed-skin panels are possible, most panels of this type span intermediate distances from 12 to 35 feet.

H. Suspension Structures

Suspension structures are most commonly seen in suspension bridges, but their use is increasing in buildings, most notably in large stadiums with suspended roofs. The suspension system was boldly used in the Federal

Reserve Bank in Minneapolis where two sets of cables were draped from towers at the ends of the building. These, in turn, support the floors and walls, leaving the space on the grade level free of columns.

Cable suspension structures are similar to arches in that the loads they support must be resisted by both vertical reactions and horizontal thrust reactions. The difference is that the vertical reactions are up and the horizontal thrust reaction is outward since the sag tends to pull the ends together. As shown in Figure 1.12 (a), the horizontal reaction is dependent on the amount of sag in the cable. Shallow sags result in high reactions while deep sags result in lower reactions.

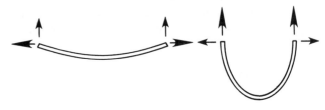

(a) horizontal reaction depends on sag

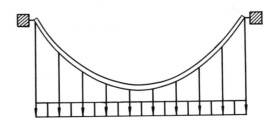

(b) uniform horizontal load results in parabolic curve

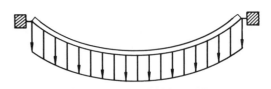

(c) uniform load on cable results in catenary curve

Figure 1.12   Cable-Supported Structures

Since suspension structures can only resist loads with tension, the shape of the cable used changes as the load changes. No bending stresses are possible. With a single concentrated load, the cable assumes the shape of two straight lines (not counting the intermediate sag due to the weight of the cable). With two concentrated loads, the shape is three straight lines, and so on.

If the cable is uniformly loaded horizontally, the shape of the curve is a parabola. If the cable is loaded along its length uniformly (such as supporting its own weight) the shape will be a catenary curve. See Figure 1.12 (b) and (c).

The fact that a suspension structure can only resist loads in tension creates one of its disadvantages: instability due to wind and other types of loading. Suspension structures must be stabilized or stiffened with a heavy infill material, with cables attached to the ground or with a secondary grid of cables either above or below the primary set.

I. Inflatable Structures

Inflatable structures are similar to suspension structures in that they can only resist loads in tension. They are held in place with constant air pressure which is greater than the outside air pressure. The simplest inflatable structure is the single membrane anchored continuously at ground level and inflated.

A variation of this is the *double-skin inflatable structure* in which the structure is created by inflation of a series of voids, much like an air mattress. With this system, the need for an "air-lock" for entry and exit is eliminated. Another variation is a double-skin structure with only one large air pocket supported on the bottom by a cable suspension system and with the top supported by air pressure.

Like cable suspension buildings, inflatable structures are inherently unstable in the wind and cannot support concentrated loads. They are often stabilized with a network of cables over the top of the membrane. Inflatable structures are used for temporary enclosures and for large, single-space buildings such as sports arenas.

3 STRUCTURAL SYSTEM SELECTION CRITERIA

The selection of an optimum structural system for a building can be a complex task. In addition to the wide variety of structural systems available and their many variations and combinations, there are dozens of other considerations that must be factored into making the final selection. The architect's job is to determine the full scope of the problem and find the best balance among often conflicting requirements. This section briefly outlines some of the major selection criteria you should be familiar with when analyzing possible systems.

A. Resistance to Loads

Of course, the primary consideration is the ability of the structural system to resist the anticipated and unanticipated loads that will be placed on it. These include the weight of the structure itself (*dead load*), loads caused by external factors such as wind, snow and earthquakes, loads caused by the use of the building such as people, furniture, and equipment (*live loads*), as well as others. These are discussed in more detail in Chapter 2.

The anticipated loads can be calculated directly from known weights of materials and equipment and from requirements of building codes that set down what is statistically probable in a given situation—the load caused by people in a church, for example. Unanticipated loads are difficult to plan for but include such things as changes in the use of a building, overloading caused by extra people or equipment, unusual snow loads, ponding of water on a roof, and degradation of the structure itself.

When deciding on what material or system to use, there is always the consideration of what is reasonable for the particular circumstance. For example, wood can be made to support very heavy loads with long spans, but only at a very high cost with complex systems. A wood system doesn't make sense if other materials and systems such as steel and concrete are available.

Often, very unusual loads will be the primary determinant of the structural system and its affect on the appearance of the building. Extremely tall high-rise buildings like the Sears Tower or the John Hancock Building in Chicago with its exterior diagonal framing are examples of load-driven structural solutions.

B. Building Use and Function

The type of *occupancy* is one of the primary determinants of a structural system. A parking garage needs spans long enough to allow the easy movement and storage of automobiles. An office building works well with spans in the 30 to 40 foot range.

Sports arenas need quite large open areas. Some buildings have a fixed use over their life span and may work with fixed bearing walls while others must remain flexible and require small columns widely spaced.

These are all examples of somewhat obvious determinates of building systems. However, there are many other needs that are not so apparent. For example, in a location where building height is limited, a client may want to squeeze as many floors into a multistory building as possible. This may require the use of concrete flat plate construction with closely spaced columns although another system is more economical.

In another instance, a laboratory building may need large spaces between usable floors in which to run mechanical services. This may suggest the use of deep span, open-web trusses. If the same laboratory were to house delicate, motion sensitive equipment, then the use of a rigid, massive concrete structure might be warranted.

C. Integration With Other Building Systems

Although a building's structure is an important element, it does not exist alone. Exterior cladding must be attached to it, ductwork and pipes run around and through it, electrical wires among it, and interior finishes must cover it. Some materials and structural systems make it easy for other services to be integrated. For instance, a steel column-and-beam system with open-web steel joists and concrete floors over metal decking yields a fairly penetrable structure for pipes, ducts, and wiring while still allowing solid attachment of ceilings, walls, and exterior cladding.

On the other hand, reinforced prestressed concrete buildings may require more consideration as to how mechanical services will be run so there is not an excess of dropped ceilings, furred-out columns, and structure-weakening penetrations. Exposed structural systems, such as glued-laminated beams and wood decking or architectural concrete, present particularly difficult integration problems.

D. Cost Influences

As with most contemporary construction, the concern over money drives many decisions. Structure is no exception. It is one portion of a building that is most susceptible to cost cutting because it quite often cannot be seen and the client sees no reason to spend more on it than absolutely necessary.

There are two primary elements of selecting a structural system based on cost. The first is *selecting materials* and systems that are most appropriate for the anticipated loads, spans required, style desired, integration needed, fire-resistance called for, and all the other factors that must be considered. This generally leads to major decisions such as using a concrete flat slab construction instead of steel, or using a steel arch system instead of glued-laminated beams.

The second part is *refining the selected system* so that the most economical arrangement and use of materials is selected regardless of the system used. In a typical situation, for example, a steel system is selected but various framing options must be compared and evaluated. Changing the direction of the beams and girders or slightly altering the spacing of beams may result in a savings in the weight of steel and therefore a savings in money. Or, a concrete frame may be needed, but the one with the simplest forming will generally cost less.

E. Fire Resistance

Building codes dictate the fire resistance of structural systems as well as other parts of a building. These range from one hour to four hours; the time is an indication of how long the member can withstand a standard fire test before becoming dangerously weakened. The structure is, of course, the most important part of a building because it holds everything else up. As a consequence, required fire resistances are generally greater for structural members than for other components in the same occupancy type and building type.

There are two considerations in the fire resistance of a structural member. One is the combustibility of the framing itself and the other is the loss of strength a member may experience when subjected to intense heat. Steel, for instance, will not burn but will bend and collapse when subjected to high temperatures. It must, therefore, be protected with other noncombustible materials. Heavy timber, on the other hand, will burn slightly and char, but still maintain much of its strength in a fire before it burns completely.

Some materials, such as concrete and masonry, are inherently fire resistant and are not substantially weakened when subjected to fire (assuming any steel reinforcing is adequately protected). Other materials, such as wood and steel, must be protected for the time period required by building codes.

Since it costs money to protect structural members from fire, this must be factored into the decision to use one material instead of another. Even though steel may be a less expensive structural material to use than concrete, it may be more expensive to fireproof and in the long run cost more than a concrete-framed building.

F. Construction Limitations

The realities of construction often are a decisive factor in choosing a structural system. Some of these include construction time, material and labor availability, and equipment availability.

Construction time is almost always a factor due to high labor costs typical in the United States. However, other things influence the need to shorten the construction period as much as possible. The cost of financing requires that the term of construction loans be as short as feasible. This may dictate the use of large, prefabricated structural elements instead of slow, labor-intensive systems such as unit masonry. Another factor can be climate and weather. In locations with short construction seasons, buildings need to be erected as fast as possible.

Material and labor are the two primary variables in all construction cost. Sometimes both are expensive, but usually one dominates the other. In the United States, labor costs are high in relation to materials; in many developing countries labor is extremely cheap while most modern materials are expensive or even unattainable. Even within the United States labor and material costs for the same material or structural system in different states many vary enough to influence the structural system decision.

Related to the cost of labor are the skills of the work force. A sophisticated structural system may require a technically skilled workforce that is not available in a remote region. The cost to transport and house the needed workers could very well make such a system unfeasible.

Finally, equipment needed to assemble a structural system may be unavailable or prohibitively expensive. The lack of heavy cranes near the job location, for example, could suggest that large, prefabricated components not be used.

G. Style

Some structural systems are more appropriate as an expression of a particular style than others. One of the most obvious examples is the International Style, which could only be achieved with a steel post-and-beam system. Even when fireproofing requirements might have implied a concrete structure, steel was used.

The architect and client usually determine what style the building will be and then require that any structural solution adapt to that need. In some instances, the structural engineer may devise a structural solution that becomes the style itself. Once again, there should be a balance between what style may be desired and what is practical and reasonable from a structural point of view.

H. Social And Cultural Influences

Related to the style of a building are the social and cultural influences on the architecture of a geographical location and particular time period. The architect must be sensitive to these influences. For example, in a historic area where most buildings are constructed of brick, a masonry bearing wall structural system certainly should be considered. In a newly developing industrial park, more contemporary and daring structural systems might be appropriate.

SAMPLE QUESTIONS

1. Rigid frames have which of the following characteristics?

   I. Rigid frames should be hinged at the column bases.

   II. Moment connections must be designed at the intersection of beam and column.

   III. Loads are transferred vertically to the foundations.

   IV. Rigid frames are more efficient than simple post-and-beam systems.

   V. Sloping the horizontal members can reduce the amount of steel required.

   A. I, II, and IV
   B. II, IV, and V
   C. II, III, IV, and V
   D. all of the above

2. Which of the following would be most important in selecting a structural system for a proposed restaurant and warming house at the mid-slope of a ski resort?

   A. cost, resistance to loads, and construction limitations

   B. style, integration with building systems, and fire resistance

   C. building occupancy, construction limitations, and style

   D. fire resistance, resistance to loads, and cost

3. Select the incorrect statement concerning exterior wall facings and building structures.

   A. Heavy materials with low coefficients of expansion require expansion joints as much as materials such as steel, aluminum, and wood.

   B. Transfer of wind loads from curtain wall systems is accomplished with clip angles connecting the facing and the structural frame.

   C. Long-term deflections of both wood and concrete can cause problems with cracking of exterior facings.

   D. Simple, lightweight exterior materials such as thin paneling or stucco can be attached directly to the exterior studs.

The answers to questions 4 through 7 can be found on the following key list. Select only one answer for each question.

   A0 arch
   A1 camber
   A2 catenary
   A3 cavity
   A4 composite construction
   A5 creep
   A6 double wythe
   A7 flat plate
   A8 flat slab
   A9 folded plate

   B0 funicular
   B1 lift slab
   B2 rigid frame
   B3 single wythe
   B4 space frame
   B5 thin shell
   B6 waffle slab

4. What type of structure resists loads through shear, tension, and compression in the plane of the structure?

5. Select the system that allows extra reinforcement at the columns.

6. A bearing wall with a high slenderness ratio would probably require what kind of construction?

7. What economical two-way system of steel or concrete would be appropriate for a span over 150 feet?

8. Which of the following is not true about arches?

   A. Horizontal thrust must be resisted by foundations or tie rods.

   B. The thrust on an arch can be decreased by doubling its height.

   C. Supporting an arch with two hinges will make it statically determinate.

   D. The funicular shape of an arch can be easily determined without calculations.

9. Which of the following statements are correct?

I. The amount of camber in a prestressed concrete beam can be varied to suit the requirements of loading.

II. Flat plate and flat slab construction should be designed for square bays while waffle slabs should be more rectangular.

III. A one-way concrete joist system is easy to form and can span 25 to 40 feet.

IV. When a long prestressed member cannot be delivered to a site, post-tensioned construction may be warranted.

V. Topping is often omitted on single tee construction if floor-to-floor heights are limited.

A. I and IV
B. I, III, and IV
C. II and IV
D. IV and V

10. Select the incorrect statement about steel framing.

A. A beam-and-girder system is efficient for spans in the range of 25 to 40 feet.

B. Open-web steel joists are best supported on steel beams.

C. The ductile properties of steel make it advantageous for intermittent lateral loading.

D. Steel is used for high-rise buildings because of its ductility and strength.

2 LOADS ON BUILDINGS

Nomenclature

A	area of floor or roof	ft^2
D	dead load	psf
L	live load	psf
P	direct wind pressure	psf
r	rate of reduction of live loads	
R	allowable reduction of live load	percent
R_s	snow load reduction per degree	psf
S	snow load	psf
V	wind velocity	mph

Determining the loads acting on buildings is basic to structural analysis and design. An accurate determination of loads is necessary to design a safe building and satisfy building code requirements while not requiring a more costly structure than necessary. The probable magnitudes of building loads have been determined over a long period of time based on successful experience and the statistical probability that a particular situation will result in a given load. They are also based on the worst case situation. For example, the common live load for residences of 40 pounds per square foot is highly unlikely to occur on every square foot in a house, but provides an allowance for safety and unusual circumstances.

Typically, loads are defined by building codes and by common practice. Codes, for example, give live load requirements, wind values, and earthquake values. Standard published tables provide accepted weights of building materials for dead load calculations. Occasionally, special situations may require custom load determination such as when building models are tested in a wind tunnel. Most loads on buildings are static, and those that are dynamic, such as wind, are assumed to have a static effect on the building structure so calculations are easier.

There are many types of loads on buildings. This chapter provides an overview of what the different types are, how they are determined, and their effects on buildings and architectural design. More detailed information concerning building code requirements is given in Chapter 8, while specific calculation procedures for lateral loads due to wind and earthquakes are described in Chapters 13 and 14, respectively.

1 GRAVITY LOADS

A. Dead Loads

Dead loads are the *vertical loads* due to the weight of the building and any permanent equipment. These include such things as beams, exterior and interior walls, floors, and mechanical equipment. Dead loads of structural elements cannot always be readily determined because the weight depends on the size, which in turn depends on the weight to be supported. Initially, the weight of the structure must be assumed to make a preliminary calculation of the size of the structural member. Then the actual weight can be used for checking the calculation.

Most dead loads are easily calculated from published lists of weights of building materials found in standard reference sources. Some common weights are given in Table 2.1. In addition to these, the Uniform Building Code requires that floors in office buildings and other buildings where partition locations are subject to change be designed to support an extra 20 pounds per square foot of dead load.

Example 2.1

Find the uniform load on a typical interior beam supporting the floor shown in the diagram. Do not include the weight of the beam.

From Table 2.1, determine the weight per square foot of the materials comprising the floor. Since the concrete

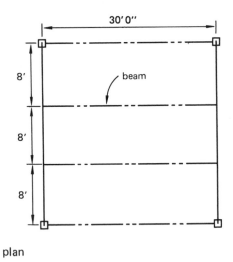

plan

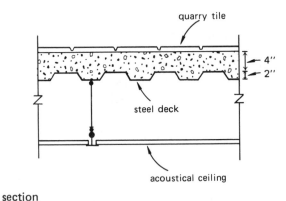

section

is on a fluted steel deck, take the average thickness of five inches.

The total weight is therefore:

quarry tile	5.8 psf
concrete	62.5 psf (5 × 12.5 psf)
steel deck	2.5 psf
suspended ceiling	1.0 psf
total	71.8 psf

The beam supports a portion of the floor half the distance of the beam spacing on either side of it, or 8 feet. 8 times 71.8 is 574 pounds per lineal foot. If you wanted the total load you would just multiply by the length of the beam.

In practice, numbers such as 71.8 are rounded to the nearest whole number, so the weight in this case would be 72 psf and the load would be 576 plf.

B. Live Loads

Live loads are those imposed on the building by its particular use and occupancy, and are generally considered

Table 2.1
Weights of Some Common Building Materials

material	weight
asphalt shingles	2 psf
brick, 4″ wall	40 psf
built-up roofing, 5-ply	6 psf
concrete block, 8″ heavy aggregate	55 psf
concrete, reinforced	150 psf
concrete slab, per inch of thickness	12.5 psf
curtain wall, aluminum and glass, average	15 psf
earth, moist and packed	100 psf
glass, 1/4″	3.3 psf
granite	170 pcf
gypsum wallboard, 1/2″	1.8 psf
hardwood floor, 7/8″	2.5 psf
marble	165 pcf
partition, 2 × 4 with 1/2″ gyp. bd. each side	8 psf
partition, metal stud with 5/8″ gyp. bd.	6 psf
plaster, 1/2″	4.5 psf
plywood, 1/2″	1.5 psf
quarry tile, 1/2″	5.8 psf
steel decking	2.5 psf
suspended acoustical ceiling	1 psf
terrazzo, 2 1/2″ sand cushion	27 psf
water	62 pcf
wood joists and subfloor, 2′ × 10″, 16″ o.c.	6 psf

movable or temporary such as people, furniture, movable equipment, and snow. It does not include wind loading or earthquake loading. Snow load is often considered a special type of live load because it is so variable. To determine snow loads, local building officials or building codes must be consulted.

Live loads are established by building codes for different occupancies. Table 2.2 gives the uniform live floor loads from the Uniform Building Code, and Table 2.3 gives minimum roof live loads not including any special snow loads. The requirements for special loads are given in Table 2.4. These include such conditions as cranes, elevators, and fire sprinkler structural support, among others.

The code also requires that floors be designed to support concentrated loads if the specified load on an otherwise unloaded floor would produce stresses greater than those caused by the uniform load. The concentrated load is assumed to be located on any space 2 1/2 feet square. The concentrated load requirements are given in the last column in Table 2.2.

There are two instances when the Uniform Building Code allows the live load to be reduced: when a structural member supports more than 150 square feet (except for floors in places of public assembly and for live

Table 2.2
Uniform and Concentrated Loads

USE OR OCCUPANCY		UNIFORM LOAD[1]	CONCEN- TRATED LOAD
CATEGORY	DESCRIPTION		
1. Access floor systems	Office use	50	2000[2]
	Computer use	100	2000[2]
2. Armories		150	0
3. Assembly areas[3] and auditoriums and balconies therewith	Fixed seating areas	50	0
	Movable seating and other areas	100	0
	Stage areas and enclosed platforms	125	0
4. Cornices, marquees and residential balconies		60	0
5. Exit facilities[4]		100	0[5]
6. Garages	General storage and/or repair	100	6
	Private or pleasure-type motor vehicle storage	50	6
7. Hospitals	Wards and rooms	40	1000[2]
8. Libraries	Reading rooms	60	1000[2]
	Stack rooms	125	1500[2]
9. Manufacturing	Light	75	2000[2]
	Heavy	125	3000[2]
10. Offices		50	2000[2]
11. Printing plants	Press rooms	150	2500[2]
	Composing and linotype rooms	100	2000[2]
12. Residential[7]		40	0[5]
13. Rest rooms[8]			
14. Reviewing stands, grandstands and bleachers		100	0
15. Roof deck	Same as area served or for the type of occupancy accommodated		
16. Schools	Classrooms	40	1000[2]
17. Sidewalks and driveways	Public access	250	6
18. Storage	Light	125	
	Heavy	250	
19. Stores	Retail	75	2000[2]
	Wholesale	100	3000[2]

[1]See Section 2306 for live load reductions.
[2]See Section 2304 (c), first paragraph, for area of load application.
[3]Assembly areas include such occupancies as dance halls, drill rooms, gymnasiums, playgrounds, plazas, terraces and similar occupancies which are generally accessible to the public.
[4]Exit facilities shall include such uses as corridors serving an occupant load of 10 or more persons, exterior exit balconies, stairways, fire escapes and similar uses.
[5]Individual stair treads shall be designed to support a 300-pound concentrated load placed in a position which would cause maximum stress. Stair stringers may be designed for the uniform load set forth in the table.
[6]See Section 2304(c), second paragraph, for concentrated loads.
[7]Residential occupancies include private dwellings, apartments and hotel guest rooms.
[8]Rest room loads shall be not less than the load for the occupancy with which they are associated, but need not exceed 50 pounds per square foot.

Reproduced from the 1988 edition of the Uniform Building Code, copyright © 1988, with permission of the publishers, the International Conference of Building Officials.

The *rate of reduction*, r, is equal to 0.08 for floors, 0.08 for roofs ranging from flat to less than 4 inches rise per foot, and 0.06 for roof slopes ranging from 4/12 to 12/12.

There are a few limitations, however. The reduction cannot exceed 40 percent for members receiving load from one level only or 60 percent for other members, nor can the reduction exceed the percentage determined by the formula:

$$R = 23.1(1 + D/L) \qquad 2.2$$

Table 2.3
Roof Live Loads

ROOF SLOPE	METHOD 1			METHOD 2		
	TRIBUTARY LOADED AREA IN SQUARE FEET FOR ANY STRUCTURAL MEMBER			UNIFORM LOAD[2]	RATE OF REDUC- TION r (Percent)	MAXIMUM REDUC- TION R (Percent)
	0 to 200	201 to 600	Over 600			
1. Flat or rise less than 4 inches per foot. Arch or dome with rise less than one eighth of span	20	16	12	20	.08	40
2. Rise 4 inches per foot to less than 12 inches per foot. Arch or dome with rise one eighth of span to less than three eighths of span	16	14	12	16	.06	25
3. Rise 12 inches per foot and greater. Arch or dome with rise three eighths of span or greater	12	12	12	12		
4. Awnings except cloth covered[3]	5	5	5	5	No Reductions Permitted	
5. Greenhouses, lath houses and agricultural buildings[4]	10	10	10	10		

[1]Where snow loads occur, the roof structure shall be designed for such loads as determined by the building official. See Section 2305 (d). For special purpose roofs, see Section 2305 (e).
[2]See Section 2306 for live load reductions. The rate of reduction r in Section 2306 Formula (6-1) shall be as indicated in the table. The maximum reduction R shall not exceed the value indicated in the table.
[3]As defined in Section 4506.
[4]See Section 2305 (e) for concentrated load requirements for greenhouse roof members.

Reproduced from the 1988 edition of the Uniform Building Code, copyright © 1988, with permission of the publishers, the International Conference of Building Officials.

loads greater than 100 pounds per square foot), and when there is a snow load in excess of 20 pounds per square foot on any roof pitched more than 20 degrees.

In the first instance, the allowable reduction from the load values shown in Table 2.2 is given by the formula:

$$R = r(A - 150) \qquad 2.1$$

Example 2.2

What live load should be used to design a structural member that supports an area of 225 square feet of single-level office space, a live load of 60 pounds per square foot, and a dead load of 72 pounds per square foot?

Since the live load is less than 100 pounds per square foot and it is not public assembly space, a reduction is permitted. First, determine the reduction and then check against the other two limitations and select the least one.

$$R = r(A - 150)$$
$$= 0.08(225 - 150)$$
$$= 6\%$$
$$= 40\% \text{ for members receiving load from one floor}$$

Check against formula 2.2:

$$R = 23.1(1 + D/L)$$
$$= 23.1(1 + 72/60)$$
$$= 50.82\%$$

Of the three values, 6% is the least so the reduced live load will be $60 - 0.06(60)$, or 56.4 pounds per square foot.

When using these formulas for roofs, the figures listed under Method 2 in Table 2.3 should be used. An alternate approach for roofs is to use Method 1 in the same table where you simply look under the appropriate column for supported area and the appropriate row for roof pitch.

The reduction allowed for snow loads greater than 20 pounds per square foot on pitched roofs over 20 degrees is given by the formula:

$$R_s = \frac{S}{40} - \frac{1}{2} \qquad\qquad 2.3$$

Example 2.3

What snow load should be used for calculation on a 6/12 roof in an area with a snow load of 60 pounds per square foot?

Since the load is greater than 20 psf and the roof pitch is more than 20 degrees, a reduction is allowed.

The roof pitch is arctan = 6/12, or 26.6 degrees.

$$R_s = \frac{60}{40} - \frac{1}{2}$$

$R_s = 1$ pound per square foot for every degree over 20.

$(26.6 - 20)1 = 6.6$ pounds per square foot reduction. The design snow load is $60 - 6.6$, or 53.4 pounds per square foot.

There is one final thing to remember when determining roof loads: loads on sloped surfaces are assumed to

act vertically on a horizontal plane projected from the slope.

C. Combination Loads

It is generally agreed that when calculating all the loads on a building, all of them probably will not act at once. For example, full snow load will not be present when full wind load exists because the wind will blow some of the snow away. The Uniform Building Code recognizes this and requires that several combinations of loads be calculated to find the most critical one.

These combination of loads are as follows:

- dead plus floor live plus roof live (or snow)

- dead plus floor live plus wind (or seismic)

- dead plus floor live plus wind plus one-half snow

- dead plus floor live plus snow plus one-half wind

- dead plus floor live plus snow plus seismic

2   LATERAL LOADS

A. Wind

Wind loading on buildings is a *dynamic* process. That is, the pressures, directions, and timing are constantly changing. For purposes of calculation, however, wind is considered a *static* force. There are several variables that affect wind loading. The first is the *wind velocity* itself. The pressure on a building varies as the square of the velocity according to the following formula:

$$p = 0.00256V^2 \qquad\qquad 2.4$$

The second variable is the *height* of the wind above the ground. Since wind acts as any fluid where a surface causes friction and slows the fluid, wind velocity is lower near the ground and increases with height. Wind speed values are taken at a standard height of 10 meters (33 feet) above the ground, so adjustments must be made when calculating pressure at different elevations.

A third variable is the nature of the building's *surroundings*. Other buildings, trees, and topography affect how the wind will finally strike the structure under consideration. Buildings in large, open areas are subject to more wind force than those in protected areas. The type of surrounds is taken in account with multiplying factors found in the building codes.

Finally, there are things like the size, shape, and surface texture of the building. Some buildings allow the wind to flow around them while others channel or focus the wind.

A building subjected to wind forces responds in several ways. These are shown diagrammatically in Figure 2.1. There is, of course, positive pressure on the windward side of the building. On the leeward side and roof there is often a negative pressure, or suction. In addition to these, there are local areas where wind pressure is greater such at building corners, overhangs, parapets, and other projections. The method of calculating these is described in detail in Chapter 13.

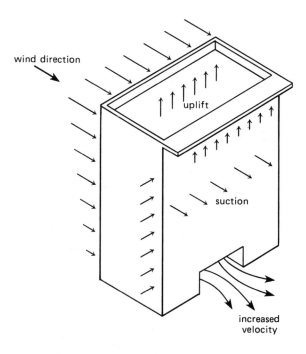

Figure 2.1 Forces on a Building Due to Wind

Of particular interest to architects are building shapes and design features that may exacerbate wind problems. These include things such as closely spaced buildings or small openings at ground level that cause normally acceptable wind speeds to increase to unacceptable levels. Because wind is a fluid, forcing a given volume at a given speed into a smaller area causes the speed to increase. There have been instances, for example, where localized winds are so great that entry doors cannot be opened or an otherwise pleasant outdoor plaza is unusable.

Other potential problems include *building drift*, which is the distance a building moves from side to side in the wind. This is particularly of concern in very tall buildings where the drift may be several feet. Generally,

a building should be designed stiff enough so that the maximum drift does not exceed 1/500 of the height of the building.

B. Earthquake

Like wind, an earthquake produces *dynamic* loads on a building. During an earthquake, the ground moves both vertically and laterally, but the lateral movement is usually most significant and the vertical movement is ignored.

For some tall buildings or structures with complex shapes or unusual conditions, a *dynamic structural analysis* is required. With this method, a computer is used to model the building and earthquakes to study the response of the structure and what forces are developed. In most cases, however, building codes allow a static analysis of the loads produced, greatly simplifying structural design.

With the *static analysis method*, the total horizontal shear at the base of the building is calculated according to a standard formula. Then, this total lateral force is distributed to the various floors of the building so the designer knows what force the structure must resist. Chapter 14 discusses calculation of earthquake loads in more detail.

3 MISCELLANEOUS LOADS

A. Dynamic Loads

When a load is applied suddenly or changes rapidly, it is called a *dynamic load*. When a force is only applied suddenly, it is often called an *impact load*. Examples of dynamic loads are automobiles moving in a parking garage, elevators traveling in a shaft, or a helicopter landing on the roof of a building. Dynamic loads do not occur on every building but are important to analyze and design for. The Uniform Building Code lists minimum requirements for many of these types of loads. See Table 2.4. In many cases, a dynamic load is simply a static load value multiplied by an impact factor.

A unique type of dynamic load is a *resonant load*. This is a rhythmic application of a force to a structure with the same fundamental period as the structure itself. The *fundamental period* is the time it takes the structure to complete one full oscillation, such as a complete swing from side to side in a tall building in the wind or one up-and-down bounce of a floor. Resonant loads are usually small compared to other types of loads but slowly build over time as the load repeatedly amplifies the motion of the structure. The principle of resonant loading is what makes it possible for a few people to overturn a heavy car by bouncing it on its springs in time with the fundamental period of the springs. The rocking motion of the car eventually is great enough so a final push makes it overturn.

Resonant loads can affect an entire structure, such as repeated gusts of wind on a tall building, or portions of a building. A common problem is a vibrating machine attached to a floor with the same period as the machine's vibrations. In such a situation, the floor can be subjected to forces larger than it was designed for. The problem can be alleviated by placing the machine on resilient pads or springs to dampen the vibration, or by stiffening the floor to change its fundamental period.

Occasionally, a tuned dynamic damper is placed at the top of tall buildings to dampen the effects of wind sway. This is a very heavy mass attached to the sides of the building with springs of the same period as the building. As the building oscillates in one direction, the spring-mounted mass moves in the opposite direction, effectively counteracting the action of the wind. With this approach, costly wind bracing normally required to stiffen the entire building can be minimized.

B. Temperature-Induced Loads

All materials expand when they are heated and contract when they are cooled. The amount of the change is dependent on the material and is expressed as the *coefficient of expansion* measured in inches per foot per degree Fahrenheit. Some materials, like wood, have a low coefficient of expansion while others, like plastic, have a high value. If a material is restrained so it cannot move and then subjected to a temperature change, a load is introduced on the material in addition to any other applied loads.

In the worst case, temperature-induced loads can so overload a structural member that failure may occur. Most often, however, failing to account for temperature-induced loads causes other types of failures such as tight-fitting glass breaking when a metal frame contracts, or masonry walls cracking when expansion joints are not provided. In nearly all cases, the solution is fairly simple: the material or assembly of materials must be allowed to expand and contract for the expected distance. This is fairly easy to calculate and detailed methods are described in Chapter 3.

C. Soil Loads

Retaining walls are required to resist the lateral pressure of the retained material in accordance with accepted engineering practice. The Uniform Building

Table 2.4
UBC Requirements for Dynamic and Special Loads

USE		VERTICAL LOAD	LATERAL LOAD
Category	Description	(Pounds per Square Foot unless Otherwise Noted)	
1. Construction, public access at site (live load)	Walkway, see Sec. 4406	150	
	Canopy, see Sec. 4407	150	
2. Grandstands, reviewing stands, bleachers, and folding and telescoping seating (live load)	Seats and footboards	120[2]	See Footnote No. 3
3. Stage accessories (live load)	Gridirons and fly galleries	75	
	Loft block wells[4]	250	250
	Head block wells and sheave beams[4]	250	250
4. Ceiling framing (live load)	Over stages	20	
	All uses except over stages	10[5]	
5. Partitions and interior walls, see Sec. 2309 (live load)			5
6. Elevators and dumbwaiters (dead and live load)		2 x Total loads[6]	
7. Mechanical and electrical equipment (dead load)		Total loads	
8. Cranes (dead and live load)	Total load including impact increase	1.25 x Total load[7]	0.10 x Total load[8]
9. Balcony railings and guardrails	Exit facilities serving an occupant load greater than 50		50[9]
	Other		20[9]
10. Handrails		See Footnote No. 10	See Footnote No. 10
11. Storage racks	Over 8 feet high	Total loads[11]	See Table No. 23-P
12. Fire sprinkler structural support		250 pounds plus weight of water-filled pipe[12]	See Table No. 23-P
13. Explosion exposure	Hazardous occupancies, see Sec. 910		

[1]The tabulated loads are minimum loads. Where other vertical loads required by this code or required by the design would cause greater stresses, they shall be used.
[2]Pounds per lineal foot.
[3]Lateral sway bracing loads of 24 pounds per foot parallel and 10 pounds per foot perpendicular to seat and footboards.
[4]All loads are in pounds per lineal foot. Head block wells and sheave beams shall be designed for all loft block well loads tributary thereto. Sheave blocks shall be designed with a factor of safety of five.
[5]Does not apply to ceilings which have sufficient total access from below, such that access is not required within the space above the ceiling. Does not apply to ceilings if the attic areas above the ceiling are not provided with access. This live load need not be considered as acting simultaneously with other live loads imposed upon the ceiling framing or its supporting structure.
[6]Where Appendix Chapter 51 has been adopted, see reference standard cited therein for additional design requirements.
[7]The impact factors included are for cranes with steel wheels riding on steel rails. They may be modified if substantiating technical data acceptable to the building official is submitted. Live loads on crane support girders and their connections shall be taken as the maximum crane wheel loads. For pendant-operated traveling crane support girders and their connections, the impact factors shall be 1.10.
[8]This applies in the direction parallel to the runway rails (longitudinal). The factor for forces perpendicular to the rail is 0.20 x the transverse traveling loads (trolley, cab, hooks and lifted loads). Forces shall be applied at top of rail and may be distributed among rails of multiple rail cranes and shall be distributed with due regard for lateral stiffness of the structures supporting these rails.
[9]A load per lineal foot to be applied horizontally at right angles to the top rail.
[10]The mounting of handrails shall be such that the completed handrail and supporting structure are capable of withstanding a load of at least 200 pounds applied in any direction at any point on the rail. These loads shall not be assumed to act cumulatively with Item 9.
[11]Vertical members of storage racks shall be protected from impact forces of operating equipment, or racks shall be designed so that failure of one vertical member will not cause collapse of more than the bay or bays directly supported by that member.
[12]The 250-pound load is to be applied to any single fire sprinkler support point but not simultaneously to all support joints.

PROFESSIONAL PUBLICATIONS ● Belmont, CA

Code allows walls retaining drained earth to be designed for pressure equal to that exerted by a fluid weighing 30 pounds per cubic foot and having a depth equal to that of the retained earth. This is in addition to any surcharge such as vertical loads near the top of the wall or other lateral loads. In addition, retaining walls must be designed to resist sliding by at least 1.5 times the lateral force, and resist overturning by at least 1.5 times the overturning moment.

To calculate the pressure at the bottom of the wall, simply multiply 30 pounds per cubic foot by the depth of the wall to get pounds per square foot. Since the pressure varies uniformly from zero at the very top of the wall where no earth is retained to a maximum at the bottom, the total load is found by calculating the area of the triangular distribution or the maximum earth pressure at the bottom times the height divided by two. This is the total horizontal load per linear foot acting on the wall. See Figure 2.2.

Example 2.4

What is the total horizontal load exerted on a retaining wall 8 feet high?

The pressure at the bottom is 8 feet times 30 pounds per cubic foot, or 240 pounds per square foot. The total horizontal load is 240/2 times 8 feet, or 960 pounds per linear foot of wall.

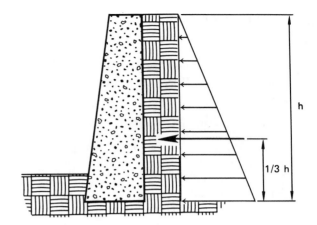

Figure 2.2   Load From Soil on Retaining Wall

It will be shown that this total load acts at the centroid of a triangle, or one-third the distance from the base. Retaining wall design is discussed in more detail in Chapter 6.

D. Water

Loads from water can occur in many situations: in water tanks, swimming pools, and against retaining walls holding back groundwater. The load developed from water and other fluids is equal to the unit weight of the fluid in pounds per cubic foot multiplied by its depth. For water, the weight is about 62 pounds per cubic foot and the water force exerted on structures is called *hydrostatic pressure*.

SAMPLE QUESTIONS

The answers to questions 1 through 5 can be found on the following key list. Select only one answer for each question.

A0 combination load
A1 concentrated load
A2 dead load
A3 drift
A4 dynamic analysis
A5 dynamic load
A6 hydrostatic pressure
A7 impact load
A8 lateral load
A9 live load

B0 resonant load
B1 seismic load
B2 snow load
B3 static analysis
B4 surcharge
B5 temperature load

1. Cars parked on a driveway at the top of a retaining wall are considered what type of load?

A9 B4

2. Cross-bracing can lessen the effects of what?

A8 or A3

3. What might be induced by an elevator?

B0 A5

4. An aerobics class could produce what type of load?

A7 B0

5. What is necessary to design for at a basement wall with undrained soil under an automobile drive-through?

A6 B4

6. A tuned dynamic damper would be used in which of the following situations?

A. a mid-rise concrete structure in an earthquake zone

B. near a mechanical room that contained several vibrating machines

C. in a high-rise building subject to earthquake resonance

D. at the top of a tall building

7. A small commercial office building has 2″ × 10″ wood joists spaced 16 inches on center supporting a hardwood floor over 1/2-inch plywood sheathing. The ceiling below is 1/2-inch gypsum wallboard. Ignoring the beam weight, what is the design live and dead load per linear foot on a beam supporting a central structural bay 14 feet long before allowance is made for live load reduction? (See diagram.)

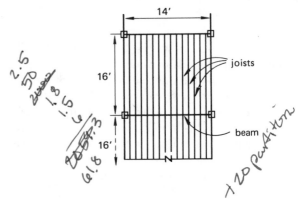

A. 965 pounds per linear foot
B. 1125 pounds per linear foot
C. 1285 pounds per linear foot
D. 1310 pounds per linear foot

8. Which of the following is not correct concerning live load calculations?

A. Live loads can be reduced when a structural member supports more than 150 square feet if the occupancy is not public assembly and if the live load is less than 80 psf.

B. Live loads include snow, people, and furniture.

C. Any live load reduction cannot exceed 40 percent for structural members supporting load from one story.

D. Snow load reduction is calculated according to the formula $R_s = S/40 - 0.5$ if the roof pitch is more than 20 degrees.

9. Select the correct statements about lateral loads.

I. Wind load varies with the height above the ground.

II. Full wind load and snow load should be calculated together to check the worst case situation.

III. Wind load varies with the square of wind velocity.

IV. Total horizontal shear at ground level is used in the dynamic analysis method of seismic design.

V. Drift should not exceed the height of the building divided by 500.

    A. II, III, and V

    B. I, III, IV, and V

    C. I, III, and V

    D. III, IV, and V

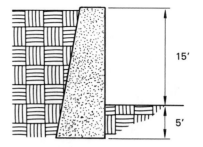

10. What is the total earth pressure acting on the left side of the retaining wall shown in the following diagram? Assume an equivalent fluid pressure of 30 pounds per square foot per foot of height.

    A. 450 plf

    B. 600 plf

    C. 3375 plf

    D. 6000 plf

3 STRUCTURAL FUNDAMENTALS

Nomenclature

a	coefficient of linear expansion	in/in-°F
A	area	in² or ft²
b	base of rectangular section	inches
d	depth of rectangular section or distance between axes	inches
e	total deformation (strain)	inches
E	modulus of elasticity	psi
f	unit stress	psi or psf
I	moment of inertia	in⁴
I_n	moment of inertia of transferred area	in⁴
I_x	moment of inertia of area about neutral axis	in⁴
L	original length	inches
P	total force	pounds or kips
x	original length	inches
ϵ	unit strain	inches per inch
Δt	change in temperature	°F

1 STATICS AND FORCES

A. Statics

Statics is the branch of mechanics that deals with bodies in a state of *equilibrium*. Equilibrium is said to exist when the resultant of any number of forces acting on a body is zero. For example, a 10-pound object on the ground is acted on by gravity to the magnitude of 10 pounds. The ground, in turn, exerts an upward force of 10 pounds and the object is in equilibrium.

Three fundamental principles of equilibrium apply to buildings:

- The sum of all vertical forces acting on a body must equal zero (as in the preceding simple example).

- The sum of all horizontal forces acting on a body must equal zero.

- The sum of all the moments acting on a body must equal zero.

B. Forces

A force is any action applied to an object. In architecture, external forces are called *loads* and result from such actions as the weight of people, wind, snow, or the weight of building materials. The internal structure of a building material must resist external loads with internal forces of their own that are equal in magnitude and of opposite sign. These are called *stresses*. The structural design of buildings is primarily concerned with selecting the size, configuration, and material of components to resist, with a reasonable margin of safety, external forces acting on them.

A force has both direction and magnitude and as such is called a *vector quantity*. Direction is shown by using a line with an arrowhead, and magnitude is indicated by establishing a convenient scale. For example, at a scale of 1 inch equals 2000 pounds, a line 2 inches long represents a force of 4000 pounds. An 8000 pound force would therefore be shown with a line 4 inches long.

The line of action of a force is a line concurrent with the force vector. You can consider a force acting anywhere along the line of action as long as the direction and magnitude do not change. This is the principle of *transmissibility*.

There are several types of forces:

- *Colinear forces* are those whose vectors lie along the same straight line. See Figure 3.1 (a). Structural members subjected to colinear forces such as tension or compression are said to be two-force members.

- *Concurrent forces* are those whose lines of action meet at a common point. See Figure 3.1 (b).

- *Nonconcurrent forces* have lines of action that do not pass through a common point. See Figure 3.1 (c). A special case of this type that is commonly found in architectural applications is a parallel force system, such as a type that may be acting on a beam. See Figure 3.1 (d).

- *Coplanar forces* are forces whose lines of action all lie within the same plane. Noncoplanar forces do not lie within the same plane.

Structural forces in buildings can be any combination of these types. For example, a truss is a collection of sets of concurrent-coplanar forces while a space frame is an example of a combination of sets of concurrent-noncoplanar forces.

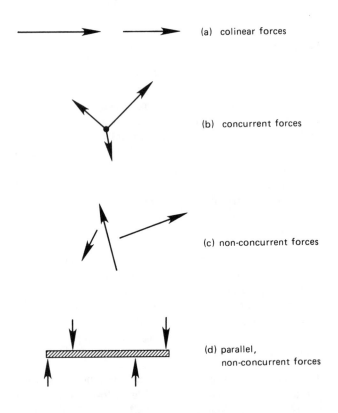

Figure 3.1   Types of Forces

It is often necessary to add two or more concurrent forces or to break down a single force into its components for purposes of structural analysis. The simplest combination of forces are colinear forces. The magnitudes of the forces are added directly in the same direction of force. See Figure 3.2.

Figure 3.2   Addition of Colinear Forces

With concurrent and noncurrent forces, the effect of the direction of the force must be taken into account. The methods used to find resultant forces or to break down a force into its components will be discussed in the section on Structural Analysis in this chapter.

C. Stresses

Stress is the internal resistance to an external force. There are three basic types of stress: tension, compression, and shear. Tension and compression stresses are known as *normal stresses*. All stresses consist of these basic types or some combination.

Tension is stress in which the particles of the member tend to pull apart under load.

Compression is stress in which the particles of the member are pushed together and the member tends to shorten.

Shear is stress in which the particles of a member slide past each other.

With tension and compression, the force acts *perpendicular* to the area of the material resisting the force. With shear, the force acts *parallel* to the area resisting the force.

For these three conditions, stress is expressed as force per unit area and is determined by dividing the total force applied to the total area:

$$f = \frac{P}{A} \qquad 3.1$$

Example 3.1

A balcony is partially supported from structure above by a steel rod 1 1/4 inches in diameter. The load on the rod is 10,000 pounds. What is the stress in the rod?

The area of the rod is:

$$A = \pi r^2$$
$$= 3.14 \times 0.63 \times 0.63 = 1.23 \text{ in}^2$$

From equation 3.1, the stress is

$$f = \frac{10,000}{1.23} = 8130 \text{ pounds per square inch}$$

Other types of stresses consist of *torsion*, *bending*, and *combined* stresses. Torsion is a type of shear in which a member is twisted. Bending is a combination of tension and compression like the type that occurs in beams. This will be discussed in more detail in Chapter 4. Combined loads can occur in many situations. For example, a column resisting loads from above and lateral wind loads is subjected to both compression and bending.

D. Thermal Stress

When a material is subjected to a change in temperature, it expands if heated or contracts if cooled. For an unrestrained material, the general formula is:

$$e = ax\Delta t \qquad 3.2$$

Some coefficients of common materials are shown in Table 3.1.

Table 3.1
Coefficients of Linear Expansion

aluminum	0.0000128	inches/inch-°F
brick	0.0000031	
bronze	0.0000101	
concrete	0.0000065	
glass	0.0000051	
marble	0.0000056	
plastic, acrylic	0.0000450	
structural steel	0.0000067	
wood, fir	0.0000021	
parallel to grain		

If the material is restrained at both ends a change in temperature causes an internal thermal stress. The formula for this stress is:

$$f = Ea\Delta t \qquad 3.3$$

Notice that the unit stress is independent of the cross-sectional area of the member if there are no other loads being applied to the member while it is undergoing thermal stress.

E. Strain and Deformation

As a force is applied to a material, it changes size. For example, a tensile force causes a rod to elongate and narrow while a compressive force causes a material to shorten and widen. Strain is the deformation of a material caused by external forces. It is the ratio of the total change in length of a material to its original length. As a formula, it is represented as:

$$\epsilon = \frac{e}{L} \qquad 3.4$$

As a force is applied to a material, the deformation (strain) is directly proportional to the stress, up to a certain point. This is known as *Hooke's Law*, named after Robert Hooke, a British mathematician and physicist who first discovered it. This relationship is shown graphically in Figure 3.3. At a certain point, however, the material will begin to change length at a faster ratio than the applied force. This point is called the *elastic limit*. At any stress up to the elastic limit, the material will return to its original size if the force is removed. Above the elastic limit there will be permanent deformation, even if the force is removed.

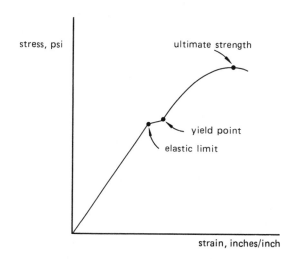

Figure 3.3 Hypothetical Stress-Strain Graph

There is also a point, with some materials, slightly above the elastic limit called the *yield point*. This is the point at which the material continues to deform with very little increase in load. Some materials, such as wood, do not have well-defined elastic limits and no yield points.

If the load is continually increased, the material will ultimately rupture. The unit stress just before this occurs is called the *ultimate strength* of the material.

Although the entire range of a material's stress/strain relationship is interesting from a theoretical point of view, the most important portion from a practical standpoint is where the stress and strain are directly proportional, up to the elastic limit. Sound engineering practices and limitations set by building codes establish the working stresses to be used in calculations at some point below the yield point.

Every material has a characteristic ratio of stress to strain. This is called the *modulus of elasticity*, E, which is a measure of a material's resistance to deformation or its stiffness. It can be expressed as the following formula:

$$E = \frac{f}{\epsilon} \qquad 3.5$$

Since stress was defined as total force divided by total area, $f = P/A$ (formula 3.1), and strain was defined as total strain divided by original length, $\epsilon = e/L$ (formula 3.4), the equation can be rewritten:

$$E = \frac{P/A}{e/L} = \frac{PL}{Ae} \qquad 3.6$$

This equation can be also be used to find the total strain (deformation) of a material under a given load by rearranging the values:

$$e = \frac{PL}{AE} \qquad 3.7$$

Example 3.2

If a load of 12,000 pounds is applied to a $3'0''$, 4×4 Douglas fir #2 wood column, how much will it compress? The modulus of elasticity for Douglas fir #2 is 1,700,000 psi.

The actual size of a 4×4 is 3 1/3″ × 3 1/2″ or 12.25 square inches. The change in length is therefore:

$$e = \frac{12,000(3)(12)}{12.25(1,700,000)} = 0.021 \text{ inches}$$

Note that the 3 foot dimension had to be multiplied by 12 to convert to inches so all dimensional units would be consistent.

0.021 inches is between 1/64 inch (0.01563) and 1/32 inch (0.03125).

Some representative values of E for various materials are given in Table 3.2 to show how they vary with material type. Actual values of E to be used in calculations should be derived from building codes or accepted tables of values.

Table 3.2
Modulus of Elasticity
of Some Common Building Materials*

material	modulus of elasticity (psi)
structural steel	29,000,000
brass	15,000,000
aluminum	10,000,000
concrete (3000 psi)	3,200,000
lumber (Douglas fir-larch)	1,700,000
lumber (western cedar)	900,000

*Note that these are representative values only. Exact values depend on such things as the alloy of the metal, mix of concrete, or species and grade of lumber.

F. Moment

Moment is a special condition of a force applied to a structure. A *moment* is the tendency of a force to cause rotation about a point. As such, it is the product of the force times the distance to the point about which it is acting. The units are in foot-pounds, inch-pounds, or kip-feet. Figure 3.4 illustrates a simple condition of moments where two downward forces are balancing a lever on one pivot point. Even though the forces are of unequal value, they balance the lever because the distances from the pivot point result in equal moments.

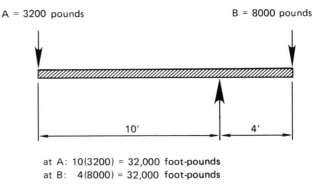

at A: 10(3200) = 32,000 foot-pounds
at B: 4(8000) = 32,000 foot-pounds

Figure 3.4 Moments in Equilibrium

Understanding the concept of moments is important in structural design because in a system in equilibrium the algebraic sum of moments about any point is zero. This concept allows you to analyze structures, determine support reactions, and design structural systems. When dealing with moments, it is necessary to be consistent with the values given to moments based on the direction in which they act. If a force tends to cause a clockwise rotation, the moment is said to be *positive*. If it tends to cause a counterclockwise rotation, the moment is said to be *negative*. This is a purely arbitrary convention and could be reversed, as long as the calculations are kept consistent.

Example 3.3

Consider a simply supported beam with two concentrated loads at the locations shown in the sketch. Determine the reactions of the two supports, ignoring the weight of the beam itself.

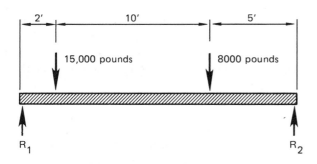

Since there are two unknowns, R_1 and R_2, select one of these points as the pivot point about which to make calculations. This eliminates one of the variables because the distance the force acts at the pivot point is zero, so the moment will be zero also. Select R_1 as the first point.

Since the algebraic sum about this point is zero, the formula becomes:

About R_1,

$$15,000(2) + 8000(12) - R_2(17) = 0$$

The two concentrated loads tend to cause rotation in a clockwise direction (positive) while the reaction of the other beam support tends to cause a counterclockwise rotation (negative) about point R_1.

Solving for R_2 gives 7412 pounds.

Since one of the principles of equilibrium is that the sum of all vertical forces equals zero, R_1 and R_2 (upward) must equal the loads (downward). Therefore,

$$R_1 = 15,000 + 8000 - 7412 = 15,588 \text{ pounds}$$

However, you can use the same procedure of summing moments about reaction R_2 to find R_1 another way:

About R_2,

$$R_1(17) - 15,000(15) - 8000(5) = 0$$
$$R_1 = 15,588 \text{ pounds}$$

Moments on beams will be discussed in more detail in Chapter 4.

2   PROPERTIES OF SECTIONS

All structural sections, regardless of material, used to support building loads have certain properties. These properties affect how efficiently they resist a load and how they are designed. The most common properties are *area*, *centroid*, *statical moment*, *moment of inertia*, *section modulus*, and *radius of gyration*. The area of a section is self-explanatory and its use in calculating stress has already been shown.

A. Centroid

In all solid bodies, there is a point at which the mass of the body can be considered concentrated. This is the *center of gravity*. Although technically a flat area cannot have a center of gravity because it has no mass, the point on a plane surface that corresponds to the center of gravity is called the *centroid*. In symmetrical sections, such as a rectangular wood beam or round bar, the centroid is located in the geometric center of the area as shown in Figure 3.5.

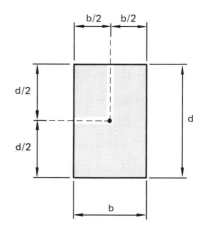

Figure 3.5 Centroid of a Symmetrical Area

The locations of centroids have been computed for simple non-symmetrical areas (see Figure 3.6).

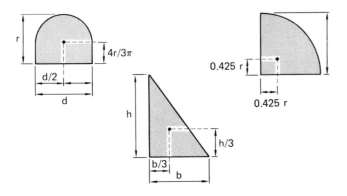

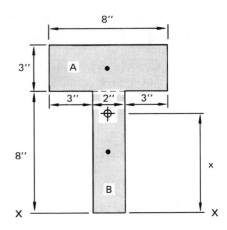

Figure 3.6 Centroids for Some Common Shapes

Manufacturers of structural members also include the location of centroids as part of their published data. Figure 3.7 illustrates one example of a steel section as found in the American Institute of Steel Construction *Manual of Steel Construction.*

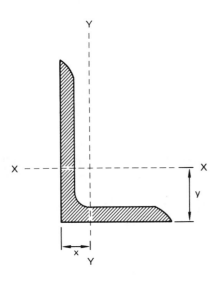

Figure 3.7 Centroidal Axes of Steel Angle with Unequal Legs

B. Statical Moment

To find the centroid of unsymmetrical areas, the statical moment must be used. The statical moment of a plane area with respect to an axis is the product of the area times the perpendicular distance from the centroid of the area to the axis. If a complex unsymmetrical area is divided into two or more simple parts, the statical moment of the entire area is equal to the sum of the statical moments of the parts.

Example 3.4

Locate the centroid of the area shown in the following figure.

Select any convenient axis. In this case, use the X-X axis at the base of the figure. Let x equal the distance from the axis to the centroid of the entire figure. Divide the area into two rectangular sections, A and B, each having their centroids in the geometric center of their respective areas.

The sum of the statical moments of the parts equals the statical moment of the entire section—all about the axis X-X. The distance from X-X to the centroid of area A is 9.5 inches, and the distance to the centroid of area B is 4 inches.

$$(9.5)(24) + (4)(16) = x(40)$$
$$x = 7.3 \text{ inches}$$

Since this figure is symmetrical about the vertical, or Y-Y axis, the centroid will be in the center of the figure between the right and left edges.

If there is a hole in the figure, treat the statical moment of the hole as a negative number.

C. Moment of Inertia

Another important property of structural sections is the moment of inertia. In general terms, this is a measure of the *bending stiffness* of a structural member's cross-sectional shape, similar to how the modulus of elasticity is a measure of the stiffness of the material of a structural member.

In more exact terms, the moment of inertia about a certain axis of a section is the summation of all the infinitely small areas of the section multiplied by the square of the distance from the axis to each of these areas. Its common designation is I and its units are inches to the fourth power. It is most common to use the neutral axis (axis passing through the centroid) as the axis of reference, but the moment of inertia about an axis through the base of a figure is also useful when calculating I for unsymmetrical sections.

The derivation of the moment of inertia for a section is done with calculus, but I for common shapes can be calculated with simple equations that have been derived with calculus. In addition, most manufacturers of structural shapes give the value of the moment of inertia with respect to both vertical and horizontal axes passing through the centroid. For example, the tables of structural steel shapes give the value for I for both the X-X and Y-Y centroidal axes.

For rectangular sections, the moment of inertia about the centroidal axis parallel to the base is:

$$I = \frac{bd^3}{12} \qquad\qquad 3.8$$

The moment of inertia about an axis through the base of a rectangular section is:

$$I = \frac{bd^3}{3} \qquad\qquad 3.9$$

Example 3.5

Find the moment of inertia of a solid wood beam 6 inches wide and 13 1/2 inches deep.

$$I = \frac{6(13.5)^3}{12}$$
$$= 1230 \text{ in}^4$$

In order to find the moment of inertia for composite areas you must transfer the moment of inertia of each section about its centroid to a new axis, typically the centroid of the composite section. The general formula for doing this as, illustrated in Figure 3.8, is:

$$I_n = I_x + Ad^2 \qquad\qquad 3.10$$

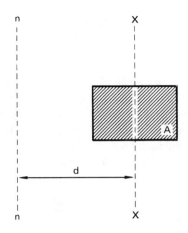

Figure 3.8   Transfer of Moment of Inertia

The transferred moments of inertia of the various sections are then added to get the moment of inertia for the entire section.

Example 3.6

Using the same composite section as shown in Example 3.4 calculate the moment of inertia.

The first step is to locate the centroid of the figure. This was done in the previous example problem and was found to be 7.3 inches.

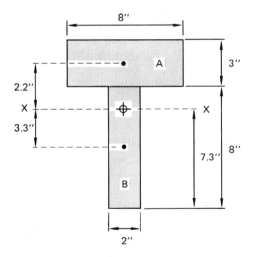

The next task is to transfer the individual moments of inertia about this centroidal axis and add them. To do this, it is helpful to set up a table so all the figures and calculations can be seen easily. This is an especially useful technique when you are dealing with several individual areas.

The moment of inertia of areas A and B are found with formula 3.8, and is denoted I_o to express the fact that it is the moment of inertia about an axis passing through the centroid of the elementary figure. d is the distance from the centroidal axis to the axes of areas A and B. Performing the calculations yields:

area	I_o	A	d	Ad^2	$I_o + Ad^2$
A	18	24	2.2	116	134
B	85	16	3.3	174	259
					$I_x = 393$ in^4

The moment of inertia is dependent on the *area* of a section and the *distance* of the area from the neutral axis, but from the statement that moment of inertia is the summation of the areas times the square of the distances of those areas from the neutral axis. From formulas 3.8 and 3.9, it is evident that the *depth* of a beam has a greater bearing on its resistance to bending than its width or total area. This explains why a board placed on edge between two supports is much stronger than the same board placed on its side.

There are two other important properties of sections: the *section modulus* and the *radius of gyration*. However, these are more appropriately discussed in Chapter 4. Section modulus will be explained in the sections on beams and the theory of bending, while radius of gyration will be discussed in the section on columns.

3   STRUCTURAL ANALYSIS

A. Resultant Forces

There are times when it is desirable to combine two or more concurrent forces into one force such that the one force produces the same effect on a body as the concurrent forces. This single force is called the *resultant*. If the forces are colinear, as described previously in this chapter, the resultant is simply the sum of the forces, with forces acting upward or to the right considered positive and forces acting downward or to the left considered negative. For example, in Figure 3.9 the three forces are added to get the resultant.

For concurrent forces (forces whose lines of action pass through a common point), both the magnitude and direction must be taken into account. Consider the two forces shown in Figure 3.10 (a). The resultant of these forces can be found graphically or algebraically.

To find it graphically, draw the lines of force to any convenient scale, such as 1 inch equals 100 pounds, and in the direction they are acting as shown in Figure 3.10 (b). Then draw a line parallel to each force starting with the head of the force vector to form a parallelogram. Connect the point of concurrence to the opposite corner of the parallelogram with a line. This is the resultant whose magnitude and direction can be found by scaling the length of it and measuring its angle.

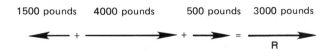

Figure 3.9   Resultant of Colinear Forces

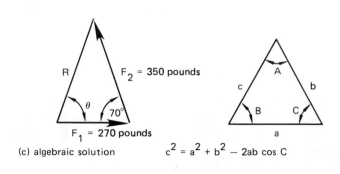

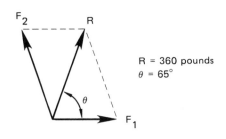

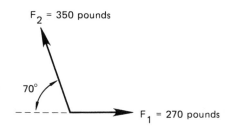

Figure 3.10   Finding the Resultant of Concurrent Coplanar Forces

To find the resultant algebraically, sketch a force triangle as shown in Figure 3.10 (c). Since the forces are in equilibrium, the triangle must close. The resultant will then be the third side of the triangle. Both the magnitude and direction can be solved with trigonometry using the law of cosines and sines, or the Pythagorean theorem for a right triangle.

To solve for the magnitude of the resultant use the law of cosines with the general form:

$$c^2 = a^2 + b^2 - 2ab\cos C \qquad 3.11$$

From Figure 3.10 (c),

$$R^2 = 350^2 + 270^2 - 2(350)(270)\cos 70$$
$$R = 122,500 + 72,900 - 2(94,500).34$$
$$R = 362.13 \text{ pounds}$$

To solve for the direction of the resultant use the law of sines with the general form:

$$\frac{a}{\sin A} = \frac{b}{\sin B} = \frac{c}{\sin C} \qquad 3.12$$

$$\frac{F_2}{\sin \theta} = \frac{R}{\sin 70}$$
$$\sin \theta = \frac{F_2(\sin 70)}{R}$$
$$\theta = 65.26°$$

B. Components of a Force

Just as a resultant can be found for two or more forces, so can a single force be resolved into two components. This is often required when analyzing loads on a sloped surface (a roof, for example) and it is necessary to find the horizontal and vertical reactions. As with finding resultant forces, both graphic and algebraic solutions are possible.

Example 3.7

Consider the diagonal force shown in the sketch. What would be the vertical and horizontal reactions necessary to resist this force?

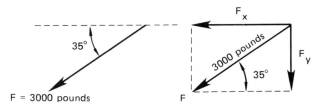

F = 3000 pounds

The reactions to the force would be equal in magnitude but opposite in direction to the vertical and horizontal components of the force. To solve the problem algebraically, construct a right triangle with the 3000 pound force as the hypotenuse and the legs of the triangle as the horizontal and vertical forces.

Then,

$$\sin 35° = \frac{F_y}{3000}$$
$$F_y = 1721 \text{ pounds}$$
$$\text{and}$$
$$\cos 35° = \frac{F_x}{3000}$$
$$F_x = 2457 \text{ pounds}$$

Note that the same solution could be obtained by drawing the triangle to scale and measuring the legs of the triangle, although this method is not as accurate.

Three or more forces can be resolved by resolving each one into their horizontal and vertical components, summing these components (taking care to be consistent with positive and negative signs), then finding the resultant of the horizontal and vertical components with the Pythagorean theorem.

C. Free-Body Diagrams

In analyzing structures it is sometimes convenient to extract a portion of the structure and represent the forces acting on it with force vectors. The portion then under study is called a *free-body diagram* to which the principles of equilibrium can be applied.

Consider the simple structure shown in Figure 3.11 (a) with a single load of 3000 pounds applied at the end. Find the load in member *BC*.

Take member *BC* as a free body as shown in Figure 3.11 (b). There are three forces acting on this member: the vertical load of 3000 pounds, the force in member *BC* (compression), and the force through member *AB* (tension). Since these forces act through a common point, and since the structure is in equilibrium, you can construct a force triangle with the force vectors as the sides of the triangle as shown in Figure 3.11 (c).

The angle, θ, can be determined from $\tan\theta = 5/8$, or 32°.

Then, the force, F, in member BC will be

$$\sin 32° = \frac{3000}{F} = 5661 \text{ pounds}$$

Knowing the force in member BC, you could find the horizontal and vertical components of the force using the methods described in the previous section.

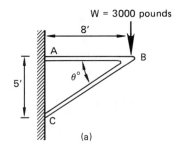

(a)

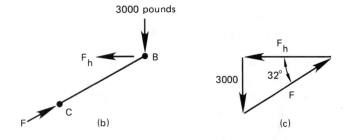

Figure 3.11 Free-Body Diagrams

SAMPLE QUESTIONS

1. What are the horizontal and vertical components of the force shown?

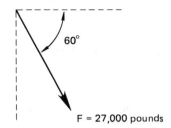

A. $F_x = 13,500$ pounds; $F_y = 23,283$ pounds

B. $F_x = 15,588$ pounds; $F_y = 22,046$ pounds

C. $F_x = 31,177$ pounds; $F_y = 54,000$ pounds

D. $F_x = 23,383$ pounds; $F_y = 13,500$ pounds

2. The elastic limit of a material is:

A. the point at which a material continues to deform without any increase in load.

B. the maximum unit stress that determines the engineering working stress to design a member.

C. the point beyond which unit stress increases faster than unit strain.

D. the unit stress below which deformation is directly proportional to stress.

The answers to questions 3 through 6 can be found on the following key list. Select only one answer for each question.

```
A0  colinear force
A1  concurrent force
A2  couple
A3  elastic limit
A4  equilibrium
A5  force
A6  modulus of elasticity
A7  moment
A8  moment of inertia
A9  nonconcurrent force

B0  resultant force
B1  statical moment
B2  strain
B3  stress
B4  transmissibility
B5  ultimate strength
```

3. The stiffness due to a structural member's shape is described by what term?

4. What are compression and bending examples of?

5. A force can be considered acting anywhere along the line of action of the force if its direction and magnitude do not change because of what principle?

6. What causes the tendency of a body to rotate?

7. A load of 3000 pounds is applied to the support struts shown. What is the compressive force in each strut?

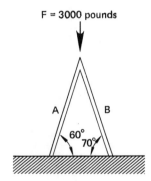

A. $A = 1320$ pounds; $B = 1680$ pounds

B. $A = 1250$ pounds; $B = 1983$ pounds

C. $A = 1339$ pounds; $B = 1958$ pounds

D. $A = 1500$ pounds; $B = 2898$ pounds

8. The bridge railing shown must support a maximum load of 600 pounds laterally. What is the compression force in the diagonal member?

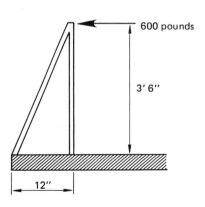

A. 2184 pounds

B. 2100 pounds

C. 624 pounds

D. 577 pounds

9. What are the magnitudes of the reactions at the beam supports shown? Assume that the weight of the uniform load acts at its center as a concentrated load.

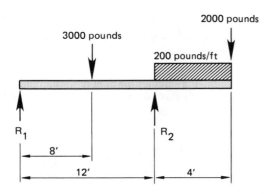

A. $R_1 = 2067$ pounds; $R_2 = 3733$ pounds

B. $R_1 = 200$ pounds; $R_2 = 5600$ pounds

C. $R_1 = 1800$ pounds; $R_2 = 4000$ pounds

D. $R_1 = 300$ pounds; $R_2 = 4900$ pounds

10. Thermal stress in a restrained member is dependent on:

I. the change in temperature

II. the area of the member

III. the coefficient of linear expansion

IV. the unit strain

V. the modulus of elasticity

A. I, II, III, and IV

B. I, III, IV, and V

C. I, III, and V

D. all of the above

4 BEAMS AND COLUMNS

Nomenclature

A	area	in^2
b	width of beam	inches
c	distance from extreme fiber in bending to neutral axis	inches
d	depth of beam	inches
E	modulus of elasticity	psi
f	allowable fiber stress in bending	psi
f_b	extreme fiber stress in bending	
F_a	allowable axial unit stress	psi
I	moment of inertia	in^4
l	length of column	inches
M	bending moment	inch-pounds or foot-pounds
P	concentrated load	pounds or kips
Q	statical moment about neutral axis of the area above the plane under consideration	in^3
r	radius of gyration	inches
S	section modulus	in^3
v_h	horizontal shear stress	psi
V	vertical shearing force	pounds
w	uniformly distributed load	pounds or kips per linear foot
W	total uniformly distributed load	pounds or kips

1 BEAMS

A. Basic Principles

When a simply supported beam is subjected to a load, it deflects as shown in the exaggerated diagram in Figure 4.1 (a).

In order for this to happen, the top of the beam compresses and the bottom of the beam stretches which causes compressive stresses to develop in the top half of the beam and tension stresses to develop in the bottom half. At the neutral axis, or centroid, which is in the geometric center of the beam if it is rectangular or symmetrical, the beam does not change length so no compressive or tension stresses are developed.

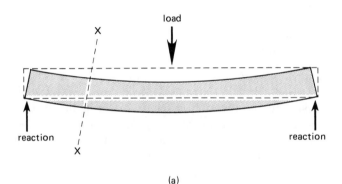

(a)

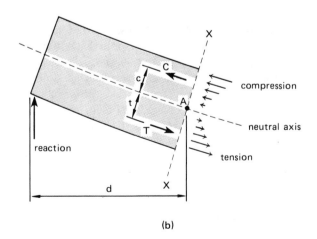

(b)

Figure 4.1 Behavior of Simply Supported Beam Under Load

The actions occurring in the beam can be seen more clearly by taking an enlarged section of the beam to the left of an arbitrary cut as shown in Figure 4.1 (b).

In this diagram there are only three forces acting on the section: the reaction of the support, the compressive forces in the top of the beam, and the tensile forces in the bottom of the beam. If the beam is in equilibrium as discussed in Chapter 3, then all the moment forces must cancel out; those acting in a clockwise rotation must equal those acting in a counterclockwise rotation. Therefore, taking moments about point A in Figure 4.1 (b):

$$R \times d = (C \times c) + (T \times t) \qquad 4.1$$

This formula represents the basic theory of bending, that the internal resisting moments at any point in a beam must equal the bending moments produced by the external loads on the beam.

As shown in Figure 4.1 (a), the moment increases as the distance from the reaction increases or as the distance from the neutral axis increases (assuming the loads stay the same). Therefore, in the case of a simply supported beam, the maximum moment occurs at the center of the span and the beam is subjected to its highest bending stresses at the extreme top and bottom fibers. (*Fibers* is a general term regardless of the beam's material.)

Therefore, in order for a beam to support loads, the material, size, and shape of the beam must be selected to sustain the resisting moments at the point on the beam where the moment is greatest. There must be some way to relate the bending moments to the actual properties of a real beam. Although the derivation will not be given here, the final formula is simple.

$$\frac{M}{f_b} = \frac{I}{c} \qquad 4.2$$

Theoretically, formula 4.2 can be used to design a beam to resist bending forces, but it gets a little cumbersome with steel sections and unusual shapes. There is another property of every structural section that simplifies the formula even further. This is the *section modulus*, which is the ratio of the beam's moment of inertia to the distance from the neutral axis to the outermost part of the section (extreme fiber).

$$S = \frac{I}{c} \qquad 4.3$$

Substituting the value of S with formula 4.2 gives:

$$S = \frac{M}{f} \qquad 4.4$$

So, knowing only the maximum moment on a beam caused by a particular loading condition and the maximum allowable fiber stress (given in tables and building codes), you can calculate the section modulus required. By looking in reference tables or manufacturer's tables of their product, you can find the minimum required section to support the bending loads. For example, the *Manual of Steel Construction* published by the American Institute of Steel Construction (AISC) gives the section modulus for all beam sections. How this formula is used will be illustrated in a sample question.

Another fundamental type of stress in beams is *shear*. This is the tendency of two adjacent portions of the beam to slide past each other in a vertical direction. See Figure 4.2 (a).

There is also *horizontal shear*, which is the tendency of two adjacent portions of a beam to slide past each other in the direction parallel to the length of the beam. This tendency can readily be seen when you consider that the top portions of a beam tend to compress and the bottom portions tend to stretch. See Figure 4.2 (b).

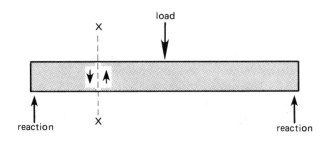

(a) vertical shear

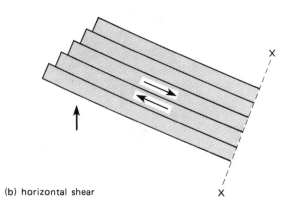

(b) horizontal shear

Figure 4.2   Shear Forces in Beams

The general equation for finding horizontal shear stress is:

$$v_h = \frac{VQ}{Ib} \qquad 4.5$$

Q is the statical moment discussed in Chapter 3.

For rectangular sections, the horizontal shear stress at mid-depth of the beam, where the stress is a maximum, is given by:

$$v_h = \frac{3V}{2bd} \qquad \text{(at neutral axis of beam)} \qquad 4.6$$

This formula is obtained by substituting applicable terms in formula 4.5 for the specific case of a rectangular beam. Usually, horizontal shear is not a problem except in wood beams where the horizontal fibers of the wood make an ideal place for the beam to split and shear in this direction.

Another important aspect of the behavior of beams is their tendency to deflect under the action of external loads. Although beam deflection usually does not control the selection of beam size (as does bending or horizontal shear stress), it is an important factor that must be calculated. In some cases, it can be the controlling factor in determining beam size. Even though a large deflection will usually not lead to a structural collapse, excessive deflection can cause finish materials to crack, pull partitions away from the floor or ceiling, crush full-height walls, and can result in a bouncy floor structure.

B. Types of Beams

There are several basic types of beams. These are shown in Figure 4.3 with their typical deflections under load shown exaggerated. The simply supported, overhanging, and continuous beam all have ends that are free to rotate as the load is applied. The cantilever and fixed end beams have one or both sides restrained against rotation. A continuous beam is one that is held up by more than two supports. Of course, there are many variations of these types, such as an overhanging beam with one end fixed, but these are the most typical situations.

There are also two typical kinds of loads on building structures: *concentrated load* and *uniformly distributed load*. Graphic representations of these loads are shown in Figure 4.4. A concentrated load is shown with an arrow and designated P, and a uniformly distributed load is shown as w pounds per linear foot or W for the total load. Loads may either be expressed in pounds or kips (one kip is 1000 pounds). The resultant of uniformly distributed loads is at the center of the loads. This principle is particularly useful when summing moments of partial uniform loads.

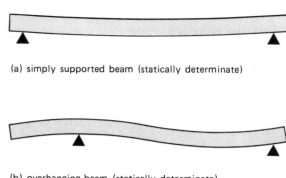

(a) simply supported beam (statically determinate)

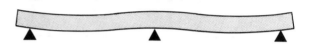

(b) overhanging beam (statically determinate)

(c) continuous beam (statically indeterminate)

(d) cantilever beam (statically determinate)

(e) fixed end beam (statically indeterminate)

Figure 4.3 Types of Beams

It is worth noting that simply supported, overhanging, and cantilever beams are *statically determinate*. This means that the reactions can be found using the equations of equilibrium. That is, the summation of horizontal, vertical, and moment forces equal zero as described in Chapter 3. Continuous and fixed-end beams are statically indeterminate and other, more complex, calculation methods are required to find reactions in these types of beams. The examination will deal primarily with determinate beams so only these types will be described here.

One of the basic requirements for the structural design of a beam is to determine what the stresses due to bending moment and vertical shear will be that are caused by the particular loading conditions. Before these are determined, however, the reactions of the supports must be calculated. The method of doing this

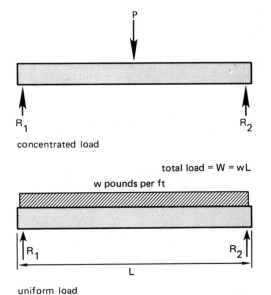

concentrated load

total load = W = wL

w pounds per ft

uniform load

Figure 4.4   Types of Loads

for statically determinate beams was introduced in Chapter 3 but will be briefly reviewed here.

Remember the three basic principles of equilibrium:

- The sum of all vertical forces acting on a body equal zero.

- The sum of all horizontal forces acting on a body equal zero.

- The sum of all moments acting on a body or the moment of all forces about a point on the body equal zero.

Additionally, as a matter of convention, if a force tends to cause a clockwise rotation, the resulting moment is said to be positive; if it tends to cause a counterclockwise rotation, it is said to be negative.

Example 4.1

Find the reactions of the beam shown.

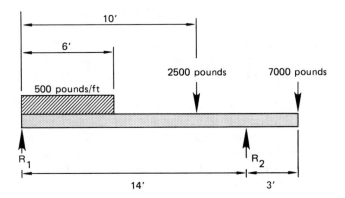

By summing the moments about R_1 you can eliminate one of the unknowns. Each of the three loads tends to cause a clockwise rotation about point R_1 so these will be positive numbers and the resisting reaction, R_2 will tend to cause a counterclockwise rotation so this will be negative. The sum must be zero. Remember that the total load of the uniform load is taken to act at its center, or 3 feet from R_1.

$$3(500 \times 6) + 2500(10) + 7000(17) - 14(R_2) = 0$$
$$R_2 = 10,929 \text{ pounds}$$

Since the summation of all vertical forces must also be equal, the reaction R_1 can be found by subtracting 10,929 from the total of all loads acting on the beam, or:

$$[(500 \times 6) + 2500 + 7000] - 10,929 = 1571 \text{ pounds}$$

The same answer for R_1 can be found by summing moments about reaction R_2.

Once all the loads and reactions are known, shear and moment diagrams can be drawn. These are graphic representations of the value of the shear and moment at all points on the beam.

Although it is not critical to know the values at every point on the beam, there are certain important points that are of interest in designing the beam—mainly where the shear and moment are at their maximum values and where they are zero.

C. Shear Diagrams

A shear diagram is a graphic representation of the values of the *vertical shear* anywhere along a beam. To find the values, take a section at any point and algebraically sum the reactions and loads to the left of the section. The same answer can be found by taking values to the right of the section, but the convention for both shear and moment is to work from left to right. Also by convention, upward forces are considered positive and downward forces are considered negative. The standard designation for shear is V.

Example 4.2

What is the vertical shear at points 4 feet and 10 feet to the right of reaction R_1 as shown in the sketch?

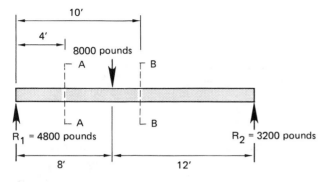

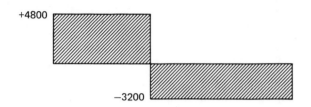

(a) beam loading and reactions

(b) shear diagram

diagram because you only have to calculate shear at a few points and then just connect the lines.

A uniformly distributed load creates a slightly different looking shear diagram. Consider the same beam loaded with a uniform load of 1500 pounds per linear foot. See Figure 4.5 (a). The total load is 1500×20, or 30,000 pounds, which is equally distributed between the two reactions. Just at the left reaction R_1 the only force is the reaction of $+15,000$ pounds. Beginning here, for the remainder of the beam, the uniform load begins to act in a downward direction. At a point 1 foot from the reaction, the shear is $15,000 - (1 \times 1500) = 13,500$ pounds. At a point 3 feet from the reaction, the shear is $15,000 - (3 \times 1500)$, or 10,500 pounds. At the midpoint of the span, the shear is zero and begins to be a negative value because the accumulating load is now larger than the reaction R_1. At reaction R_2, the positive value of the reaction brings the shear back to zero which is consistent with the principles of equilibrium.

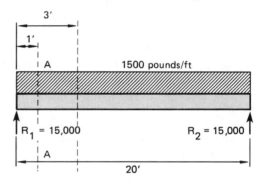

(a) beam loading and reactions

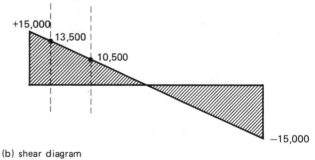

(b) shear diagram

Figure 4.5 Shear Diagram of Uniformly Loaded Beam

First, compute the reaction using the summation of moments as discussed previously. $R_1 = 4800$ pounds, and $R_2 = 3200$ pounds.

Now, consider the point 4 feet from the left reaction marked as A-A in the sketch. At this point there is only the reaction of 4800 pounds acting in an upward direction so the shear is 4800 pounds. At the point 10 feet from the reaction there are two forces to the left of the section, the reaction of $+4800$ pounds and the load of -8000 pounds for a net shear of -3200 pounds. Notice that this is exactly the same as the reaction R_2. This makes sense because there are no other loads and reactions, so the summation of all vertical loads must equal zero as dictated by the principles of equilibrium.

To draw the shear diagram of a beam, first draw the beam and its loads to scale as shown in the upper portion of the sketch. Below the beam sketch, draw a horizontal line the same length as the beam and decide on a convenient vertical scale to represent the loading. Beginning from the left, the values of the shear are plotted above and below this line, the positive values above and the negative values below. The lower portion of the sketch shows the shear diagram for the beam.

You should notice two things about the shear diagram. First, when there are no intervening loads between a reaction and a load (or between two loads) the portion of the shear diagram between them is a horizontal line. Second, a concentrated load or reaction causes the shear diagram to change abruptly in the vertical direction. Knowing these two facts makes it easy to draw a shear

Once again, notice a simple fact: a uniform load creates a shear diagram with a uniformly sloping line. In the case of the example shown in Figure 4.5 (b), you only need to calculate the shears at the reactions, plot the one on the left as positive and the one on the right as negative, and connect the two points with a straight line. If the diagram is drawn to scale, you can find the shear at any point by simply scaling the drawing. For a more exact value, you can use the principle of similar triangles to find the shear at any distance along the beam.

With a shear diagram in hand you have two important pieces of information vital to designing the beam. First, you know what the *maximum shear* is. In the case of Example 4.2, the maximum shear is 4800 pounds; in Figure 4.5, the maximum is 15,000 pounds. You also know where the value of shear is zero, which is the point on the beam where maximum moment occurs and where the beam has its greatest tendency to fail in bending. This will be shown in drawing moment diagrams.

D. Moment Diagrams

Like shear diagrams, moment diagrams are a graphic representation of the *moment* at all points along a beam. To find the moment at any point, remember that the bending moment is the algebraic sum of the moments of the forces to the left of the section under consideration and that moment is the value of force times distance. As mentioned in Chapter 3, moments tending to cause a clockwise rotation are considered positive, and those causing a counterclockwise rotation are considered negative.

Example 4.3

Using the same beam and loading as shown in Example 4.2, find the moments at sections *A-A* and *B-B*.

To visualize the situation a little easier, draw free-body diagrams of the two conditions. See the accompanying illustration. Of course, the moment at the reaction is zero since the moment arm distance is zero. At point *A-A*, 4 feet from the left reaction, the moment is:

$$4 \times 4800 = 19,200 \text{ foot-pounds}$$

At point *B-B*, the moment is:

$$(4800 \times 10) - (8000 \times 2) = 32,000 \text{ foot-pounds}$$

Because the maximum moment occurs where the shear diagram crosses zero, it is wise to calculate moment at this point also. From the shear diagram shown in Example 4.2, this is the point where the concentrated load occurs. The moment just to the left of this point is $4800 \times 8 = 38,400$ foot-pounds. Just to the right of this point the concentrated load begins to act in a counterclockwise rotation so the moment begins to decrease from the maximum until it is again zero at the right-hand support.

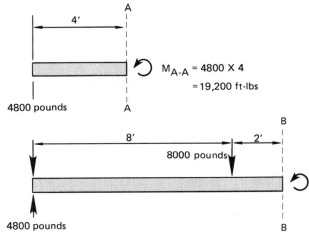

$$M_{A-A} = 4800 \times 4 = 19,200 \text{ ft-lbs}$$

$$M_{B-B} = 4800 \times 10 - 8000 \times 2 = 32,000 \text{ ft-lbs}$$

To draw the moment diagram, you can calculate moments at several points and connect them with a line in a way similar to drawing the shear diagram. This is shown in Figure 4.6 along with the beam loading and shear diagrams from Example 4.2 repeated to show the relationship between the three drawings. Positive moment is shown above the base line and negative moment (if any) shown below the line. Negative moment will be illustrated in a later example.

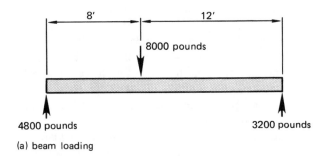

(a) beam loading

(b) shear diagram

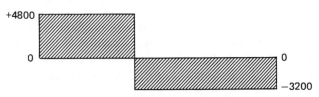

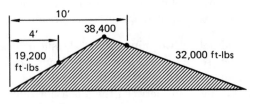

(c) moment diagram

Figure 4.6 Relationship of Shear and Moment Diagrams

As with shear diagrams, you should notice some important facts about the moment diagram. First, the *maximum moment* does occur where the shear diagram passes through zero and this is indicated by the highest point of the moment diagram. Second, when the shear diagram is a constant horizontal line between two concentrated loads or reaction, the shear diagram between these two points is a straight, constant sloped line. Third, where the shear changes abruptly as shown by a vertical line, the slope of the line representing moment also changes abruptly.

Also note, as in the next example, that when there is a uniformly distributed load, and the shear diagram is a sloped line, the moment diagram will be composed of one or more parabolic curves.

Example 4.4

Draw the moment diagram of the example previously shown in Figure 4.5. The beam loading, reactions, and shear diagrams are repeated in the sketch for convenience along with the moment diagram to illustrate the relationship between the three.

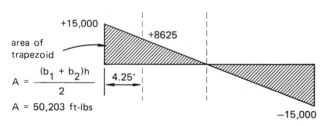

(a) beam loading

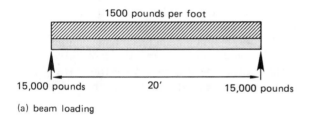

(b) shear diagram

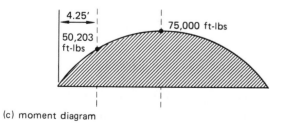

(c) moment diagram

Since the distance of the moment arm at each reaction is zero, the moment at these two points will also be zero.

The maximum moment will occur where the shear diagram passes through zero, so start here. The moment is:

$$M = (15,000 \times 10) - [(1500 \times 10) \times 5]$$
$$= 75,000 \text{ foot-pounds}$$

Remember, when calculating moments due to uniform loads, their resultant is at the center of the loads and therefore the moment of those loads is calculated as if the total load was concentrated at their midpoints. This is why the uniform load on the beam is multiplied by 5 feet in the preceding calculation. It is recorded as a negative number because it tends to cause a counterclockwise rotation about the center of the beam where moments are taken.

To find other points of the moment diagram curve you could calculate several moments and connect the points with a smooth curve, but the curve of a moment diagram of a uniformly loaded beam is parabolic so this is usually not necessary.

Note one final interesting point: The area of the shear diagram at any point along the beam is numerically equal to the moment of the beam at that same point. Thus, at the midpoint of the beam in shown in the sketch, the area of the triangle is $(15,000 \times 10)/2$, or 75,000, exactly the same as calculating it with moment arms. Since the shear diagram is drawn to scale in pound units in the vertical direction and foot units in the horizontal direction, the result is in foot-pounds.

If, in the example shown in the sketch, you wanted to find the moment at a point 4.25 feet from the left reaction, you would only need to find the area of the trapezoid with a height of 4.25 feet, the larger base of 15,000 pounds and the smaller base of 8625 pounds. This latter figure can easily be found by the law of proportions of similar triangles.

Example 4.5

Find the reactions and draw the shear and moment diagrams of the beam shown in the following illustration.

This example is more complicated that previous ones and illustrates negative moment and combinations of load types.

First, find the reactions. As before, find the sum of moments about one of the reactions and set them equal to zero. About reaction R_1 the equation is:

$$[(1000 \times 10) \times 5] + (3000 \times 6) - R_2(12)$$
$$+ (5000 \times 15) = 0$$
$$50,000 + 18,000 + 75,000 = R_2(12)$$
$$R_2 = 11,916.7 \text{ pounds}$$

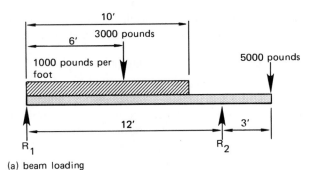

(a) beam loading

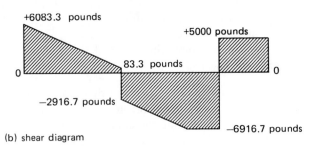

(b) shear diagram

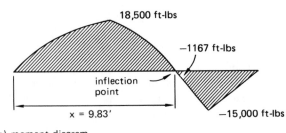

(c) moment diagram

R_1 is the difference between the total load and R_2, or 6083 pounds.

Next, find the vertical shears and draw the shear diagram.

Starting with the left reaction, the shear is 6083.3 pounds in the upward direction. The shear just to the left of the 3000 pound load is the sum of the loads and reactions so at this point it is:

$$V = 6083.3 - (1000 \times 6) = 83.3 \text{ pounds}$$

At the 3000 pound load, the shear is:

$$V = 6083.3 - (1000 \times 6) - 3000 = -2916.7 \text{ pounds}$$

Since the load between R_1 and the 3000 pound load is uniformly distributed, the two points connect with a sloped line as shown in the sketch. The shear at the end of the uniform load is found in the same way. From this point to the reaction R_2 there are no loads or reactions (ignoring the weight of the beam), so the line is horizontal. At the support, reaction R_2, the load changes abruptly in the magnitude of the reaction, or 11,916.7

pounds which is added to the negative shear of 6916.7 pounds giving a net value of +5000 pounds.

No other loads are encountered until the 5000 pound load at the end of the overhang. Since it is in the downward direction it is negative and brings the shear to zero at the end of the beam, which is what we would expect because of the principles of equilibrium.

Finally, calculate and draw the moment diagram. In this example, there are two points where the shear diagram crosses zero so there will be two maximum moments: one positive, as in a simply supported beam, and one negative. A negative moment simply means that the beam is bending upward above a support instead of downward because of the way the loads are applied. Both moment values need to be calculated to determine which one is the greater of the two because it is not always clear from visual inspection. The highest value is the one that must be used to design the beam.

There are two ways to find the moments. One way is to draw free-body diagrams at each point of interest and take the moments about that point as was done in previous examples.

Another, sometimes simpler way, is to find the area of the shear diagram at the point of interest.

To find the maximum moment at the 3000 pound load, find the area of the trapezoid with the bases of 6083.3 pounds and 83.3 pounds and the height of 6 feet.

$$\begin{aligned} A &= 1/2(b_1 + b_2) \times h \\ &= 1/2[(6083.3 + 83.3) \times 6] = 18,500 \text{ foot-pounds} \end{aligned}$$

To find the moment 10 feet to the right of reaction R_1, find the area of the trapezoid from the 3000 pound load to the end of the uniform load and subtract it from the previous moment. This is because this area is below the baseline of the shear diagram and is negative.

$$A = 1/2[(2916.7 + 6916.7) \times 4] = 19,667 \text{ foot-pounds}$$

The moment is, therefore:

$$18,500 - 19,667 = -1167 \text{ foot-pounds}$$

Next, find the area of the rectangle from the end of the uniform load to the reaction R_2 which is 13,833 foot-pounds and subtract this from the last value. The maximum negative moment is then 15,000 foot-pounds.

Now, connect the points just found. The lines connecting points below a sloped line in the shear diagram will be sections of parabolas and the lines below horizontal lines in the shear diagram will be straight sloped lines as shown in the moment diagram of the sketch.

Notice that the slopes of the parabolas change abruptly where the concentrated load of 3000 pounds occurs. Also notice that the curve of the moment diagram between the 6 foot point and 10 foot point crosses the zero line a little to the left of the 10 foot point. Where this occurs in a moment diagram is called the *inflection point*. Knowing where this point occurs is often important in designing beams. For instance, the inflection point is where reinforcing rods in concrete beams are bent to change from carrying positive moment to negative moment. In this example, the inflection point just happens to be very close to the end of the uniform load, but it can occur anywhere depending on the distribution of loads.

To find the inflection point, let the distance from reaction R_1 be x. Then, knowing the moment at this point is zero, draw a free-body diagram cut at this point, sum the moments to the left of this point, and set them equal to zero:

$$6083(x) - [1000(x)(x/2)] - 3000(x - 6) = 0$$

This reduces to the quadratic equation

$$500x^2 - 3083x - 18,000 = 0$$

Using the general formula for the solution of a quadratic equation:

$$x = \frac{-b \pm \sqrt{b^2 - 4ac}}{2a} \qquad 4.7$$

$$= \frac{-(-3083) \pm \sqrt{(-3083)^2 - 4(500)(-18,000)}}{2(500)}$$

$$= 9.83 \text{ feet}$$

E. Deflection

Deflection is the change in vertical position of a beam due to a load. The amount of deflection depends on the load, the beam length, the moment of inertia of the beam, and the beam's modulus of elasticity. Generally, the amount of *allowable deflection* is limited by building code requirements or practical requirements such as how much a beam can deflect before ceiling surfaces begin to crack or before the spring of the floor becomes annoying to occupants.

In many cases, the deflection due to live load is limited to 1/360 of the beam's span, whereas the deflection due to total load (dead load plus live load) is usually limited to 1/240 of the beam's span. If there are two or more loads on a beam such as a uniform load and concentrated load, the deflections caused by the loads individually are added to find total deflection.

Deriving the formulas for beam deflection under various loads is a complex mathematical process. However, standard formulas for deflection as well as shear and moment are given in reference sources such as the *AISC Manual of Steel Construction*. These apply to beams of any material. A few of the more common loading situations with accompanying formulas are given in Figure 4.7.

2   COLUMNS

A. Basic Principles

Although columns resist axial compressive forces, there are other considerations that must be taken into account. The first is the tendency of a long slender column to *buckle* under a load. Even though the column's material and size can withstand the load according to the formula

$$F_a = \frac{P}{A} \qquad 4.8$$

the column will fail in buckling under a much smaller load.

The second consideration is the *combined loading* that occurs on many columns. This can be due to the normal compressive force plus lateral load, such as wind, on the column. Combined loading can also be induced by an eccentric compressive load, one that is applied off the centroidal axis of the column. In this case, the column acts a little like a beam on standing end with one face in compression and the other in tension. The compressive forces due to the eccentric load add to the normal compressive stresses on one side and subtract from the normal compressive stresses on the other. The *flexural stress* caused by eccentricity is given by the flexural formula (see formula 4.2):

$$f = \frac{Mc}{I} \qquad 4.9$$

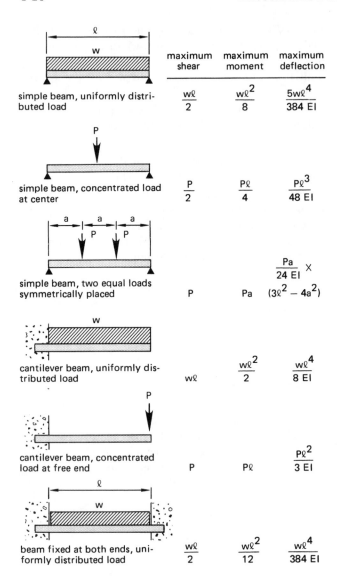

	maximum shear	maximum moment	maximum deflection
simple beam, uniformly distributed load	$\dfrac{w\ell}{2}$	$\dfrac{w\ell^2}{8}$	$\dfrac{5w\ell^4}{384\,EI}$
simple beam, concentrated load at center	$\dfrac{P}{2}$	$\dfrac{P\ell}{4}$	$\dfrac{P\ell^3}{48\,EI}$
simple beam, two equal loads symmetrically placed	P	Pa	$\dfrac{Pa}{24\,EI} \times (3\ell^2 - 4a^2)$
cantilever beam, uniformly distributed load	$w\ell$	$\dfrac{w\ell^2}{2}$	$\dfrac{w\ell^4}{8\,EI}$
cantilever beam, concentrated load at free end	P	$P\ell$	$\dfrac{P\ell^2}{3\,EI}$
beam fixed at both ends, uniformly distributed load	$\dfrac{w\ell}{2}$	$\dfrac{w\ell^2}{12}$	$\dfrac{w\ell^4}{384\,EI}$

Figure 4.7 Static Formulas for Some Common Loads

Because of the inexact nature of how columns respond to loads, various column formulas have been developed and adopted for different conditions and for various materials. These have been established through experience and are standardized in building codes. The methods for designing columns in different materials will be discussed in the individual chapters on specific structural materials. This chapter focuses on the general principles of column design.

B. Radius of Gyration

The ability of a column to withstand a load is dependent on its length, cross-sectional shape and area, and its moment of inertia. There is a convenient way to combine the properties of area and moment of inertia that is useful in column design. This is called the *radius*

of gyration and is expressed with the formula:

$$r = \sqrt{I/A} \qquad 4.10$$

For non-symmetric sections, such as rectangular columns, there are two radii of gyration, one for each axis. The one of most interest in column design is the least radius of gyration since it is in this axis that a column will fail by buckling. For example, a $4'' \times 8''$ wood column will bend under a load parallel to the 4 inch dimension before it will bend in the other dimension.

C. Slenderness Ratio

The slenderness ratio is the most important factor in column design and is equal to:

$$\text{slenderness ratio} = \frac{l}{r} \qquad 4.11$$

Example 4.6

A $4'' \times 6''$ structural steel column is 9 feet 6 inches long. What is its slenderness ratio if its least radius of gyration is 1.21 inches?

The slenderness ratio is:

$$\frac{l}{r} = \frac{9.5(12)}{1.21} = 94.2$$

Remember, the length must be multiplied by 12 to convert to inches.

The slenderness ratio is used in a basic equation that applies to all columns and gives the maximum stress a column can resist without buckling. It is called Euler's equation and predicts the actual load just prior to failure.

$$\frac{P}{A} = \frac{\pi^2 E}{(l/r)^2} \qquad 4.12$$

However, because various materials behave differently, end conditions vary, and slenderness ratios affect loads, this equation is theoretical and not used without modification in actual column design. For simple wood column design, for example, the thinnest dimension of the column is used in place of the least radius of gyration.

D. Categories of Columns

Compression members are categorized into three groups based on their slenderness ratios: *short compressive members, intermediate columns,* and *slender columns.* For short compressive members, the basic stress formula $s = P/A$ holds true (that is, column buckling is not a problem). For slender columns, Euler's equation generally holds true modified to account for safety factors and for end conditions. For intermediate columns, there are several formulas that attempt to predict column behavior. Building codes and sound engineering practices give the formulas used in actual design for various materials. These will be discussed in later chapters on specific materials.

E. End Conditions

The method by which the ends of columns are fixed affects their load-carrying capacity. These are shown diagrammatically in Figure 4.8. The end of any column may be in one of four states: it may be fixed against both rotation and movement from side to side (translation), it may be able to rotate but not translate, it may be able to move from side to side but not rotate, or it may be free to both rotate and translate.

The strongest type of column is one that is fixed against both rotation and translation; the weakest is one that is free to move at one end. Column formulas generally assume a condition in which both ends are fixed in translation but free to rotate. When other conditions exist, the load-carrying capacity is increased or decreased so the allowable stress must be increased or decreased or the slenderness ratio increased. For example, for steel columns, a factor, K, is used to multiply by the actual length to give an effective length. The theoretical K values are listed in Figure 4.8, but more

conservative recommended values are often used. For steel design these are discussed in Chapter 10.

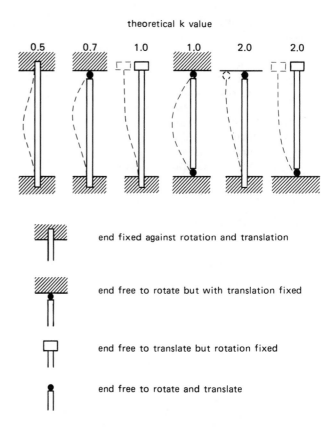

theoretical k value

| 0.5 | 0.7 | 1.0 | 1.0 | 2.0 | 2.0 |

end fixed against rotation and translation

end free to rotate but with translation fixed

end free to translate but rotation fixed

end free to rotate and translate

Figure 4.8   End Conditions for Columns

SAMPLE QUESTIONS

The answers to questions 1 through 4 can be found on the following key list. Select only one answer for each question.

    A0 bending moment
    A1 deflection
    A2 end conditions
    A3 effective length
    A4 Euler's equation
    A5 flexure formula
    A6 horizontal shear
    A7 moment diagram
    A8 negative moment
    A9 neutral axis

    B0 point of inflection
    B1 radius of gyration
    B2 section modulus
    B3 shear diagram
    B4 slenderness ratio
    B5 vertical shear

1. What is the most important factor in determining the load-carrying capacity of a column?

2. Identify the following formula: $r = \sqrt{I/A}$

3. What stress is more important to check in wood beams than in steel beams?

4. What theoretically determines the stress on a column just prior to failure?

5. The reaction for which of the following types of beams cannot be found using the principles of equilibrium?

    A. continuous beams

    B. cantilevered beams

    C. simply supported beams

    D. overhanging beams

6. Select the correct statements about a simply supported beam with a uniform load.

    I. The maximum bending stresses occur at the extreme fibers.

II. Moment is maximum where vertical shear is zero.

III. The shear stress remains constant for one-half the beam's length.

IV. The higher the value of the beam's modulus of elasticity, the more it will deflect.

V. Horizontal shear is at its greatest at the neutral surface.

    A. I, II, and III

    B. II, III, and VI

    C. I, II, and V

    D. I, II, III, and V

7. What is the maximum moment in the beam shown? Ignore the weight of the beam.

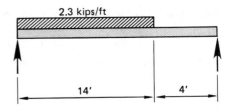

    A. 68.88 foot-kips

    B. 84.2 foot-kips

    C. 50.12 foot-kips

    D. 137.76 foot-kips

8. The maximum bending stress a wood beam must resist is 3000 ft-pounds. If the maximum allowable bending stress is 1500 psi, what is the minimum section modulus the beam must have to resist bending?

    A. 6 in^3

    B. 12 in^3

    C. 20 in^3

    D. 24 in^3

9. Which of the following statements are true about designing beams?

    I. If the vertical shear on a simply supported beam is different at each reaction, both values are critical to know.

    II. The point where the shear diagram crosses zero is important.

III. If negative moment occurs, it is not critical to know its value.

IV. Most beams are designed for maximum moment.

V. Moment at any point on a beam can be found by calculating the area under the shear diagram up to the same point.

A. II, IV, and V

B. I, II, IV, and V

C. III, IV, and V

D. II, III, and V

10. A nominal $6'' \times 8''$ wood column supports a load of 2500 pounds. If the column is 8 feet 0 inches long and has a moment of inertia of 104 in^4 about the axis parallel to the 8 inch dimension, what is the slenderness ratio?

A. 5.0

B. 16.0

C. 17.5

D. 60.4

5 TRUSSES

1 BASIC PRINCIPLES

A *truss* is a structure generally formed of straight members to form a number of triangles with the connections arranged so that the stresses in the members are either tension or compression. Trusses are very efficient structures and are used as an economical method to span long distances. Typical depth-to-span ratios range from 1:10 to 1:20, with flat trusses requiring less overall depth than pitched trusses. Spans generally range from 40 feet to 200 feet. However, some wood-trussed rafters are used to span shorter distances.

Some typical truss types are shown in Figure 5.1 with nomenclature of the various parts. Generally, roof loads on a truss are transferred from the decking to purlins, which are attached to the truss at the panel points to avoid putting any bending stresses in the top chord of the truss. If concentrated loads are placed between panel points, or uniform loads are applied directly to the top chords, the member must be designed for the axial loading as well as for bending.

Trusses act much like beams in that there is usually compression in the top chords and tension in the bottom chords, with the web members being either in compression or tension, depending on the loading and type of truss used. Like a beam, the forces in a parallel chord truss increase toward the center. In a bowstring truss, on the other hand, the chord forces remain fairly constant because the truss depth varies from a minimum at the supports to a maximum in the center.

In designing a trussed roof, trusses are placed from 10 to 40 feet on centers, depending on the loads and the spanning capabilities of the purlins. In residential and light commercial construction, trussed rafters made of $2'' \times 4''$ or $2'' \times 6''$ members are often placed 2 feet on center. Open-web steel joists are usually placed 2 to 3 feet on center for floor construction and 4 to 6 feet on center for roof construction, depending on the spanning capabilities of the roof deck. Since trusses are thin and deep and subject to buckling, they must be laterally supported with bridging along the bottom chord. In some cases, diagonal bracing is required along the top chords of pitched roofs if the roof deck is not adequate to act as a diaphragm.

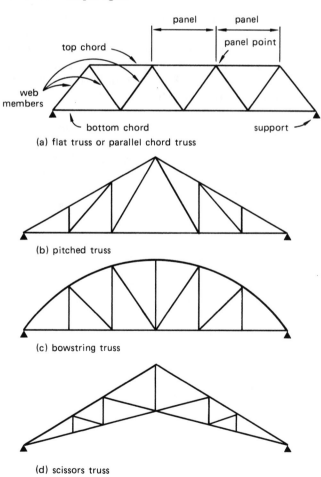

(a) flat truss or parallel chord truss

(b) pitched truss

(c) bowstring truss

(d) scissors truss

Figure 5.1 Types of Trusses

Individual truss members are designed as columns if they are in compression. If in tension, they must have adequate net area (after deducting for the area of fasteners) to resist the unit tensile stress allowed by the material being used. If concentrated loads or uniform loads are placed on any chord member between the panel points, the member must also be designed to resist bending stresses.

As with columns, the effective length of chord members in compression is important; that is, Kl in which K is determined by the restraint of the ends of the members. For steel trusses, K is usually taken as 1.0 so the effective length is the same as the actual length. Also for steel trusses, the ratio of length to least radius of gyration, l/r, should not exceed 120 for main members and 200 for secondary and bracing members.

When designing steel trusses with double angles as is usually the case, allowable concentric loads and other properties for various double angle combinations can be found in the American Institute of Steel Construction (AISC) *Manual of Steel Construction*. By knowing the compressive load, the length of the member, and strength of steel, you can determine the size and thickness of a double angle combination.

For members in tension, the net area must be determined. This is the actual area of the member less the area of bolt holes which is taken to be 1/8 inch larger than the diameter of the bolt.

Regardless of material, truss members should be designed so they are concentric; that is, so the member is symmetric on both sides of the centroid axis in the plane of the truss. To accomplish this, steel truss members are often built with two angles back-to-back separated by 3/8-inch or 1/2-inch gusset plates, with tee sections, or with wide flange sections. See Figure 5.2.

With light loads, bars or rods can be used for tension members. Wood trusses are often constructed with web members between double top and bottom chord members or with all members in the same plane connected with steel gusset plates. See Figure 5.3.

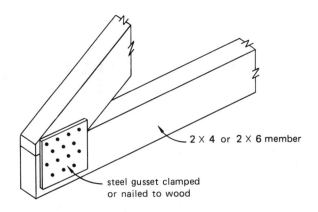

Figure 5.3 Typical Wood Trussed Rafter Construction

The centroidal axes of all intersecting members must also meet at a point to avoid eccentric loading. For steel members composed of angles, it is standard practice to have the gage lines rather than the centroidal axes meet at a common point as shown in Figure 5.4. The *gage line* is a standard dimension from the corner edge of an angle to the centerline of the bolt hole or holes. Its value depends on the size of the angle, and the standard dimensions are published in the AISC manual.

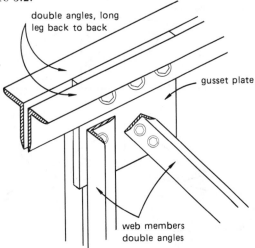

Figure 5.2 Typical Steel Truss Construction

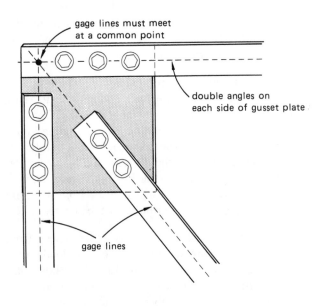

Figure 5.4 Alignment of Lines of Force in a Truss

2 TRUSS ANALYSIS

The first step in designing a truss is to determine the loads in the various members. Before reviewing the methods to do this, there are some general guidelines for truss analysis that you should know.

- The sum of vertical forces at any point equals zero.

- The sum of horizontal forces at any point equals zero.

- The sum of the moments about any point equals zero.

- Forces in each member are shown by an arrow away from a joint or cut section if in tension and toward a joint or cut section if in compression.

- Forces acting upward or to the right are considered positive (+) and forces acting downward or to the left are considered negative (−).

- All forces should be indicated acting in their known direction. If you are unsure when beginning the analysis, show the force in tension, acting away from the joint or cut section. If your calculation of the force is negative, this indicates that the direction is reversed.

- For analysis, trusses are assumed to have pivoting or rolling supports to avoid other stresses at these points.

Since truss analysis often requires you to resolve forces into their horizontal and vertical components, and to find the resultant of two forces, the following guidelines will be helpful. See Figure 5.5.

The x component of a force (horizontal) is equal to the force times the cosine of the angle the force vector makes with the x-axis.

$$F_x = F \cos a \qquad\qquad 5.1$$

The y component of a force (vertical) is equal to the force times the cosine of the angle the force vector makes with the y-axis.

$$F_y = F \cos b \qquad\qquad 5.2$$

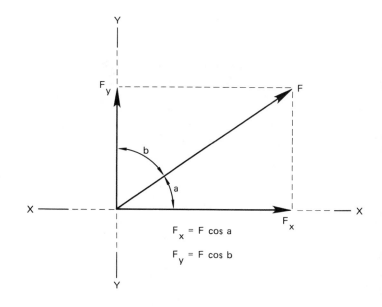

Figure 5.5 Determining Horizontal
and Vertical Truss Components

Also note that the X-Y axis can be titled to any convenient angle if required by the problem.

There are three methods that can be used to determine the forces in truss members: the *method of joints*, the *method of sections*, and the *graphic method*. The method of joints is useful when you need to determine the forces in all the members or when you only need to calculate the forces in members near the supports. The method of sections is convenient when you only need to find the forces in a few members, particularly ones that are not at or near the supports. The graphic method is useful for complex trusses and avoids all the calculation inherent in analytic solutions but, of course, is not as accurate.

A. Method of Joints

With this method, each joint is considered separately as a free-body diagram to which the equations of equilibrium are applied. Starting from one support, the force in each member is determined, joint by joint, until all have been calculated.

Example 5.1

Consider the simple truss shown in the sketch. Find the forces in the members using the method of joints. Neglect the weight of the structure.

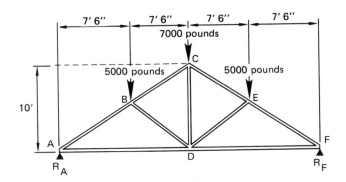

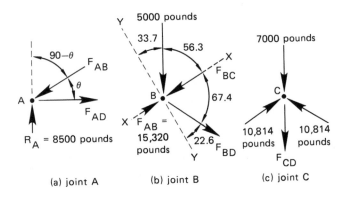

(a) joint A   (b) joint B   (c) joint C

First, find the reactions. Since the loads are symmetric, $R_A = R_F = 1/2(17,000) = 8500$ pounds. If the loads were not symmetric, you could find the reactions by taking the moments about one reaction and setting the moments equal to zero.

Next, start with joint A at reaction R_A and draw this joint as a free-body diagram as shown in (a) below the truss diagram. The direction of the reaction is known (upward), and the type of forces in the top chord and bottom chord can be assumed to be in compression and tension, respectively. Therefore, using the labeling convention, show force F_{AB} with an arrow toward the joint and force F_{AD} with an arrow away from the joint. Calculate the angle between member AB and AD.

$$\tan\theta = \frac{10}{15}$$
$$\theta = 33.7°$$

The complement of this angle is $56.3°$.

Since the sum of vertical forces at any point equals zero, and since the vertical component of F_{AB} equals the force times the cosine of the angle with the y-axis (formula 5.2), then,

$$8500 - F_{AB}\cos 56.3 = 0$$

Remember, the reaction force is positive since it is acting upward and the y-component of F_{AB} is negative

since it is acting downward. Force F_{AD} has no vertical component.

Solving for F_{AB},

$$F_{AB} = \frac{8500}{\cos 56.3}$$
$$= 15,320 \text{ pounds (compression)}$$

Since the answer is positive, the assumption that force AB is in compression is correct.

The force in member AD is found in a similar way, knowing that the sum of the horizontal forces also equals zero.

$$F_{AD} - F_{AB}\cos 33.7 = 0$$
$$F_{AD} = 12,746 \text{ pounds (tension)}$$

Now, consider joint B as a free-body diagram as shown in (b) in the sketch. Since the direction of the force in member BD is not clear, assume it is in tension and draw it with the arrow away from the joint. (Actually, since the 5000 pound load is acting down, there must be a force acting upward to counteract this, so member BD would have to be in compression. For purposes of illustration, however, assume it is in tension.)

In this case, tilt the X-Y axes so the X-axis aligns with the top chord of the truss. The angles between the X-Y axes and the forces can easily be determined by trigonometry and are shown in (b). With the axes tilted, force F_{BC} has no vertical component in this free-body diagram so force F_{BD} can be found easily.

$$-5000\cos 33.7 - F_{BD}\cos 22.6 = 0$$

(Since both forces are acting downward, they are both negative values.)

$$F_{BD} = -4506 \text{ pounds}$$

The negative number indicates that the assumption that member BD was in tension is incorrect; it is in compression.

Now, find the force in BC knowing that the summation of forces in the x-axis equals zero.

$$15,320 - 5000(\cos 56.3) - F_{BC} - 4506(\cos 67.4) = 0$$
$$F_{BC} = 10,814 \text{ pounds (compression)}$$

Finally, draw joint C as a free-body diagram as shown in (c). The sum of the forces in the y-direction are zero, so:

$$10,814(\cos 56.3) - 7000 + 10,814(\cos 56.3) - F_{CD} = 0$$
$$F_{CD} = 5000 \text{ pounds (tension)}$$

Since the truss and loading are symmetric, the forces in the right half are identical to those in the left half.

B. Method of Sections

With this method, a portion of the truss is cut through three members, one of which is the member under analysis. The cut section is then drawn as a free-body diagram and the force in the members found by taking moments about various points knowing that $\Sigma M = 0$. You can also use the equations $\Sigma F_x = 0$ and $\Sigma F_y = 0$ when you have more than one unknown, but this is not usually necessary if you select the center of moment in such a way as to eliminate two unknowns.

Example 5.2

Using the same truss as shown in Example 5.1, determine the forces in members BD and BC using the method of sections.

First, solve for the reactions as in the previous problem. These were determined to be 8500 pounds at each reaction.

Next, cut a section through the two members under analysis as shown in the sketch. In this free-body diagram there are five forces acting, two that are known and three that are unknown. To find the force in member BD, take moments about point A. Selecting this point eliminates the unknowns of F_{BC} and F_{AD} because their lines of action pass through the point so their moment is zero. This leaves only F_{BD} acting about A.

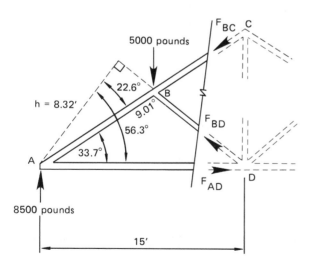

Remember, by convention, moments acting in a clockwise direction are positive and those acting in a counterclockwise direction are negative.

Before you take moments, you must find the dimension of the moment arm of BD, a line passing through A perpendicular to BD. With some simple trigonometry, the length of AB is found to be 9.01 feet and the angle between AB and the moment arm of BD is found to be 22.6°. Then,

$$\cos 22.6 = \frac{h}{9.01}$$
$$h = 8.32 \text{ feet}$$

Then, the sum of moments about A equals zero, or

$$5000(7.5) - F_{BD}(8.32) = 0$$
$$F_{BD} = 4507 \text{ pounds}$$

This is the same value (within one pound) that was calculated by the method of joints in the previous example.

Now, find the value of F_{BC}. In this case, to eliminate two unknowns, take moments about point D. This is acceptable even though it is outside the free-body diagram because the equation of moment equilibrium holds at any point in the truss. The moment arm from D perpendicular to BC must be found. It is the same dimension as the previous moment arm calculated: 8.32 feet. Then, the sum of moments about joint D is:

$$8500(15) - 5000(7.5) - F_{BC}(8.32) = 0$$
$$F_{BC} = 10,817 \text{ pounds}$$

In both cases, the answer was a positive number, indicating that the original assumption of direction of force (compression) was correct. If either had been negative, it would simply mean that the assumption was incorrect and the arrow or arrows should be reversed. (This answer is within 3 pounds of that found by the method of joints allowing for some minor inaccuracies due to rounding off when calculating the length of moment arms.)

C. Graphic Method

Finding forces in truss members with graphics is a quick method and is particularly suited for complex trusses. However, its accuracy depends on the scale selected and the accuracy with which the diagram is drawn. A truss is analyzed graphically by drawing a stress diagram. This is a carefully drawn diagram, to scale, showing all the force polygons for each joint on one drawing.

When developing a stress diagram there are a few things to keep in mind:

- Since the truss is in equilibrium, the force polygon of each joint must close.

- When developing the force polygon for a joint, work in a clockwise direction around the joint. Do this consistently for every joint.

- To determine whether a member is in compression or tension, trace the rays of the force polygon. Imagine that the ray was transposed onto the truss diagram. If the direction of the ray is toward the joint, the member is in compression. If it is away from the joint, the member is in tension.

- There will be as many sides to each force polygon as there are truss members entering a joint.

Example 5.3

Consider the same truss as used in the previous two examples. Draw a diagram of the truss and allow room below to draw the stress diagram as shown in the illustration. Label the spaces between each load and reaction with a letter of the alphabet, *A*, *B*, *C*, and so on. Number each triangle of the truss with a number. Then, each load or reaction can be identified with a two-letter combination and each structural member can be identified with a letter/number combination.

Begin the diagram by drawing a force polygon of the loads and reactions. In the sketch, start with reaction *AB*. With a convenient scale, in this case 1 inch = 3000 pounds, draw a line parallel to the reaction in the truss drawing (in this case vertical) to a scale of 8500 pounds. Working clockwise, the next load is the 5000 pound load *BC*. Draw a line downward, parallel to a scale of 5000 pounds. Continue until you are back at point *A*. Since the loads and reactions are all vertical, the force polygon is a straight line but it does close on itself.

Next, draw a force polygon for the joint at the left reaction, *AB*1. You already have the load *AB* drawn, so working clockwise draw a line parallel to *B*1 from point *B* on the stress diagram. Then, draw a line representing member 1*A* horizontally from point *A*. Where these two lines intersect is point 1. To determine the type of force, trace the lines of the polygon beginning with point *A*. *AB* is the reaction and is acting upward. *B*1 runs down and to the left toward point 1, which in the truss drawing is toward the joint, so *B*1 must be in compression. From point 1, line 1*A* runs to the right

which in the truss drawing is away from the joint, so 1*A* must be in tension.

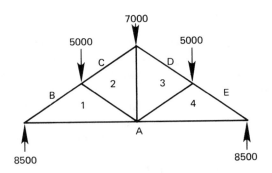

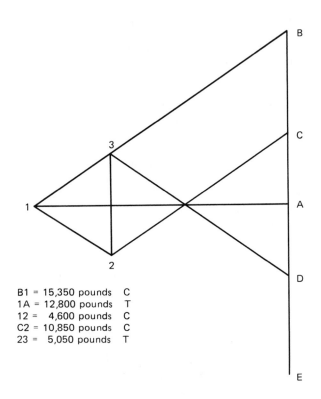

B1 = 15,350 pounds   C
1A = 12,800 pounds   T
12 =   4,600 pounds   C
C2 = 10,850 pounds   C
23 =   5,050 pounds   T

Now, study joint *BC*21. Since lines 1*B* and *BC* have already been drawn, start with point *C* and draw a line parallel with *C*2. From point 1 draw a line parallel with member 12. Where these intersect is point 2 and the force polygon closes. Measuring line 12 and *C*2 to scale gives the magnitude of the forces in these members.

Continue the procedure until all joints have been solved. A tabulation of the forces is given in the sketch. Compare these values with those found by the method of joints and sections in the previous examples.

TRUSSES 5-7

SAMPLE QUESTIONS

1. Select the incorrect statement.

   A. Trusses are usually required to have lower chord bridging.

   B. Spacing of trusses depends entirely on the spanning capabilities of purlins and the type of truss used.

   C. Parallel chord trusses usually have greater stresses toward the center of the span.

   D. The method of joints is often used to find all the forces in a truss.

2. What is wrong with the wood truss detail shown?

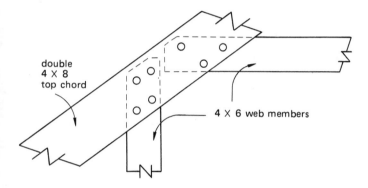

   A. There is eccentric loading.

   B. There are not enough bolts.

   C. The ends of the web members are not cut properly.

   D. A gusset plate should be used instead of direct connections.

The answers to questions 3 through 6 can be found on the following key list. Select only one answer for each question.

   A0 bowstring truss
   A1 center line
   A2 centroidal axis
   A3 chord members
   A4 concentric load
   A5 effective length
   A6 flat truss
   A7 gage line
   A8 graphic analysis
   A9 gusset plates

   B0 method of joints
   B1 method of sections
   B2 panel point
   B3 pitched truss

   B4 trussed rafter
   B5 summation of horizontal components
   B6 summation of moments
   B7 web member

3. Which truss usually requires a larger depth?

4. What is used in place of the centroidal axis in detailing some steel trusses?

5. What design procedure is best for finding the force in the first horizontal member next to a support?

6. What are loads on a truss generally placed on?

7. What is the force in diagonal member A in the truss shown?

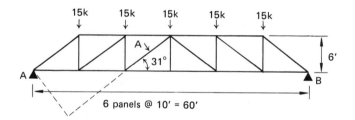

   A. 17.38 kips compression

   B. 17.38 kips tension

   C. 14.58 kips compression

   D. 14.58 kips tension

8. The most common depth-to-span ratio for a steel truss is:

   A. 1:5 to 1:15

   B. no more than 1:12

   C. dependent on its type

   D. 1:10 to 1:20

9. The following truss would best be analyzed with:

    A. method of joints

    B. graphic method

    C. method of sections

    D. any of the above

10. What is the force in member *AB* as illustrated?

    A. 21.2 kips, compression

    B. 21.2 kips, tension

    C. 28.3 kips, compression

    D. 28.3 kips, tension

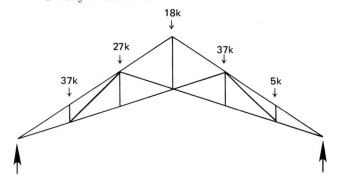

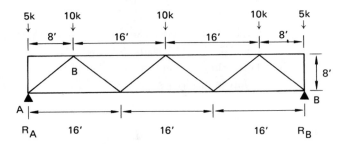

6 SOIL AND FOUNDATIONS

Nomenclature

a	depth of rectangular stress block	inches
A_s	area of steel	in^2
B	bearing capacity of soil	psf
C_o	coefficient of earth pressure	
d	effective depth—distance from top of footing to centroid of reinforcing steel	inches
d_b	diameter of reinforcing steel	inches
D	actual dead load	pounds
f_c'	specified compressive strength	psi
f_y	specified yield strength of reinforcing steel	psi
h	height of retaining wall below grade	feet
l_d	development length	inches
L	actual live load	pounds
M_u	moment	inch-pounds
P	pressure	pounds
q_s	design soil pressure	psf
U	required strength load	pounds
V	shear	psf
V_c	maximum allowable shear	psf
w	width of foundation wall	inches
W	unit weight of soil behind retaining wall	pcf
x	distance from face of foundation wall to edge of footing	feet
ϕ	capacity reduction factor	

The *foundation* is the part of the building that transmits all the gravity and lateral loads to the underlying soil. Selection and design of foundations depends on two primary elements: the required strength of the foundation to transmit the loads on it, and the ability of the soil to sustain the loads without excessive total settlement or differential settlement among different parts of the foundation.

1 SOIL PROPERTIES

Soil is a general term used to describe the material that supports a building. It is generally classified into four groups: Sands and gravels, clays, silts, and organics. *Sands and gravels* are granular materials that are non-plastic. *Clays* are composed of smaller particles that have some cohesion, or tensile strength, and are plastic in their behavior. *Silts* are of intermediate size between clays and sands, and behave as granular materials but are sometimes slightly plastic in their behavior. *Organics* are materials of vegetable or other organic matter.

In addition to these general types, there is *solid rock*, which has the highest bearing capacity of all soil types.

A. Subsurface Exploration

The first step in designing a foundation is to determine the bearing capacity of the underlying soil through subsurface exploration and testing. Several exploration methods are used. The two most common are *borings* and *test pits*.

With typical core borings, undisturbed samples of the soil are removed at regular intervals and the type of material recovered is recorded in a boring log. This log shows the material, the depth at which it was encountered, its standard designation, and other information such as moisture content, density, and the results of any borehole tests that might have been conducted at the bore site.

One of the most common borehole tests is the *Standard Penetration Test* (SPT) which is a measure of the density of granular soils and consistency of some clays. In this test, a 2-inch diameter sampler is driven into the bottom of the borehole by a 140-pound hammer falling

30 inches. The number of blows, N, required to drive the cylinder 12 inches is recorded. A typical boring log is shown in Figure 6.1.

The recovered bore samples can be tested in the laboratory. Some of the tests include strength tests of bearing capacity, resistance to lateral pressure, and slope stability. In addition, compressibility tests, grain size, specific gravity, and density tests are sometimes performed. Since laboratory tests are expensive and not always necessary, they are not performed for every building project.

The number of borings taken at a building site is determined by many factors such as the size of the building, suspected subsurface geological conditions, and requirements by local codes. Usually, a minimum of four borings are taken, one near each corner of the proposed building. If wide variations are found in the initial boring logs, additional tests may be warranted.

Test pits are the second common type of subsurface exploration. These are simply trenches dug at the job site that allow visual inspection of the soil strata and direct collection of undisturbed samples. Because they are open pits, the practical limit on depth is about ten feet so the soil below that cannot be directly examined.

The location of each test boring or test pit is shown on the plot plan and given a number corresponding to the boring log in the soil test report. Soil tests are requested by the architect but paid for by the owner. They are typically shown on the drawings for information only. However, soil tests are not part of the contract documents.

B. Soil Types And Bearing Capacities

Soils are classified according to the *Unified Soil Classification System* (USC). This system divides soils into major divisions and subdivisions based on grain size and laboratory tests of physical characteristics, and provides standardized names and symbols. A summary chart of the USC is shown in Figure 6.2.

Bearing capacities are generally specified by code. A summary chart of the allowable bearing capacities of the Uniform Building Code is shown in Figure 6.3. Other bearing capacities may be used if acceptable tests are conducted and show that higher values are appropriate.

C. Water In Soil

The presence of water in soil can cause several problems for foundations as well as other parts of a building.

Water can reduce the load-carrying capacity of the soil in general, so larger or more expensive foundation systems may be necessary. If more moisture is present under one area of the building than another, differential settlement may occur causing cracking and weakening of structural and non-structural components. In the worst case, structural failure may occur.

Foundations below the groundwater line, often called the *water table*, are also subjected to hydrostatic pressure. This pressure from the force of the water-saturated soil can occur against vertical foundation walls as well as under the floor slabs. Hydrostatic pressure creates two difficulties: it puts additional loads on the structural elements, and it makes waterproofing more difficult because the pressure tends to force water into any crack or imperfection in the structure.

Even if hydrostatic pressure is not present, moisture in the soil can leak into the below-grade structure if not properly dampproofed, and can cause general deterioration of materials.

There are several ways to minimize the problems caused by excess soil moisture. The first is to slope the ground away from the building sufficiently to drain away any rainwater or other surface moisture. Generally, a minimum slope of 1/4 inch per foot is recommended. Secondly, all water from roofs and decks should be drained away from the building with gutters, drainpipes, and other appropriate methods.

Below grade, several steps can be taken. If ground water is a significant problem, drain tile can be laid around the footings as shown in Figure 6.4. This tile has open joints or is perforated plastic pipe and is drained to the atmosphere, dry wells, or storm sewers. A layer of gravel is placed on top of the tile and is sometimes extended up the foundation wall to relieve the hydrostatic pressure against the wall.

An alternative method of relieving pressure against a wall is to place a continuous layer of open-web matting against the wall. Water forced against the wall loses its pressure when it encounters the matting and drips to the drain tile.

To relieve pressure against floor slabs, a layer of large gravel can be placed below the slab. If the presence of water is a significant problem, the gravel layer can be used in conjunction with a waterproofing membrane and drain tiles placed below the slab.

D. Soil Treatment

In order to increase bearing capacity or decrease settlement, or both, several methods of soil treatment are used.

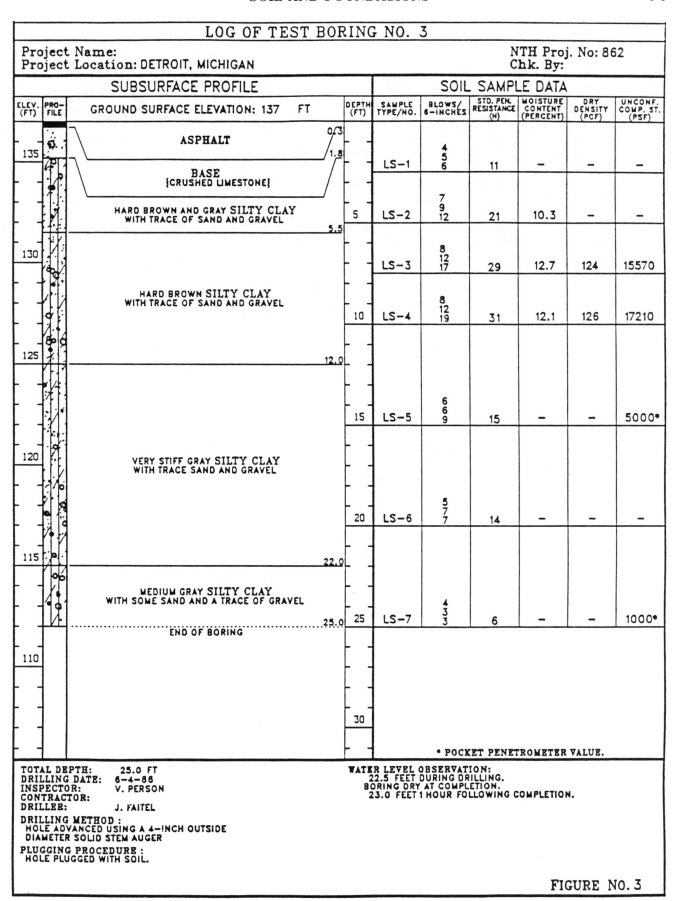

LOG OF TEST BORING NO. 3											

Project Name:
Project Location: DETROIT, MICHIGAN

NTH Proj. No: 862
Chk. By:

SUBSURFACE PROFILE				SOIL SAMPLE DATA					
ELEV. (FT)	PRO- FILE	GROUND SURFACE ELEVATION: 137 FT	DEPTH (FT)	SAMPLE TYPE/NO.	BLOWS/ 6-INCHES	STD. PEN. RESISTANCE (N)	MOISTURE CONTENT (PERCENT)	DRY DENSITY (PCF)	UNCONF. COMP. ST. (PSF)
135		ASPHALT 0.3 1.8		LS-1	4 5 6	11	–	–	–
		BASE {CRUSHED LIMESTONE}							
		HARD BROWN AND GRAY SILTY CLAY WITH TRACE OF SAND AND GRAVEL 5.5	5	LS-2	7 9 12	21	10.3	–	–
130				LS-3	8 12 17	29	12.7	124	15570
		HARD BROWN SILTY CLAY WITH TRACE OF SAND AND GRAVEL	10	LS-4	8 12 19	31	12.1	126	17210
125		12.0							
			15	LS-5	6 6 9	15	–	–	5000*
120		VERY STIFF GRAY SILTY CLAY WITH TRACE SAND AND GRAVEL							
			20	LS-6	5 7 7	14	–	–	–
115		22.0							
		MEDIUM GRAY SILTY CLAY WITH SOME SAND AND A TRACE OF GRAVEL							
		25.0 END OF BORING	25	LS-7	4 3 3	6	–	–	1000*
110									
			30						
					* POCKET PENETROMETER VALUE.				

TOTAL DEPTH: 25.0 FT
DRILLING DATE: 6-4-86
INSPECTOR: V. PERSON
CONTRACTOR:
DRILLER: J. FAITEL

DRILLING METHOD :
  HOLE ADVANCED USING A 4-INCH OUTSIDE
  DIAMETER SOLID STEM AUGER
PLUGGING PROCEDURE :
  HOLE PLUGGED WITH SOIL.

WATER LEVEL OBSERVATION:
  22.5 FEET DURING DRILLING.
  BORING DRY AT COMPLETION.
  23.0 FEET 1 HOUR FOLLOWING COMPLETION.

FIGURE NO. 3

Figure 6.1   Typical Boring Log

coarse grained soils more than 50% of material is larger than No. 200 sieve	gravels more than 50% of coarse fraction retained on No. 4 sieve	clean gravels less than 5% fines	GW	well-graded gravel
			GP	poorly graded gravel
		gravels with fines more than 12% fines	GM	silty gravel
			GC	clayey gravel
	sands 50% or more of coarse fraction passes No. 4 sieve	clean sands less than 5% fines	SW	well-graded sand
			SP	poorly-graded sand
		sands with fines more than 12% fines	SM	silty sand
			SC	clayey sand
fine grained soils 50% or more passes the No. 200 sieve	silts and clays liquid limit less than 50	inorganic	CL	lean clay
			ML	silt
		organic	OL	organic silty
	silts and clays liquid limit 50 or more	inorganic	CH	fat clay
			MH	elastic silt
		organic	OH	organic clay
highly organic soils	primary organic matter, dark in color, and organic odor		PT	peat

Figure 6.2 Unified Soil Classification System

CLASS OF MATERIALS[2]	ALLOWABLE FOUNDATION PRESSURE LBS./SQ. FT.[3]	LATERAL BEARING LBS./SQ. FT./ FT. OF DEPTH BELOW NATURAL GRADE[4]	LATERAL SLIDING[1]	
			COEF- FICIENT[5]	RESISTANCE LBS./SQ. FT.[6]
1. massive crystalline bedrock	4000	1200	.70	
2. sedimentary and foliated rock	2000	400	.35	
3. sandy gravel and/or gravel (GW and GP)	2000	200	.35	
4. sand, silty sand, clayey sand, silty gravel and clayey gravel (SW, SP, SM, SC, GM and GC)	1500	150	.25	
5. clay, sandy clay, silty clay and clayey silt (CL, ML, MH and CH)	1000[7]	100		130

[1] Lateral bearing and lateral sliding resistance may be combined.

[2] For soil classifications OL, OH, and PT (i.e., organic clays and peat), a foundation investigation shall be required.

[3] All values of allowable foundation pressure are for footings having a minimum width of 12 inches and a minimum depth of 12 inches into natural grade. Except as in Footnote 7 below, increase of 20 percent allowed for each additional foot of width and/or depth to a maximum value of three times the designated value.

[4] May be increased the amount of the designated value for each additional foot of depth to a maximum of 15 times the designated value. Isolated poles for uses such as flagpoles or signs and poles used to support buildings which are not adversely afffected by a 1/2-inch motion at ground surface due to short-term lateral loads may be designed using lateral bearing values equal to two times the tabulated values.

[5] Coefficient to be multiplied by the dead load.

[6] Lateral sliding resistance value to be multiplied by the contact area. In no case shall the lateral sliding resistance exceed one-half the dead load.

[7] No increase for width is allowed.

Figure 6.3 UBC Allowable Soil Bearing Pressures

Reproduced from the 1988 edition of the Uniform Building Code, copyright © 1988, with permission of the publishers, the International Conference of Building Officials.

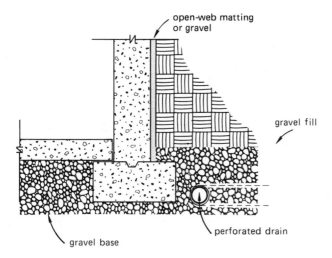

Figure 6.4 Methods of Controlling Subsurface Water

Drainage. As mentioned in the section above, drainage can solve several types of problems. It can increase the strength of the soil and prevent hydrostatic pressure.

Fill. If existing soil is unsuitable for building, the undesirable material is removed and new fill brought in. This may be soil, sand, gravel, or other material as appropriate. In nearly all situations, the fill must be compacted before building commences. Controlled compaction requires moisture to lubricate the particles. With all types of fill, there is an optimum relationship between the fill's density and its optimum moisture content. The method of determining this is the *Proctor test*. With the Proctor test, fill samples are tested in the laboratory to determine a standard for compaction. Specifications are then written that call for fill to be compacted between 90 percent to 100 percent of the optimum Proctor density. Higher values are necessary for heavily loaded structures, and lower values are appropriate for other loadings. Moisture contents within 2 to 4 percent of the optimum moisture content at the time of compaction must also be specified.

Fill is usually placed in lifts of 8 to 12 inches, with each lift being compacted before placement of the next.

Compaction. Sometimes existing soil can simply be compacted to provide the required base for construction. The same requirements for compaction of fill material apply to compaction of existing soil.

Densification. This is a type of on-site compaction of existing material using one of several techniques involving vibration, dropping of heavy weights, or pounding piles into the ground and filling the voids with sand. The specific technique used depends on the grain size of the soil.

Surcharging. Surcharging is the preloading of the ground with fill material to cause consolidation and set-tlement of the underlying soil before building. Once the required settlement has taken place, the fill is removed and construction begins. Although suitable for large areas, the time and cost required for sufficient settlement often preclude this method of soil improvement.

E. Other Considerations

Frost. Because most soils expand and heave when they freeze, footings and foundations must be placed below the frost line to prevent the structure from lifting up. The depth of the frost line varies, of course, with location and local climatic conditions. It is usually specified by the local building code or building official.

Expansive soil. Many clays, such as bentonite, expand when they get wet and shrink when they dry. If such soils are below a proposed building, the foundations must be isolated from them. One method of doing this is to use pile or caisson foundation piers that bear on material below the expansive soil. Concrete grade beams span between the piers with voids below the beams so any expansion does not cause stress on the foundation. The building walls are then built on the grade beams. The remainder of the ground level slab is usually built over select fill material, although in some instances is suspended from beams and piers.

Repose. When sands, gravels, and other types of soils are piled up, they come to rest with a characteristic slope. The angle of the slope depends on the granular size of the material and its moisture content. The slope is known as the *angle of natural repose* and is the maximum practical angle for changing grades without using retaining walls or other stabilization techniques. However, even though a slope may conform to the angle of repose of a material, it may still be unsuitable to prevent erosion or allow for the desired type of landscaping.

2 FOUNDATION SYSTEMS

Foundations can be categorized into two broad divisions: *spread footings* and *pile* or *caisson foundations*. Spread footings do just what their name implies—they spread the load from the structure and the foundation walls over a large area, so the load-carrying capacity of the soil is not exceeded and settlement is minimized. Pile and caisson foundations (often referred to as piers) distribute the load from the building to the ends of the piles which often bear on bedrock, or to the surrounding soil in contact with the pile through skin friction, or a combination of both.

A. Spread Footings

There are several types of spread footings. These are shown in Figure 6.5. One of the most common is the *wall footing* which is placed under a continuous foundation wall which in turn supports a bearing wall. Both the footing and foundation are reinforced (except where very small loads are supported), and the joint between the footing and foundation wall is strengthened with a keyed joint (Figure 6.5 (a)).

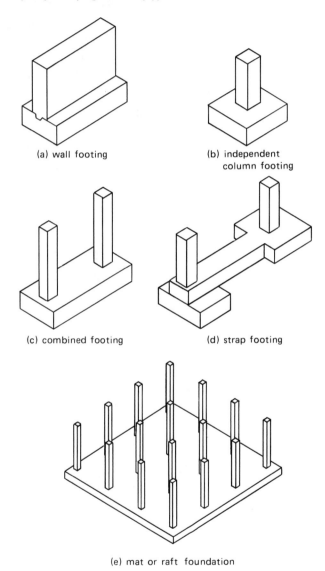

(a) wall footing

(b) independent column footing

(c) combined footing

(d) strap footing

(e) mat or raft foundation

Figure 6.5 Types of Spread Footings

The *independent column footing* is similar in concept but supports only one column. The footing is usually square but may be rectangular if the column is rectangular or if there is not enough room to form a square footing.

The required size of both wall and independent column footings is found by dividing the total load on the foot-

ing by the load-carrying capacity of the soil. A safety factor is often used as well. For wall footings, design is based on a linear foot basis.

Combined footings support two or more columns in situations where the columns are spaced too close together for separate ones, or where one column is so close to the property line that a symmetrically loaded footing could not be poured. If the two columns are far apart, a variation of the combined footing is used for economy. This is the *strap footing* or *cantilever footing* (see Figure 6.5 (d)) which uses a concrete strap beam to distribute the column loads to each footing to equalize the soil pressures on each footing. The beam itself is poured on compressible material so it does not bear on the soil. Strap footings are also used where the exterior column is next to the property line but the footing cannot extend beyond the property line.

A *mat* or *raft foundation* (see Figure 6.5 (e)) is used when soil bearing is low or where loads are heavy in relation to soil pressures. With this type of foundation, one large footing is designed as a two-way slab and supports the columns above it. Walls or beams above the foundation are sometimes used to give added stiffness to the mat.

B. Pile Foundations

When soil near grade level is unsuitable for spread footings, pile foundations are used. These transmit building loads through the unsuitable soil to more secure bearing with end bearing or side friction. Piles are either driven or drilled. Driven piles may be of timber or steel and are placed with pile-driving hammers powered with drop hammers, compressed air, or diesel engines. Drilled piles or caissons are usually called *piers*. Some common types of piers are shown in Figure 6.6.

Drilled piers are formed by drilling out a hole to the required depth and then filling it with concrete. If the soil is soft, a metal lining is used to keep the soil from caving in during drilling. It is removed as the concrete is poured or may be left in. If the soil pressure is not sufficient for a drilled pier of normal dimensions, the bottom is "belled" out to increase the surface area for bearing (see Figure 6.6 (c)).

Piles are usually placed in groups or in a line under a bearing wall with the loads from the building transferred to them with pile caps. See Figure 6.7. The piles are embedded from 4 to 6 inches into the pile cap which is designed and reinforced to safely transmit the loads and resist shear and moment stresses developed. When two or more piles are used to support one column, the centroid of the pile group is designed to coincide with the center of gravity of the column load.

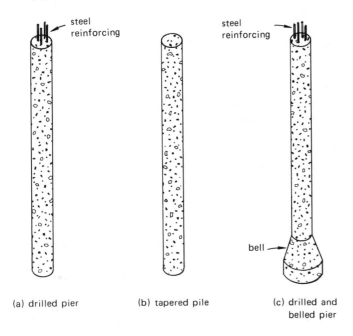

Figure 6.6 Pile Types

One type of pile foundation system frequently used is the *grade beam*. See Figure 6.7 (b). With this system, piles are driven or drilled in line at regular intervals and connected with a continuous grade beam. The grade beam is designed and reinforced to transfer the loads from the building wall to the piles.

This system is often used where expansive soils or clay, such as bentonite, are encountered near the surface. In this case, the grade beams are poured on carton forms that support the concrete during pouring but do not transmit any upward pressures from the soil when they expand because they disintegrate and form a void shortly thereafter.

C. Designing Footings

There are three primary factors to investigate when designing footings. The first is the *unit loading*, so that the allowable bearing pressure of the soil is not exceeded and differential settlement in various parts of the structure is eliminated as much as possible. The other two are *shear* and *bending*. There are two kinds of shear failure. A footing fails in punching or two-way shear when the column or wall load punches through the footing. A footing can also fail in flexural shear or diagonal tension the same as regular beams. Footings fail in bending when the lower surface cracks under flexural loading.

Simple spread footings act much like inverted beams with the upward soil pressure being a continuous load that is resisted by the downward column load (although in reality, the column load is the action, and the upward pressure is the reaction). See Figure 6.8. This tends to cause bending in the upward direction, which induces compression near the top of the footing and tension near the bottom of the footing. If the tension is great enough, tension reinforcing must be added near the bottom of the footing.

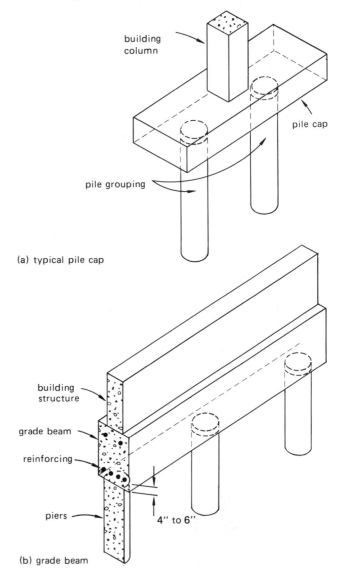

Figure 6.7 Pile Caps

The area of a spread footing is determined by dividing the total wall or column load on it plus its own weight plus any soil on top of the footing by the allowable soil bearing pressure. Then, the footing itself is designed for shear, moment, and other loads with factored loads as required by the *American Concrete Institute* (ACI) code. These, in effect, are safety factors to make sure the footing is of sufficient size and design to resist all loads.

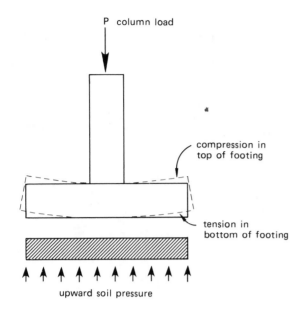

Figure 6.8   Load Action on Simple Spread Footings

There are various formulas to take into account combinations of live loads, dead loads, wind, earthquake, earth pressure, fluids, impact loads, and settlement, creep, and temperature change effects.

For foundations, the following formula is used:

$$U = 1.4D + 1.7L \qquad 6.1$$

The two most basic kinds of spread footings are the wall footing and the single column footing (see Figure 6.5 (a) and (b)). Each behaves a little differently and each is designed based on slightly different conditions.

When designing wall footings, there are two critical sections that must be investigated. These are at the face of the wall where bending moment is greatest and at a distance, d, from the face of the wall in wall footings where flexural shear is of most concern. These sections are shown in Figure 6.9 (a) and (b). However, the critical two-way shear section for column footings is a distance $d/2$ from the face of the wall. See Figure 6.10.

d is the distance from the top of the footing to the centroid of the reinforcing steel, called the *effective depth* of the footing since the concrete below the steel does not contribute any structural properties. The distance, d, for masonry and concrete foundation walls is a little different as shown in the two sketches. For concrete walls, it is measured from the face of the wall.

For lightly loaded walls where the total width of the footing is not too great, the bending action is not as critical as the shear which must be resisted by the thickness of the footing. Generally, it is not economical to

provide tension reinforcement in wall footings, so the width and thickness are designed to resist the wall load and shear forces using only the strength of unreinforced concrete. Usually, however, longitudinal reinforcing is included (parallel to the length of the wall) for temperature reinforcing and to help the footing span any intermittent, weaker soil conditions.

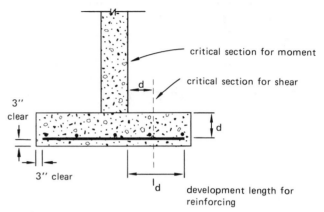

(a) concrete foundation wall

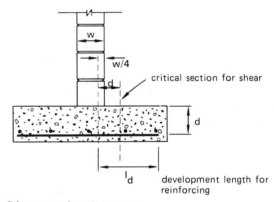

(b) masonry foundation wall

Figure 6.9   Critical Sections for Wall Footings

Where heavy loads or weak soil conditions are present, the width of the footing may become great enough to require tension reinforcement. In most cases, however, maximum allowable flexural shear governs the design depth of wall footings.

Individual column footings are subject to two-way action much like flat slabs near columns as well as one-way shear. Because of this, both types of shear must be calculated and the depth of the footing designed to resist these shear forces. When both are calculated, the greater shear value is used for design.

Figure 6.10 shows the two locations where shear must be calculated. For one-way shear at distance d from the face of the column, the factored soil design pressure is calculated over the rectangular area indicated as *abcd* in Figure 6.10. For two-way shear, the soil design pressure is calculated over the area outside the square $efgh$ indicated in Figure 6.10.

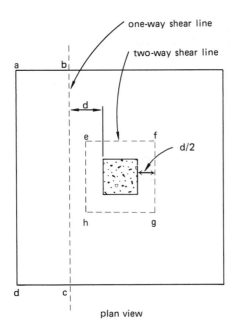

Figure 6.10   Individual Column Footings

In addition, bottom reinforcing in both directions is usually required to resist the moment forces at the face of the column.

Example 6.1

Find the required depth, width, and transverse reinforcing for the footing shown in the sketch. The bottom of the footing is five feet below grade and carries a load per linear foot of 14,000 pounds dead load and 7000 pounds live load on a 12-inch wide foundation wall. The concrete strength is 3000 psi, and the steel yield point is 60,000 psi. Soil tests have shown the allowable soil bearing pressure to be 3500 pounds per square foot.

> *step 1:* In the design, consider a one-foot long section of wall and footing. To find the width of the footing, divide the total load plus an allowance for the weight of the footing and an allowance for the soil on top of the footing by the allowable soil bearing pressure. Estimate the footing width as 7 feet and its depth as 12 inches. With concrete weighing about 150 pounds per cubic foot, a one-foot long section weighs 1050 pounds. Soil weighs about 100 pounds per square

foot so the soil weight is 4 feet times 100, or 400 pounds per square foot, or 1200 pounds for the three-foot section on either side of the foundation wall.

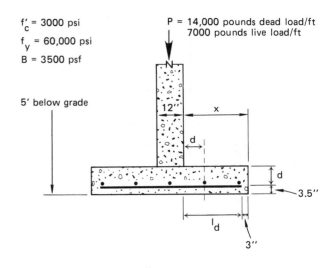

So, the width of the footing should be:

$$b_w = \frac{14,000 + 7000 + 1050 + 2400}{3500} = 6.99 \text{ feet}$$

Use a 7-foot wide footing.

step 2: To begin the design of the footing, the ACI code requires the design soil pressure to be calculated based on factored loads according to formula 6.1:

$$U = 1.4D + 1.7L$$
$$= 1.4(14,000) + 1.7(7000) = 31,500 \text{ pounds}$$

Note that this excludes the weight of the footing and the soil above the footing because they do not contribute to producing moment or shear in the footing.

The design soil pressure is then equal to the factored design load divided by the area.

$$q_s = \frac{31,500}{7} = 4500 \text{ psf}$$

step 3: Assuming a footing depth of 12 inches, check the flexural shear at the critical section since flexural shear almost always governs footing design. This section is at a distance, d, (the effective depth of the footing) from the face of the wall (see Figure 6.9 (a)). The distance is from the top of the footing to the centroid of reinforcing steel. Since the ACI code requires a 3-inch clear dimension from steel to the bottom of a footing cast against the earth, use this plus an allowance (guess at this point) of 1/2 inch for one-half the diameter of reinforcing steel. The rebars will probably be less than #8's but this gives an easy number of 3 1/2 inches to work with. Distance, d, is then $12 - 3.5$, or 8.5.

Shear at this point is the distance to the end of the footing times the design soil pressure. Remember, we are still working with a one-foot long section of wall, so units are in square feet and pounds per square foot.

$$V = (x - d)q_s$$
$$= (3 - 0.708)4500$$

(Note: 0.708 is 8 1/2 inches converted to a fraction of a foot.)

$$V = 10,314 \text{ psf}$$

The ACI code limits one-way shear on plain or reinforced sections to a maximum of:

$$V_c = \phi 2\sqrt{f_c'}\, b_w d \qquad 6.2$$
$$= (0.85)2\sqrt{3000}(12)(8.5) = 9497 \text{ lbs}$$

The actual shear of 10,314 pounds is more than the allowable of 9497 so the section needs to be revised.

Try a 14-inch deep footing with $d = 14 - 3.5$, or 10.5.

$$V_c = (90.85)2\sqrt{3000}(12)(10.5) = 11,732 \text{ psf}$$

A 14-inch thick footing will work since the allowable shear is now more than the actual shear.

step 4: Find the moment at the face of the wall. The leg of the footing acts as an inverted cantilevered beam so the moment is:

$$M_u = \frac{q_s l^2}{2} = \frac{(4500)(3)^2}{2} = 20,250 \text{ foot-pounds}$$

step 5: Find the area of the steel required according to the formula:

$$A_s = \frac{M_u}{\phi f_y(d - a/2)} \qquad 6.3$$

a is the depth of rectangular stress block determined by:

$$a = \frac{A_s f_y}{0.85 f_c b} \qquad 6.4$$

Since steel area is not known, you have to assume a value for a. Refer to Chapter 11 for a full discussion of this value. Try 1 inch to begin with.

The capacity reduction factor, ϕ, is 0.90 for flexure members.

$$A_s = \frac{20,250(12)}{0.90(60,000)(10.5 - 1/2)}$$
$$= 0.45 \text{ square inches per linear foot of footing}$$

There are several possible combinations of bar sizes and spacings that will satisfy this requirement. Number 5 bars at 8 inches on center gives a steel area of 0.46 square inches per foot, so use this. Refer to Figure 11.1 for various bar/spacing combinations.

Check to see that the value of a is less than that used in the assumption by using formula 6.4:

$$a = \frac{0.46(60,000)}{0.85(3000)12} = 0.90$$

This is less than the 1 inch assumed in finding the area of the steel, so this will work.

step 6: Find the development length required for the steel. This is the minimum length required to develop a sufficient bond between the steel and the concrete. It is measured from the face of the wall to the end of the steel as shown in Figure 6.9 and is found by the formula:

$$l_d = \frac{0.04 A_s f_y}{\sqrt{f_c'}} \geq 0.0004 d_b f_y \qquad 6.5$$

However, the length must be equal to or greater than the value determined by the second part of the formula.

The area of a #5 bar is 0.31 inch and its diameter is 0.625 inch (see Figure 11.1).

$$l_d = \frac{0.04(0.31)60,000}{\sqrt{3000}} = 13.58 \text{ inches}$$

However, the minimum length is 0.0004(0.625)60,000, or 15 inches, so this value governs. Since the actual length is $36 - 3$, or 33, there is sufficient length of steel.

step 7: Find the longitudinal temperature reinforcement required.

ACI code requires at least 0.002 times the area of the section to be steel, so $A_s = 0.002(12)(14) = 0.34$ square inches.

Number 4 bars at 7 inches on center provide 0.34 square inches per foot (see Table 11.1).

3 RETAINING WALLS

Retaining walls are used to hold back soil or other material when the desired change in elevation between two points is greater than can be achieved by letting the soil rest at its normal angle of repose.

A. Types of Retaining Walls

There are three types of retaining walls: the *gravity wall*, the *cantilever wall*, and the *counterfort wall*. See Figure 6.11. The gravity wall resists the forces on it by its own weight and by soil pressure and soil friction against its surface opposite to the earth forces. It is commonly used for low retaining walls up to about 10 feet where the forces on it are not too great.

The cantilever wall is the most common type and is constructed of reinforced concrete. This type resists forces by the weight of the structure as well as by the weight of the soil on the heel of the base slab. It is often constructed with a key projecting from the bottom of the slab to increase the wall's resistance to sliding as shown in Figure 6.11 (b). Occasionally, the toe is omitted if the wall is next to a property line or some other obstruction. Since the arm, heel, and toe act as cantilevered slabs, the thickness and reinforcement increase with increased length because of the larger moments developed.

Because of this, cantilevered walls are economically limited to about 20 to 25 feet in height.

For walls higher than 20 to 25 feet, the counterfort wall is used. This is similar to the cantilevered wall, but with counterforts placed at distances equal to or a little larger than one-half the height. The counterforts are simply reinforced concrete webs that act as diagonal bracing for the wall.

B. Forces on Retaining Walls

In the simplest case, the force on a retaining wall results entirely from the pressure of the earth retained acting in a horizontal direction to the wall. The earth pressure increases proportionally with the depth from the surface, ranging from zero at ground level to a maximum at the lowest depth of the wall in a triangular distribution pattern. See Figure 6.12.

The earth pressure at any point is given by the formula:

$$P = C_o W h \qquad 6.6$$

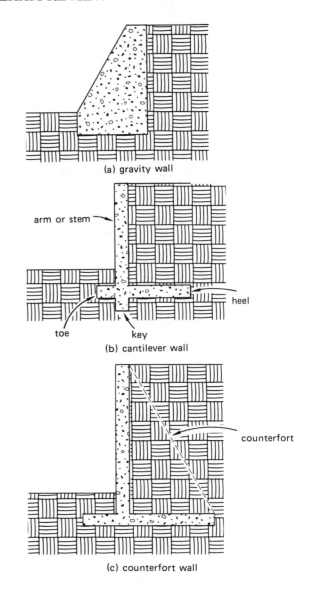

Figure 6.11 Types of Retaining Walls

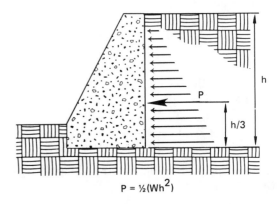

Figure 6.12 Forces Acting on a Retaining Wall

The coefficient of earth pressure, C_o, depends on the soil type and the method of backfilling and compacting it.

The value may range from 0.4 for uncompacted soils like sands and gravels to 1.0 for cohesive, compacted soils. In many situations, the formula is simplified so that C_o is eliminated and the weight of the soil is considered to be equivalent to a fluid weighing 30 pounds per cubic foot. Therefore, the pressure at any point is:

$$P = 30h \qquad 6.7$$

In the situation shown in Figure 6.12, since the pressure acts in a triangular form, the total pressure against the wall can be assumed to be acting through the centroid of the triangle, or one-third the distance from the base. Therefore, to find this value, you only need to find the pressure at the base of the wall and multiply by one-half the height (the area of a triangle). The formula for this is:

$$P = \frac{1}{2}Wh^2 \qquad 6.8$$

Or, if you use the 30 pounds per cubic foot assumption for the equivalent weight of the soil, the formula reduces to:

$$P = 15h^2 \qquad 6.9$$

Example 6.2

What is the total pressure on a retaining wall 9.5 feet high?

Assuming the soil has an equivalent fluid weight of 30 psf per foot of height, the total force acts at a point 9.5/3 or 3.17 feet above the base.

$$P = 15(9.5)^2 = 1354 \text{ pounds}$$

Additional forces may act on retaining walls. The earth being retained may slope upward from the top of the wall resulting in the total force acting through the centroid of the pressure triangle, but in a direction parallel to the slope of the soil. Additional loads, called surcharges, may result from driveways or other forces being imposed on the soil next to the wall. If the ground behind the wall becomes wet, there is additional pressure resulting from the water which must be added to the soil pressure.

C. Design Considerations

A retaining wall may fail in two ways: it may fail as a whole by overturning or by sliding, or its individual components may fail, such as when the arm or stem breaks due to excessive moment. In order to prevent failure by overturning or sliding, the resisting moment or forces that resist sliding are generally considered sufficient if there is a safety factor of 1.5. For example,

the total dead load of the wall plus the weight of the earth backfill acting on the footing of a cantilevered retaining wall should be at least 1.5 times the overturning moment caused by earth pressure to be safe. See Figure 6.13 (a). To prevent sliding, the friction between the footing and surrounding soil and the earth pressure in front of the toe (and key, if any) must be 1.5 times the pressures tending to cause the wall to slide. See Figure 6.13 (b).

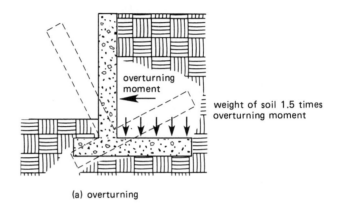

(a) overturning

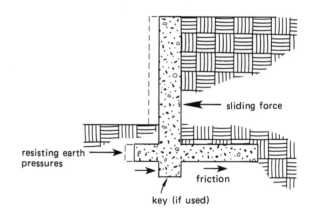

(b) sliding

Figure 6.13   Resisting Forces on Retaining Walls

To prevent failure of individual components, the thickness, width, and reinforcing of the retaining wall must be designed to resist the moment and shear forces induced by soil pressures, surcharges, and any hydrostatic pressures.

Retaining walls should be designed to eliminate or reduce the buildup of water behind them. This can be accomplished by providing weep holes near the bottom of the wall and by providing a layer of gravel next to the back of the wall. In some cases, it is necessary to install a drain tile above the heel of the wall to carry away excess water.

SAMPLE QUESTIONS

1. Soil tests made prior to construction have indicated that excessive groundwater is present. If the project has a basement, what suggestions would you make to your client to alleviate the potential problem and in what order of priority?

I. Specify that drainage matting be placed against all basement foundation walls.

II. Add extra drain pipes from the roof and drain away from the building.

III. Detail and specify drain tile around the footings and connect to atmosphere or a dry well.

IV. Use 1-inch to 2-inch gravel under the basement slab.

V. Draw the site plan so the ground has a positive slope away from the building on all sides.

A. V, IV, III, I, II

B. III, IV, I, V, II

C. V, I, IV, III, II

D. III, I, IV, II, V

2. Which of the following techniques would be most appropriate to prepare the soil for a building site that tests have shown to be primarily composed of silt and organic silt?

A. compaction

B. surcharging

C. densification

D. fill

3. The retaining wall shown holds back compacted soil with a coefficient of earth pressure of 1.0 and an equivalent fluid weight of 30 pcf. What is the total earth pressure against the retaining wall per foot and at what point is it considered to be acting for design purposes?

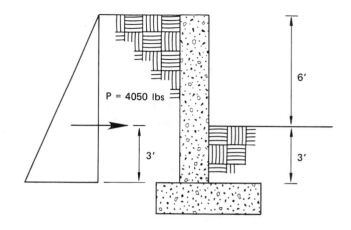

P = 4050 lbs

A. 270 pounds at the top of the footing

B. 1215 pounds at the level of the lower grade

C. 1215 pounds 2 feet above the lower grade level

D. 1080 pounds at the level of the lower grade

4. The footing and foundation wall shown support a live load of 500 pounds per linear foot and a dead load of 1000 pounds per linear foot. Assuming concrete weighs 150 pounds per cubic foot and the soil weighs about 100 pounds per cubic foot, how wide should the footing be if the allowable soil bearing pressure is 1500 psf?

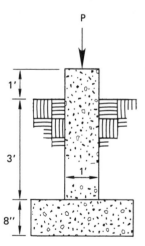

A. 1 foot

B. 1 1/2 feet

C. 2 feet

D. 3 feet

5. Soil tests are:

A. ordered by the architect and included in the sitework portion of the specifications.

B. ordered by the structural engineer and made part of the structural drawings.

C. not part of the contract documents, but test locations and boring logs are often shown for information only.

D. paid for by the client and included on the site plan as part of the architectural drawings.

6. Bearing capacities are determined by:

I. building codes

II. the amount of water present in the soil

III. unified soil classification system

IV. field tests

V. extent and amount of compaction

A. I, II, and IV

B. I, II, and V

C. II, III, and IV

D. all of the above

The answers to questions 7 through 10 can be found on the following key list. Select only one answer for each question.

A0 belled pier
A1 boring log

A2 combined footing
A3 grade beam
A4 gravels
A5 hydrostatic pressure
A6 organics
A7 Proctor test
A8 raft foundation
A9 repose

B0 sands
B1 silts
B2 spread footing
B3 standard penetration test
B4 strap footing
B5 test pip report
B6 water table

7. What is used to specify the required compaction of fill material?

8. Which soil type would be best for heavily loaded spread footings?

9. Information on what item is necessary if retaining walls are not to be used?

10. If a soil test confirmed the presence of bentonite, what type of foundation would probably be best for a one-story building?

7 CONNECTIONS

Nomenclature

F_c unit stress in compression perpendicular   psi
      to the grain

F_g design value for end grain in bearing   psi
      parallel to grain

F_n unit compressive stress at inclination   psi
      θ with the direction of grain

F_p allowable bearing stress   ksi

F_t allowable tensile stress   ksi

F_u minimum tensile strength of steel or   ksi
      fastener

F_v allowable shear stress   ksi

F_y specified minimum yield stress of steel   ksi

θ angle between the direction of grain and
      direction of load normal to face considered

The majority of structural failures occur in the connections of members, not in the members themselves. Either the incorrect types of connectors are used, they are undersized, too few in number, or improperly installed. It is therefore important for A.R.E. test candidates to have a good understanding of the various types of connectors and how they are used.

1 WOOD CONNECTIONS

There are several variables that affect the design of wood connections. The first, of course, is the load-carrying capacity of the connector itself. Nails and screws, for example, carry relatively light loads while timber connectors can carry large loads. Other variables that apply to all connections include the species of wood, the type of load, the condition of the wood, the service conditions, whether or not the wood is fire-retardant treated, and the angle of the load to the grain. Additional design considerations are the critical net section, the type of shear the joint is subjected to, the

spacing of the connectors, and the end and edge distances to connectors.

A. Species of Wood

The species and density of wood affects the holding power of connectors. Species are classified into four groups. There is one grouping for timber connectors, such as split ring connectors and shear plates, and another grouping for lag screws, nails, spikes, wood screws and metal plate connector loads. The four groups for timber connectors are designated Group A, B, C, and D, while the grouping for other connectors are designated Group I, II, III, and IV. Tables that give the allowable loads for connectors have separate columns for each group. Design values for connectors in a particular species apply to all grades of that species unless otherwise noted in the tables.

B. Type of Load

The design values for connectors can be adjusted for the duration of loading just as wood members can be (see Chapter 9). This is because wood can carry greater maximum loads for short durations than for long durations. The tables of allowable connector loads are for normal duration of ten years. For other conditions, the allowable values can be multiplied by the following factors:

- 0.90 for permanent loading over 10 years

- 1.15 for 2 months' duration (snow loading, for example)

- 1.25 for 7 days' duration

- 1.33 for wind or earthquake loads

- 2.00 for impact loads

C. Condition of Wood

Tabulated design values found in building codes and elsewhere are for fastenings in wood seasoned to a moisture content of 19 percent or less. This is adequate for most use, but partially seasoned or wet wood (either at the time of fabrication or in service) reduces the holding power of the connector.

D. Service Conditions

Service conditions refer to the environment in which the wood joint will be used. These conditions can either be dry, wet, exposed to the weather, or subject to wetting and drying. Any service conditions other than dry or continuously wet reduce the holding power of the connector.

E. Fire-Retardant Treatment

Wood that has been fire-retardant treated does not hold connectors as well as wood that has not been treated. The adjustment factor for fastener design loads is 0.90.

F. Angle of Load

One of the most important variables affecting allowable loads carried by connectors is the angle of the load to the grain, which is defined as the angle between the direction of load acting on the member and the longitudinal axis of the member. Wood connectors can carry more load parallel to the grain than perpendicular to it, so tables of design values include both. If the load is acting other than parallel or perpendicular to the grain, it must be calculated using the *Hankinson formula* or by using one of the graphs that gives the same results.

The Hankinson formula gives the unit compressive stress at angle θ:

$$F_n = \frac{F_g F_c}{F_g \sin^2 \theta + F_c \cos^2 \theta} \qquad 7.1$$

Example 7.1

A $2'' \times 6''$ truss member bears on a $4'' \times 6''$ member at an angle of 40 degrees. Both pieces of lumber are select structural Douglas fir ($F_g = 1400$ psi, and $F_c = 625$ psi). What is the allowable unit compressive stress for the connection?

Using the Hankinson formula,

$$F_n = \frac{1400(625)}{1400 \sin^2 40 + 625 \cos^2 40}$$
$$= \frac{875,000}{1400(0.413) + 625(0.587)} = 926 \text{ psi}$$

G. Critical Net Section

When a wood member is drilled for one of the many types of connectors (except for nails and screws) there is a decrease in area of wood to carry the imposed load. The section where the most wood has been removed is called the *critical net section*. Once the size of the drilled area is known, the member must be checked for load-carrying capacity at this section. It may be necessary to increase the size of the member just to compensate for this decrease in area. See Figure 7.1 (a).

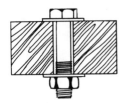

(a) critical net area

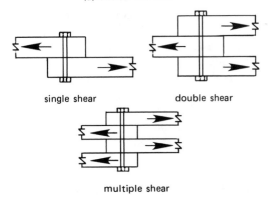

single shear   double shear

multiple shear

(b) types of shear conditions

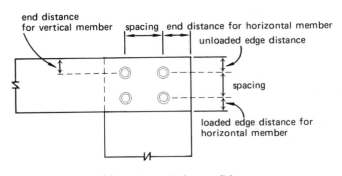

(c) spacing and edge conditions

Figure 7.1 Wood Connector Design Variables

H. Type of Shear

Connectors such as bolts and lag screws can be in single shear, double shear, or multiple shear as shown in Figure 7.1 (b). The type of shear condition and the relative thickness of each piece to the others are especially important when designing bolted connections.

I. Spacing Connectors

Connector spacing is the distance between centers of connectors measured along a line joining their centers as shown in Figure 7.1 (c). Minimum spacing is given for various types of connectors in building codes and in the *National Design Specification for Wood Construction* published by the National Forest Products Association.

J. End and Edge Distances to Connectors

End distance is the distance measured parallel to the grain from the center of the connector to the square-cut end of the member. *Edge distance* is the distance from the edge of the member to the center of the connector closest to the edge of the member measured perpendicular to the edge. See Figure 7.1 (c).

For loading perpendicular to the grain, a distinction is made between the loaded and unloaded edges. The loaded edge is the edge toward which the fastener load acts, and the unloaded edge is the edge opposite from this. Minimum values for these distances are given in tables of allowable loads for the various types of connectors.

K. Nails

Although they are the weakest of wood connectors, nails are the most common for light frame construction. The types used most frequently for structural applications include common wire nails, box nails, and common wire spikes. Wire nails range in size from six penny (6d) to sixty penny (60d). Box nails range from 6d to 40d. 6d nails are two inches in length while 60d nails are six inches long. Common wire spikes range from 10d (three inches long) to 8 1/2 inches long and 3/8-inch diameter. For the same penny weight, box nails have the smallest diameter, common wire nails have the next largest diameter, and wire spikes have the greatest diameter.

For engineered applications, that is, where each nailed joint is specifically designed, there are tables of values giving the allowable withdrawal resistance and lateral load (shear) resistance for different sizes and penetrations of nails depending on the type of wood used. The most typical situation of most nailed wood construction is to simply use nailing schedules found in the building code. These give the minimum size, number, and penetration of nails for specific applications such as nailing studs to sole plates, joists to headers, and so forth.

There are several orientations that nails, screws, and lag screws have with wood members. These are shown in Figure 7.2 and affect the holding power of the fastener. The preferable orientation is to have the fastener loaded

laterally in side grain where the holding power is the greatest. If one of the pieces is metal rather than wood, allowable values may be increased by 25 percent. For nails, the design values for shear are the same regardless of the angle of load to grain.

Fasteners may also be driven or screwed so that there is withdrawal from side grain. Fasteners loaded in withdrawal from end grain are not allowed by building codes.

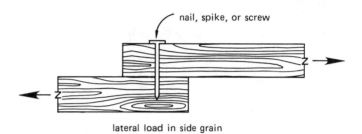

lateral load in side grain

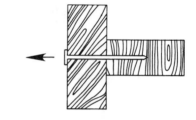

withdrawal from side grain

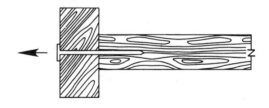

withdrawal from end grain (avoid)

Figure 7.2   Orientation of Wood Fasteners

L. Screws

Wood screws used for structural purposes are available in sizes from #6 (0.138-inch shank diameter) to #24 (0.372-inch shank diameter) in lengths up to five inches. The most common types are flat head and round head. As with nails, design tables give withdrawal and lateral load values for screws of different sizes, penetrations, and type of wood in which they are used. Also like nails, screws are best used laterally loaded in side grain rather than in withdrawal from side grain. Withdrawal from end is not permitted.

Design values given in the tables are for a penetration into the main member of approximately 7 diameters. In no case should the penetration be less than 4 diameters. Like nails, design values can be increased by 25 percent if a metal side plate is used.

Lead holes must be drilled into the wood to permit the proper insertion of the wood screw. The recommended size of the lead hole depends on the species group of the wood being used and whether the screw is in lateral resistance or withdrawal resistance. Soap or other lubricant may be used to facilitate insertion.

M. Lag Screws

A lag screw is threaded with a pointed end like a wood screw but has a head like a bolt. It is inserted by drilling lead holes and screwing the fastener into the wood with a wrench. A washer is used between the head and the wood. Lag screws are also called *lag bolts*.

Sizes range from 1/4 inch to 1 1/4 inches in diameter and from 1 inch to 16 inches in length. Diameters are measured at the non-threaded shank portion of the screw.

The design values for lateral loading and withdrawal resistance depend on the species group, the angle of load to grain, the diameter of the lag screw, the thickness of the side member, and the length of the screw. These variables are summarized in allowable load tables for loading parallel and perpendicular to the grain. Unlike nails and spikes, if the load is other than at a zero degree or 90 degree angle, the design value must be determined from the Hankinson formula. Spacings, end distances, and edge distance for lag screw joints are the same as for bolts of the same diameter as the shank of the lag screw.

N. Bolts

Bolts are one of the most common forms of wood connectors for joints of moderate to heavy loading. The design requirements for bolted joints are a little more complicated than those for screwed or nailed joints. Variables such as the thicknesses of the main and side members, ratio of bolt length in main member to bolt diameter, and the number of members joined affect the allowable design values and the spacing of the bolts.

The two typical conditions are joints in single shear and double shear as illustrated in Figure 7.3.

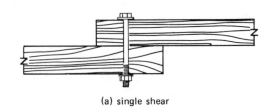
(a) single shear

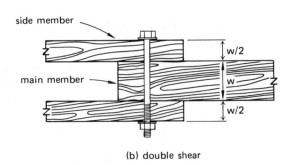
(b) double shear

Figure 7.3 Typical Bolted Connection Conditions

Design values given in tables are usually for conditions where the side members in double shear joints are one-half the thickness of the main member. If a value is given for only double shear joints, values for single shear joints of members of equal widths are taken as one-half the values for double shear joints. In some cases, such as the table from the Uniform Building Code shown in Table 7.1, values for both single and double shear are given.

When steel plates are used for side members or main members loaded parallel to the grain, the tabulated values can be increased 75 percent for joints made with bolts 1/2 inch or less, and 25 percent for joints made with bolts 1 1/2 inch with intermediate diameter values interpolated. No increase is allowed for loading perpendicular to the grain.

If loading is at an angle to the grain, the Hankinson formula must be used to determine allowable loading on a bolt. When side member dimensions vary from those shown in Figure 7.3 (b), or the bolt grouping consists of rows of multiple bolts, procedures for modifying the design values are given in the *National Design Specification for Wood Construction*.

Example 7.2

A nominal 4″ × 6″ redwood beam is to be supported by two 2″ × 6″ members acting as a spaced column as shown in the illustration. The minimum spacing and edge distances for 1/2-inch bolts are shown. How many 1/2-inch bolts will be required to safely carry a load of 1500 pounds?

Table 7.1
Holding Power of Bolts

p = Safe loads parallel to grain in pounds
q = Safe loads perpendicular to grain in pounds

Length of Bolt in Main Wood Member[3] (in inches)		DIAMETER OF BOLT (IN INCHES)					
		3/8	1/2	5/8	3/4	7/8	1
1½	Single p	325	470	590	710	830	945
	Shear q	185	215	245	270	300	325
	Double p	650	940	1180	1420	1660	1890
	Shear q	370	430	490	540	600	650
2½	Single p		630	910	1155	1370	1575
	Shear q		360	405	450	495	540
	Double p	710	1260	1820	2310	2740	3150
	Shear q	620	720	810	900	990	1080
3½	Single p			990	1400	1790	2135
	Shear q			565	630	695	760
	Double p	710	1270	1980	2800	3580	4270
	Shear q	640	980	1130	1260	1390	1520
5½	Single p					1950	2535
	Shear q					1090	1190
	Double p		1270	1990	2860	3900	5070
	Shear q		930	1410	1880	2180	2380
7½	Single p						
	Shear q						
	Double p			1990	2860	3890	5080
	Shear q			1260	1820	2430	3030
9½	Single p						
	Shear q						
	Double p				2860	3900	5080
	Shear q				1640	2270	2960
11½	Single p						
	Shear q						
	Double p					3900	5080
	Shear q					2050	2770
13½	Single p						
	Shear q						
	Double p						5100
	Shear q						2530

[1]Tabulated values are on a normal load-duration basis and apply to joints made of seasoned lumber used in dry locations. See U.B.C. Standard No. 25-17 for other service conditions.

[2]Double shear values are for joints consisting of three wood members in which the side members are one half the thickness of the main member. Single shear values are for joints consisting of two wood members having a minimum thickness not less than that specified.

[3]The length specified is the length of the bolt in the main member of double shear joints or the length of the bolt in the thinner member of single shear joints.

[4]See U.B.C. Standard No. 25-17 for wood-to-metal bolted joints.

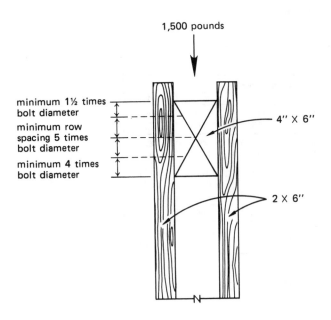

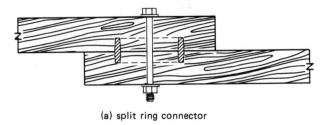

(a) split ring connector

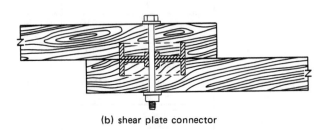

(b) shear plate connector

Figure 7.4   Timber Connectors

plate is flush with one surface. See Figure 7.4 (b). Because of this configuration, shear plate connections can either hold two pieces of wood together or one piece of wood and a steel plate.

Split ring connectors and shear plates can transfer larger loads than bolts or screws alone, and are often used in connecting truss members. Shear plates are particularly suited for constructions that must be disassembled. Tables of design values for loads, spacing, end and edge distances are published by the National Forest Products Association.

P. Miscellaneous Connection Hardware

Because wood is such a common building material, there are dozens of types of special connectors especially designed to make assembly easy, fast, and structurally sound. Hardware is available for both standard sizes of wood members as well as special members like wood truss joists. Manufacturers publish allowable design values for each of their pieces. Some of the common types of connection hardware are shown in Figure 7.5.

2   STEEL CONNECTIONS

Bolting and *welding* are the two most common methods in use today for making steel connections. Riveting was once widely used but has been generally replaced with bolting because bolting is less expensive and does not take such a large crew of skilled workers to accomplish.

Look in Table 7.1 under the column labeled 1/2-inch bolt diameter. Since the length of the bolt in the main member is 3 1/2 inches (4 inch nominal width), use that row and the portion of the row labeled double shear. The lower of the two values governs, so use this row. This is the load perpendicular to the grain. This value is 980 pounds. Two bolts will allow for a load of 980 times 2, or 1960 pounds, well above the 1500 required.

Using the spacing and edge distances given in the illustration, there must be a spacing of 2 1/2 inches, a top edge distance of 3/4 inch, and a bottom edge distance of 2 inches, for a total of 5 1/4 inches, within the total actual depth of 5 1/2 inches of the 4 × 6 member.

O. Timber Connectors

There are two types of timber connectors: *split rings* and *shear plates*. Split rings are either 2 1/2 inches or 4 inches in diameter and are cut through in one place in the circumference to form a tongue and slot. The ring is beveled from the central portion toward the edges. Grooves are cut in each piece of the wood members to be joined so that half the ring is in each section. The members are held together with a bolt concentric with the ring as shown in Figure 7.4 (a).

Shear plates are either 2 5/8 inches or 4 inches in diameter, and are flat plates with a flange extending from the face of the plate. There is a hole in the middle through which a either a 3/4-inch or 7/8-inch bolt is placed to hold the two members together. Shear plates are inserted in precut grooves in a piece of wood so that the

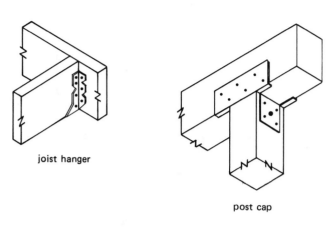

joist hanger

post cap

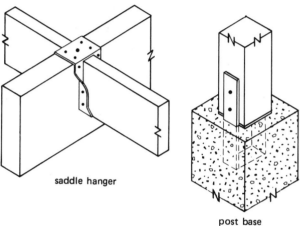

saddle hanger

post base

Figure 7.5 Special Connection Hardware

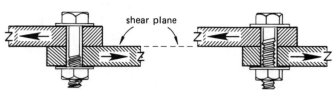

threads excluded from shear plane   threads included in shear plane

Figure 7.6 Location of Bolt Threads in Relation to Shear Plane

less area to resist the load through the threaded portion. See Figure 7.6. Like wood connections, bolts may be in either single shear or double shear.

There are three basic types of bolts used in modern steel construction. Bolts designated with the American Society of Testing and Materials (ASTM) number A307 are called *unfinished bolts* and have the lowest load-carrying capacity. They are used only for bearing-type connections. Bolts designated A325 and A490 are *high-strength bolts* and may be used in bearing-type connections but must be used in slip-critical connections. In slip-critical connections, the nuts are tightened to develop a high tensile stress in the bolt, thus causing the connected members to develop a high friction between them which resists the shear.

Bolts range in diameter from 5/8 inch to 1 1/2 inches in 1/8 inch increments, but the most typically used diameters are 3/4 inch and 7/8 inch. Bolts are installed with a washer under the head and nut. In addition to the ASTM designations, there are standard codes for the condition of use:

- SC: slip-critical connection

- N: bearing-type connection with threads included in the shear plane

- X: bearing-type connection with threads excluded from the shear plane

- S: bolt in single shear

- D: bolt in double shear

The American Institute of Steel Construction (AISC) *Manual of Steel Construction* gives the allowable loads for various types of connectors in both shear and bearing. For bearing connections, different values are given

A. Bolts

There are two types of bolted connections: *bearing type* and *slip-critical*. Bearing-type connections resist the shear load on the bolt through friction between surfaces, but may also produce direct bearing between the steel being fastened and the sides of the bolts. This is due to the fact that bolt holes are slightly larger than the bolts, and under load the two pieces of steel being connected may shift until they are bearing against the bolt.

Slip-critical connections are those where any amount of slip would be detrimental to the serviceability of the structure, such as joints subject to fatigue loading or joints with oversized holes. With slip-critical joints, the entire load is carried by friction.

Bolts are further classified as to whether the bolt threads are included or excluded from the shear plane. This affects the strength of the connection because there is based on the minimum tensile strength of the base material of the connected part. For A36 steel, this value is 58 ksi. The maximum allowable bearing stress between the bolt and the side of the hole is given by the equation

$$F_p = 1.2F_u \qquad\qquad 7.2$$

The allowable loads for shear are given in Table 7.2, and the allowable loads for bearing for A36 steel are given in Table 7.3. To use the tables, you simply need to know the diameter of the bolt, its designation, the type of hole being used, the connection type, and the loading condition. Procedures for using these tables will be shown in following examples.

There are several types of holes for bolted connections. *Standard round holes* are 1/16 inch larger than the diameter of the bolt. Other kinds of holes as listed below may be used with high-strength bolts 5/8 inch in diameter and larger.

Oversize holes may have nominal diameters up to 3/16 inch larger than bolts 7/8 inch and less in diameter, 1/4 inch larger than 1 inch bolts, and 5/16 inch larger than bolts 1 1/8 inch and greater in diameter. These holes may only be used in slip-critical connections.

Short slotted holes are 1/16 inch wider than the bolt diameter and have a length that does not exceed the oversize hole dimensions by more than 1/16 inch. They may be used in either bearing- or slip-critical connections, but if used in bearing, the slots have to be perpendicular to the direction of load.

Long slotted holes are 1/16 inch wider than the bolt diameter and a length not exceeding 2 1/2 times the bolt diameter. They may be used in slip-critical connections without regard to direction of load, but must be perpendicular to the load direction in bearing-type connections.

Slotted holes are used where some amount of adjustment is needed. Long slotted holes can only be used in one of the connected parts of a joint. The other part must use standard round holes or be welded.

In addition to the load-carrying capacities of the bolts, the effect of reducing the cross-sectional area of the members must be checked. Figure 7.7 shows a typical example of this. In this case, a beam is framed into a girder with an angle welded to the girder bolted to the beam. With a load applied to the beam, there is a tendency for the web of the beam to tear where the area of the flange has been reduced by the bolt holes. This area is known as the *net area*. As shown in the figure, there is both shear failure parallel to the load and tension failure perpendicular to the load.

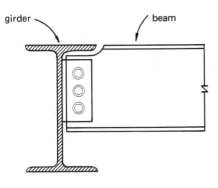

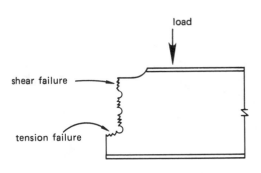

Figure 7.7 Tearing Failures at Bolted Connection

The AISC specifications limit the allowable stress on the net tension area to

$$F_t = 0.50F_u \qquad\qquad 7.3$$

The allowable stress on the net shear area is limited to

$$F_v = 0.30F_u \qquad\qquad 7.4$$

For A36 steel, $F_u = 58$ ksi.

The total tearing force is the sum required to cause both forms of failure.

The stress on net tension area must be compared with the allowable stress on the gross section, which is

$$F_t = 0.60F_y \qquad\qquad 7.5$$

Example 7.3

A 3/8-inch A36 steel plate is suspended from a 1/2-inch plate with three 3/4-inch A325 bolts in standard holes spaced as shown in the drawing. The threads are excluded from the shear plane and the connection is bearing type. What is the maximum load-carrying capacity of the 3/8-inch plate?

Table 7.2
Allowable Loads in Shear for Connectors

BOLTS, THREADED PARTS AND RIVETS
Shear
Allowable load in kips

SHEAR													
	ASTM Desig- nation	Conn- ection Type[a]	Hole Type[b]	F_v ksi	Load- ing[c]	Nominal Diameter d, in.							
						5/8	3/4	7/8	1	1 1/8	1 1/4	1 3/8	1 1/2
						Area (Based on Nominal Diameter) in.[2]							
						.3068	.4418	.6013	.7854	.9940	1.227	1.485	1.767
Bolts	A307	—	STD NSL	10.0	S D	3.1 6.1	4.4 8.8	6.0 12.0	7.9 15.7	9.9 19.9	12.3 24.5	14.8 29.7	17.7 35.3
	A325	SC[a] Class A	STD	17.0	S D	5.22 10.4	7.51 15.0	10.2 20.4	13.4 26.7	16.9 33.8	20.9 41.7	25.2 50.5	30.0 60.1
			OVS, SSL	15.0	S D	4.60 9.20	6.63 13.3	9.02 18.0	11.8 23.6	14.9 29.8	18.4 36.8	22.3 44.6	26.5 53.0
			LSL	12.0	S D	3.68 7.36	5.30 10.6	7.22 14.4	9.42 18.8	11.9 23.9	14.7 29.4	17.8 35.6	21.2 42.4
		N	STD, NSL	21.0	S D	6.4 12.9	9.3 18.6	12.6 25.3	16.5 33.0	20.9 41.7	25.8 51.5	31.2 62.4	37.1 74.2
		X	STD, NSL	30.0	S D	9.2 18.4	13.3 26.5	18.0 36.1	23.6 47.1	29.8 59.6	36.8 73.6	44.5 89.1	53.0 106.0
	A490	SC[a] Class A	STD	21.0	S D	6.44 12.9	9.28 18.6	12.6 25.3	16.5 33.0	20.9 41.7	25.8 51.5	31.2 62.4	37.1 74.2
			OVS, SSL	18.0	S D	5.52 11.0	7.95 15.9	10.8 21.6	14.1 28.3	17.9 35.8	22.1 44.2	26.7 53.5	31.8 63.6
			LSL	15.0	S D	4.60 9.20	6.63 13.3	9.02 18.0	11.8 23.6	14.9 29.8	18.4 36.8	22.3 44.6	26.5 53.0
		N	STD, NSL	28.0	S D	8.6 17.2	12.4 24.7	16.8 33.7	22.0 44.0	27.8 55.7	34.4 68.7	41.6 83.2	49.5 99.0
		X	STD, NSL	40.0	S D	12.3 24.5	17.7 35.3	24.1 ⊤48.1	31.4 62.8	39.8 79.5	49.1 98.2	59.4 119.0	70.7 141.0
Rivets	A502-1	—	STD	17.5	S D	5.4 10.7	7.7 15.5	10.5 21.0	13.7 27.5	17.4 34.8	21.5 42.9	26.0 52.0	30.9 61.8
	A502-2 A502-3	—	STD	22.0	S D	6.7 13.5	9.7 19.4	13.2 26.5	17.3 34.6	21.9 43.7	27.0 54.0	32.7 65.3	38.9 77.7
Threaded Parts	A36 (F_u=58 ksi)	N	STD	9.9	S D	3.0 6.1	4.4 8.7	6.0 11.9	7.8 15.6	9.8 19.7	12.1 24.3	14.7 29.4	17.5 35.0
		X	STD	12.8	S D	3.9 7.9	5.7 11.3	7.7 15.4	10.1 20.1	12.7 25.4	15.7 31.4	19.0 38.0	22.6 45.2
	A572, Gr. 50 (F_u=65 ksi)	N	STD	11.1	S D	3.4 6.8	4.9 9.8	6.7 13.3	8.7 17.4	11.0 22.1	13.6 27.2	16.5 33.0	19.6 39.2
		X	STD	14.3	S D	4.4 8.8	6.3 12.6	8.6 17.2	11.2 22.5	14.2 28.4	17.5 35.1	21.2 42.5	25.3 50.5
	A588 (F_u=70 ksi)	N	STD	11.9	S D	3.7 7.3	5.3 10.5	7.2 14.3	9.3 18.7	11.8 23.7	14.6 29.2	17.7 35.3	21.0 42.1
		X	STD	15.4	S D	4.7 9.4	6.8 13.6	9.3 18.5	12.1 24.2	15.3 30.6	18.9 37.8	22.9 45.7	27.2 54.4

[a]SC = Slip critical connection.
  N: Bearing-type connection with threads *included* in shear plane.
  X: Bearing-type connection with threads *excluded* from shear plane.
[b]STD: Standard round holes (d + 1/16 in.)   OVS: Oversize round holes
  LSL: Long-slotted holes   SSL: Short-slotted holes
  NSL: Long-or short-slotted hole normal to load direction
        (required in bearing-type connection).
[c]S: Single shear   D: Double shear.
For threaded parts of materials not listed, use $F_v = 0.17F_u$ when threads are included in a shear plane, and $F_v = 0.22F_u$ when threads are excluded from a shear plane.
To fully pretension bolts 1 1/8-in. dia. and greater, special impact wrenches may be required.
When bearing-type connections used to splice tension members have a fastener pattern whose length, measured parallel to the line of force, exceeds 50 in., tabulated values shall be reduced by 20%. See AISC ASD Commentary Sect. J3.4.

Reprinted from Manual of Steel Construction 9th ed.,
American Institute of Steel Construction

Table 7.3
Allowable Loads in Bearing for Connectors (A36 Steel)

BOLTS AND THREADED PARTS
Bearing
Allowable loads in kips

BEARING Slip-critical and Bearing-type Connections											
Material Thickness	F_u = 58 ksi Bolt dia.			F_u = 65 ksi Bolt dia.			F_u = 70 ksi Bolt dia.			F_u = 100 ksi Bolt dia.		
	3/4	7/8	1	3/4	7/8	1	3/4	7/8	1	3/4	7/8	1
1/8	6.5	7.6	8.7	7.3	8.5	9.8	7.9	9.2	10.5	11.3	13.1	15.0
3/16	9.8	11.4	13.1	11.0	12.8	14.6	11.8	13.8	15.8	16.9	19.7	22.5
1/4	13.1	15.2	17.4	14.6	17.1	19.5	15.8	18.4	21.0	22.5	26.3	30.0
5/16	16.3	19.0	21.8	18.3	21.3	24.4	19.7	23.0	26.3	28.1	32.8	37.5
3/8	19.6	22.8	26.1	21.9	25.6	29.3	23.6	27.6	31.5	33.8	39.4	45.0
7/16	22.8	26.6	30.5	25.6	29.9	34.1	27.6	32.2	36.8		45.9	52.5
1/2	26.1	30.5	34.8	29.3	34.1	39.0	31.5	36.8	42.0			60.0
9/16	29.4	34.3	39.2	32.9	38.4	43.9		41.3	47.3			
5/8	32.6	38.1	43.5		42.7	48.8		45.9	52.5			
11/16		41.9	47.9		46.9	53.6			57.8			
3/4		45.7	52.2			58.5						
13/16			56.6									
7/8			60.9									
15/16												
1	52.2	60.9	69.6	58.5	68.3	78.0	63.0	73.5	84.0	90.0	105.0	120.0

Notes:

This table is applicable to all mechanical fasteners in both slip-critical and bearing-type connections utilizing standard holes. Standard holes shall have a diameter nominally 1/16-in. larger than the nominal bolt diameter (d + 1/16 in.).

Tabulated bearing values are based on F_p = 1.2 F_u.

F_u = specified minimum tensile strength of the connected part.

In connections transmitting axial force whose length between extreme fasteners measured parallel to the line of force exceeds 50 in., tabulated values shall be reduced 20%.

Connections using high-strength bolts in slotted holes with the load applied in a direction other than approximately normal (between 80 and 100 degrees) to the axis of the hole and connections with bolts in oversize holes shall be designed for resistance against slip at working load in accordance with AISC ASD Specification Sect. J3.8.

Tabulated values apply when the distance l parallel to the line of force from the center of the bolt to the edge of the connected part is not less than 1½ d and the distance from the center of a bolt to the center of an adjacent bolt is not less than 3d. See AISC ASD Commentary J3.8.

Under certain conditions, values greater than the tabulated values may be justified under Specification Sect. J3.7.

Values are limited to the double-shear bearing capacity of A490-X bolts.

Values for decimal thicknesses may be obtained by multiplying the decimal value of the unlisted thickness by the value given for a 1-in. thickness.

Reprinted from Manual of Steel Construction 9th ed.,
American Institute of Steel Construction

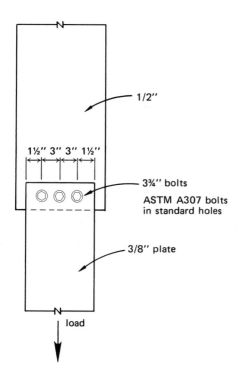

There are many kinds of framed connections depending on the type of connector being used, the size and shape of the connected members, and the magnitude of the loads that must be transferred. Figure 7.8 illustrates some of the more typical kinds of steel connections. In most cases, the angle used to connect one piece with another is welded to one member in the shop and bolted to the other member during field erection. Slotted holed are sometimes used to allow for minor field adjustments.

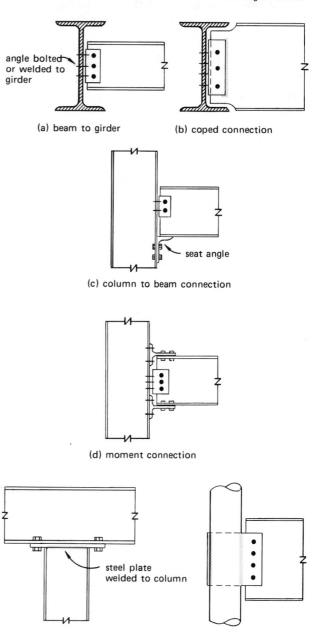

Figure 7.8 Typical Steel Framing Connections

First, check the shear capacity of the bolts. From Table 7.2, one bolt can carry a load of 13.3 kips or three bolts can carry 3 × 13.3, or 39.9 kips.

Next, check bearing capacity. The thinner material governs, so use the 3/8-inch row in Table 7.3. From this row, read under the 3/4-inch diameter column (with $F_u = 58$). The allowable load is 19.6 kips. Three bolts will then carry 3 × 19.6, or 58 kips.

Finally, determine the maximum stress on the net section through the holes. Once again, the thinner material is the most critical component. The allowable unit stress is:

$$F_t = 0.50F_u = 0.50 \times 58 = 29 \text{ ksi}$$

The diameter of each hole is 1/16 inch larger than the bolt, or 13/16 inch, which is 0.8125 inch. The net width of the 3/8-inch plate is:

$$\text{net width} = 9 - (3 \times 0.8125) = 6.56 \text{ inches}$$

The allowable stress on the net section is:

$$F_t = (6.56 \times 0.375) \times 29 = 71.34 \text{ kips}$$

From these three loads, the minimum governs, which is the shear capacity of the bolts, or 39.9 kips.

If the top flange of one beam needs to be flush with another, the web is coped as shown in Figure 7.8 (b).

Simple beam-to-column connections are often made as illustrated in Figure 7.8 (c). The seat angle carries most of the gravity load, and the clip angle is used to provide stability from rotation. If a moment connection is required, a detail similar to Figure 7.8 (d) is used, although welding is more suitable for moment connections. For tubes and round columns, a single plate can be welded to the column and connected with beams as shown in Figure 7.8 (f). When the loads are heavy, some engineers prefer to slot the column and run the shear plate through, welding it at the front and back of the column.

Since connecting beams to columns and other beams with angles and bolts is such a common method of steel framing, the AISC manual gives tables of allowable loads for various types and diameters of bolts and lengths and thicknesses of angles. Two such tables are reproduced in Tables 7.4 and 7.5. The first is for bearing-type connections and the second is for friction-type connections.

One of the important considerations in bolted steel connections, just as in wood connections, is the spacing of bolts and the edge distance from the last bolt to the edge of the member. The AISC specifies minimum dimensions. The absolute minimum spacing is 22/3 times the diameter of the bolt being used with 3 times the diameter being the preferred dimension. Many times, a dimension of 3 inches is used for all sizes of bolts up to 1 inch diameter.

The required edge distance varies with the diameter of the bolt being used: at the edges of plates, shapes, or bars the dimension is 1 inch for a 3/4-inch bolt and 1.25 inches for a 1-inch bolt. To simplify detailing and tabulated values, a dimension of 1.25 inches is often used for all bolts up to 1 inch in diameter.

Example 7.4

A W24 × 104 girder supports a W18 × 55 beam with two 3 1/2 × 3 1/2 × 5/16 × 14 1/2 inch long angles. The connection is made with 7/8 inch, A325 bolts in a slip-critical connection. What is the maximum allowable load that can be supported?

Look in Table 7.5 in the A325-F bolt type column. Since 7/8-inch bolts are being used, read down that subcolumn until you find the row corresponding to the angle length of 141/2 inches. Read the allowable load directly as 102 kips.

B. Welds

Welded connections are quite frequently used in lieu of bolts for several reasons:

- The gross cross section of the members can be used instead of the net section.

- Construction is often more efficient because there are no angles, bolts, or washers to deal with and no clearance problems with wrenches.

- Welding is more practical for moment connections.

Since members must be held in place until welding is completed, welding is often used in combination with bolting. Connection angles and other pieces are welded to one member in the shop with the outreach leg punched or slotted for field connection with bolts.

There are several types of welding processes, but the one most commonly used in building construction is the *electric arc process*. One electrode from the power source is attached to the steel members being joined, and the other electrode is the welding rod the welder holds in his or her hand. The intense heat generated by the electric arc formed when the welding rod is brought close to the members causes some of the base metal and the end of the electrode to melt into the joint, so the material of the electrode and both pieces of the joint are fused together. *Penetration* refers to the depth from the surface of the base metal to the point where fusion stops.

Two types of electrodes are in common use today: the E60 and the E70. The allowable shear stress for E60 electrodes is 18 kips per square inch (kips), and for E70 electrodes it is 21 ksi.

There are many types of welds. Which one to use depends on the configuration of the joint, the magnitude and direction of the load, the cost of preparing the joint, and what the erection process will be. The three most common types of welded joints are the *lap*, the *butt*, and the *tee*. Some of the common welding conditions for these joints are shown in Figure 7.9 along with the standard welding symbol used on drawings. In addition to the welds shown, plug or slot welds are frequently used to join two pieces. In these welds, a hole is cut or punched in one of the members and the area filled with the weld.

The fillet weld is one of the most common types. In section, its form is an isosceles triangle with the two equal legs of the triangle being the size of the weld. The perpendicular distance from the 90 degree corner to the hypotenuse of the triangle is called the *throat*. See Figure 7.10 (a). Because the angles are 45 degrees, the dimension of the throat is 0.707 times the leg dimension.

Table 7.4
Allowable Loads for Framed Beam Connections—Bearing Type

FRAMED BEAM CONNECTIONS
Bolted
Allowable loads in kips

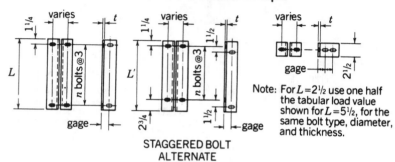

STAGGERED BOLT
ALTERNATE

Note: For $L=2\frac{1}{2}$ use one half
the tabular load value
shown for $L=5\frac{1}{2}$, for the
same bolt type, diameter,
and thickness.

Bolt Shear[a]													
For bolts in **bearing-type** connections with standard or slotted holes.													

Bolt Type			A325-N			A490-N			A325-X			A490-X		
F_v, Ksi			21.0			28.0			30.0			40.0		
Bolt Dia., d In.			$\frac{3}{4}$	$\frac{7}{8}$	1	$\frac{3}{4}$	$\frac{7}{8}$	1	$\frac{3}{4}$	$\frac{7}{8}$	1	$\frac{3}{4}$	$\frac{7}{8}$	1
Angle Thickness t, In.			$\frac{5}{16}$	$\frac{3}{8}$	$\frac{5}{8}$	$\frac{3}{8}$	$\frac{1}{2}$	$\frac{5}{8}$	$\frac{3}{8}$	$\frac{5}{8}$	$\frac{5}{8}$	$\frac{1}{2}$	$\frac{5}{8}$	$\frac{5}{8}$
L In.	L' In.	n												
$29\frac{1}{2}$	31	10	186	253	330	247	337	440[b]	265	361	[d]	353	453[c]	[d]
$26\frac{1}{2}$	28	9	167	227	297	223	303	396[b]	239	325	[d]	318	408[c]	[d]
$23\frac{1}{2}$	25	8	148	202	264	198	269	352[b]	212	289	[d]	283	363[c]	[d]
$20\frac{1}{2}$	22	7	130	177	231	173	236	308[b]	186	253	[d]	247	317[c]	[d]
$17\frac{1}{2}$	19	6	111	152	198	148	202	264[b]	159	216	272[c]	212	272[c]	272[c]
$14\frac{1}{2}$	16	5	92.8	126	165	124	168	220[b]	133	180	227[c]	177	227[c]	227[c]
$11\frac{1}{2}$	13	4	74.2	101	132	99.0	135	176[b]	106	144	181[c]	141	181[c]	181[c]
$8\frac{1}{2}$	10	3	55.7	75.8[b]	99.0	74.2	101[b]	132[b]	79.5[b]	108	136[c]	106[b]	136[c]	136[c]
$5\frac{1}{2}$	7	2	37.1	50.5[b]	66.0	49.5	67.3[b]	88.0[b]	53.0[b]	72.2	90.6[c]	70.7[b]	90.6[c]	90.6[c]

[a]Tabulated load values are based on double shear of bolts unless noted. See RCSC Specification for other surface conditions.

[b]Capacity shown is based on double shear of the bolts; however, for length L, net shear on the angle thickness specified is critical. See Table II-C.

[c]Capacity shown is based on bearing capacity of $1\frac{1}{4}$ in. end distance [Specification Equation (J3-6)] on A36 angles of thickness specified; however, for length L, net shear on this angle is critical. See Table II-C.

[d]Capacity is governed by net shear on angles for lengths L and L'. See Table II-C.

Reprinted from Manual of Steel Construction 9th ed.,
American Institute of Steel Construction

Table 7.5
Allowable Loads for Framed Beam Connections—Slip Critical

FRAMED BEAM CONNECTIONS
Bolted
Allowable loads in kips

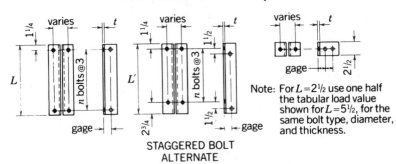

STAGGERED BOLT
ALTERNATE

Note: For $L = 2\frac{1}{2}$ use one half
the tabular load value
shown for $L = 5\frac{1}{2}$, for the
same bolt type, diameter,
and thickness.

Bolt Shear[a]

For A307 bolts in standard or slotted holes and for A325 and A490 bolts in **slip-critical**
connections with standard holes and Class A, clean mill scale surface condition.

Bolt Type			A307			A325-SC			A490-SC			
F_v, Ksi			10.0			17.0			21.0			Note:
Bolt Dia., d In.			$\frac{3}{4}$	$\frac{7}{8}$	1	$\frac{3}{4}$	$\frac{7}{8}$	1	$\frac{3}{4}$	$\frac{7}{8}$	1	For slip-critical
Angle Thickness t, In.			$\frac{1}{4}$	$\frac{1}{4}$	$\frac{1}{4}$	$\frac{1}{4}$	$\frac{5}{16}$	$\frac{1}{2}$	$\frac{5}{16}$	$\frac{1}{2}$	$\frac{5}{8}$	connections with oversize or slotted
L In.	L' In.	n										holes, see Table II-B.
$29\frac{1}{2}$	31	10	88.4	120	157	150	204	267	186	253	330	
$26\frac{1}{2}$	28	9	79.5	108	141	135	184	240	167	227	297	
$23\frac{1}{2}$	25	8	70.7	96.2	126	120	164	214	148	202	264	
$20\frac{1}{2}$	22	7	61.9	84.2	110	105	143	187	130	177	231	
$17\frac{1}{2}$	19	6	53.0	72.2	94.2	90.1	123	160	111	152	198	
$14\frac{1}{2}$	16	5	44.2	60.1	78.5	75.1	102	134	92.8	126	165	
$11\frac{1}{2}$	13	4	35.3	48.1	62.8	60.1	81.8	107	74.2	101	132	
$8\frac{1}{2}$	10	3	26.5	36.1	47.1[b]	45.1	61.3	80.1	55.7	75.8	99.0	
$5\frac{1}{2}$	7	2	17.7	24.1	31.4[b]	30.0	40.9	53.4	37.1	50.5	66.0	

Notes:

[a]Tabulated load values are based on double shear of bolts unless noted. See RCSC Specification for other surface conditions.

[b]Capacity shown is based on double shear of the bolts; however, for length L, net shear on the angle thickness specified is critical. See Table II-C.

Reprinted from Manual of Steel Construction 9th ed.,
American Institute of Steel Construction

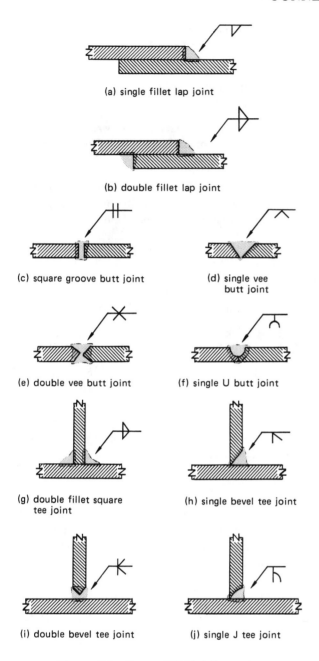

(a) single fillet lap joint

(b) double fillet lap joint

(c) square groove butt joint

(d) single vee butt joint

(e) double vee butt joint

(f) single U butt joint

(g) double fillet square tee joint

(h) single bevel tee joint

(i) double bevel tee joint

(j) single J tee joint

Figure 7.9 Types of Welded Connections

The type of weld is indicated with one of the standard symbols and placed below the line if the weld is on the side near the arrow and above the line if it is on the side away from the arrow. If the members are to be welded on both sides, the symbol is repeated above and below the line. Other data placed with the weld symbol are the size, weld symbol, length of weld, and spacing, in that order, reading from left to right. Field welds are indicated with a flag placed at the junction of the horizontal line and the arrowhead line and pointing toward the tail of the reference line. A circle at the same point indicates that the weld should be made all around. The perpendicular legs of the filled, bevel, J, and flare bevel welds must be at the left.

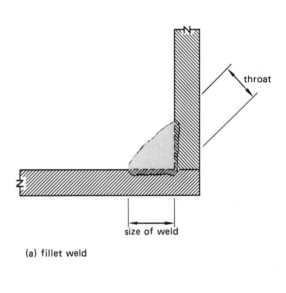

(a) fillet weld

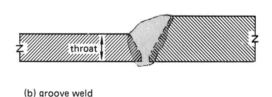

(b) groove weld

Figure 7.10 Weld Dimensions

For a butt joint, the throat dimension is the thickness of the material if both pieces are the same thickness, or the size of the thinner of two materials if they are unequal as shown in Figure 7.10 (b).

There are common symbols used for welding. These are listed in the AISC *Manual of Steel Construction*. A few are reproduced in Figure 7.11 (a). The full range of symbols gives information regarding the type, size, location, finish, welding process, angle for grooves, and other information. To indicate information about a weld, a horizontal line is connected to an arrowhead line which points to the weld. This is shown in Figure 7.11 (b).

Designing a welded joint requires that you know the load to be resisted and the allowable stress in the weld. For fillet welds, the stress is considered as shear on the throat regardless of the direction of the load. For butt welds, the allowable stress is the same as for the base metal. As previously mentioned, the allowable stress for fillet welds of E60 electrodes is 18 ksi, and for E70 electrodes it is 21 ksi. These stresses apply to A36 steel. For any size fillet weld you can multiply the size by 0.707 and by the allowable stress to get the allowable working strength per linear inch of weld, but these have been tabulated for quicker calculations. The allowable strengths are listed in Table 7.6.

Table 7.6
Allowable Working Strengths of Fillet Welds

allowable load (kips per inch)

size of weld, inches	E 60 electrodes	E 70 electrodes
3/16	2.4	2.8
1/4	3.2	3.7
5/16	4.0	4.6
3/8	4.8	5.6
1/2	6.4	7.4
5/8	8.0	9.3
3/4	9.5	11.1

Source: Manual of Steel Construction, 8th ed., American Institute of Steel Construction

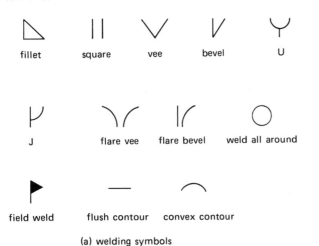

(a) welding symbols

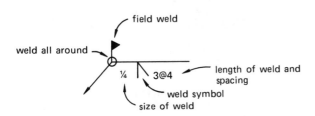

(b) typical welding symbol

Figure 7.11 Welding Symbols

In addition to knowing the allowable stresses, some AISC code provisions apply to weld design. The following are some of the requirements.

- The maximum size of a fillet weld is 1/16 inch less than the nominal thickness of the material being joined if it is 1/4-inch thick or more. If the material is less than 1/4-inch thick, the maximum size is the same as the material.

- The minimum size of fillet welds is shown in Table 7.7.

- The minimum length of fillet welds must not be less than 4 times the weld size plus 1/4 inch for starting and stopping the arc.

- For two or more welds parallel to each other, the length must be at least equal to the perpendicular distance between them.

- For intermittent welds, the length must be at least 1 1/2 inches.

Table 7.7
Minimum Size of Fillet Welds

material thickness of the thicker part joined, inches	minimum size of fillet weld, inches
to 1/4 inclusive	1/8
over 1/4 to 1/2	3/16
over 1/2 to 3/4	1/4
over 3/4	5/16

Source: Manual of Steel Construction, 8th ed., American Institute of Steel Construction

Example 7.5

An A36 steel bar, $3/8'' \times 4''$, is welded to a tube section with E70 electrodes as shown in the illustration. What is the maximum load-carrying capacity if the maximum size of weld is used?

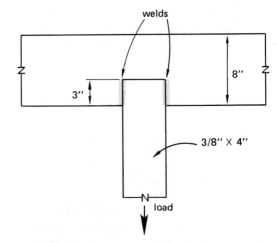

Since the maximum weld size is 1/16 inch less than the member being joined, a weld of 5/16 inch will be used. From Table 7.6, the allowable load is 4.6 kips per inch. The total load is therefore:

$$2 \times 3 \times 4.6 = 27.6 \text{ kips}$$

Example 7.6

A $3'' \times 3'' \times 1/4''$ angle (area of 1.44 in^2) is to be welded to a gusset plate to serve as a tension member as shown in the diagram. If A36 steel and E60 electrodes are used, what is the required size and length of welds of both sides of the angle if the full load-carrying capacity of the angle is to be developed?

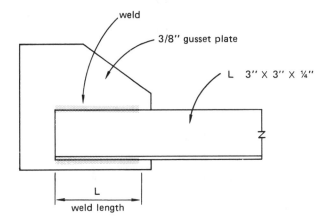

First, the maximum allowable capacity of the angle must be determined. The allowable unit stress is 0.60 times the minimum yield point of steel (formula 7.5). The total maximum capacity is the unit stress times the area of the angle.

$$0.60 \times 36 \times 1.44 = 31.1 \text{ kips}$$

For a 1/4-inch angle, the maximum size of weld is 3/16 inch which, from Table 7.6, has a load carrying of 2.4 kips per inch with E60 electrodes. The total length of weld is

$$\frac{31.1}{2.4} = 12.96 \text{ inches}$$

Round up to 13 inches. Since the welding will be on both sides of the angle, each weld should be at least 6 1/2 inches long.

3   CONCRETE CONNECTIONS

In most cast-in-place concrete construction there are generally no connectors as with wood or steel. Different pours of concrete are tied together with reinforcing bars or with keyed sections. For precast concrete construction, however, there must be some way of rigidly attaching one piece to another. This is accomplished with weld plates.

A. Rebars and Keyed Sections

The most typical type of cast-in-place concrete joint is one where the reinforcing bars are allowed to extend past the formwork to become part of the next pour. Continuity is achieved through the bonding of the two pours of concrete with the rebars that extend through the joint. These types of joints are found in many situations: footing to foundation wall, walls to slabs, beams to beams, columns to beams, and several others. When the reinforcing is only for the purpose of tying two pours of concrete together rather than transmitting large loads, they are called *dowels*. Some typical conditions are shown in Figure 7.12. The length of the dowels or extensions of rebar from one section of concrete to the next is determined by the minimum development length required to transmit the loads or by the ACI code.

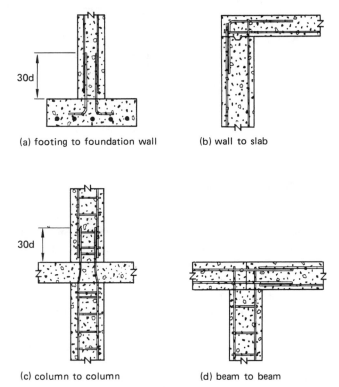

(a) footing to foundation wall   (b) wall to slab

(c) column to column   (d) beam to beam

Figure 7.12   Concrete Joints Tied with Rebars

Keyed sections are used either alone or with rebars to provide a stronger joint between two pours of concrete. Keyed sections are often used in footings and floor slabs as shown in Figure 7.13.

B. Weld Plates

Because precast structures are built in sections, there must be some way to transmit horizontal, vertical, and moment forces from one piece to the next. This is usually accomplished by casting weld plates, angles, and

other types of steel pieces into the concrete members
at the factory. At the site, the members are placed in
position and corresponding plates are welded together.
When allowance must be made for horizontal movement
due to temperature changes, concrete shrinkage, and
the like, precast members often bear on elastomeric
pads rather than being rigidly fastened. Figure 7.14
shows two of the many possible types of precast connections.

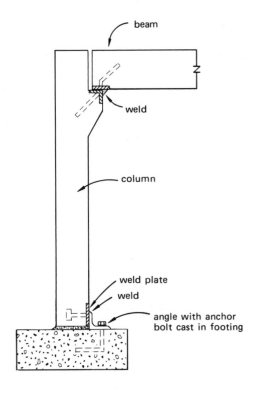

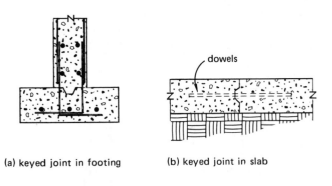

(a) keyed joint in footing   (b) keyed joint in slab

Figure 7.13 Keyed Concrete Connections

Figure 7.14 Precast Concrete Connections

C. Shear Connectors

Shear connectors are not really connectors in the usual
sense, but are used to tie steel and concrete together in
composite sections so forces are transmitted from one
to the other. They are available in diameters of 5/8
inch, 3/4 inch, and 7/8 inch. One of the typical applications of shear connectors is with concrete slab/steel
beam composite sections as shown in Figure 7.15. Here,
the connectors are welded to the top of the steel beam
in the fabricating shop at a fairly close spacing which is
determined by engineering calculations to transmit the
forces created by the applied loads.

When the beam is erected, forms are placed and the
concrete is poured around the connectors (along with
any tensile and temperature steel). The enlarged head
of the connector is provided to give extra bearing surface. These are often called *headed anchor studs* and
abbreviated HAS on the drawings.

Figure 7.15 shows a single row of studs but two rows
may be used if required. Metal decking instead of re-
movable forms is often used for forming the concrete.

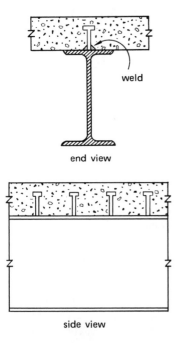

Figure 7.15 Shear Connectors

SAMPLE QUESTIONS

1. Which of the following are the most important variables in designing a bolted wood connection?

I. the angle of the load to the grain

II. the thickness of the members through which the bolt is placed

III. the species of wood

IV. the type of washers used under the head and nut

V. the area of the net section at the bolt holes

    A. I, III, and V
    B. I, II, III, and V
    C. I, II, IV, and V
    D. I, III, IV, and V

The answers to questions 2 through 5 can be found on the following key list. Select only one answer for each question.

    A0 bevel
    A1 common bolt
    A2 dowel
    A3 edge distance
    A4 fillet
    A5 Hankinson formula
    A6 headed anchor stud
    A7 high strength bolt
    A8 lag screw
    A9 oversize hole
    A0 penetration

    B1 plug
    B2 shear plate
    B3 split ring connector
    B4 vee
    B5 weld plate

2. What connector would be best for a wood truss covering a temporary building with a long span?

3. What is used to account for wood members that are loaded at an angle to each other?

4. What type of weld would most likely be used to connect two overlapping steel plates in compression?

5. In designing a composite section, what device would most likely be used?

6. Two 1/4″ × 6″ A36 steel bars are welded, as shown in the figure, with E70 electrodes. What is the maximum allowable tensile load that this joint can resist?

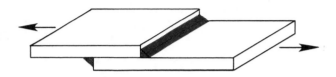

    A. 44.4 kips
    B. 33.6 kips
    C. 30.8 kips
    D. 32.4 kips

7. Which of the welding symbols would indicate that the weld shown should be made at the job site?

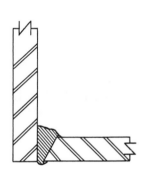

A.

B.

C.

D.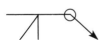

8. A 2″ × 6″ Douglas fir member is suspended from a 4″ × 8″ member as shown in the illustration with four

5/8-inch bolts. Assuming the edge, end, and spacing distances are adequate, what is the allowable load on this joint?

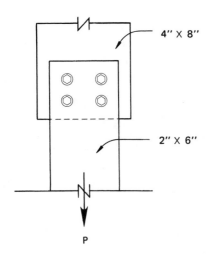

4″ × 8″

2″ × 6″

P

A. 980 pounds

B. 2260 pounds

C. 2360 pounds

D. 3960 pounds

9. Which of the following types of bolts should be used in a joint with long slotted holes where the load perpendicular to the length of the hole is repeatedly reversed?

A. A325 slip-critical

B. A490 bearing-type

C. A307 bearing-type

D. none of the above

10. Which of the following should be avoided when designing wood joints?

I. bolted joints with load perpendicular to grain

II. screws attached to the end grain

III. nails with penetration more than 12 times the nail diameter

IV. nails attached in withdrawl from side grain

V. steel plates bolted to wood members

A. I, II, and IV

B. I, III, and IV

C. IV and V

D. II and IV

BUILDING CODE REQUIREMENTS ON STRUCTURAL DESIGN

8

Nomenclature

C_F	size factor	
d	depth of beam	inches
F_b	allowable bending stress	ksi
F_t	allowable axial tensile stress	ksi
F_v	allowable shear stress	ksi
F_y	specified minimum yield stress of the type of steel being used	ksi

Building code provisions related to structural design deal with how loads must be determined, what stresses are allowed in structural members, formulas for designing members of various materials, and miscellaneous requirements for construction. This chapter provides an overview of the requirements with which the candidate should be familiar. Specific provisions and calculation methods are presented in other chapters. Loads on buildings are covered in Chapter 2, wind loading and calculation methods in Chapter 13, and seismic design methods are reviewed in Chapter 14. The code provisions outlined here are based on the Uniform Building Code (UBC), but similar provisions are included in the other two model codes.

1 LOADING

Chapter 23 of the UBC details how loads must be calculated. In general terms, the code requires that any construction method be based on a rational analysis in accordance with well-established principles of mechanics, and that such an analysis provides a path for all loads and forces from their point of origin to the load-resisting elements. The analysis must include distribution of horizontal shear, horizontal torsional moments, stability against overturning, and anchorage. Horizontal torsional moment results from torsion due to eccentricity between the center of application of a lateral force and the center of rigidity of the force-resisting system. Anchorage resists the uplift and sliding forces on a structure.

When the building design is based on allowable stress or working stress design, each component must be designed to resist the most critical effect resulting from the combination of loads listed. When other design methods are used for concrete or steel, each component must be designed to resist the most critical effects of load combinations as prescribed in each chapter of the code related to the specific material used.

- dead plus floor live plus roof live (or snow)

- dead plus floor live plus wind (or seismic)

- dead plus floor live plus wind plus one-half snow

- dead plus floor live plus snow plus one-half wind

- dead plus floor live plus snow plus seismic

In addition, lateral earth pressure must be included in the design when it results in a more critical combination.

A. Live Loads

Required floor live loads are given in UBC Table 23-A, roof loads in Table 23-C, and special loads in Table 23-B. These are reproduced in Tables 2.2, 2.3, and 2.4, respectively.

Some reductions in live loads are permitted. The loads given in the Uniform Building Code may be reduced on any member supporting more than 150 square feet except for floors in places of public assembly and for live loads greater than 100 pounds per square foot. Snow loads in excess of 20 pounds per square foot may also be reduced for each degree of pitch over 20 degrees. The formulas for determining these reductions are given in Chapter 2 in formulas 2.1 and 2.3, respectively, along with examples for their use.

Additional code provisions related to live loads include the following:

- Provisions must be made for designing floors to accommodate concentrated loads as shown in Figure 2.1 (UBC Table 23-A). If these loads, acting on any space 2 1/2 feet square on an otherwise unloaded floor, would result in stresses greater than those caused by the uniform load, then the floor must be designed accordingly.

- Where uniform live floor and roof loads are involved, the design may be limited to full dead load on all spans in combination with full live load on adjacent spans and on alternate spans. This is particularly important where structural continuity of adjacent spans is involved. In any case, the code requires the investigation of loading conditions that would cause maximum shear and bending moments along continuous members.

- Live loads for each floor or portion thereof in commercial or industrial buildings must be conspicuously posted.

- Interior walls, permanent partitions, and temporary partitions over 6 feet high must be designed to resist all loads on them but in no case less than a force of 5 pounds per square foot applied perpendicular to the wall.

B. Dead Loads

The UBC defines dead load as the vertical load due to the weight of all permanent structural and non-structural components of a building, such as walls, floors, roofs, and fixed service equipment. The code does not specifically state required dead loads; rather, the designer must use standard unit weights for various building materials published in standard reference sources.

However, two specific provisions are mentioned. First, floors in office buildings where partition locations are subject to change must be designed to support a uniformly distributed dead load equal to 20 pounds per square foot. Second, access floor systems may be designed to support an additional 10 pounds per square foot of uniformly distributed dead load over all other loads.

C. Lateral Loads

Lateral loads include wind loads and seismic loads. Wind is assumed to come from any direction, and the design wind pressure used for calculations is dependent on the height of the structure above the ground, exposure of the structure, a wind stagnation pressure at a standard height of 30 feet above the ground, the portion of the structure under consideration, and a factor related to the importance of the building during an emergency, such as a fire station. These are established as values and coefficients given in tables at the end of Chapter 23 of the UBC. The formula for determining design wind pressure and a full explanation of the factors involved are given in Chapter 13.

When special conditions exist, such as structures sensitive to dynamic effects, structures sensitive to wind-excited oscillations, and buildings over 400 feet in height, the buildings must be designed in accordance with approved national standards. This basically means using accepted wind tunnel testing procedures to determine the actual wind forces on the structure.

For earthquake loads, the code requires that stresses be calculated as the effect of a force applied horizontally at each floor or roof level above the base. The designer must assume that the force can come from any direction. Although the UBC gives detailed methods and concepts for designing structures to resist seismic forces, it does allow that other methods can be approved by the local building official if it can be shown that equivalent ductility and energy absorption can be provided. In the event that wind loads produce higher stresses, they must be used in place of those resulting from earthquake forces.

Seismic forces and methods of design are discussed in more detail in Chapter 14.

2   ALLOWABLE STRESSES

The Uniform Building Code establishes basic allowable stresses for various types of construction materials. The design of any structural member must be such that these stresses are not exceeded. Although some provisions of the code are extremely complex (such as with concrete), this section outlines some of the more important provisions with which you should be familiar.

A. Wood

Tables in Chapter 25 of the Uniform Building Code give allowable unit stresses in structural lumber and glued-laminated timber. These include allowable stresses for extreme fiber in bending, tension parallel to the grain, horizontal shear, and compression perpendicular and parallel to the grain. The stresses given are for normal loading and must be adjusted according to various conditions of use as follows.

Single or repetitive use: Two values for allowable stress in extreme fiber are given in UBC Tables 25-A-1 and 25-A-2. One is for a wood member used by itself, such as a beam, and one is for several members used together such as joists or rafters. Examples of these tables are shown in Chapter 9. The value for repetitive use is higher than for single use. In order to use the higher value, the member cannot be over 4 inches in nominal thickness, cannot be spaced more than 24 inches on center, must be joined by transverse load-distributing elements (such as bridging or decking), and there must be at least three members in a group.

Duration of load: The amount of stress a wood member can withstand is dependent on the time during which the load producing the stress acts. This relation of strength to duration of load is shown graphically in Figure 8.1. Allowable design loads are based on what is called *normal duration of load* which is assumed to be ten years. For duration of loads shorter than this, the allowable stress may be increased according to the following percentages:

- 15 percent for two months' duration, as for snow

- 25 percent for seven days' duration, as for roof loads

- 33 1/3 percent for wind or earthquake loads

- 100 percent for impact loads

If a structural member is fully stressed to the maximum allowable stress for more than ten years under conditions of maximum design load, the allowable stress cannot exceed 90 percent of those listed in the tables.

Fire-retardant treatment: Allowable stress values for horizontal shear, compression, and modulus of elasticity must be decreased by 10 percent for lumber pressure impregnated with approved fire-retardant chemicals.

Values must be reduced by 15 percent for extreme fiber in bending and 20 percent for tension parallel to grain. Plywood values must be reduced according to approved test methods.

Size factor adjustment: Design values for bending, tension, and compression parallel to grain for visually graded dimension lumber 2 to 4 inches thick must be multiplied by size factors given at the end of Tables 25-A-1 to 25-A-5. When the depth of a rectangular sawn bending member 5 inches or thicker exceeds 12 inches, the bending design values, F_b, must be multiplied by a size factor determined by the formula:

$$C_F = \left(\frac{12}{d}\right)^{\frac{1}{9}} \qquad 8.1$$

There is also a slenderness factor adjustment for unsupported beams. However, most wood members are supported either with bridging or with continuous decking material, so this adjustment is not usually required.

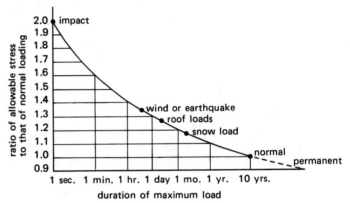

Figure 8.1 Relation of Strength to Duration of Load for Wood Structural Members

B. Steel

Allowable stresses for structural steel are expressed as a fraction of the yield stress of the steel. They vary with the type of stress the member is under (shear, compression, bending, and tension) and with conditions such as unsupported lengths and geometry of the section. Some of the more common code requirements for allowable stress are:

For tension on the gross area,

$$F_t = 0.6F_y \qquad 8.2$$

For tension on the net effective area,

$$F_t = 0.5F_y \qquad 8.3$$

For shear on gross sections,

$$F_v = 0.40F_y \qquad 8.4$$

At beam end connections where the top flange is coped, and similar conditions where failure might occur along a plane through the fasteners, allowable shear stress is:

$$F_v = 0.30F_y \qquad 8.5$$

For bending where the beam is laterally supported, and the section meets the requirements of a compact section and is loaded in the plane of the minor axis,

$$F_b = 0.66F_y \qquad 8.6$$

For bending where the beam is not a compact section, but where it is supported laterally,

$$F_b = 0.60F_y \qquad 8.7$$

Allowable stresses for bolts, rivets, and threaded parts are based on the type of load placed on them and are given as values in kips per square inch based on the ASTM designation of the fastener or as a fraction of the minimum tensile strength of the type of fastener. These are shown in Tables 7.2 and 7.3 in Chapter 7.

Allowable stresses for welds are based either on the yield strength of the base metal or the nominal tensile strength of the weld metal. The allowable stress is then multiplied by the area of the weld. Chapter 27 of the Uniform Building Code along with the AISC *Manual of Steel Construction* describe the requirements for welds in great detail. Table 7.6 in Chapter 7 summarizes the allowable working strengths for welds of various sizes.

C. Concrete

Building code requirements for reinforced concrete are very complex and detailed, and cover all aspects of formwork, reinforcing, mixing, placing, and curing. UBC Chapter 26 concerns concrete construction. It contains specific requirements too numerous to mention here. In addition, it makes reference to *Building Code Requirements for Reinforced Concrete, ACI 318*, published by the American Concrete Institute, as well as to other ACI publications.

The candidate is not expected to know all the code provisions for concrete design, but to have a general understanding of the more important limitations. Two of the most important concepts are the safety factors of increased ultimate load above the calculated dead and live loads, and the strength reduction factor. These are discussed in detail in Chapter 11 along with other code requirements.

Concrete construction is based on the specified compressive strength, f'_c expressed in pounds per square inch. Many of the formulas for concrete design use this as a part of the equation.

Because concrete is a highly variable material, the UBC goes to great lengths to specify how concrete is to be mixed and then how quality control is to be maintained. This is to ensure that a building is actually constructed of concrete that meets or exceeds the original design strength.

The UBC requires that samples for strength tests are taken for each class of concrete placed. Samples must be taken not less than once per day, nor less than once for each 150 cubic yards of concrete, nor less than once for each 5000 square feet of surface area for slabs or walls. The average of all sets of three consecutive strength tests must equal or exceed f'_c, and no individual test can be less than 500 psi below the f'_c value.

3 CONSTRUCTION REQUIREMENTS

In addition to allowable stresses and other requirements related to structural calculations, the UBC places many restrictions on how various materials may be used. The following sections outline some of the more important ones with which you should be familiar.

A. Wood

Since the structural integrity of wood is dependent on such factors as moisture, fire, insect attack, and connections, the UBC goes to great lengths to specify wood construction techniques. You should be familiar with the following requirements.

- The bottom of wood joists must be at least 18 inches above exposed ground, and the bottom of wood girders must be at least 12 inches above ground, unless they are treated or made of a species with a natural resistance to decay.

- Ends of wood girders entering masonry or concrete walls must be provided with a 1/2-inch air space on top, sides, and end, unless the wood is of natural resistance to decay or it is treated.

- Foundation plates and sills must be treated or made of foundation redwood.

- Under-floor areas such as crawl spaces must be ventilated with openings having a net area of not less than one square foot for each 150 square feet of under-floor area, and they must be placed to provide cross-ventilation.

- Wood used for construction of permanent structures located nearer than 6 inches to earth must be treated or wood of natural resistance to decay.

- All wood used as structural members must be protected from exposure to the weather and water with approved protection.

- Fire stops are required in walls at the ceiling and floor levels and at 10-foot intervals both vertical and horizontal.

- Fire stops are required at interconnections between concealed vertical and horizontal spaces such as soffits and dropped ceilings.

- Fire stops are required in concealed spaces in stairway construction and in vertical openings between floors and the roof that could afford a passage for fire.

B. Steel

Two provisions in the UBC relate to an important consideration in steel design. The first requires that roof systems without sufficient slope for drainage be investigated to assure stability under ponding conditions. This is to prevent failure when an amount of water collects on a roof causing it to deflect, which allows a further accumulation of water which leads to further deflection.

The second provision requires that horizontal framing members be designed for deflection criteria and ponding requirements. It also requires that trusses longer than **80 feet be cambered for the dead load deflection.**

C. Concrete

In addition to allowable stresses, the UBC and *ACI 318* set forth highly detailed requirements for other aspects of concrete use. In addition to those mentioned in Chapter 11, some of the more important ones include the following.

- Construction loads cannot be supported nor any shoring removed until the concrete has sufficient strength to safely support its weight and loads placed on it. However, some formwork can be removed if the structure in combination with remaining formwork can support the loads.

- There are limitations on the amount and placement of conduits and other pipes embedded in concrete so as not to decrease the load-resisting area. Aluminum conduits cannot be embedded unless effectively coated or covered to prevent aluminum-concrete reaction or electrolytic action between steel and aluminum. Pipes carrying fluids or gases must be pressure-tested prior to placement of concrete.

- The size and bending of reinforcement is clearly spelled out to ensure that sufficient bond is developed between the concrete and steel and that all reinforcement acts together.

- Minimum concrete cover over reinforcing is specified. This is to protect the steel from rusting and to ensure proper bonding of the concrete to the steel. Concrete exposed to the weather or in direct contact with the ground requires more cover than concrete members in a protected area.

4   FIREPROOFING

One of the primary purposes of any building code is to ensure that buildings are adequately protected from fire and that if a fire does occur, structural members are sufficiently protected. Chapter 17 of the UBC defines fire-resistive requirements for various building elements based on types of construction. Chapter 43 and Table 43-A define the minimum protection of structural portions of a building based on time periods for various noncombustible insulating materials.

Although steel is noncombustible, it loses strength at high temperatures and must be protected with approved insulating materials, such as sprayed-on fireproofing or gypsum wallboard. The exception to this is for roof framing, other than the structural frame, which is more than 25 feet above the floor. This framing may be of unprotected noncombustible materials.

Wood framing, of course, is combustible, but may be used in certain types of construction if adequately protected. A unique property of wood is that while it is combustible, thick pieces of wood exposed to fire will char but not immediately loose structural integrity. The UBC recognizes this by having a separate type of construction, Type IV, for heavy timber construction. In this type of construction, columns must be at least 8 inches in any dimension, beams and girders must be at **least 6 inches wide and 10 inches deep, and floor decking must be at least 3 inches thick.**

SAMPLE QUESTIONS

1. Select the correct statement about lateral loads.

    A. For both wind and earthquake loads, forces must be calculated as though loads can come from any direction and act on the building.

    B. In zones of high earthquake probability, the forces produced by seismic loads always take precedence over wind loads.

    C. Wind stagnation pressure is assumed to act at a point 50 feet above ground.

    D. Buildings can only be designed to resist seismic forces according to specified procedures in the UBC or with approved wind tunnel tests.

2. The maximum possible allowable stress for steel members is:

    A. $F_t = 0.60F_y$ (on net effective area)

    B. $F_t = 0.66F_y$ (on net effective area)

    C. $F_b = 0.66F_y$ (for laterally supported compact sections)

    D. $F_b = 0.75F_y$ (for laterally supported compact sections)

3. Select the incorrect statements about wood construction.

    I. Foundation sills may be any type wood if located more than 6 inches above the earth.

    II. Fire stops are not required in vertical openings of two-story residential construction.

    III. Untreated wood joists over crawl spaces must have their bottom edges at least $1'6''$ above ground, while beams only need $1'0''$ clearance.

    IV. Concrete beam pockets must be sized to allow for 1/2-inch air space at the sides and tops, and 1 inch at the ends, unless the wood is treated or of a species with a natural resistance to decay.

    V. Each 150 square feet of crawl space area requires a one square foot net vent opening.

    A. I, II, and III

    B. I, II, and IV

    C. II, IV, and V

    D. III, IV, and V

The answers to questions 4 through 7 can be found on the following key list. Select only one answer for each question.

    A0 camber
    A1 clearance from embedded conduit
    A2 combination loading
    A3 concrete cover
    A4 deflection criteria
    A5 duration of load factor
    A6 fire retardant factor
    A7 minimum tensile stress
    A8 rebar bending requirements
    A9 shoring removal

    B0 size factor
    B1 slenderness factor
    B2 ten percent
    B3 ultimate strength
    B4 working stress
    B5 yield stress

4. What is important to protect the structural integrity of reinforcing bars?

5. What building code provision attempts to minimize the likelihood of roof failure through ponding?

6. What is one of the bases for defining allowable stresses on bolts?

7. A $6'' \times 14''$ wood beam supporting solid wood decking would have its allowable stress modified by what?

8. If the allowable stress on a wood beam is 1450 psi, what is the required section modulus if the beam must resist a moment of 4518 ft-lbs caused by snow loading?

    A. 27.8 in^3

    B. 28.1 in^3

    C. 29.9 in^3

    D. 32.5 in^3

9. Which of the following loading conditions does not have to be investigated?

    A. dead plus floor live plus snow plus one-half seismic

    B. dead plus floor live plus snow

C. dead plus floor live plus wind plus one-half snow

D. dead plus floor live plus one-half wind plus snow

10. Which of the following are true statements?

I. 20 pounds per square foot of dead load must be factored into normal dead loading when designing speculative office buildings.

II. Live loads can be reduced on structural components supporting more than 150 square feet in all occupancies except educational.

III. Structural continuity affects load calculations.

IV. Pitched roofs over 5 in 12 allow for a reduction in snow loads over 20 pounds per square foot.

V. Required live loads are clearly stated in the UBC.

    A. II, III, and V
    B. II, III, and IV
    C. I, III, and V
    D. I, III, IV, and V

9 WOOD CONSTRUCTION

Nomenclature

A	area of a member	in^2
b	width of beam	inches
C_f	size factor	
d	depth of beam	inches
d'	depth of beam remaining at a notch	inches
E	modulus of elasticity	psi
f_b	actual value for extreme fiber in bending stress	psi
F_b	design value for extreme fiber in bending	psi
F_c	design value for compression parallel to grain	psi
F_c'	design value for compression parallel to grain, adjusted for l/d ratio	psi
$F_{c\perp}$	design value for compression perpendicular to grain	psi
f_t	actual unit stress in tension parallel to grain	psi
F_t	design value for tension parallel to grain	psi
f_v	actual unit stress in horizontal shear	psi
F_v	design value for horizontal shear	psi
I	moment of inertia	in^4
K	largest slenderness ratio, l/d, at which intermediate column formula applies	
K_e	effective buckling length factor	
l	span of bending member or effective length of column	inches
L	span of bending member	feet
P	total concentrated load or total axial load	pounds
V	vertical shear	pounds
w	uniform load per foot	plf
Δ	deflection	inches

1 PROPERTIES OF STRUCTURAL LUMBER

A. Sizes

Structural lumber is referred to by its nominal dimension in inches such as 2 × 4 or 2 × 10. However, after surfacing at the mill and drying, its actual dimension is somewhat less.

Table 9.1 gives the actual dimensions for various nominal sizes of sawn lumber. Also shown in Table 9.1 are the actual areas, section modulus, and moment of inertia, which are all based on the actual size. The majority of structural lumber used is surfaced and dried to the actual sizes listed in Table 9.1, so these are the values that must be used in structural calculations.

B. Grading

Since a log yields lumber of varying quality, the individual sawn pieces must be categorized to allow selection of the quality that best suits the purpose. For structural lumber, the primary concern is the amount of stress that a particular grade of lumber of a species will carry. The load-carrying ability is affected by such things as size and number of knots, splits, and other defects, as well as the direction of grain and the specific gravity of the wood.

Grading of structural lumber is done under standard rules established by several different agencies certified by the American Lumber Standards Committee. The grading is done at the sawmill either by visual inspection or by machine. The resulting allowable stress values are published in tables referred to as design values for visually graded structural lumber and design values for machine-stress-rated structural lumber.

Table 9.1
Sectional Properties of Standard Dressed Lumber

nominal size	standard dressed size, inches $b \times d$	area A	moment of inertia I	section modulus S
2×3	$1\,1/2 \times 2\,1/2$	3.750	1.953	1.563
2×4	$1\,1/2 \times 3\,1/2$	5.250	5.359	3.063
2×6	$1\,1/2 \times 5\,1/2$	8.250	20.797	7.563
2×8	$1\,1/2 \times 7\,1/4$	10.875	47.635	13.141
2×10	$1\,1/2 \times 9\,1/4$	13.875	98.932	21.391
2×12	$1\,1/2 \times 11\,1/4$	16.875	177.979	31.641
4×4	$3\,1/2 \times 3\,1/2$	12.250	12.505	7.146
4×6	$3\,1/2 \times 5\,1/2$	19.250	48.526	17.646
4×8	$3\,1/2 \times 7\,1/4$	25.375	111.148	30.661
4×10	$3\,1/2 \times 9\,1/4$	32.375	230.840	49.911
4×12	$3\,1/2 \times 11\,1/4$	39.375	415.283	73.828
4×14	$3\,1/2 \times 13\,1/4$	46.375	678.475	102.411
6×6	$5\,1/2 \times 5\,1/2$	30.250	76.255	27.729
6×8	$5\,1/2 \times 7\,1/2$	41.250	193.359	51.563
6×10	$5\,1/2 \times 9\,1/2$	52.250	392.963	82.729
6×12	$5\,1/2 \times 11\,1/2$	63.250	697.068	121.229
6×14	$5\,1/2 \times 12\,1/2$	74.250	1127.672	167.063
6×16	$5\,1/2 \times 15\,1/2$	85.250	1706.776	220.229
8×8	$7\,1/2 \times 7\,1/2$	56.250	263.672	70.313
8×10	$7\,1/2 \times 9\,1/2$	71.250	535.859	112.813
8×12	$7\,1/2 \times 11\,1/2$	86.250	950.547	165.313

Visually graded lumber is divided into categories based on nominal size, so the same grade of lumber in a species may have different allowable stresses depending on which category it is in. This can be confusing, but is critical in selecting the correct allowable stress for a particular design condition. For example, one of the most common categories is 2 inches to 4 inches thick, 5 inches and wider. This includes wood members like 2×6s, 2×8s, and the like, but not 2×4s. 2×4 members are in two separate categories: 2 inches to 4 inches thick, 2 inches to 4 inches wide; and 2 inches to 4 inches thick, 4 inches wide. The first category is based on structural grades, and the second category is based on appearance grades.

There are also categories for beams and stringers, and posts and timbers. Beams and stringers are defined as members 5 inches and wider, having a depth more than 2 inches greater than the width. Posts and timbers are defined as members 5 inches by 5 inches and larger, with a depth not more than 2 inches greater than the width.

Machine-stress-rated lumber is based on grade designations which depend on the allowable bending stress and modulus of elasticity of the wood.

C. Design Values

For visually graded lumber, allowable design values are based on the species of the wood, the size category, the grade, and the direction of loading. Different values are required based on the direction of loading because wood has different strengths depending on how loads are applied. The tables give values for extreme fiber stress in bending, F_b, tension parallel to grain, F_t, horizontal shear, F_v, compression perpendicular to grain, $F_{c\perp}$, and compression parallel to grain, F_c. Table 9.2 shows a portion of a table of design values for Douglas fir-larch as published by the National Forest Products Association. Similar tables are found in Chapter 25 of the Uniform Building Code.

One additional variable for selecting the extreme fiber in bending stress is whether or not the member is being used alone or with other members such as a row of joists. The design values for repetitive member use, as shown in Table 9.2, are slightly higher than those for single member use. In order to qualify for repetitive member use, there must be at least three members spaced not more than 24 inches apart, and there must be some method to distribute the load among them such as bridging or sheathing.

As mentioned in Chapter 8, the amount of stress a wood member can withstand is also dependent on the length of time the load acts on the member. Design values given in the tables are based on what is considered a normal duration of loading, ten years. However, for shorter duration of loading, the allowable unit stresses may be increased as follows:

- 15% for two months' duration, as for snow

- 25% for seven days' duration, as for roof loading

- 33 1/3% for wind or earthquake loading

- 100% for impact loads

D. Moisture Content

Moisture content is defined as the weight of water in wood as a fraction of the weight of oven dry wood. Moisture content is an important variable because it affects the amount of shrinkage, weight, strength, and withdrawal resistance of nails.

Moisture exists in wood both in the individual cell cavities and bound chemically within cell walls. When the cell walls are completely saturated, but no water exists in the cell cavities, the wood is said to have reached its fiber saturation point. This point averages about 30 percent moisture content in all woods. Above this point, the wood is dimensionally stable, but as the wood dries below this point it begins to shrink.

When wood is used for structural framing and other construction purposes, it tends to absorb or lose moisture in response to the temperature and humidity of the surrounding air. As it loses moisture it shrinks, and as it gains moisture it swells. Ideally, the moisture content of wood when it is installed should be the same as the prevailing humidity to which it will be exposed. However, this is seldom possible, so lumber needs to be dried—either air dried or kiln dried—to reduce the moisture content to acceptable levels.

To be considered dry lumber, moisture content cannot exceed 19 percent. To be grademarked kiln dry, the maximum moisture content permitted is 15 percent. Design values found in tables assume that the maximum moisture content will not exceed 19 percent. If it does, the allowable stresses must be decreased slightly.

Wood shrinks most in the direction perpendicular to the grain and very little parallel to the grain. Perpendicular to the grain wood shrinks most in the direction of the annual growth rings (tangentially) and about half as much across the rings (radially).

Table 9.2
Design Values for Visually Graded Structural Lumber

Species and commercial grade	Size classification	Extreme fiber in bending "F_B"		Tension parallel to grain "F_T"	Horizontal shear "F_V"	Compression perpendicular to grain "$F_{C\perp}$"	Compression parallel to grain "F_C"	Modulus of elasticity "E"	Grading rules agency
		Single-member uses	Repetitive-member uses						
COTTONWOOD (Surfaced dry or surfaced green. Used at 19% max. m.c.)									NHPMA (See footnotes 1–12)
Stud	2" to 3" thick 2" to 4" wide	525	600	300	65	320	350	1,000,000	
Construction	2" to 4" thick 4" wide	675	775	400	65	320	650	1,000,000	
Standard		375	425	225	65	320	525	1,000,000	
Utility		175	200	100	65	320	350	1,000,000	
DOUGLAS FIR-LARCH (Surfaced dry or surfaced green. Used at 19% max. m.c.)									WCLIB WWPA (See footnotes 1–12 and 20)
Dense Select Structural	2" to 4" thick 2" to 4" wide	2450	2800	1400	95	730	1850	1,900,000	
Select Structural		2100	2400	1200	95	625	1600	1,800,000	
Dense No. 1		2050	2400	1200	95	730	1450	1,900,000	
No. 1		1750	2050	1050	95	625	1250	1,800,000	
Dense No. 2		1700	1950	1000	95	730	1150	1,700,000	
No. 2		1450	1650	850	95	625	1000	1,700,000	
No. 3		800	925	475	95	625	600	1,500,000	
Appearance		1750	2050	1050	95	625	1500	1,800,000	
Stud		800	925	475	95	625	600	1,500,000	
Construction	2" to 4" thick 4" wide	1050	1200	625	95	625	1150	1,500,000	
Standard		600	675	350	95	625	925	1,500,000	
Utility		275	325	175	95	625	600	1,500,000	
Dense Select Structural	2" to 4" thick 5" and wider	2100	2400	1400	95	730	1650	1,900,000	
Select Structural		1800	2050	1200	95	625	1400	1,800,000	
Dense No. 1		1800	2050	1200	95	730	1450	1,900,000	
No. 1		1500	1750	1000	95	625	1250	1,800,000	
Dense No. 2		1450	1700	775 (See Footnote 3)	95	730	1250	1,700,000	
No. 2		1250	1450	650	95	625	1050	1,700,000	
No. 3		725	850	375	95	625	675	1,500,000	
Appearance		1500	1750	1000	95	625	1500	1,800,000	
Stud		725	850	375	95	625	675	1,500,000	
Dense Select Structural	Beams and Stringers	1900	—	1100	85	730	1300	1,700,000	WCLIB (See footnotes 1–12 and 20)
Select Structural		1600	—	950	85	625	1100	1,600,000	
Dense No. 1		1550	—	775	85	730	1100	1,700,000	
No. 1		1300	—	675	85	625	925	1,600,000	
No. 2		875	—	425	85	625	600	1,300,000	
Dense Select Structural	Posts and Timbers	1750	—	1150	85	730	1350	1,700,000	
Select Structural		1500	—	1000	85	625	1150	1,600,000	
Dense No. 1		1400	—	950	85	730	1200	1,700,000	
No. 1		1200	—	825	85	625	1000	1,600,000	
No. 2		750	—	475	85	625	700	1,300,000	
Select Dex	Decking	1750	2000	—	—	625	—	1,800,000	
Commercial Dex		1450	1650	—	—	625	—	1,700,000	
Dense Select Structural	Beams and Stringers	1900	—	1250	85	730	1300	1,700,000	WWPA (See footnotes 1–13 and 20)
Select Structural		1600	—	1050	85	625	1100	1,600,000	
Dense No. 1		1550	—	1050	85	730	1100	1,700,000	
No. 1		1350	—	900	85	625	925	1,600,000	
Dense No. 2		1000	—	500	85	730	700	1,400,000	
No. 2		875	—	425	85	625	600	1,300,000	
Dense Select Structural	Posts and Timbers	1750	—	1150	85	730	1350	1,700,000	
Select Structural		1500	—	1000	85	625	1150	1,600,000	
Dense No. 1		1400	—	950	85	730	1200	1,700,000	
No. 1		1200	—	825	85	625	1000	1,600,000	
Dense No. 2		800	—	550	85	730	550	1,400,000	
No. 2		700	—	475	85	625	475	1,300,000	
Selected Decking	Decking	—	2000	—	—	—	—	1,800,000	
Commercial Decking		—	1650	—	—	—	—	1,700,000	
Selected Decking	Decking	—	2150	(Surfaced at 15% max. m.c. and used at 15% max. m.c.)			—	1,900,000	
Commercial Decking		—	1800				—	1,700,000	

From Design Values for Wood Construction, NDS Supplement,
National Forest Products Association, Washington, D.C.

In developing wood details, an allowance must be made for the fact that wood will shrink and swell during use regardless of its initial moisture content. Of particular importance is the accumulated change in dimension of a series of wood members placed one on top of the next. The shrinkage of an individual member may not be significant, but the total shrinkage of several may result in problems such as sagging floors, cracked plaster, distortion of door openings, and nail pops in gypsum board walls.

2   WOOD BEAMS

The design of wood beams is a fairly simple procedure. First, the loads and stresses on the beam are determined as described in Chapter 4. This includes finding the support reactions, vertical shear stresses, and bending moments. Then, the basic flexure formula is used to find the required section modulus needed to resist the bending moment. A beam size is then selected that has the required section modulus. Second, horizontal shear stresses are calculated and compared with the allowable horizontal shear for the species and grade of lumber being used. This is especially important because wood beams have a tendency to fail parallel to the grain where their strength is lowest. Finally, deflection is checked to see if it is within acceptable limits. This, too, is important because wood is not as stiff as steel or concrete. Even though a beam may be strong enough to resist bending moment, the deflection may be outside of tolerable limits.

A. Design for Bending

To design wood beams for bending, the basic flexure formula is used:

$$S = \frac{M}{F_b} \qquad 9.1$$

The allowable extreme fiber stress in bending is found in Table 9.2 or similar tables in the building code or from other reference sources, and the section modulus is found in Table 9.1. Since moment is usually calculated in foot-pounds, you must be sure to convert to inch-pounds by multiplying by 12 because the value of F_b is in pounds per square inch. Also, if any increase in stress is allowed due to short duration of loading, the value of F_b is multiplied by the allowable percentage increase.

Example 9.1

A simply supported wood beam spans 12 feet and carries a load of 350 pounds per linear foot. If the beam is Douglas fir-larch, #2, what size beam should be used?

First, find the maximum bending moment. From Figure 4.7, the moment for a uniformly loaded beam is $wL^2/8$. The moment is:

$$M = \frac{350(12)^2}{8}$$
$$= 6300 \text{ ft-lbs}$$

Using Table 9.2, find the column labeled "Extreme Fiber in Bending." Since this is a single beam, use the subcolumn for single member use. At this point, you do not know if the beam will be in the 2 inches to 4 inches thick category, or if it will be a 6-inch or wider member and therefore be in the beams and stringers category. However, assume the beam will be either a nominal 2-inch or 4-inch wide member. Reading across from the no. 2 grade, the allowable stress is 1250 psi. The required section modulus is:

$$S = \frac{6300(12)}{1250}$$
$$= 60.48 \text{ in}^3$$

Remember, the moment must be multiplied by 12 to convert foot-pounds to inch-pounds.

Looking in Table 9.1, the smallest beam that will provide this section modulus is a 4 × 12 with an S of 73.828 in^3. Notice that a 6 × 10 would also provide the required value (82.729), but this has more area and therefore costs more than the 4 × 12. In addition, if a 6-inch wide beam was used, a different value for F_b would have to be used in the beams and stringers category. This value from Table 9.2 is 875 psi.

Recalculating the required section modulus using this value gives

$$S = \frac{6300(12)}{875}$$
$$= 86.40 \text{ in}^3$$

This is greater than the section modulus of a 6 × 10, so the necessary choice is a 4 × 12 anyway.

Example 9.2

What is the maximum moment-carrying capacity, in foot-pounds, of a 2 × 10 select structural Douglas fir-larch beam spanning 15 feet?

Rearranging formula 9.1 and dividing by 12 to convert inch-pounds to foot-pounds,

$$M = \frac{SF_b}{12}$$

The allowable unit stress from Table 9.2 is 1800 psi, and the section modulus (from Table 9.1) of a 2 × 10 is 21.391.

$$M = \frac{1800(21.391)}{12}$$
$$= 3209 \text{ ft-lbs}$$

Sometimes, either the width or depth of a beam is established by some limiting factor (such as ceiling clearance) and the other beam dimension must be found. This is easy to calculate if you remember that the section modulus of a rectangular beam is:

$$S = \frac{bd^2}{6} \qquad \qquad 9.2$$

Example 9.3

A wood beam spanning 10 feet must be designed to support a concentrated load of 2900 pounds in the center of the span, but there is only enough room for a nominal 8-inch deep beam. If the beam can be dense select structural Douglas fir-larch, what beam width is necessary?

The moment of a beam with a concentrated load is $PL/4$ (from Figure 4.7). The moment is:

$$M = \frac{2900(10)(12)}{4}$$
$$= 87,000 \text{ inch-pounds}$$

The allowable unit stress for dense select structural from Table 9.2 is 1900 psi (assuming beams and stringers classification), so the required section modulus is:

$$S = \frac{87,000}{1900}$$
$$= 45.79$$

If there was no limitation on the depth of the beam, a 4×10 would work with a section modulus of 49.911. However, if the maximum depth is 7.25 inches (the actual depth of a nominal 8-inch member) then the required width is:

$$S = \frac{bd^2}{6}$$

Rearranging the formula gives

$$b = \frac{6S}{d^2}$$
$$= \frac{6(45.79)}{(7.25)^2}$$
$$= 5.23 \text{ inches}$$

A nominal 6-inch wide beam will work with an actual width of 5.50 inches.

Example 9.4

A Douglas fir-larch no. 2 beam supports a roof with a dead load of 100 pounds per linear foot and a snow load of 150 pounds per linear foot. If the beam must span 8 feet, what is the most economical size to use?

For the snow load, an increase of 15 percent in allowable stress is permitted. However, when there are loads of different durations on wood members, each load combination should be checked. In this case, the moment due to dead load only is:

$$M = \frac{100(8)^2(12)}{8}$$
$$= 9600 \text{ in-lbs}$$

The moment due to dead load and snow load is:

$$M = \frac{250(8)^2(12)}{8}$$
$$= 24,000 \text{ in-lbs}$$

Remember, the factor of 12 must be used to convert foot-pounds to inch-pounds.

The required section modulus for dead load only is:

$$S = \frac{9600}{1250}$$
$$= 7.68 \text{ in}^3$$

The required section modulus for the combined load using the 15 percent increase allowed is:

$$S = \frac{24,000}{1250(1.15)}$$
$$= 16.70 \text{ in}^3$$

Use the greater of the calculated section moduli. You would need to use a 2×10 with a section modulus of 21.391 (from Table 9.1).

B. Design for Horizontal Shear

Because it is easy for wood to shear along the lines of the grain, actual horizontal shear must always be checked against the allowable unit shear stress, F_v. This is especially important for short spans with large loads. Frequently, a beam that is sufficient in size to resist bending stresses must be made larger to resist horizontal shear stresses.

Because horizontal shear failure will always occur before vertical shear failure, it is not necessary to check for vertical shear except for beams notched at their supports.

For rectangular beams, the maximum unit horizontal shear stress is:

$$f_v = \frac{3V}{2bd} \qquad 9.3$$

When calculating the vertical shear, V, the loads within a distance from the supports equal to the depth of the member may be neglected.

Example 9.5

Using the beam found in Example 9.1, check it for horizontal shear.

The load is 350 pounds per linear foot for 12 feet or 4200 pounds total. The vertical shear at each reaction is 2100 pounds. Subtract the load within a distance equal to the depth of the beam, 11 1/4 inches.

$$V = 2100 - \left(\frac{11.25}{12}\right) 350 = 1772 \text{ pounds}$$

The value of bd is the area of the member which equals 39.375 in^2.

Actual horizontal shear is:

$$f_v = \frac{3(1772)}{2(39.375)}$$
$$= 67.50 \text{ psi}$$

Looking at Table 9.2, the allowable horizontal shear, F_v, is 85 psi for Douglas fir-larch #2, so the beam is adequate to resist the imposed horizontal shear. If the actual value was greater than the allowable, a larger beam would be needed.

C. Design for Deflection

Since wood is not as stiff as steel or concrete, deflection is always a concern. Detrimental effects of deflection can include nail popping in gypsum ceilings, cracking of plaster, bouncy floors, and visible sagging. In many cases, a wood member can be selected that will satisfy bending requirements but will not satisfy deflection criteria. Therefore, the design of wood beams must always include a check for deflection.

The formulas for deflection are the same ones used for other materials and are outlined in Figure 4.7. The criteria for maximum deflection is given in the Uniform Building Code and requires that two different conditions of loading be checked. The first limits deflection due to live load only to $L/360$ of the span. The second limits deflection due to live load and dead load for unseasoned wood to $L/240$ of the span. In both cases, the

units of deflection will be the same as the units used for the value of L.

The Uniform Building Code does allow a reduction by one-half of the dead load for the condition of live load and dead load if seasoned wood is used. *Seasoned wood* is defined as wood with a moisture content of less than 16 percent at the time of installation and used under dry conditions. This is typically the case, but since wood will deflect under long-term use beyond its initial deflection, it is common practice to use the full value of dead load and live load when checking deflection against the $L/240$ criterion. This provides for the extra stiffness necessary to limit deflection under long-term loading.

Example 9.6

Using the same beam found in Example 9.1, check to see that its deflection is within allowable limits. Assume that of the total load of 350 pounds per foot, dead load is 150 pounds and live load is 200 pounds per foot.

From Figure 4.7, the deflection for a uniformly loaded beam is:

$$\Delta = \frac{5wl^4}{384EI} \qquad 9.4$$

The modulus of elasticity of Douglas fir-larch #2 is 1,700,000 psi as found in Table 9.2, and the moment of inertia of a 4×12 is 415.283 as found in Table 9.1.

In this case, it is important to keep units consistent in order for the answer to be in inches. Remember that in formula 9.4, w is the weight per unit length and l is the length. If l is in inches, the weight must be in pounds per inch, not feet. For calculating the total dead and live load, 350 pounds per foot is 350/12 or 29.167 pounds per inch. The beam length of 12 feet must be converted to inches and then raised to the fourth power:

$$\Delta = \frac{5(29.167)(12 \times 12)^4}{384(1,700,000)(415.283)}$$
$$= 0.23 \text{ inches}$$

Another way to arrive at the same answer is to remember that formula 9.4 can also take the form

$$\Delta = \frac{5Wl^3}{384EI} \qquad 9.5$$

W is the total uniformly distributed weight on the beam. The length still needs to be converted to inches and then raised to the third power, so the calculation is:

$$\Delta = \frac{5(350 \times 12)(12 \times 12)^3}{384(1,700,000)(415.283)}$$
$$= 0.23 \text{ inches for dead and live load}$$

For deflection of live load only,

$$\Delta = \frac{5(200 \times 12)(12 \times 12)^3}{384(1,700,000)(415.283)}$$
$$= 0.13 \text{ inches}$$

Next, determine the allowable deflection limits. For live load only,

$$\frac{12 \times 12}{360} = 0.40 \text{ inches}$$

This is more than the actual deflection under live load only of 0.13, so this is acceptable. For total load,

$$\frac{12 \times 12}{240} = 0.60 \text{ inches}$$

This is also more than the actual deflection under total load of 0.23 inches, so the 4 × 12 beam is acceptable for deflection requirements.

3 MISCELLANEOUS PROVISIONS

A. Notched Beams

Notching of beams should be avoided, but if it is done, the UBC states that notches in sawn lumber bending members cannot exceed one-sixth the depth of the member and cannot be located in the middle third of the span. When the notches are at the supports as shown in Figure 9.1, the depth cannot exceed one-fourth of the beam depth.

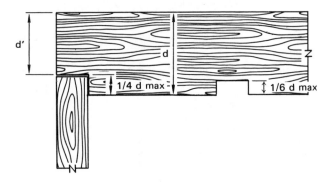

Figure 9.1 Notching of Beams

If beams are notched, the vertical shear cannot exceed the value determined by the formula

$$V = \left(\frac{2bd'F_v}{3}\right)\left(\frac{d'}{d}\right) \qquad 9.6$$

Example 9.7

If the beam in Example 9.1 is notched 2 inches, is it still an acceptable size?

The beam found in Example 9.1 is a 4 × 12, so its actual depth is 11.25 inches. Subtracting 2 inches gives a d' value of 9.25 inches with a width of 3.5 inches. From Table 9.2, the allowable horizontal shear for Douglas fir-larch #2 is 85 psi.

$$V = \frac{2(3.5)(9.25)(85)}{3} \times \frac{9.25}{11.25}$$
$$= 1508 \text{ pounds}$$

From Example 9.5, the vertical shear was found to be 2100 pounds, so this beam could not be notched 2 inches without exceeding the allowable vertical shear limitation.

B. Size Factor

As the depth of a beam increases, there is a slight decrease in bending strength. The Uniform Building Code requires that the allowable unit stress in bending, F_b, be decreased by a size factor as determined by the formula

$$C_f = \left(\frac{12}{d}\right)^{1/9} \qquad 9.7$$

This applies only to rectangular sawn bending members exceeding 12 inches in depth. Design values for bending, tension, and compression parallel to grain for visually graded dimension lumber 2 to 4 inches thick must be multiplied by size factors given at the end of Tables 25-A-1 to 25-A-5 in the Uniform Building Code. The size factor does not affect the allowable strength to any great amount. C_f for a 14-inch deep beam, for example, is only 0.987, and for a 16-inch deep beam, it is 0.972.

C. Lateral Support

When a wood beam is loaded in bending, there is a tendency for it to buckle laterally. The UBC provides that a decrease in allowable bending strength be made if certain conditions are not met. For the vast majority of wood construction, this is not required if proper lateral support is provided. This amounts to providing continuous support at the compression edge, such as with sheathing or subflooring, and providing restraint against rotation at the ends of the members and at intervals with bridging. Most wood construction meets these conditions, so adjustments are not required.

D. Bearing

The load on a wood beam compresses the fibers where the weight is concentrated at the supports. To determine the required bearing area, the total reaction load is divided by the allowable compression perpendicular to grain, $F_{c\perp}$, found in Table 9.2. For joists, the UBC states that there must be at least 1 1/2 inches bearing on wood or metal, and at least 3 inches bearing on masonry. Beams or girders supported on masonry must have at least 3 inches of bearing surface.

Example 9.8

What is the required bearing area for the beam selected in Example 9.1?

The total reaction of the beam is:

$$R = \frac{350(12)}{2}$$
$$= 2100 \text{ pounds}$$

The required bearing area is:

$$A = \frac{2100}{625}$$
$$= 3.36 \text{ square inches}$$

Since the beam is 3 1/2 inches wide, the required length of bearing is 3.36/3.5, or 0.96 inches. However, since this is less than the code requirement of 3 inches, 3 inches must be used.

4 WOOD COLUMNS

As discussed in Chapter 4, columns have a tendency to buckle under a load, so even though a column may have enough cross-sectional area to resist the unit compressive forces, it may fail in buckling. For wood columns, the ratio of the column length to its width is just as important as it is for concrete and steel columns. However, for wood columns, the slenderness ratio is defined as the laterally unsupported length in inches divided by the least dimension of the column. This is a little different than the length divided by the radius of gyration as discussed in Chapter 4, but the same principles apply.

Wood columns can be solid members of rectangular, round, or other shapes, or spaced columns built up from two or more individual solid members separated by blocking. Since almost all wood columns are solid

rectangular sections, the method of design in this section will be limited to these types.

As mentioned in Chapter 4, the load-carrying capacity of a wood column depends on the way the ends of the column are fixed. For design, the *effective length* must be determined. This is the total unsupported length multiplied by an effective buckling length factor, K_e. These factors for various end conditions are shown in Figure 9.2. Notice that this diagram is very similar to Figure 4.8, but the values are slightly different.

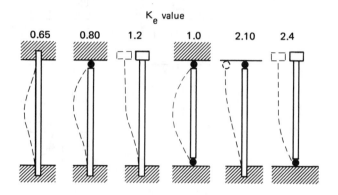

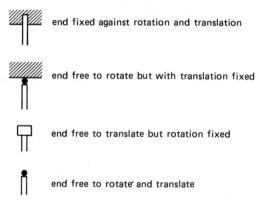

Figure 9.2 K_e Values for Wood Columns

Because of the way most wood construction is detailed, columns are usually fixed in translation but free to rotate, so the K value is taken as 1, and the effective length is taken as the actual unsupported length. For the purposes of this chapter, the letter l indicates the effective length of a column in inches.

The allowable unit stress in pounds per square inch of cross-sectional area of square or rectangular solid columns is determined according to a complex formula that considers the effective length, whether the wood is visually graded or machine graded, and whether the wood is sawn lumber, round timber piles, or glued-laminated timber. Because of the complexity of the formula, it is unlikely that the test will ask for specific values to be calculated.

Table 9.3

Allowable Spans for Floor Joists

DESIGN CRITERIA: Deflection—For 40 lbs. per sq. ft. live load. Limited to span in inches divided by 360. **Strength**—Live load of 40 lbs. per sq. ft. plus dead load of 10 lbs. per sq. ft. determines the required fiber stress value.

JOIST SIZE (IN)	SPACING (IN)	Modulus of Elasticity, E, in 1,000,000 psi													
		0.8	0.9	1.0	1.1	1.2	1.3	1.4	1.5	1.6	1.7	1.8	1.9	2.0	2.2
2x6	12.0	8-6 720	8-10 780	9-2 830	9-6 890	9-9 940	10-0 990	10-3 1040	10-6 1090	10-9 1140	10-11 1190	11-2 1230	11-4 1280	11-7 1320	11-11 1410
	16.0	7-9 790	8-0 860	8-4 920	8-7 980	8-10 1040	9-1 1090	9-4 1150	9-6 1200	9-9 1250	9-11 1310	10-2 1360	10-4 1410	10-6 1460	10-10 1550
	24.0	6-9 900	7-0 980	7-3 1050	7-6 1120	7-9 1190	7-11 1250	8-2 1310	8-4 1380	8-6 1440	8-8 1500	8-10 1550	9-0 1610	9-2 1670	9-6 1780
2x8	12.0	11-3 720	11-8 780	12-1 830	12-6 890	12-10 940	13-2 990	13-6 1040	13-10 1090	14-2 1140	14-5 1190	14-8 1230	15-0 1280	15-3 1320	15-9 1410
	16.0	10-2 790	10-7 850	11-0 920	11-4 980	11-8 1040	12-0 1090	12-3 1150	12-7 1200	12-10 1250	13-1 1310	13-4 1360	13-7 1410	13-10 1460	14-3 1550
	24.0	8-11 900	9-3 980	9-7 1050	9-11 1120	10-2 1190	10-6 1250	10-9 1310	11-0 1380	11-3 1440	11-5 1500	11-8 1550	11-11 1610	12-1 1670	12-6 1780
2x10	12.0	14-4 720	14-11 780	15-5 830	15-11 890	16-5 940	16-10 990	17-3 1040	17-8 1090	18-0 1140	18-5 1190	18-9 1230	19-1 1280	19-5 1320	20-1 1410
	16.0	13-0 790	13-6 850	14-0 920	14-6 980	14-11 1040	15-3 1090	15-8 1150	16-0 1200	16-5 1250	16-9 1310	17-0 1360	17-4 1410	17-8 1460	18-3 1550
	24.0	11-4 900	11-10 980	12-3 1050	12-8 1120	13-0 1190	13-4 1250	13-8 1310	14-0 1380	14-4 1440	14-7 1500	14-11 1550	15-2 1610	15-5 1670	15-11 1780
2x12	12.0	17-5 720	18-1 780	18-9 830	19-4 890	19-11 940	20-6 990	21-0 1040	21-6 1090	21-11 1140	22-5 1190	22-10 1230	23-3 1280	23-7 1320	24-5 1410
	16.0	15-10 790	16-5 860	17-0 920	17-7 980	18-1 1040	18-7 1090	19-1 1150	19-6 1200	19-11 1250	20-4 1310	20-9 1360	21-1 1410	21-6 1460	22-2 1550
	24.0	13-10 900	14-4 980	14-11 1050	15-4 1120	15-10 1190	16-3 1250	16-8 1310	17-0 1380	17-5 1440	17-9 1500	18-1 1550	18-5 1610	18-9 1670	19-4 1780

NOTES:

(1) The required extreme fiber stress in bending (F_b) in pounds per square inch is shown below each span.

(2) Use single or repetitive member bending stress values (F_b) and modulus of elasticity values (E) from Tables Nos. 25-A-1 and 25-A-2.

(3) For more comprehensive tables covering a broader range of bending stress values (F_b) and modulus of elasticity values (E), other spacing of members and other conditions of loading, see U.B.C. Standard No. 25-21.

(4) The spans in these tables are intended for use in covered structures or where moisture content in use does not exceed 19 percent.

5   JOISTS

Joists are a very common type of wood construction. They are small, closely spaced members used to support floor, ceiling, and roof loads, and are usually lumber nominally 2 inches wide by 6, 8, 10, and 12 inches deep, spaced 12, 16, or 24 inches on center. Of course, they are beams and can be designed using the methods described earlier in this section, but since they are used so frequently, their size and spacing is usually selected from tables. When they are designed as beams, the design value of F_b from Table 9.2 should be selected from the column labeled "Repetitive Member Uses." The design value is slightly larger for multiple member use than for single members.

Table 9.3 shows one joist table from the Uniform Building Code. Similar tables are published by the National Forest Products Association, the Southern Forest Products Association, other trade groups, and reference sources. For a given joist size and spacing, and a given modulus of elasticity, the table gives the maximum allowable span when the deflection is the limiting factor. Below the span is the required extreme fiber stress in bending. Most tables are established for typical floor and roof loads, so if you have unusual circumstances you need to calculate the required size and spacing using the methods of beam design.

To use the table, you can either begin with a known span and lumber species and find the required size and spacing of joists, or begin with the span and joist design and determine what design values are required to satisfy your requirements. Then you can specify a lumber species and grade that have the design values you need. The design values are found in Table 9.2.

Example 9.9

A floor must be designed to support a live load of 40 pounds per square foot and a dead load of 10 pounds per square foot. The joists will span 13 feet. If the most readily available grade of wood joist is Douglas fir-larch #2, what size and spacing is required?

Since joists are being used, they fall in the size classification of 2 inches to 4 inches thick, 5 inches and wider. From Table 9.2, Douglas fir-larch #2 has a modulus of elasticity of 1,700,000 psi and an F_b value for repetitive member use of 1450 psi.

Table 9.3 gives E in multiples of 1,000,000 psi, so look down the 1.7 column until you find a span of 13 feet or more. The first value to fit this requirement is 13'1" corresponding to a 2 × 8 inch joist 16 inches on center. Below the span is a value of 1310 psi for the minimum F_b. Since this is less than the actual value of 1450, this size and spacing will work.

6 GLUED LAMINATED CONSTRUCTION

Glued laminated wood members consist of a number of individual pieces of lumber glued together and finished under factory conditions for use as beams, columns, purlins, and other structural uses. Glued laminated construction, or *glue-lam* as it is usually referred to, is used when larger wood members are required for heavy loads or long spans, and simple sawn timber pieces are not available or cannot meet the strength requirements. Glue-lam construction is also used where unusual structural shapes are required and appearance is a consideration. In addition to being fabricated in simple rectangular shapes, glue-lam members can be formed into arches, tapered forms, and pitched shapes.

Glue-lam members are manufactured in standard sizes of width and depth. In most cases, 1 1/2 inch actual depth pieces are used, so the overall depth is some multiple of 1 1/2 depending on how many laminations are used. Three-quarter inch thick pieces are used if a tight curve must be formed. Standard widths and depths are shown in Figure 9.3.

Because individual pieces can be selected free from certain defects and seasoned to the proper moisture content, and the entire manufacturing process is conducted under carefully controlled conditions, the allowable stresses for glue-lam construction are higher than for

solid, sawn lumber. Although glue-lam beams are usually loaded in the direction perpendicular to the laminations, they can be loaded in either direction to suit the requirements of the design. Tables of design values give allowable stresses about both axes.

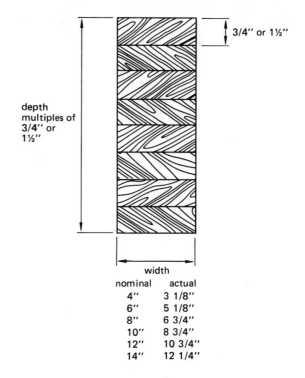

Figure 9.3 Glued Laminated Beam

For structural purposes, glue-lams are designated by size and a commonly used symbol that specifies its stress rating. For design purposes, glue-lams are available in three appearance grades: *industrial*, *architectural*, and *premium*. These do not affect the structural properties but only designate the final look and finishing of the member. Industrial is used where appearance is not a primary concern, while premium is used where the finest appearance is important. Architectural grade is used where appearance is a factor but the best grade is not required.

7 PLANKING

Wood planking, or *decking* as it is often called, is solid or laminated lumber laid on its face spanning between beams. Planking is available in nominal thicknesses of

2, 3, 4, and 5 inches with actual sizes varying with manufacturer and whether the piece is solid or laminated. All planking has some type of tongue and groove edging, so the pieces fit solidly together and load can be distributed among adjacent pieces.

The allowable span depends on the thickness of the planking and load to be supported, and ranges from 4 feet to 20 feet. Planking is often used in heavy timber construction with glued laminated beams and purlins. Planking has the advantages of easy installation, attractive appearance, and efficient use of material since the planking serves as floor structure, finish floor, and finish ceiling below. Its primary disadvantages are that there is no place to put additional insulation or conceal mechanical and electrical services.

SAMPLE QUESTIONS

1. Which of the following statements is correct?

   A. Glue-laminated beams may shrink excessively once on the job site.
   B. Selecting a premium appearance grade glue-lam allows an increase in allowable bending stress.
   C. 3/4-inch laminations are used in glue-lam beams primarily when a tight curve must be formed.
   D. A nominal 8-inch wide glue-lam is actually 7 1/2 inches wide.

2. An outdoor deck in a mountain region is supported on #2 western red cedar joists with an F_b of 1050 psi for repetitive members and an F_v of 75 psi. The joists are cantilevered 2 feet as shown in the figures. If the snow load creates a uniform load on each joist of 173 pounds per foot, what size joist is required (neglecting the weight of the joist and considering both bending and horizontal shear)?

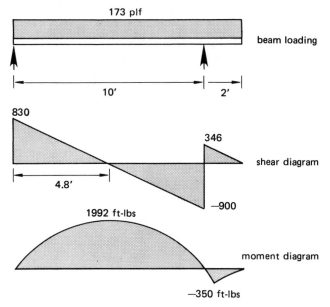

   A. 2 × 6
   B. 2 × 8
   C. 2 × 10
   D. 2 × 12

3. Which of the following is usually not checked when designing floor joists for heavy loads?

   A. vertical shear

   B. horizontal shear
   C. moment effects
   D. deflection

The answers to questions 4 through 6 can be found on the following key list. Select only one answer for each question.

   A0 appearance grade
   A1 buckling length factor
   A2 compression parallel to grain
   A3 compression perpendicular to grain
   A4 deflection cracking
   A5 extreme fiber in bending
   A6 fiber saturation point
   A7 lateral support
   A8 machine grading
   A9 modulus of elasticity

   B0 moisture content
   B1 size categories
   B2 slenderness ratio
   B3 vertical shear
   B4 visual grading

4. What must be used in designing bearing plates for girders?

5. What would be used to design a column with its lower end encased in concrete?

6. What is as important as wood species in selecting allowable stresses?

7. Which of the following affect the selection of a value for allowable tension parallel to the grain, before modification due to duration of loading?

   I.   wood species

   II. size of member

   III. single or multiple member use

   IV. grade of lumber

   V.   duration of loading

   A. I, II, and IV
   B. I, III, and IV
   C. II, IV, and V
   D. all of the above

8. A wood column is anchored solidly in concrete at its base and supports a rigid beam in such a way that the top of the column is free to rotate. If the actual length is 12 feet, what is the effective length?

    A. 7.8 feet

    B. 9.6 feet

    C. 12.0 feet

    D. 25.2 feet

9. The maximum bending moment on a 20-foot long beam is 8200 ft-lbs. If the beam is Douglas fir-larch dense no. 1, and lateral support is provided, what is the most economical size that should be used? (Neglect effects of deflection.)

    A. 4×10

    B. 4×12

    C. 6×8

    D. 6×10

10. Select the incorrect statement below.

    A. Design values can be increased 33 1/3 percent for wind loading on wood structures.

    B. Structural lumber should be specified at an absolute maximum moisture content of 19 percent.

    C. Horizontal shear is almost always more critical than deflection or bending in short, heavily loaded beams.

    D. Beams can be notched a maximum of one-sixth of their depth at end supports.

10 STEEL CONSTRUCTION

Nomenclature

A	cross-sectional area	in^2
d	actual depth of beam	inches
D_c	uniform load deflection constant	in/ft^2
E	modulus of elasticity	psi
F_a	allowable axial compressive stress	ksi or psi
F_b	bending stress permitted in a member in the absence of axial force	ksi or psi
F_t	allowable tensile stress	ksi or psi
f_v	unit shear stress	ksi or psi
F_v	allowable shear stress	ksi or psi
F_y	specified minimum yield point of the type of steel being used	ksi
I	moment of inertia	in^4
K	effective length factor	
l	span	inches
L	span or column length	feet
L_c	maximum unbraced length of the compression flange at which the allowable bending stress may be taken at 0.66 F_y	feet
L_u	maximum unbraced length of the compression flange at which the allowable bending stress may be taken at $0.60F_y$	feet
L_v	span length below which shear, V, in beam web governs	feet
M	moment	foot-kips or inch-pounds
M_R	resisting moment	foot-kips
P	concentrated load	pounds or kips
r	governing radius of gyration	inches
R	end beam reaction	kips or pounds
S	section modulus	in^3
t_w	thickness of web	inches

V	maximum web shear	kips
w	weight per foot	pounds or kips
W	total uniform load on a beam	kips
W_c	uniform load constant	foot-kips
Δ	deflection	inches

There are currently two accepted methods of structural steel design in the United States: the *allowable stress design* (ASD) method and the *load and resistance factor design* (LRFD) method. The use of either method is allowed by the Uniform Building Code, but the UBC text is based on the ASD method. The material in this chapter is also based on the ASD method.

1 PROPERTIES OF STRUCTURAL STEEL

Steel is one of the most widely used structural materials because of its many advantages, which include high strength, ductility, uniformity of manufacture, variety of shapes and sizes, and ease and speed of erection. Steel has a high strength-to-weight ratio. This makes it possible to reduce a building's dead load and to minimize the space taken up by structural elements. In addition, steel has a high modulus of elasticity, which means it is very stiff.

Ductility of steel is a property that allows it to withstand excessive deformations due to high tensile stresses without failure. This property makes it useful for earthquake-resistant structures.

Because steel is manufactured under carefully controlled conditions, the composition, size, and strength can be uniformly predicted so that structures do not have to be overdesigned to compensate for manufacturing or erection variables as with concrete.

The variety of available sizes and shapes of steel also allows the designer to select a member that is the most efficient for the job and that is not larger than it needs to be. These properties make possible a cost-efficient structure.

Finally, because most of the cutting and preparation of members can occur in the fabricating plant, steel structures can be erected very quickly and easily, thus reducing overall construction time.

In spite of the advantages, however, steel does have negative properties that must be accounted for. Most notable are its reduction in strength when subjected to fire and the tendency to corrode in the presence of moisture. Steel itself does not burn, but deforms in the presence of high temperatures. As a result, steel must be protected with fire-resistant materials such as sprayed-on cementitious material or gypsum board, or it must be encased in concrete. This adds to the overall cost, but is usually justified when the many advantages are considered.

As with any ferrous material, steel will rust and otherwise corrode if not protected. This can be accomplished by including alloys in the steel to protect it (e.g., stainless steel), or by covering it with paint or other protective coatings.

A. Types and Composition of Steel

Steel is composed primarily of iron with small amounts of carbon and other elements that are part of the alloy, either as impurities left over from manufacturing or deliberately added to impart certain desired qualities to the alloy. In *medium-carbon steel* used in construction, these other elements include manganese (from 0.5 to 1.0 percent), silicon (from 0.25 to 0.75 percent), phosphorus, and sulfur. Phosphorus and sulfur in excessive amounts are harmful in that they affect weldability and make steel brittle.

The percentage of carbon present affects the strength and ductility of steel. As carbon is added, the strength increases but the ductility decreases. Percentages of carbon range from about 0.15 percent for very mild steel to 0.70 percent for high-carbon steel. Standard structural steel has from 0.20 to 0.50 percent carbon.

The most common type of steel for structural use is ASTM A36 which means that the steel is manufactured according to the *American Society for Testing and Materials (ASTM)* specification number A36. The yield point for this steel is 36 kips per square inch

(ksi). Other high-strength steels include A242, A440, and A441 steel, which have yield points of 46 ksi or 50 ksi.

B. Shapes and Sizes of Structural Steel

Structural steel comes in a variety of shapes, sizes, and weights. This gives the designer a great deal of flexibility in selecting an economical member that is geometrically correct for any given situation. Figure 10.1 shows the most common shapes of structural steel.

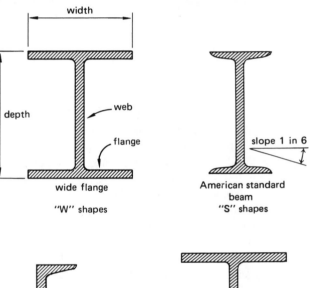

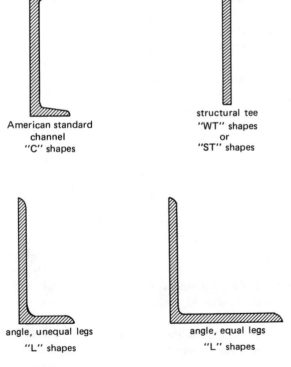

Figure 10.1   Structural Steel Shapes

Wide flange members are H-shaped sections used for both beams and columns. They are called "wide flange" because the width of the flange is greater than that of standard I-beams. The outside and inside faces of the flanges are parallel. Many of the wide flange shapes are particularly suited for columns because the width of the flange is very nearly equal to the depth of the section, so they have about the same rigidity in both axes. Fourteen-inch deep wide flange sections are often used for columns on high-rise multistory structures. On low-rise and mid-rise multistory buildings, usually the smallest column used is an 8-inch deep wide flange.

Wide flange sections are designated with the letter W followed by the nominal depth in inches and the weight in pounds per linear foot. For example, a W 18 × 85 is a wide flange nominally 18 inches deep and weighing 85 pounds per linear foot. Because of the way these sections are rolled in the mill, the actual depth varies slightly from the nominal depth.

American Standard I-beams have a relatively narrow flange width in relation to their depth, and the inside face of the flanges have a slope of 16 2/3 percent, or 1/6. Unlike the wide flanges, the actual depth of an I-beam in any size group is also the nominal depth. Heavier sections are made by adding thickness to the flanges on the inside face only. The designation of depth and weight per foot for these sections is preceded with the letter S. These sections are usually used for beams only.

American Standard channel sections have a flange on one side of the web only and are designated with the letter C followed by the depth and weight per foot. Like the American Standard I-beams, the depth is constant for any size group. Extra weight is added by increasing the thickness of the web and the inside face of the flanges. Channel sections are typically used to frame openings, form stair stringers, or in other applications where a flush side is required. They are seldom used by themselves as beams or columns because they tend to buckle due to their asymmetrical shape.

Structural tees are made by cutting either a wide flange section or I-beam in half. If cut from a wide flange section, a tee is given the prefix designation WT, and if cut from an American Standard I-beam, it is given the designation ST. A WT 9 × 57, for example, is cut from a W 18 × 114. Because they are symmetrical about one axis and have an open flange, tees are often used for chords of steel trusses.

Steel angles are available either with equal or unequal legs. They are designated by the letter L followed by the lengths of the angles, and then followed by the thickness of the legs. Angles are used in pairs for members for steel trusses or singly as lintels in a variety of appli-cations. They are also used for miscellaneous bracing of other structural members.

Square and rectangular tube sections and round pipe are also available. These are often used for light col-umns and as members of large trusses or space frames. Structural tubing of various sizes is available in several different wall thicknesses, while structural pipe is avail-able in standard weight, extra strong, and double-extra strong. Each of the three weights has a standard wall thickness depending on the size. Pipe is designated by its nominal diameter, but the actual outside dimension is slightly larger, while the size designation for square or rectangular tubing refers to its actual outside dimen-sions.

Finally, steel is available in bars and plates. Bars are considered any rectangular section 6 inches or less in width with a thickness of 0.203 inches and greater, or sections 6 to 8 inches in width with a thickness of 0.230 and greater.

Plates are considered any section over 8 inches in width with a thickness of 0.230 inches and over, or sections over 48 inches in width with a thickness of 0.180 inches and over.

Table 10.1 summarizes the standard designations for structural steel shapes.

Table 10.1
Standard Designations for Structural Shapes

wide flange shapes	W 12 × 22
American Standard beams	S 12 × 35
miscellaneous shapes	M 12 × 11.8
American Standard channels	C 15 × 40
miscellaneous channels	MC 12 × 37
angles, equal legs	L 3 × 3 × 3/8
angles, unequal legs	L 3 × 4 × 1/2
structural tees—cut from wide flange shapes	WT 7 × 15
structural tees—cut from American Standard beams	ST 9 × 35
plate	PL 1/2″ × 10
structural tubing, square	TS 8 × 8 × 0.3750
pipe	pipe 4 std.

C. Allowable Stresses

Allowable unit stresses for structural steel are expressed as percentages of the minimum specified yield point of the grade of steel used. For A36 steel, the yield point is 36 ksi. The percentages used depend on the type of stress, the condition of use, and other factors. Al-lowable unit stresses are established by the American Institute of Steel Construction (AISC) and are com-monly adopted by reference by model codes such as the

Uniform Building Code and by local codes. Table 10.2 summarizes some of the more common AISC values for A36 steel.

2   STEEL BEAMS

The design of steel beams involves finding the lightest weight section (and therefore the least expensive) that will resist bending and shear forces within allowable limits of stress, and one that will not have excessive deflection for the condition of use. Beam design can be accomplished either through the use of the standard formulas for flexure, shear, and deflection, or by using tables in the *Manual of Steel Construction* published by the AISC. Both methods will be reviewed in the following sections.

A. Lateral Support and Compact Sections

Before proceeding with methods for steel beam design, you should have a firm understanding of two important concepts: lateral support and compact sections. When a simply supported beam is subjected to a load, the top flange is in compression and the bottom flange is in tension as discussed in Chapter 4. At the compression flange, there is a tendency for it to buckle under load, just as a column can buckle under an axial load. For overhanging beams, when the bottom flange is in compression the same potential problem exists.

To resist this tendency, either the compression flange needs to be supported or the beam needs to be made larger. In many cases, steel beams are automatically laterally supported because of standard construction methods. This occurs with beams supporting steel decking welded to the beams, beams with the top flange embedded in a concrete slab, or composite construction. In some instances, a girder is only supported laterally with intermittent beams.

If a beam is continuously supported or supported at intervals no greater than L_c, the full allowable stress of $0.66\,F_y$ may be used. If the support is greater than L_c, but not greater than L_u, then the allowable stress must be reduced to $0.60\,F_y$. The values of L_c and L_u are given in tables in the AISC manual and will be illustrated in later example problems.

Sections are determined to be either *compact* or *noncompact* based on the yield strength of the steel and the width-to-thickness ratios of the web and flanges. If a section is non-compact, a lower allowable bending stress must be used. Identification of non-compact sections and the reduced stresses are incorporated into the design tables in the AISC manual.

B. Design for Bending

There are two approaches to designing steel beams: with the flexure formula as discussed in Chapter 4 or with the tables found in the AISC manual. Both will be discussed here.

The basic flexure formula is:

$$S = \frac{M}{f_b} \qquad 10.1$$

This formula from Chapter 4 is the same for steel design, except that the AISC uses the nomenclature F_b for the allowable bending stress instead of f_b, which it reserves for computed bending stress.

The basic formula is used in two forms to either select a beam by finding the required section modulus, S, or to calculate the maximum resisting moment, M, when a beam is being analyzed. These two forms are, respectively:

$$S = \frac{M}{F_b} \qquad 10.2$$

and

$$M = SF_b \qquad 10.3$$

Moments are calculated using the static formulas for various types of loading conditions as shown in Figure 4.12, or by using the methods described in Chapters 3 and 4 with shear and moment diagrams, or with the summation of moments method.

There is one very important point to remember: keep the units consistent! It is typical in steel design to use the units of kips instead of pounds, and feet instead of inches. However, allowable stresses are often listed in kips per square inch, so you often have to covert to kip-inches from kip-feet. In addition, many of the tables used in the AISC manual are in kips while problems are often given in pounds. The best way to avoid problems is to adopt a consistent procedure of using kips and feet in all your problems. If a problem is stated in pounds or inches, the first step should be to convert them. The following example problems will illustrate this point.

Example 10.1

An A36 steel beam that is laterally supported is to span 26 feet, supporting a uniform load of 1500 pounds per foot not including its own weight. What is the most economical wide flange section that can be used?

The weight of a beam can be accounted for in one of two ways. You can assume a weight and add it to the

Table 10.2
Selected Allowable Unit Stresses for A36 Steel

type of stress and condition	stress nomenclature	AISC specification	value for A36 steel
bending			
tension and compression on extreme fibers of laterally supported compact sections symmetrical about and loaded in the plane of their minor axis	F_b	$0.66\,F_y$	24 ksi
tension and compression on extreme fibers of other rolled shapes braced laterally	F_b	$0.60\,F_y$	22 ksi
solid round and square bars bending about their weak axis and doubly symmetrical I and H shapes bent about their minor axis	F_b	$0.75\,F_y$	27 ksi
shear on gross sections	F_v	$0.40\,F_y$	14.5 ksi
tension			
on net section	F_t	$0.60\,F_y$	22 ksi
on effective net area, except at pinholes	F_t	$0.50\,F_u$	29 ksi

load and then calculate moment, or you can ignore it, solve the problem to find the actual weight of the beam, and then recheck your work. Since the weight of steel beams is usually a very small percentage of the total weight, it can usually be ignored for preliminary calculations. For example, the heaviest wide flange section used for a beam is a W 36 × 300, so the most additional weight you can have is 0.3 kips per foot.

Find the maximum moment ignoring the weight of the beam.

From Figure 4.12, the formula for moment is:

$$M = \frac{wL^2}{8}$$

Converting 1500 pounds per linear foot to 1.5 kips per linear foot,

$$M = 1.5 \times \frac{(26)^2}{8}$$
$$= 127 \text{ foot-kips}$$

For A36 steel, the allowable bending stress is 24 ksi (Table 10.2). Use formula 10.2 to find the required section modulus:

$$S = 127 \times \frac{12}{24}$$
$$= 63.5 \text{ in}^3$$

Note that the value of 127 foot-kips had to be converted to inch-kips to work with the value of 24 ksi and yield an answer in in^3 for the section modulus.

To find the most economical section (the lightest weight), you can look in the various AISC tables showing properties of sections (Table 10.3, for example) or you can look in the section modulus table in the AISC manual. A portion of this table is reproduced in Table 10.4. This table lists the various sections in the order of descending section modulus value with the lightest weight member in a group shown in boldface type. For this problem, the lightest weight section that satisfies the required section modulus is a W 16 × 40 with an S of 64.7 in^3.

Table 10.4 also lists the maximum resisting moment that the beam can carry and the length limits, L_c and L_u, for unsupported sections. The columns on the right

are for A36 steel. The maximum moment this beam can resist, assuming A36 steel, is 129 foot-kips. If an additional 40 pounds (0.004 kips) of beam weight is added to the load and the moment recalculated, the resulting moment is 127.1 foot-kips, well under the maximum allowable of 129.

The other way to select the beam is to use the Allowable Loads on Beams tables in the AISC manual. One page is reproduced in Table 10.5. These tables make it very easy to calculate allowable loads for a given size beam, select a beam for a given span and loading, find deflections and shear values, and check for unbraced lengths. The tables take into account the weight of the beams, but these should be deducted to determine the net load that the beam will support.

The tables are for uniformly loaded beams, but they can be used for concentrated loads by using the table of concentrated load equivalents in the AISC manual, which gives factors for converting concentrated loads to uniform loads. In Table 10.5, the notation L_c is used to denote the maximum unbraced length of the compression flange, in feet, for which the allowable loads for compact symmetrical shapes are calculated with an allowable stress of $0.66F_y$. The tables are not applicable for beams with an unbraced length greater than L_u.

Keep in mind that for relatively short spans, the allowable loads for beams may be limited by the shear stress in the web instead of by the maximum bending stress. Loads above the heavy line in the tables are limited by the maximum allowable web shear.

When the spacing of lateral bracing exceeds L_c but is less than L_u, the tabulated loads must be reduced by a ratio of F_b for non-compact sections to F_b for compact sections, or 21.6/23.8, which is 0.91. (Note that the values for F_b shown in Table 10.2 have been rounded off.) To use the tables, take the tabulated load and multiply by 0.91.

Example 10.2

An A36 beam, fully laterally supported, spans 15 feet and carries a uniform load of 1700 pounds per foot. If there is only space for a 12-inch deep beam, what size section should be used? If the beam is only laterally supported at its third points, could the same beam be used?

1700 pounds per foot is 1.7 kips per foot, so the total load on the beam is 1.7 times 15 feet or 25.5 kips.

Table 10.3
Properties of Wide Flange Shapes

W SHAPES — Properties

Designation	Nom. Wt. per Ft. (Lb)	$b_f/2t_f$	F'_y (Ksi)	d/t_w	F'''_y (Ksi)	r_T (In)	d/A_f	I_x (In⁴)	S_x (In³)	r_x (In)	I_y (In⁴)	S_y (In³)	r_y (In)	J (In⁴)	Z_x (In³)	Z_y (In³)
W 12x336	336	2.3	—	9.5	—	3.71	0.43	4060	483	6.41	1190	177	3.47	243	603	274
x305	305	2.4	—	10.0	—	3.67	0.46	3550	435	6.29	1050	159	3.42	185	537	244
x279	279	2.7	—	10.4	—	3.64	0.49	3110	393	6.16	937	143	3.38	143	481	220
x252	252	2.9	—	11.0	—	3.59	0.53	2720	353	6.06	828	127	3.34	108	428	196
x230	230	3.1	—	11.7	—	3.56	0.56	2420	321	5.97	742	115	3.31	83.8	386	177
x210	210	3.4	—	12.5	—	3.53	0.61	2140	292	5.89	664	104	3.28	64.7	348	159
x190	190	3.7	—	13.6	—	3.50	0.65	1890	263	5.82	589	93.0	3.25	48.8	311	143
x170	170	4.0	—	14.6	—	3.47	0.72	1650	235	5.74	517	82.3	3.22	35.6	275	126
x152	152	4.5	—	15.8	—	3.44	0.79	1430	209	5.66	454	72.8	3.19	25.8	243	111
x136	136	5.0	—	17.0	—	3.41	0.87	1240	186	5.58	398	64.2	3.16	18.5	214	98.0
x120	120	5.6	—	18.5	—	3.38	0.96	1070	163	5.51	345	56.0	3.13	12.9	186	85.4
x106	106	6.2	—	21.1	—	3.36	1.07	933	145	5.47	301	49.3	3.11	9.13	164	75.1
x 96	96	6.8	—	23.1	—	3.34	1.16	833	131	5.44	270	44.4	3.09	6.86	147	67.5
x 87	87	7.5	—	24.3	—	3.32	1.28	740	118	5.38	241	39.7	3.07	5.10	132	60.4
x 79	79	8.2	62.6	26.3	—	3.31	1.39	662	107	5.34	216	35.8	3.05	3.84	119	54.3
x 72	72	9.0	52.3	28.5	—	3.29	1.52	597	97.4	5.31	195	32.4	3.04	2.93	108	49.2
x 65	65	9.9	43.0	31.1	—	3.28	1.67	533	87.9	5.28	174	29.1	3.02	2.18	96.8	44.1
W 12x 58	58	7.8	—	33.9	57.6	2.72	1.90	475	78.0	5.28	107	21.4	2.51	2.10	86.4	32.5
x 53	53	8.7	55.9	35.0	54.1	2.71	2.10	425	70.6	5.23	95.8	19.2	2.48	1.58	77.9	29.1
W 12x 50	50	6.3	—	32.9	60.9	2.17	2.36	394	64.7	5.18	56.3	13.9	1.96	1.78	72.4	21.4
x 45	45	7.0	—	36.0	51.0	2.15	2.61	350	58.1	5.15	50.0	12.4	1.94	1.31	64.7	19.0
x 40	40	7.8	—	40.5	40.3	2.14	2.90	310	51.9	5.13	44.1	11.0	1.93	0.95	57.5	16.8
W 12x 35	35	6.3	—	41.7	38.0	1.74	3.66	285	45.6	5.25	24.5	7.47	1.54	0.74	51.2	11.5
x 30	30	7.4	—	47.5	29.3	1.73	4.30	238	38.6	5.21	20.3	6.24	1.52	0.46	43.1	9.56
x 26	26	8.5	57.9	53.1	23.4	1.72	4.95	204	33.4	5.17	17.3	5.34	1.51	0.30	37.2	8.17
W 12x 22	22	4.7	—	47.3	29.5	1.02	7.19	156	25.4	4.91	4.66	2.31	0.847	0.29	29.3	3.66
x 19	19	5.7	—	51.7	24.7	1.00	8.67	130	21.3	4.82	3.76	1.88	0.822	0.18	24.7	2.98
x 16	16	7.5	—	54.5	22.2	0.96	11.3	103	17.1	4.67	2.82	1.41	0.773	0.10	20.1	2.26
x 14	14	8.8	54.3	59.6	18.6	0.95	13.3	88.6	14.9	4.62	2.36	1.19	0.753	0.07	17.4	1.90

W SHAPES — Dimensions

Designation	Area A (In²)	Depth d (In)	Depth d (fraction)	Web Thickness t_w (In)	$t_w/2$ (In)	Flange Width b_f (In)	Flange Width (fraction)	Flange Thickness t_f (In)	Flange Thickness (fraction)	T (In)	k (In)	k_1 (In)
W 12x336	98.8	16.82	16 7/8	1.775	7/8	13.385	13 3/8	2.955	2 15/16	9 1/2	3 11/16	1 1/2
x305	89.6	16.32	16 3/8	1.625	13/16	13.235	13 1/4	2.705	2 11/16	9 1/2	3 7/16	1 7/16
x279	81.9	15.85	15 7/8	1.530	3/4	13.140	13 1/8	2.470	2 1/2	9 1/2	3 3/16	1 3/8
x252	74.1	15.41	15 3/8	1.395	11/16	13.005	13	2.250	2 1/4	9 1/2	2 15/16	1 5/16
x230	67.7	15.05	15	1.285	11/16	12.895	12 7/8	2.070	2 1/16	9 1/2	2 3/4	1 1/4
x210	61.8	14.71	14 3/4	1.180	5/8	12.790	12 3/4	1.900	1 7/8	9 1/2	2 5/8	1 1/4
x190	55.8	14.38	14 3/8	1.060	1/2	12.670	12 5/8	1.735	1 3/4	9 1/2	2 7/16	1 3/16
x170	50.0	14.03	14	0.960	1/2	12.570	12 5/8	1.560	1 9/16	9 1/2	2 1/4	1 1/8
x152	44.7	13.71	13 3/4	0.870	7/16	12.480	12 1/2	1.400	1 3/8	9 1/2	2 1/8	1 1/16
x136	39.9	13.41	13 3/8	0.790	3/8	12.400	12 3/8	1.250	1 1/4	9 1/2	1 15/16	1
x120	35.3	13.12	13 1/8	0.710	3/8	12.320	12 3/8	1.105	1 1/8	9 1/2	1 13/16	1
x106	31.2	12.89	12 7/8	0.610	5/16	12.220	12 1/4	0.990	1	9 1/2	1 11/16	15/16
x 96	28.2	12.71	12 3/4	0.550	5/16	12.160	12 1/8	0.900	7/8	9 1/2	1 5/8	7/8
x 87	25.6	12.53	12 1/2	0.515	1/4	12.125	12 1/8	0.810	13/16	9 1/2	1 1/2	7/8
x 79	23.2	12.38	12 3/8	0.470	1/4	12.080	12 1/8	0.735	3/4	9 1/2	1 7/16	7/8
x 72	21.1	12.25	12 1/4	0.430	1/4	12.040	12	0.670	11/16	9 1/2	1 3/8	7/8
x 65	19.1	12.12	12 1/8	0.390	3/16	12.000	12	0.605	5/8	9 1/2	1 5/16	13/16
W 12x 58	17.0	12.19	12 1/4	0.360	3/16	10.010	10	0.640	5/8	9 1/2	1 3/8	13/16
x 53	15.6	12.06	12	0.345	3/16	9.995	10	0.575	9/16	9 1/2	1 1/4	13/16
W 12x 50	14.7	12.19	12 1/4	0.370	3/16	8.080	8 1/8	0.640	5/8	9 1/2	1 3/8	13/16
x 45	13.2	12.06	12	0.335	3/16	8.045	8	0.575	9/16	9 1/2	1 1/4	13/16
x 40	11.8	11.94	12	0.295	3/16	8.005	8	0.515	1/2	9 1/2	1 1/4	3/4
W 12x 35	10.3	12.50	12 1/2	0.300	3/16	6.560	6 1/2	0.520	1/2	10 1/2	1	9/16
x 30	8.79	12.34	12 3/8	0.260	1/8	6.520	6 1/2	0.440	7/16	10 1/2	15/16	1/2
x 26	7.65	12.22	12 1/4	0.230	1/8	6.490	6 1/2	0.380	3/8	10 1/2	7/8	1/2
W 12x 22	6.48	12.31	12 1/4	0.260	1/8	4.030	4	0.425	7/16	10 1/2	7/8	1/2
x 19	5.57	12.16	12 1/8	0.235	1/8	4.005	4	0.350	3/8	10 1/2	13/16	1/2
x 16	4.71	11.99	12	0.220	1/8	3.990	4	0.265	1/4	10 1/2	3/4	1/2
x 14	4.16	11.91	11 7/8	0.200	1/8	3.970	4	0.225	1/4	10 1/2	11/16	1/2

Reprinted from Manual of Steel Construction, 8th ed., American Institute of Steel Construction

Table 10.4
Section Modulus and Moment of Resistance
of Selected Structural Shapes

S_X ALLOWABLE STRESS DESIGN SELECTION TABLE
For shapes used as beams

$F_y = 50$ ksi			S_x	Shape	Depth d	F_y'	$F_y = 36$ ksi		
L_c	L_u	M_R					L_c	L_u	M_R
Ft.	Ft.	Kip-ft.	In.^{3}		In.	Ksi	Ft.	Ft.	Kip-ft.
5.6	**6.0**	**260**	94.5	**W 21x50**	$20\frac{7}{8}$	—	**6.9**	**7.8**	**189**
6.4	10.3	254	92.2	W 16x57	$16\frac{3}{8}$	—	7.5	14.3	184
9.0	15.5	254	92.2	W 14x61	$13\frac{7}{8}$	—	10.6	21.5	184
6.7	**7.9**	**244**	88.9	**W 18x50**	18	—	**7.9**	**11.0**	**178**
10.7	20.0	238	87.9	W 12x65	$12\frac{1}{8}$	43.0	12.7	27.7	176
4.7	**5.9**	**224**	81.6	**W 21x44**	$20\frac{5}{8}$	—	**6.6**	**7.0**	**163**
6.3	9.1	223	81.0	W 16x50	$16\frac{1}{4}$	—	7.5	12.7	162
5.4	6.8	217	78.8	W 18x46	18	—	6.4	9.4	158
9.0	17.5	215	78.0	W 12x58	$12\frac{1}{4}$	—	10.6	24.4	156
7.2	12.7	214	77.8	W 14x53	$13\frac{7}{8}$	—	8.5	17.7	156
6.3	8.2	200	72.7	W 16x45	$16\frac{1}{8}$	—	7.4	11.4	145
9.0	15.9	194	70.6	W 12x53	12	55.9	10.6	22.0	141
7.2	11.5	193	70.3	W 14x48	$13\frac{3}{4}$	—	8.5	16.0	141
5.4	**5.9**	**188**	68.4	**W 18x40**	$17\frac{7}{8}$	—	**6.3**	**8.2**	**137**
9.0	22.4	183	66.7	W 10x60	$10\frac{1}{4}$	—	10.6	31.1	133
6.3	**7.4**	**178**	64.7	**W 16x40**	16	—	**7.4**	**10.2**	**129**
7.2	14.1	178	64.7	W 12x50	$12\frac{1}{4}$	—	8.5	19.6	129
7.2	10.4	172	62.7	W 14x43	$13\frac{5}{8}$	—	8.4	14.4	125
9.0	20.3	165	60.0	W 10x54	$10\frac{1}{8}$	63.5	10.6	28.2	120
7.2	12.8	160	58.1	W 12x45	12	—	8.5	17.7	116
4.8	**5.6**	**158**	57.6	**W 18x35**	$17\frac{3}{4}$	—	**6.3**	**6.7**	**115**
6.3	6.7	155	56.5	W 16x36	$15\frac{7}{8}$	64.0	7.4	8.8	113
6.1	8.3	150	54.6	W 14x38	$14\frac{1}{8}$	—	7.1	11.5	109
9.0	18.7	150	54.6	W 10x49	10	53.0	10.6	26.0	109
7.2	11.5	143	51.9	W 12x40	12	—	8.4	16.0	104
7.2	16.4	135	49.1	W 10x45	$10\frac{1}{8}$	—	8.5	22.8	98
6.0	**7.3**	**134**	48.6	**W 14x34**	14	—	**7.1**	**10.2**	**97**
4.9	5.2	130	47.2	W 16x31	$15\frac{7}{8}$	—	5.8	7.1	94
5.9	9.1	125	45.6	W 12x35	$12\frac{1}{2}$	—	6.9	12.6	91
7.2	14.2	116	42.1	W 10x39	$9\frac{7}{8}$	—	8.4	19.8	84
6.0	**6.5**	**116**	42.0	**W 14x30**	$13\frac{7}{8}$	55.3	**7.1**	**8.7**	**84**
5.8	**7.8**	**106**	38.6	**W 12x30**	$12\frac{3}{8}$	—	**6.9**	**10.8**	**77**
4.0	**5.1**	**106**	38.4	**W 16x26**	$15\frac{3}{4}$	—	**5.6**	**6.0**	**77**
4.5	5.1	97	35.3	W 14x26	$13\frac{7}{8}$	—	5.3	7.0	71
7.1	11.9	96	35.0	W 10x33	$9\frac{3}{4}$	50.5	8.4	16.5	70
5.8	**6.7**	**92**	33.4	**W 12x26**	$12\frac{1}{4}$	57.9	**6.9**	**9.4**	**67**
5.2	9.4	89	32.4	W 10x30	$10\frac{1}{2}$	—	6.1	13.1	65
7.2	16.3	86	31.2	W 8x35	$8\frac{1}{8}$	64.4	8.5	22.6	62

Reprinted from Manual of Steel Construction, 8th ed.,
American Institute of Steel Construction

Table 10.4 (cont'd)
Section Modulus and Moment of Resistance
of Selected Structural Shapes

ALLOWABLE STRESS DESIGN SELECTION TABLE S_x
For shapes used as beams

$F_y = 50$ ksi			S_x	Shape	Depth d	F_y'	$F_y = 36$ ksi		
L_c	L_u	M_R					L_c	L_u	M_R
Ft.	Ft.	Kip-ft.	In.^{3}		In.	Ksi	Ft.	Ft.	Kip-ft.
4.1	4.7	80	29.0	W 14x22	13¾	—	5.3	5.6	58
5.2	8.2	77	27.9	W 10x26	10⅜	—	6.1	11.4	56
7.2	14.5	76	27.5	W 8x31	8	50.0	8.4	20.1	55
3.6	4.6	70	25.4	W 12x22	12¼	—	4.3	6.4	51
5.9	12.6	67	24.3	W 8x28	8	—	6.9	17.5	49
5.2	6.8	64	23.2	W 10x22	10⅛	—	6.1	9.4	46
3.6	3.8	59	21.3	W 12x19	12⅛	—	4.2	5.3	43
2.6	3.4	58	21.1	M 14x18	14	—	3.6	4.0	42
5.8	10.9	57	20.9	W 8x24	7⅞	64.1	6.9	15.2	42
3.6	5.2	52	18.8	W 10x19	10¼	—	4.2	7.2	38
4.7	8.5	50	18.2	W 8x21	8¼	—	5.6	11.8	36
2.9	3.6	47	17.1	W 12x16	12	—	4.1	4.3	34
5.4	14.4	46	16.7	W 6x25	6⅜	—	6.4	20.0	33
3.6	4.4	45	16.2	W 10x17	10⅛	—	4.2	6.1	32
4.7	7.1	42	15.2	W 8x18	8⅛	—	5.5	9.9	30
2.5	3.6	41	14.9	W 12x14	11⅞	54.3	3.5	4.2	30
3.6	3.7	38	13.8	W 10x15	10	—	4.2	5.0	28
5.4	11.8	37	13.4	W 6x20	6¼	62.1	6.4	16.4	27
5.3	12.5	36	13.0	M 6x20	6	—	6.3	17.4	26
1.9	2.6	33	12.0	M 12x11.8	12	—	2.7	3.0	24
3.6	5.2	32	11.8	W 8x15	8⅛	—	4.2	7.2	24
2.8	3.6	30	10.9	W 10x12	9⅞	47.5	3.9	4.3	22
3.6	8.7	28	10.2	W 6x16	6¼	—	4.3	12.0	20
4.5	14.0	28	10.2	W 5x19	5⅛	—	5.3	19.5	20
3.6	4.3	27	9.91	W 8x13	8	—	4.2	5.9	20
5.4	8.7	25	9.72	W 6x15	6	31.8	6.3	12.0	19
4.5	13.9	26	9.63	M 5x18.9	5	—	5.3	19.3	19
4.5	12.0	23	8.51	W 5x16	5	—	5.3	16.7	17
3.4	3.7	21	7.81	W 8x10	7⅞	45.8	4.2	4.7	16
1.9	2.3	21	7.76	M 10x 9	10	—	2.6	2.7	16
3.6	6.2	20	7.31	W 6x12	6	—	4.2	8.6	15
3.5	4.8	15	5.56	W 6x 9	5⅞	50.3	4.2	6.7	11
3.6	11.2	15	5.46	W 4x13	4⅛	—	4.3	15.6	11
3.5	12.2	14	5.24	M 4x13	4	—	4.2	16.9	10
1.8	2.0	13	4.62	M 8x 6.5	8	—	2.4	2.5	9
1.7	1.8	7	2.40	M 6x 4.4	6	—	1.9	2.4	5

Reprinted from Manual of Steel Construction, 8th ed.,
American Institute of Steel Construction

Table 10.5
Allowable Loads on Beams

Fy = 36 ksi

BEAMS
W Shapes
Allowable uniform loads in kips
for beams laterally supported
For beams laterally unsupported, see page 2-146

W 12

Designation	W 12			W 12			W 12				Deflection In.
Wt./ft	50	45	40	35	30	26	22	19	16	14	
Flange Width	8⅛	8	8	6½	6½	6½	4	4	4	4	
L_c	8.50	8.50	8.40	6.90	6.90	6.90	4.30	4.20	4.10	3.50	
L_u	19.6	17.7	16.0	12.6	10.8	9.40	6.40	5.30	4.30	4.20	
Span in Feet											
3									76	69	.02
4							92	82	68	59	.03
5							80	67	54	47	.05
6				108	92	81	67	56	45	39	.07
7	130	116		103	87	76	57	48	39	34	.10
8	128	115	101	90	76	66	50	42	34	30	.13
9	114	102	91	80	68	59	45	37	30	26	.17
10	102	92	82	72	61	53	40	34	27	24	.20
11	93	84	75	66	56	48	37	31	25	21	.25
12	85	77	69	60	51	44	34	28	23	20	.29
13	79	71	63	56	47	41	31	26	21	18	.35
14	73	66	59	52	44	38	29	24	19	17	.40
15	68	61	55	48	41	35	27	22	18	16	.46
16	64	58	51	45	38	33	25	21	17	15	.52
17	60	54	48	42	36	31	24	20	16	14	.59
18	57	51	46	40	34	29	22	19	15	13	.66
19	54	48	43	38	32	28	21	18	14	12	.74
20	51	46	41	36	31	26	20	17	14	12	.82
21	49	44	39	34	29	25	19	16	13	11	.90
22	47	42	37	33	28	24	18	15	12	11	.99
23	45	40	36	31	27	23	17	15	12	10	1.08
24	43	38	34	30	25	22	17	14	11	10	1.18
25	41	37	33	29	24	21	16	13	11	9	1.28
26	39	35	32	28	24	20	15	13	10	9	1.38
28	37	33	29	26	22	19	14	12	10	8	1.61
30	34	31	27	24	20	18	13	11	9	8	1.84

Properties and Reaction Values

	50	45	40	35	30	26	22	19	16	14	
S_x in.^{3}	64.7	58.1	51.9	45.6	38.6	33.4	25.4	21.3	17.1	14.9	
V kips	65	58	51	54	46	40	46	41	38	34	For explanation of deflection, see page 2-32
R_1 kips	30.2	24.9	21.9	17.8	14.5	12.0	13.5	11.3	9.80	8.17	
R_2 kips/in.	8.79	7.96	7.01	7.13	6.18	5.46	6.18	5.58	5.23	4.75	
R_3 kips	36.7	30.0	23.5	24.2	17.9	13.9	17.6	13.7	10.8	8.65	
R_4 kips/in.	3.97	3.32	2.56	2.54	1.98	1.60	2.06	1.87	2.05	1.83	
R kips	51	42	32	33	25	20	25	20	18	15	

Load above heavy line is limited by maximum allowable web shear.

Reprinted from Manual of Steel Construction 9th ed.,
American Institute of Steel Construction

Example 10.2 (cont'd)

Looking in Table 10.5, the lightest weight 12-inch section that can support 25.5 kips is a W 12 × 22 (which has a uniform load value of 27 kips).

If the beam was only supported at its third points (every 5 feet), this distance would exceed the L_c value for a W 12 × 22 (4.3 feet, from Table 10.5). Because the unsupported length is more than 4.3 feet but less than the L_u of the same beam (6.4 feet), the allowable load must be reduced by the ratio of 0.91. The new allowable load is now 27 × 0.91, or 24.57 kips. This is less than the 25.5 kips required by the problem, so try the next larger beam that can support 35 kips. More importantly, its L_c is 6.9, which is more than the 5 foot distance of lateral bracing. Therefore, this beam is acceptable.

Example 10.3

A W 12 × 45 beam of A36 steel spans 21 feet. What is the maximum load per foot this beam can carry?

Looking in Table 10.5 for a W 12 × 45 beam, the total allowable load for a 21-foot span is 44 kips. Dividing by 21, the allowable load per foot is

$$\frac{44}{21} = 2.09 \text{ kips per foot}$$

C. Design for Shear

In most cases, shear is not a factor when designing steel beams. The section selected to resist the required bending stresses is typically more than adequate to resist shear. However, shear should be checked, especially for short, heavily loaded beams or beams with heavy loads near the supports. In these cases, shear may govern the design of the beam.

Because shearing stresses are not distributed evenly over the cross section and are zero at the extreme fibers, the flanges are discounted in calculating resistance to shear; only the area of the web is used. The unit shearing stress is given by the formula:

$$f_v = \frac{V}{d} \times t_w \qquad 10.4$$

Example 10.4

Check the shear in the beam in Example 10.2.

Since the total load on the beam is 25.5 kips, the maximum vertical shear at one support is one-half this, or 12.25 kips. Looking in Table 10.3 for a W 12 × 22 beam, the actual depth is 12.31 inches, and the web thickness is 0.260 inches. The actual unit shear stress is:

$$f_v = 12.25/12.31 \times 0.260$$
$$= 3.83 \text{ ksi}$$

From Table 10.2, the allowable shear on gross sections is 14.5 ksi. The area of the web is 12.31 × 0.260 = 3.2 square inches. The allowable shear force is:

$$V = 14.5 \times 3.2 = 46.4 \text{ kips}$$

This allowable shear can also be found at the bottom of Table 10.5 under the row labeled V. In this case it is rounded to 46 kips.

D. Design for Deflection

Steel beams need to be checked for deflection. Although a beam may be sufficient to resist bending stresses, it may sag enough to be objectionable or create problems such as cracking of finished ceilings or ponding of water on a roof. The maximum allowable deflection is partly determined by codes and partly by design judgment. For example, the AISC limits the live load deflection of beams supporting plaster ceilings to 1/360 of the span.

Deflection can be calculated in one of two ways: by using the deflection formulas for various static loads as given in Figure 4.12 and in the AISC manual, or by using tables. Both methods will be illustrated here.

Example 10.5

Find the actual deflection of the W 12 × 22 beam used in Example 10.2.

Using the formula for maximum deflection of a uniformly loaded beam as given in Figure 4.12:

$$\Delta = \frac{5wl^4}{384EI}$$

Note that all units must be consistent. In this example, the units are converted to inches. Since the load in Example 10.2 was 1700 pounds per foot and the weight of the beam is 22 pounds per foot, the total load is 1722 pounds per foot, or 143.5 pounds per linear inch (1722/12). The span must also be converted to inches. From Table 10.3, the moment of inertia for a W 12 × 22 beam is 156 in^4. The modulus of elasticity for steel is 29,000,000 psi.

$$\Delta = \frac{5 \times 143.5 \times (15 \times 12)^4}{384 \times 29,000,000 \times 156}$$

$$= 0.434 \text{ inches}$$

The other way to find deflection is to use the deflection constant in the allowable load tables in the AISC manual (Table 10.5). The maximum deflection under the maximum allowable load is shown in the last column in Table 10.5 as 0.46 for a 15-foot span.

However, remember that this formula gives the deflection under the maximum loading based on the uniform load constant and not on the actual load which is usually somewhat less. The actual deflection can be found by multiplying the maximum deflection by the ratio of the total design load to the total allowable load.

The design load is 25.5 kips. Dividing this by the maximum allowable load of 27 kips found in the table, a ratio of 0.944 is obtained. 0.944 × 0.46 (the deflection from the table) is 0.434 inches, the same as found by using the standard deflection formula.

If deflection was to be limited to 1/360 of the span, the maximum allowable deflection would be:

$$\Delta = \frac{15 \times 12}{360}$$

$$= 0.50 \text{ inches}$$

The actual deflection in this example is less than the maximum, so the selected beam works in deflection. Note that the beam length of 15 feet had to be converted to inches by multiplying by 12.

3 STEEL COLUMNS

As with columns of any material, the amount of load a steel column can support depends not only on its area and allowable unit stress, but also the unbraced length of the column. As discussed in Chapter 4, columns of moderate to long length tend to fail first by buckling under load. The properties of a column that resist buckling are the area and the moment of inertia. These are mathematically combined into the radius of gyration. For a non-symmetrical column, the radius of gyration is different in each axis. Review the section on columns in Chapter 4 for a further explanation.

The effect of a column's unbraced length and radius of gyration is combined in the slenderness ratio which is defined for steel columns as the ratio of a column's length in inches to the radius of gyration:

$$\text{slenderness ratio} = l/r \qquad 10.5$$

In general, the greater the slenderness ratio, the greater the tendency for the column to fail under buckling, and, therefore, the less load the column can carry. Because most steel columns are not symmetrical about both axes (such as with a wide flange shape), the least radius of gyration governs for design purposes because it is about this axis that the column will fail first. The radii of gyration, r, about both axes are given in the AISC manual, and some representative values are shown in Table 10.3.

Ideally, for the most efficient column, the radius of gyration should be the same in each direction such as with a pipe column or a square tube column. For light to moderate loads, these types of sections are often used as columns for this reason. However, they are not appropriate for heavy loads and where many beam connections must be made. Wide flange sections are most often used because the radius of gyration in the y-y axis is close to the radius of gyration in the x-x axis. There are special wide flange sections specifically manufactured to provide nearly symmetrical columns with large load-carrying capacities. Most of these are 12 and 14 inches in nominal depth.

The allowable axial compressive stress, F_a, in steel columns depends on the slenderness ratio and the allowable yield stress of the steel. The exact value of the allowable stress is calculated with several rather complex equations based on the Euler equation discussed in Chapter 4. The specific equation to be used depends on the slenderness ratio of the column. Once the allowable stress is determined, the basic equation for axial loading can be used:

$$P = F_a A \qquad 10.10$$

A. End Conditions

There is one additional variable that affects steel column design: the method in which the ends of the columns are fixed. Columns ends can be in one of four states. They can be fixed against both rotation and translation (side-to-side movement) such as with a column embedded in concrete or with a moment resisting connection. They can be fixed in rotation but free in translation. They can be fixed in translation but free to rotate. Finally, they can be free to both rotate and move side to side like the top of a flag pole.

How the ends are fixed affects the ability of a column to resist axial loads, so the AISC introduces a value, K, to modify the unbraced length of a column when calculating the slenderness ratio. Multiplying the K value by the actual unbraced length gives the effective length of the column. The entire formula for slenderness ratio then becomes:

$$\text{slenderness ratio } = \frac{Kl}{r} \qquad 10.11$$

Value for the various end conditions are given in Figure 10.2. For most building conditions, the value of K is taken as 1.0.

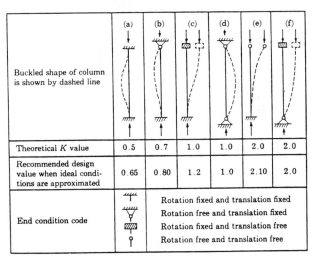

	(a)	(b)	(c)	(d)	(e)	(f)
Buckled shape of column is shown by dashed line						
Theoretical K value	0.5	0.7	1.0	1.0	2.0	2.0
Recommended design value when ideal conditions are approximated	0.65	0.80	1.2	1.0	2.10	2.0
End condition code	Rotation fixed and translation fixed					
	Rotation free and translation fixed					
	Rotation fixed and translation free					
	Rotation free and translation free					

Reprinted from Manual of Steel Construction, 8th ed., American Institute of Steel Construction

Figure 10.2 K Values for Various End Conditions

Example 10.6

A W 12 × 120 column 13 feet high is fixed at the top and bottom in both rotation and translation. What is the effective slenderness ratio?

Looking in Table 10.3, the radius of gyration for a W 12 × 120 section is 5.51 in the x-axis and 3.13 in the y-axis. Figure 10.2 gives the recommended K value for fixed top and bottom ends as 0.65. The slenderness ratio is:

$$\text{slenderness ratio } = \frac{0.65 \times 13 \times 12}{3.13} = 32.4$$

Note that the length must be converted to inches and that the least radius of gyration must be used.

B. Design for Axial Compression

As with most steel design, calculation can be done with formulas or with tables in the AISC manual. Both will be illustrated here. Even though the column formulas to determine allowable axial stress are complicated, the AISC manual has tabulated allowable stress values based on the slenderness ratio and the allowable yield stress of the steel being used. One of these tables is shown in Table 10.6 for Kl/r values of 1 to 200. Kl/r values over 200 are not allowed.

Example 10.7

A W 12 × 26 column of A36 steel has an unsupported length of 18 feet. If it is free to rotate but fixed in translation at both ends, what is the column's maximum load-carrying capacity?

Looking in Table 10.3, a W 12 × 26 section has an area of 7.65 square inches and a least radius of gyration of 1.51 inches.

The K value for this type of column is 1.0, so the Kl/r is:

$$\frac{1.0 \times 18 \times 12}{1.51} = 143$$

Looking in Table 10.6, the allowable axial stress, F_a, is 7.30 ksi. Using formula 10.10, the maximum load is then:

$$P = F_a A$$
$$= 7.30 \times 7.65$$
$$= 55.85 \text{ kips}$$

The other design method involves use of tables of allowable column loads. These are found in the AISC

Table 10.6
Allowable Stress for Compression Members Based on Kl/r Ratio

$F_y = 36$ ksi

Allowable Stress For Compression Members of 36-ksi Specified Yield Stress Steel[a]									
$\frac{Kl}{r}$	F_a (ksi)	$\frac{Kl}{r}$	F_a (ksi)	$\frac{Kl}{r}$	F_a (ksi)	$\frac{Kl}{r}$	F_a (ksi)	$\frac{Kl}{r}$	F_a (ksi)
1	21.56	41	19.11	81	15.24	121	10.14	161	5.76
2	21.52	42	19.03	82	15.13	122	9.99	162	5.69
3	21.48	43	18.95	83	15.02	123	9.85	163	5.62
4	21.44	44	18.86	84	14.90	124	9.70	164	5.55
5	21.39	45	18.78	85	14.79	125	9.55	165	5.49
6	21.35	46	18.70	86	14.67	126	9.41	166	5.42
7	21.30	47	18.61	87	14.56	127	9.26	167	5.35
8	21.25	48	18.53	88	14.44	128	9.11	168	5.29
9	21.21	49	18.44	89	14.32	129	8.97	169	5.23
10	21.16	50	18.35	90	14.20	130	8.84	170	5.17
11	21.10	51	18.26	91	14.09	131	8.70	171	5.11
12	21.05	52	18.17	92	13.97	132	8.57	172	5.05
13	21.00	53	18.08	93	13.84	133	8.44	173	4.99
14	20.95	54	17.99	94	13.72	134	8.32	174	4.93
15	20.89	55	17.90	95	13.60	135	8.19	175	4.88
16	20.83	56	17.81	96	13.48	136	8.07	176	4.82
17	20.78	57	17.71	97	13.35	137	7.96	177	4.77
18	20.72	58	17.62	98	13.23	138	7.84	178	4.71
19	20.66	59	17.53	99	13.10	139	7.73	179	4.66
20	20.60	60	17.43	100	12.98	140	7.62	180	4.61
21	20.54	61	17.33	101	12.85	141	7.51	181	4.56
22	20.48	62	17.24	102	12.72	142	7.41	182	4.51
23	20.41	63	17.14	103	12.59	143	7.30	183	4.46
24	20.35	64	17.04	104	12.47	144	7.20	184	4.41
25	20.28	65	16.94	105	12.33	145	7.10	185	4.36
26	20.22	66	16.84	106	12.20	146	7.01	186	4.32
27	20.15	67	16.74	107	12.07	147	6.91	187	4.27
28	20.08	68	16.64	108	11.94	148	6.82	188	4.23
29	20.01	69	16.53	109	11.81	149	6.73	189	4.18
30	19.94	70	16.43	110	11.67	150	6.64	190	4.14
31	19.87	71	16.33	111	11.54	151	6.55	191	4.09
32	19.80	72	16.22	112	11.40	152	6.46	192	4.05
33	19.73	73	16.12	113	11.26	153	6.38	193	4.01
34	19.65	74	16.01	114	11.13	154	6.30	194	3.97
35	19.58	75	15.90	115	10.99	155	6.22	195	3.93
36	19.50	76	15.79	116	10.85	156	6.14	196	3.89
37	19.42	77	15.69	117	10.71	157	6.06	197	3.85
38	19.35	78	15.58	118	10.57	158	5.98	198	3.81
39	19.27	79	15.47	119	10.43	159	5.91	199	3.77
40	19.19	80	15.36	120	10.28	160	5.83	200	3.73

[a]When element width-to-thickness ratio exceeds noncompact section limits of Sect. B5.1, see Appendix B5.
Note: $C_c = 126.1$

Reprinted from Manual of Steel Construction 9th ed.,
American Institute of Steel Construction

manual and give allowable axial loads in kips for various wide flange shapes, pipe columns, and square structural tubing of steel with yield values of both 36 ksi and 50 ksi. One page of the AISC tables is shown in Table 10.7. The loads are arranged according to the effective length, Kl. Load values are omitted when Kl/r exceeds 200. For wide flange sections, the values are calculated with respect to the minor axis.

Example 10.8

Select the lightest 12-inch wide flange shape of A36 steel to support a concentric axial load of 225 kips if the unbraced length is 12 feet and the K value is 1.0.

Looking in Table 10.7 in the rows designated as KL equal to 12, look across under the F_y columns marked 36 to find the sections with an allowable load of 225 or greater.

Some of the possible sections include:

W 12 × 58	301 kips
W 12 × 53	275 kips
W 12 × 50	236 kips

Since the W 12 × 50 is the lightest section in this group, this is the best choice.

Note that the same design procedures apply for columns of allowable loads for pipe and tube columns.

4 BUILT-UP SECTIONS

There are many times when standard rolled sections are inadequate or uneconomical to support heavy loads or the span is exceptionally long. In these cases, special built-up sections can be fabricated to meet the special needs of the structure. One of the most typical is a *plate girder section*, which consists of a steel plate as a web and steel plates welded to it for flanges. It is similar to a wide flange or I-section in shape but is much heavier. These can easily be fabricated deeper than the maximum 36-inch deep rolled section available in the United States.

Because the web of a plate girder is thin relative to its depth, it must usually be reinforced with vertical stiffeners to prevent buckling. These are usually angle sections welded to the web perpendicular to the depth of the section as shown in Figure 10.3.

Another common built-up section is a *standard rolled section* with cover plates welded to the top and bottom flanges to provide additional cross-sectional area where the bending moment is the greatest. This combines the

advantages of using a standard section with minimizing total weight of the beam. Cover plates can also be welded to columns to provide extra cross-sectional area or to equalize the radius of gyration in one axis with that of the other axis.

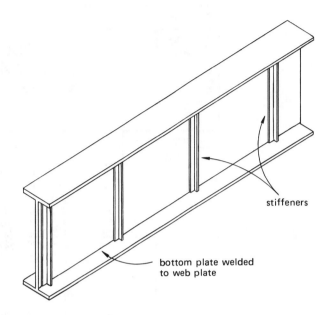

Figure 10.3 Plate Girder

5 OPEN-WEB STEEL JOISTS

Open-web steel joists are standardized, shop-fabricated trusses with webs comprised of linear members and chords which are typically parallel. However, some types have top chords which are pitched for roof drainage. See Figure 10.4.

There are three standard series of open-web joists: the *K-series*, *LH-series*, and the *DLH-series* with the properties as summarized in Table 10.8. The depths in the K-series depths increase in 2-inch increments, and the depths in the LH- and DLH-series increase in 4-inch increments. The standard designation for an open-web joist consists of the depth, the series designation, and the particular type of chord used. For example, a 36LH13 joist is a 36-inch deep joist of the LH-series with a number 13 chord type. Within any size group, the chord type number increases as the load-carrying capacity of that depth joist increases.

Open-web steel joists have many advantages for spanning medium to long distances. They are lightweight and efficient structural members, easy and quick to erect, and the open webbing allows for ductwork and other building services to be run through the joists

Table 10.7
Allowable Axial Loads for Selected
Wide Flange Columns

F_y = 36 ksi										
F_y = 50 ksi		**COLUMNS**								
		W shapes								
		Allowable axial loads in kips								

Designation		W12								
Wt./ft		58		53		50		45		40
F_y		36	50	36	50	36	50	36	50	36	50‡
Effective length in ft KL with respect to least radius of gyration r_y	0	367	510	337	468	318	441	285	396	255	354
	6	341	464	312	425	286	386	256	346	229	309
	7	335	454	307	416	279	374	250	335	223	299
	8	329	443	301	406	271	360	243	322	217	288
	9	322	432	295	395	263	346	235	309	210	276
	10	315	420	288	384	254	331	228	296	203	264
	11	308	407	282	372	246	315	220	281	196	251
	12	301	394	275	360	236	298	211	266	188	237
	13	293	380	268	347	226	281	202	250	180	222
	14	285	365	260	333	216	262	193	233	172	207
	15	276	351	252	319	206	243	183	216	163	191
	16	268	335	244	305	195	223	173	197	154	175
	18	249	302	227	274	171	181	152	159	135	141
	20	230	267	209	241	146	146	129	129	114	114
	22	209	229	189	206	121	121	106	106	94	94
	24	187	193	169	173	102	102	89	89	79	79
	26	164	164	147	147	87	87	76	76	67	67
	28	142	142	127	127	75	75	66	66	58	58
	30	123	123	111	111	65	65	57	57	51	51
	32	108	108	97	97	57	57	50	50	45	45
	34	96	96	86	86						
	38	77	77	69	69						
	41	66	66	59	59						

Properties										
U		3.21	3.21	3.24	2.94	4.10	4.10	4.12	3.75	3.77	3.77
P_{wo} (kips)		89	124	78	108	92	127	75	105	66	92
P_{wi} (kips/in.)		13	18	12	17	13	19	12	17	11	15
P_{wb} (kips)		121	142	106	125	131	155	97	115	66	78
P_{fb} (kips)		92	128	74	103	92	128	74	103	60	83
L_c (ft)		10.6	9.0	10.6	9.0	8.5	7.2	8.5	7.2	8.4	7.2
L_u (ft)		24.4	17.5	22.0	15.9	19.6	14.1	17.7	12.8	16.0	11.5

A (in.^{2})	17.0	15.6	14.7	13.2	11.8
I_x (in.^{4})	475	425	394	350	310
I_y (in.^{4})	107	95.8	56.3	50.0	44.1
r_y (in.)	2.51	2.48	1.96	1.94	1.93
Ratio r_x/r_y	2.10	2.11	2.64	2.65	2.66
B_x } Bending	0.218	0.221	0.227	0.227	0.227
B_y } factors	0.794	0.813	1.058	1.065	1.073
$a_x/10^6$	70.6	63.6	58.8	52.2	46.3
$a_y/10^6$	16.0	14.3	8.4	7.4	6.5
$F'_{ex} (K_x L_x)^2/10^2$ (kips)	289	284	278	275	273
$F'_{ey} (K_y L_y)^2/10^2$ (kips)	65.3	63.8	39.8	39.0	38.6

‡Web may be noncompact for combined axial and bending stress;
  see AISC ASD Specification Sect. B5.1.
Note: Heavy line indicates Kl/r of 200.

Reprinted from Manual of Steel Construction 9th ed.,
American Institute of Steel Construction

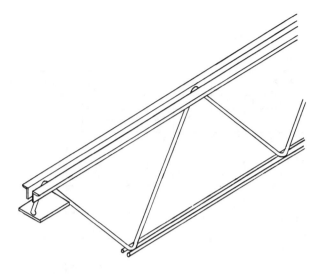

Figure 10.4   Open-Web Steel Joist

rather than under them. In addition, a variety of floor decking types can be used, from wood systems to steel and concrete deck systems. They can easily be supported by steel beams, masonry or concrete bearing walls, or by heavier open-web joist girders.

Table 10.8
Open-Web Steel Joists Series

series	name	span limits	depths in series
K	standard	8–60 feet	8″ to 30″
LH	long span	25–96 feet	18″ to 48″
DLH	deep long span	89–144 feet	52″ to 96″

Because open-web joists are deep and slender, they are subject to buckling and must be laterally supported both at the top and bottom chords. All the tables are based on the assumption that there is continuous lateral support at the top chord. The Steel Joist Institute gives minimum requirements for horizontal or diagonal bridging based on the span length and chord size.

Exact configurations of open-web joists vary with manufacturers, but certain standards have been established by the Steel Joist Institute which also publishes standard load tables for design purposes. The design tables give the load-carrying capacities in pounds per linear foot of the various joist designations based on span. In

the tables, two numbers are given. The top number gives the total safe uniformly distributed load-carrying capacity. The bottom number gives the live load per linear foot of joist, which will produce an approximate deflection of 1/360 of the span. Live loads that will produce a deflection of 1/240 of the span may be obtained by multiplying the bottom number by 1.5.

When using the tables, both the total load and live load must be determined so both of the allowable load numbers can be compared with actual loads. To use the tables, determine the span in feet and the live load and total load per linear foot. Look at the row of the required span in the table and read across until a load equal to or greater than the required total load is reached. Then look at the bottom number to determine if the allowable live load is greater than the actual live load. If either of these conditions are not met, you must look for a heavier joist in the same depth group or use a deeper section.

A portion of the design tables for the K-series is shown in Table 10.9. For the K-series, there is also an economy table which lists the various sections in order of increasing weight, so it is easier to select the most economical section in this series.

Example 10.9

Open-web joists spaced 2 feet on center span 30 feet. They support a dead load of 50 psf including an allowance for their own weight and a live load of 60 psf. If the maximum allowable deflection due to live load is 1/360 of the span, what is the most economical section to use?

First, the load must be converted to load per linear foot of joist. Since the joists are 2 feet on center, the dead load is $50 \times 2 = 100$ pounds per linear foot, and the live load is $60 \times 2 = 120$ pounds per linear foot, for a total load of 220 pounds per linear foot.

Looking in Table 10.9 across the row of 30 foot spans, there is an 18K4 which will support 245 pounds total load and 144 pounds live load. There is also a 20K3 which will support 227 pounds total load and 153 pounds live load. Both of these will work, but looking at the weight per foot you can see that the first section weighs 7.2 pounds per foot and the second section weighs 6.7 pounds per foot. Therefore, the 20K3 is the more economical section. (There is also a 16K5 joist that will work, but it is not shown in Table 10.9.)

Table 10.9

Standard Load Table for Open-Web Steel Joists, K-Series

(Based on a Maximum Allowable Tensile Stress of 30,000 psi)

Joist Designation	18K3	18K4	18K5	18K6	18K7	18K9	18K10	20K3	20K4	20K5	20K6	20K7	20K9	20K10	22K4	22K5	22K6	22K7	22K9	22K10	22K11
Depth (In.)	18	18	18	18	18	18	18	20	20	20	20	20	20	20	22	22	22	22	22	22	22
Approx. Wt. (lbs./ft.)	6.6	7.2	7.7	8.5	9.0	10.2	11.7	6.7	7.6	8.2	8.9	9.3	10.8	12.2	8.0	8.8	9.2	9.7	11.3	12.6	13.8
Span (ft.)																					
18	550	550	550	550	550	550	550														
	550	550	550	550	550	550	550														
19	514	550	550	550	550	550	550														
	494	523	523	523	523	523	523														
20	463	550	550	550	550	550	550	517	550	550	550	550	550	550							
	423	490	490	490	490	490	490	517	550	550	550	550	550	550							
21	420	506	550	550	550	550	550	468	550	550	550	550	550	550							
	364	426	460	460	460	460	460	453	520	520	520	520	520	520							
22	382	460	518	550	550	550	550	426	514	550	550	550	550	550	550	550	550	550	550	550	550
	316	370	414	438	438	438	438	393	461	490	490	490	490	490	548	548	548	548	548	548	548
23	349	420	473	516	550	550	550	389	469	529	550	550	550	550	518	550	550	550	550	550	550
	276	323	362	393	418	418	418	344	402	451	468	468	468	468	491	518	518	518	518	518	518
24	320	385	434	473	526	550	550	357	430	485	528	550	550	550	475	536	550	550	550	550	550
	242	284	318	345	382	396	396	302	353	396	430	448	448	448	431	483	495	495	495	495	495
25	294	355	400	435	485	550	550	329	396	446	486	541	550	550	438	493	537	550	550	550	550
	214	250	281	305	337	377	377	266	312	350	380	421	426	426	381	427	464	474	474	474	474
26	272	328	369	402	448	538	550	304	366	412	449	500	550	550	404	455	496	550	550	550	550
	190	222	249	271	299	354	361	236	277	310	337	373	405	405	338	379	411	454	454	454	454
27	252	303	342	372	415	498	550	281	339	382	416	463	550	550	374	422	459	512	550	550	550
	169	198	222	241	267	315	347	211	247	277	301	333	389	389	301	337	367	406	432	432	432
28	234	282	318	346	385	463	548	261	315	355	386	430	517	550	348	392	427	475	550	550	550
	151	177	199	216	239	282	331	189	221	248	269	298	353	375	270	302	328	364	413	413	413
29	218	263	296	322	359	431	511	243	293	330	360	401	482	550	324	365	398	443	532	550	550
	136	159	179	194	215	254	298	170	199	223	242	268	317	359	242	272	295	327	387	399	399
30	203	245	276	301	335	402	477	227	274	308	336	374	450	533	302	341	371	413	497	550	550
	123	144	161	175	194	229	269	153	179	201	218	242	286	336	219	245	266	295	349	385	385
31	190	229	258	281	313	376	446	212	256	289	314	350	421	499	283	319	347	387	465	550	550
	111	130	146	158	175	207	243	138	162	182	198	219	259	304	198	222	241	267	316	369	369
32	178	215	242	264	294	353	418	199	240	271	295	328	395	468	265	299	326	363	436	517	549
	101	118	132	144	159	188	221	126	147	165	179	199	235	276	180	201	219	242	287	337	355
33	168	202	228	248	276	332	393	187	226	254	277	309	371	440	249	281	306	341	410	486	532
	92	108	121	131	145	171	201	114	134	150	163	181	214	251	164	183	199	221	261	307	334
34	158	190	214	233	260	312	370	176	212	239	261	290	349	414	235	265	288	321	386	458	516
	84	98	110	120	132	156	184	105	122	137	149	165	195	229	149	167	182	202	239	280	314
35	149	179	202	220	245	294	349	166	200	226	246	274	329	390	221	249	272	303	364	432	494
	77	90	101	110	121	143	168	96	112	126	137	151	179	210	137	153	167	185	219	257	292
36	141	169	191	208	232	278	330	157	189	213	232	259	311	369	209	236	257	286	344	408	467
	70	82	92	101	111	132	154	88	103	115	125	139	164	193	126	141	153	169	201	236	269
37								148	179	202	220	245	294	349	198	223	243	271	325	386	442
								81	95	106	115	128	151	178	116	130	141	156	185	217	247
38								141	170	191	208	232	279	331	187	211	230	256	308	366	419
								74	87	98	106	118	139	164	107	119	130	144	170	200	228
39								133	161	181	198	220	265	314	178	200	218	243	292	347	397
								69	81	90	98	109	129	151	98	110	120	133	157	185	211
40								127	153	172	188	209	251	298	169	190	207	231	278	330	377
								64	75	84	91	101	119	140	91	102	111	123	146	171	195
41															161	181	197	220	264	314	359
															85	95	103	114	135	159	181
42															153	173	188	209	252	299	342
															79	83	96	106	126	148	168
43															146	165	179	200	240	285	326
															73	82	89	99	117	138	157
44															139	157	171	191	229	272	311
															68	76	83	92	109	128	146

Reproduced from "Standard Specifications, Load Tables, and Weight Tables for Steel Joists and Joist Girders," with permission from the Steel Joist Institute. The Steel Joist Institute publishes both Specifications and Load Tables; each of these contains standards which are to be used in conjunction with one another.

SAMPLE QUESTIONS

The answers to questions 1 through 3 can be found on the following key list. Select only one answer for each question.

    A0 A36 steel
    A1 American Standard sections
    A2 buckling
    A3 built-up sections
    A4 carbon steel
    A5 compact sections
    A6 double-extra strong pipe
    A7 ductility
    A8 flexure
    A9 high modulus of elasticity

    B0 lateral support
    B1 plate girders
    B2 radius of gyration
    B3 slenderness ratio
    B4 uniform load constant
    B5 wide flanges

1. What is most often used for columns in steel construction?

2. What is the most important consideration in column design?

3. What property of steel makes it good for earthquake-resistant structures?

4. A steel girder supports a concentrated load of 12 kips at its center. If the girder is A36 steel, spans 16 feet, and is laterally supported, what is the most economical section that can support the load?

    A. W 8 × 24
    B. W 8 × 28
    C. W 12 × 16
    D. W 12 × 22

5. Open-web steel joists are to span 27 feet and are placed 2 1/2 feet on center. A maximum depth of 20 inches is allowed for the joist. The live load is 80 psf, the dead load is 40 psf, and the maximum deflection is limited to 1/360 of the span. What is the best joist to use?

    A. 18K4
    B. 18K5

    C. 20K4
    D. 20K6

6. A W 12 × 50 beam of A36 steel spans 22 feet. What maximum load per foot can the beam support, and what is the maximum allowable unsupported length?

    A. 2.1 kips per foot; 8.5 feet
    B. 2.1 kips per foot; 19.6 feet
    C. 2.2 kips per foot; 8.5 feet
    D. 2.2 kips per foot; 19.6 feet

7. A W 12 × 50 column of steel with $F_y = 50$ ksi has an unbraced length of 10 feet. It is rigidly fixed at the base, fixed in translation at the top, but free to rotate at the top. What is the allowable concentric load?

    A. 271 kips
    B. 360 kips
    C. 374 kips
    D. 386 kips

8. Which of the following is not true about open-web steel joists?

    A. Proper bridging is important for joists.
    B. All components of open-web joist construction conform to standards of the Steel Joist Institute.
    C. Open web joists can span up to 144 feet.
    D. The K-series is for spanning the shortest distances up to 60 feet.

9. A uniformly loaded W 12 × 45 beam spans 13 feet. If it is A36 steel, laterally supported, and carries a total load of 65,000 pounds, how much will it deflect?

    A. 0.29 inches
    B. 0.32 inches
    C. 0.35 inches
    D. 0.38 inches

10. Which of the following statements about shear in steel beams are true?

I. Shear is evenly distributed throughout the web and flanges of the beam.

II. Unit shearing stress is partly a function of the maximum vertical shear.

III. Shear stresses can be significant for beams with concentrated loads at mid-span.

IV. Shear is not usually a problem in steel beam design.

V. It is necessary to know the actual depth of a beam rather than the nominal depth when calculating the unit shearing stress.

    A. I, II, and V

    B. I, II, IV, and V

    C. II, III, and IV

    D. II, IV, and V

11 CONCRETE CONSTRUCTION

Nomenclature

a	height of rectangular stress block	inches
A_s	area of steel reinforcing	in^2
A_v	area of web reinforcement	in^2
b	width of beam	inches
b_w	width of beam, rectangular or T-beam	inches
C	resultant of compressive forces	pounds
d	effective depth of beam	inches
d_b	diameter of reinforcing bar	inches
D	calculated dead load	psf or plf
f_c'	design strength of concrete	psf
f_y	yield strength of steel	psf
l_{db}	minimum development length	inches
L	calculated live load	psf or plf
M_u	ultimate moment capacity	ft-lbs or foot-kips
p_b	percentage of steel for balanced design	
p_s	percentage of steel	
p_{max}	maximum allowable percentage of steel	
p_{min}	minimum allowable percentage of steel	
s	spacing of web reinforcement	inches
T	resultant of tension forces	pounds
U	factored load	psf, plf, or klf
V_c	design shear stress	pounds
V_u	actual shear stress	pounds
β_c	distance from top of beam to resultant of compressive force	inches
β_1	constant for finding percentage of steel	
ϕ	strength reduction factor	

Structural design of concrete is more complicated than design with steel or wood because there are more variables and the choices depend on the experience and trained judgment of the designer. In modern construction, concrete is always reinforced. This results in a non-homogeneous section with two materials of differing strengths, and structural shapes that are not symmetrical about the neutral axis. Because of these facts, concrete design is an iterative process; certain design assumptions have to be made and then tested to see if they work. If not, the assumption must be changed and new calculations made.

Currently, the strength design method is used for concrete instead of the working stress method. Although some building inspection departments still allow the working stress method in some instances, it has generally been supplanted by the newer procedure. The latest revision to the American Concrete Institute's (ACI) Building Code Requirements is based on the strength design method.

This chapter will discuss some of the basic principles of structural reinforced concrete design and show how to make some common, fairly simple design calculations.

1 CONCRETE MATERIALS AND PLACEMENT

A. Composition of Concrete

Concrete is a combination of cement, aggregates, and water mixed in the proper portions and allowed to cure to form a hard, durable material. As a construction material, it is a mixture of portland cement, sand, gravel, and water. In addition, *admixtures* are used to impart particular qualities to the mix. Since the strength of concrete depends on the materials and their proportions, it is important to understand the relationship between the constituent parts.

Cement is the binding agent in concrete. It chemically interacts with water to form a paste that binds the other aggregate particles together in a solid mass. Portland cement is a finely powdered material manufactured primarily from limestones and clays or shales. It is supplied in bulk or in 94-pound bags containing one cubic foot.

Although water is required for hydration (the chemical hardening of concrete) and to make it possible to mix and place the concrete into forms, too much water can decrease its strength. This is because excess water not used in the chemical process remains in the paste and forms pores which, of course, cannot resist compressive forces. Generally, for complete hydration to occur, an amount of water equal to 25 percent of the weight of the cement is required. An extra 10 to 15 percent or more is required to make a workable mix. The water itself must be potable, or drinkable, to ensure that it is free of any foreign matter that could interfere with adhesion of the aggregates to the cement paste.

For most concrete mixes, the minimum water-cement ratio is about 0.35 to 0.40 by weight. Based on the weight of water, this works out to about 4 to 4.5 gallons of water per 94-pound sack of cement. Because of the way water and cement interact, the water-cement ratio is the most critical factor in determining the strength of concrete. For a given mix, there should be just enough water to give a workable mix without being excessive.

Aggregates consist of coarse and fine aggregates. *Fine aggregates* are those that pass through a no. 4 sieve (one with four openings per linear inch). Since cement is the most expensive component of concrete, the best mix is one that uses a combination of aggregate sizes that fill most of the volume with a minimum amount of cement while still achieving the desired strength. Typically, aggregates occupy about 70 to 75 percent of the total volume of the concrete.

Generally, aggregates are sand and gravel, but others are used. Materials such as expanded clays, slags, and shales are used for lightweight structural concrete. Pumice or cinders are used for insulating concretes. While standard reinforced stone concrete weighs about 150 pounds per cubic foot, lightweight mixes can range from 50 pounds per cubic foot for insulating concretes to 120 pounds per cubic foot for lightweight reinforced structural concrete.

The size of *coarse aggregates* is determined by the size of the forms and the spacing between the reinforcing. In most instances, it should not be larger than three-fourths of the smallest distance between reinforcing bars, nor larger than one-fifth of the smallest dimension of forms, nor more than one-third of the depth of slabs.

Several methods are used to specify the proportions of the concrete mix. One is to define the ratio of cement to sand to gravel by weight using three numbers such as 1:2:4 which means one part cement, 2 parts sand, and 4 parts gravel. In addition, the amount of water must also be specified. Another method is to specify the weight of materials, including water, per 94-pound bag of cement. Yet another method is to define the weight of the materials needed to make up one cubic yard of concrete. This is useful for large batch quantities.

The strength of the final mix is specified by the compressive strength of the concrete after it has cured and hardened for 28 days—this is known as the *design strength of concrete.* Typical specified design strengths, indicated with the symbol, f'_c, are 2000 psi, 3000 psi (one of the most common), and 4000 psi. Higher strengths up to 12,000 psi are now available for special applications, but are more expensive than the standard mixes.

B. Admixtures

Admixtures are chemicals or other material added to concrete to impart certain qualities. Admixtures are used to speed hydration, retard hardening, improve workability, add color, improve durability, and for a variety of other purposes. The following are some of the more common admixtures.

Air-entraining agents are used to form tiny dispersed bubbles in the concrete. These agents increase the workability and durability of the concrete and improve its resistance to freezing and thawing cycles. They also help reduce segregation of the components during placing of the mix into forms.

Accelerators speed up the hydration of the cement so the concrete achieves strength faster. This allows for faster construction and reduces the length of time needed for protection in cold weather.

Plasticizers are used to reduce the amount of water needed while maintaining the consistency needed for correct placement and compaction. Reducing the water, of course, makes it possible to mix higher strength concrete.

C. Reinforcing Steel

There are three forms of reinforcing steel: bars for standard cast-in-place concrete, wire or strands for prestressing and post-tensioning, and welded wire fabric for reinforcement of slabs. Reinforcing bars, often called *rebars*, are available in diameters from 3/8 inch to 2 1/4 inches, in 1/8-inch increments up to 1 3/8 inches, and then two special large sizes of 1 3/4 inches and 2 1/4 inches. Bars are designated by numbers which represent the number of 1/8-inch increments in the nominal diameter of the bar. Thus, a number 6 bar is 6/8 inch in diameter, or 3/4 inch. A listing of the available bars and their dimensional properties is shown in the first part of Table 11.1.

Because reinforcing steel and concrete must be bonded together to provide maximum strength, rebars are deformed to provide a mechanical interlocking of the two materials. Additional bonding is provided by the chemical adhesion of the concrete to steel and by the normal roughness of the steel. There are several different types of deformation patterns, depending on the mill that manufactures the bar, but they all serve the same purpose. In order to clearly identify bars on the job site, standard designations have been developed for marking bars at the mill. These are shown in Figure 11.1.

Rebars come in two common grades: grade 40 and grade 60. Grades 50 and 75 are also sometimes available. These numbers refer to the yield strengths in kips per square inch. Grade 60 is the type most used in construction. Wire for prestressing has a much higher tensile strength—up to 250 or 270 kips per square inch.

Welded wire fabric is used for temperature reinforcement in slabs and consists of cold-drawn steel wires at right angles to each other which are welded at their intersections. The wires are usually in a square pattern with spacings of 4 and 6 inches. Designations for welded wire fabric consist of the size first and then the gage.

A new system is currently replacing the old system, but both are in use. The old system uses a designation grid size and gage. For example, 6×6–10/10 means the grid is six inches by six inches and both wires are 10 gage. The new designation for the same material is 6×6–W1.4 $\times$ 1.4. The first part is still the grid size, but the gage designation has been replaced with a letter, either W or D, to indicate smooth (W) or deformed (D), and a number which gives the cross-sectional wire area in hundredths of a square inch. The 1.4 in the example means that the area is 1.4 hundredths of a square inch, or 0.014 in^2.

D. Placing and Curing

Two important parts of the entire process of concrete design and construction are getting the concrete to the forms and ensuring that it is allowed to cure properly. Transporting the material from the truck or mixer actually involves several steps. First it must be conveyed to the formwork. This is done with bottom-dump buckets, by pumping, or in small buggies or wheelbarrows.

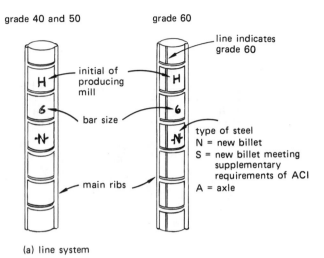

(a) line system

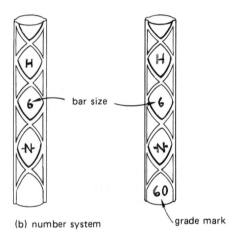

(b) number system

Figure 11.1 Reinforcing Bar Identification

Then, the concrete must be placed in the formwork in such a way as to avoid segregation which is the separation of the aggregates, water, and sand from each other because of their inherent dissimilarity. Dropping concrete long distances from the conveying device to the forms is one of the typical ways segregation can occur. Excessive lateral movement of the concrete in forms or slab work is another practice that should be minimized.

Finally, the concrete must be compacted to make sure the wet material has flowed around all the forms and rebars, that it has made complete contact with the steel, and to prevent *honeycombing*, which is the formation of air pockets within the concrete and next to the forms. For small jobs, hand compaction can be used. More typically, various types of vibrators are used.

Since concrete hardens and gains strength by curing through chemical reaction between the water and the

Table 11.1
Properties of Reinforcing Bars

Dimensional Properties of Individual Bars

bar no.	diameter	area, in^2	perimeter, in^2	wt. per foot
3	0.375	0.11	1.18	0.376
4	0.500	0.20	1.57	0.668
5	0.625	0.31	1.96	1.043
6	0.750	0.44	2.36	1.502
7	0.875	0.60	2.75	2.044
8	1.000	0.79	3.14	2.670
9	1.128	1.00	3.54	3.400
10	1.270	1.27	3.99	4.303
11	1.410	1.56	4.43	5.313
14	1.693	2.25	5.32	7.650
18	2.257	4.00	7.09	13.600

Areas of Bars in Reinforced Concrete, Square Inches per Foot

spacing, inches	3	4	5	6	7	8	9	10	11
3	0.44	0.78	1.23	1.77	2.40	3.14	4.00	5.06	6.25
3 1/2	0.38	0.67	1.05	1.51	2.06	2.69	3.43	4.34	5.36
4	0.33	0.59	0.92	1.32	1.80	2.36	3.00	3.80	4.68
4 1/2	0.29	0.52	0.82	1.18	1.60	2.09	2.67	3.37	4.17
5	0.26	0.47	0.74	1.06	1.44	1.88	2.40	3.04	3.75
5 1/2	0.24	0.43	0.67	0.96	1.31	1.71	2.18	2.76	3.41
6	0.22	0.39	0.61	0.88	1.20	1.57	2.00	2.53	3.12
6 1/2	0.20	0.36	0.57	0.82	1.11	1.45	1.85	2.34	2.89
7	0.19	0.34	0.53	0.76	1.03	1.35	1.71	2.17	2.68
7 1/2	0.18	0.31	0.49	0.71	0.96	1.26	1.60	2.02	2.50
8	0.17	0.29	0.46	0.66	0.90	1.18	1.50	1.89	2.34
9	0.15	0.26	0.41	0.59	0.80	1.05	1.33	1.69	2.08
10	0.13	0.24	0.37	0.53	0.72	0.94	1.20	1.52	1.87
12	0.11	0.20	0.31	0.44	0.60	0.78	1.00	1.27	1.56

cement rather than by drying, it is critical that the proper conditions of moisture and temperature be maintained for at least seven days and up to two weeks for critical work. If concrete dries out too fast, it can lose strength—up to 30 percent or more in some instances. With high-early-strength cements, of course, the time can be reduced. This is because concrete gains about 70 percent of its strength during the first week of curing, and final 28-day design strength depends on the initial curing conditions.

There are many techniques for maintaining proper moisture levels, including covering with plastic, using sealing compounds, or by continual sprinkling of the surfaces with water.

Concrete must also be kept from freezing while curing or it will also lose strength, sometimes as much as half. Since concrete produces heat while it cures (known as *heat of hydration*), it is often sufficient to cover the fresh material with insulated plastic sheets for a few days. In very cold conditions, external heat may need to be supplied or other construction techniques employed.

E. Testing Concrete

Because there are so many variables in concrete construction, the material must be continually tested at various stages to maintain quality. There are three tests that the architect must be familiar with: the *slump test*, the *cylinder test*, and the *core cylinder test*.

The slump test measures the consistency of the concrete, usually at the job site. In this test, concrete is placed in a 12-inch high truncated cone, 8 inches at the base and 4 inches at the top. It is compacted by hand with a rod and then the mold is removed from the concrete and placed next to it. The distance the concrete slumps from the original 12-inch height is then measured in inches. The amount of slump desired depends on how the concrete is going to be used, but is typically in the range of 2 to 6 inches. Too great a slump indicates excessive water in the mix, and a very small slump indicates the mixture will be too difficult to place properly.

The cylinder test measures compressive strength. As the concrete is being placed, samples are put in cylinder molds, 6 inches in diameter and 12 inches high, and are moist-cured for 28 days at which time they are laboratory-tested according to standardized procedures. The compressive strength in pounds per square inch is calculated and compared with the f'_c value used in the design of the structure. Almost always, cylinders are tested at seven days when their strength is about 60 to 70 percent of the 28-day strength.

The core cylinder test is used when a portion of the structure is in place and cured, but needs to be tested. Usually, if regular cylinder tests do not come up to the specified design strength, core cylinder tests are requested by the architect or structural engineer. A cylinder is drilled out of the concrete and then tested in the laboratory to determine its compressive strength. Drilled core cylinders are about 2 1/2 inches in diameter, and their length varies depending on the location they are drilled from, but usually they are about 6 inches long.

2 SAFETY FACTORS

Because of the many variables with reinforced concrete and the loads applied to concrete structures, there are two fundamental ways that safety provisions are built into the ACI code. The first is the recognition that the structure should be designed to support the loads that would cause it to fail. However, since these are not known with certainty, load factors are applied to the calculated loads to increase them to values that in all probability would never be reached, but which represent an acceptable factor of safety.

The ACI code gives a variety of load factor formulas to account for various combinations of dead loads, live loads, wind, earthquake, earth pressure, fluids, impact, settlement, creep, shrinkage, and temperature change effects. The most basic formula is:

$$U = 1.4D + 1.7L \qquad 11.1$$

This formula accounts for the concept that dead loads can be calculated with more accuracy than live loads, so the dead load needs to be increased less than the potential live load. Other formulas are used for other loading situations.

The second safety provision is known as the *strength reduction factor*, commonly symbolized by the Greek letter ϕ. This factor accounts for the accuracy with which actual strengths can be calculated in different kinds of structural members, quality control achievable with concrete, and the importance of various kinds of structural members. For example, columns are more important than beams to prevent catastrophic collapse.

The strength reduction factors for various types of loading are given in Table 11.2.

The combination of load factors and strength reduction factors is designed to reduce the probability of failure to about 1 in 100,000.

Table 11.2
Strength Reduction Factors

type of loading	strength reduction factor, ϕ
flexure and axial tension	0.90
shear and torsion	0.85
bearing on concrete	0.70
spirally reinforced columns	0.75
tied columns	0.70
flexure in plain concrete	0.65

3   CONCRETE BEAMS

Candidates for the architectural registration examination need to have a general understanding of the particular requirements of reinforced concrete construction and how it differs from building with other materials such as steel or timber. Since beams are one of the many common uses of concrete, they will be used to illustrate some of the unique aspects of concrete design.

A. Basic Concepts of Design

Concrete design is complex because of the many variables involved. Some of these variables include the strength of the concrete, the strength of the reinforcing steel, the amount of reinforcing used, and the size of the member. In addition, building code conditions change depending on the type of structural member being designed, its condition of use, and the strength of the basic materials.

Because of the many combinations possible with these variables, there is usually no single structural solution to a concrete design problem. Many combinations of design elements can support the same loading conditions. In most cases, concrete design is an iterative process where the designer must make some assumptions to start the process, work through the calculations, and then check the results against code requirements and cost efficiency. If the initial assumptions yield a less than optimum result, they are modified and new calculations are made. Fortunately, design aids such as graphs, tables, and computers make the process easier than it once was.

As discussed in Chapter 4, when a load is applied to a simply supported rectangular beam there are compression forces in the top half and tension forces in the lower half. If the beam is constructed from a homogeneous material such as timber, the neutral axis is at the center of the beam where no compression or tension forces exist. These forces increase in proportion to the distance from the neutral axis until they reach their maximum value at the extreme fibers of the beam.

In a simply supported concrete beam, the same general action occurs. However, because the beam is non-homogeneous, that is, composed of two materials, concrete and steel, the neutral axis is not at the midpoint of the beam's depth. In fact, the location of the neutral axis changes as the load on the beam is increased.

In concrete design, it is assumed that the concrete only resists compressive forces, and the reinforcing steel only resists the tension forces. Because of this assumption, none of the concrete on the tension side (lower side) of the beam below the centroid of the steel is assumed to have any structural value—it only serves to protect the steel from moisture and fire. Therefore, the *effective depth of the beam*, commonly referred to as d in formulas, is the distance from the top of the beam to the centroid of the steel. See Figure 11.2 (a).

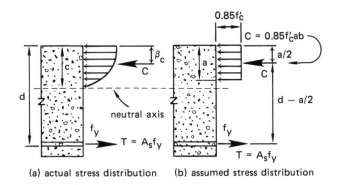

(a) actual stress distribution   (b) assumed stress distribution

Figure 11.2   Stress Distribution in Concrete Beams

In order to resist bending moments in a beam, the internal compressive and tension forces form a couple with the resultant of the tension forces, T, at the centroid of the steel and the resultant of the compressive forces, C, at some fraction of the distance from the top of the beam to the neutral axis, β_c. See Figure 11.2 (a). The shape of the distribution of the compressive forces varies considerably, with one of many possible shapes shown in Figure 11.2 (a). However, the stress distribution curve can be replaced with a more regular shape if the resultant C acts in the same position.

The assumed distribution pattern that is used is called the *rectangular stress block* as shown in Figure 11.2 (b), and although its resultant still acts at a distance β_c from the top of the beam, its height is somewhat less than the distance to the neutral axis, and is referred to as a, while its width is the width of the beam, or b. Through extensive testing of concrete beams it has been determined that the compressive force is equal to:

$$C = 0.85 f'_c ab \qquad 11.2$$

The 0.85 value is a stress intensity factor that has been determined through testing to be independent of f'_c.

The tensile force, T, is simply the strength of the steel, f_s, times the area of the steel, A_s:

$$T = A_s f_s \qquad 11.3$$

These two values of T and C, shown in the preceding formulas, give the forces in the steel and concrete just as the beam is about to fail. This is part of the current theoretical approach to concrete design known as the *strength method*. In order to resist the bending moment caused by a load, the values of T and C will be equal, but of course, act in opposite directions.

However, if a beam was designed with T and C equal, presumably the concrete would fail (crush) at the same time the steel failed (yielded). This is what is known as balanced design. This is not desirable since concrete fails by crushing without warning, and rather explosively, resulting in immediate collapse of the member. Steel, on the other hand, fails in a concrete beam more slowly, giving advance warning with excessive cracking of the concrete on the tension side and excessive deflection. Therefore, current thinking (and code requirements) is that the reinforcing steel should fail before the concrete crushes so building occupants have some advance warning.

In order to do this, the amount of steel in a given beam to support a given load must be determined. Then, the ACI code requires that the actual maximum amount of steel that can be used is equal to three-fourths of that. The amount of steel is expressed in terms of percentage of the area of the concrete according to the formula:

$$p_s = \frac{A_s}{bd} \qquad 11.4$$

The maximum amount of steel is given by the formula:

$$p_{max} = 0.75 p_b \qquad 11.5$$

This results in a beam that is actually under-reinforced.

The formula for finding the percentage of steel for a balanced design is given by:

$$p_b = 0.85 \beta_1 \frac{f'_c}{f_y} \cdot \frac{87,000}{87,000 + f_y} \qquad 11.6$$

β_1 is a constant which is 0.85 for concrete equal to or less than 4000 psi strength.

There are, however, limits to the minimum amount of steel. The ACI code sets this minimum at:

$$p_{min} = \frac{200}{f_y} \qquad 11.7$$

for concrete strength up to 6000 psi. For higher strength concretes, a slightly more complex formula is used.

Even though the steel may be designed to yield first, the actual design cannot be based on the assumption that the resisting forces, T and C, will be reached under the expected design load. Factors of safety must be included. These are the load factors and the strength reduction factor, ϕ, as discussed in the previous section. The idea is to find out what the design of the beam must be at failure under increased loads, which will likely never be reached, and at a reduced strength, which is probably less than what the designed member will actually provide.

B. Design for Flexure

Since the design of simple concrete members can be complex and time consuming, it is unlikely that problems will be given on the test that require detailed calculations. However, this section shows how to design a simple concrete beam to illustrate the iterative process and how the formulas are used.

For design, a few additional formulas are needed. The moment-carrying capacity of a beam is given by the formula

$$M_u = \phi A_s f_y (d - a/2) \qquad 11.8$$

ϕ is 0.90 for flexure.

In formula 11.8, a is found with the formula:

$$a = \frac{A_s f_y}{0.85 f'_c b} \qquad 11.9$$

With substitutions, and using the percentage of steel instead of the area, formula 11.8 can be rewritten:

$$M_u = \phi p f_y bd^2 [1 - 0.59(p f_y / f'_c)] \qquad 11.10$$

Example 11.1

Design a reinforced concrete beam to support a live load of 3.4 kip/ft and a dead load of 1.5 kip/ft. The beam is simply supported and 20 feet long. Concrete strength is $F_c' = 4000$ psi, and steel strength is $f_y = 60,000$ psi.

step 1: Determine the factored load from formula 11.1.

$$U = 1.4D + 1.7L$$
$$= 1.4(1.5) + 1.7(3.4)$$
$$= 7.88 \text{ kip/ft}$$

step 2: Determine the moment to be carried.

$$M_u = \frac{w\,l^2}{8}$$
$$= 7.88(20)^2 \times 12/8 \quad (12 \text{ converts to inch-kips})$$
$$= 4728 \text{ in-kips}$$

step 3: At this point, there are three unknowns: the beam width, beam depth, and steel area. Using the formulas previously given, you can assume a value for one or two unknowns and find the others. Since there are minimum and maximum guidelines for finding the percentage of steel, begin with that.

The maximum percentage allowed is $0.75p_b$.

From formula 11.6, the balanced steel percentage is:

$$p_b = 0.85(0.85)\frac{4000}{60,000} \times \frac{87,000}{87,000 + 60,000}$$
$$= 0.0285$$
$$p_{\max} = 0.75(0.0285)$$
$$= 0.0214$$

This percentage can be used to design an adequate beam but will result in a beam that is shallower than necessary since the steel is at its maximum. If there are no functional or architectural needs for a shallow beam, reducing the steel percentage and increasing the beam depth generally results in a more economical design and may reduce deflection. For economy of material, a concrete beam with a depth 2 to 3 times the width is desirable.

The minimum steel percentage is $p_{\min} = 200/f_y$, or 0.0033. Try a percentage of 0.0180 as a starting point, which is a little less than $p_{\max}$ calculated above.

step 4: Find the dimensions of the beam using the assumed steel percentage and formula 11.10. With this formula, you can assume a beam width and solve for d, the effective depth, or solve for the quantity bd^2

so you can more easily try different width-to-depth proportions. Reduce pounds per square inch to kips per square inch to keep units consistent.

$$M_u = \phi p f_y bd^2[1 - 0.59(p f_y/f_c')]$$
$$4728 = 0.90(0.0180)(60)bd^2[1 - 0.59(0.0180 \times 60/4)]$$
$$bd^2 = 5786 \text{ in}^3$$

Assume a 12-inch wide beam. Then,

$$d = 21.96 \text{ inches}$$

Round up to 22 inches, and with a cover below the centroid of the steel of about 2 1/2 inches, this will give an overall beam depth of 24 1/2 inches minimum. At this point, such a beam would seem reasonable so use this.

step 5: Find the actual area of steel using the minimum dimensions.

$$A_s = pbd$$
$$= 0.0180(12)(21.96)$$
$$= 4.74 \text{ in}^2$$

Using Table 11.1, six no. 8 bars will give exactly 4.74 in^2, or five no. 9 bars will give 5.00 in^2.

Unfortunately, this number of bars will not fit in a single layer in a 12-inch wide beam. This is because of the minimum cover and spacing requirement of the ACI code. The code requires a minimum of 11/2 inches clear between the steel and exterior of concrete in beams and columns. It also requires a minimum clear dimension of one inch or one bar diameter (whichever is greater) between bars to allow proper placement of the concrete. For a 12-inch beam (assuming no. 4 bars for shear reinforcement) the clearance requirements leave a width of only 8 inches for the tension steel. This only leaves room for four no. 8 bars; an additional 3 inches would be needed to accommodate six no. 8 bars. Actually, the beam would probably be made 16 inches wide rather than 15 inches, because widths are usually multiples of 2 inches.

Either the beam must be increased in width, or the percentage of steel must be reduced. It would be more economical to reduce the steel percentage and increase the depth of the beam, so try a new percentage of 0.0130 and recalculate.

$$4728 = 0.90(0.0130)(60)bd^2[1 - 0.59(0.0130 \times 60/4)]$$
$$bd^2 = 7611 \text{ in}^3$$

Since at this point we know that the width of the beam is important simply to accommodate the steel, try a width of 14 inches this time.

$$(14)d^2 = 7611$$
$$d = 23.32 \text{ inches}$$

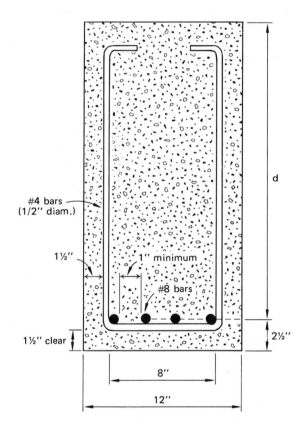

Rounding up to 23 1/2 inches and assuming a cover of 2 1/2 gives a total beam depth of 26 inches. A $14'' \times 26''$ beam seems reasonable, so use this.

Find the actual area of steel with this new size and new assumed percentage of steel.

$$A_s = 0.0130(14)(23.5)$$
$$= 4.28 \text{ in}^2$$

This can be satisfied with four no. 10 bars (A = 5.06 in^2) or five no. 9 bars (A = 5.00 in^2). However, once again, 5 bars will not quite fit in a 14-inch wide beam (required minimum width 14.15 inches), so we need to use four no. 10 bars in a $14'' \times 26''$ beam.

C. Shear

In the previous section only, stresses due to bending were discussed. However, forces caused by shear can also be significant and must be checked and provided for with additional reinforcement if the concrete itself is not capable of resisting them. It is especially important that concrete beams be adequately designed for shear, because, like compressive failure, shear collapse occurs suddenly and without warning.

Actually, what is commonly referred to as shear stress is really *diagonal tension stress* caused by the combination of shear and longitudinal flexural stress. The result is a characteristic diagonal cracking of the concrete beam in the areas of high shear forces, usually close to the beam supports as shown in Figure 11.3.

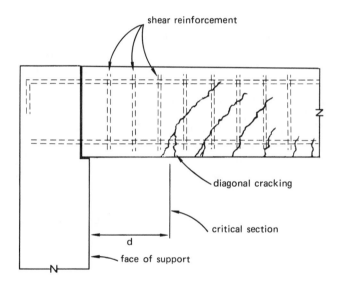

Figure 11.3 Typical Shear Cracking Pattern
Near End of Beam

When calculating for shear forces, the critical section is usually taken at the distance, d, from the support. This is because the reactions from the supports or from a monolithic column introduce vertical compression into the beam which mitigates excessive shear in that area.

There are two ways shear reinforcement, correctly called *web reinforcement*, is provided for. One way is to bend up some of the tension steel near the supports at a 45 degree angle as shown in Figure 11.4 (a). This is possible since most of the tension steel is required in the center of the beam where the moment is the greatest. The other, more common way, is to use vertical stirrups as shown in Figure 11.4 (b). These are small diameter bars (usually no. 3, no. 4, or no. 5 bars) that form a U-shaped cage around the tension steel.

(a) inclined web reinforcement

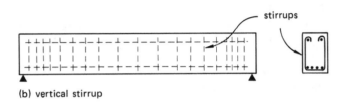

(b) vertical stirrup

Figure 11.4 Methods of Providing Web Reinforcement

The theories behind shear and diagonal tension in beams are still not completely understood. Exact, rational-analysis formulas do not exist. The existing formulas are based on tests, experience, and some mathematical analysis, and can become quite complicated.

The following formulas are a few of the basic ones with which you should be familiar.

$$V_c = 2\sqrt{f_c'}\,b_w d \qquad 11.11$$

The minimum area of web reinforcement required by the ACI code is given by the formula

$$A_v = 50\frac{b_w s}{f_y} \qquad 11.12$$

This formula must be used if the actual shear stress, V_u, is more than one-half of the shear capacity, which is V_c times the strength reduction factor, ϕ. For shear, ϕ is 0.85.

To design the area of steel required for vertical stirrups the following formula is used:

$$s = \frac{\phi A_v f_y d}{V_u - \phi V_c} \qquad 11.13$$

D. Compression Steel

In most reinforced concrete construction, reinforcement is added to the top, compression side of a beam or other section. Such beams are often called *doubly reinforced*

beams. There are several reasons for this. First, the concrete alone may not be able to resist the compressive forces. This is especially true if the concrete is of low strength or if the cross-sectional area is small in proportion to the applied loads. Second, compression steel reduces long-term deflections caused by concrete creep. Third, steel in the compression zone may simply be used to support stirrups before the concrete is poured. Finally, it may be included to provide for expected or unexpected negative moment in a member normally stressed with only positive moment. This can happen when an imposed load on one portion of a continuous span causes an adjacent unloaded span to bend upward.

If the member is designed for compression, the steel must be restrained to prevent its buckling outward just as with a column. Lateral ties are used for this purpose and must encircle the compression and tension steel on all four sides and be spaced for the entire length of the member. The shear reinforcement can serve part of this purpose, but instead of being U-shaped bars, it must continue across the top of the compression reinforcement to form a secure tie.

E. Development Length and Reinforcement Anchorage

In order for concrete reinforcement to do its job, there must be a firm bond between the two materials so that they act together to resist loads. As mentioned earlier, this is accomplished by mechanical bonding due to the deformations of the rebars and through chemical bonding between the two materials. One of the primary requirements for safety is that there is a sufficient length of steel bar from any point of stress to the end of the bar to develop the necessary bond.

The required length is primarily dependent on the strength of the concrete, the strength of the steel, and the size of the bar. The basic formula for minimum development length for steel in tension is:

$$l_{db} = \frac{0.04 A_b f_y}{\sqrt{f_c'}} \qquad 11.14$$

However, the ACI code requires that the length not be less than $0.0004 d_b f_y$, where d_b is the diameter of the bar. The ACI code also requires that in no case shall the length be less than 12 inches.

Formula 11.14 holds for no. 11 bars and smaller. Larger bars require a slightly shorter development length.

There are also some other variables that affect development length:

- the amount of concrete cover over the steel and the spacing of the bars. If rebars are spaced at least 6 inches on center and there is at least 3 inches clear from the edge bar to the face of the concrete, the development length may be reduced by a factor of 0.8.

- presence of lateral reinforcement. If spiral reinforcement of not less than 1/4 inch and not more than 4 pitch encloses the tensile bars, the development length may be reduced by a factor of 0.75.

- lightweight aggregate. Lightweight aggregates require longer development length than those determined by formula 11.14.

- top reinforcement. If there is more than 12 inches of concrete cast in a member below the bar in question, the development length must be increased by a factor of 1.4. This is because excess water tends to rise during pouring and curing, so that air and water accumulate near the underside of the bars, weakening the bond a little.

- high-strength reinforcing steel. Steels with yield stresses greater than 60,000 psi require longer development lengths.

F. Deflections

Although concrete may seem to be a very stiff material and not subject to much deflection, this is not the case. This is true because the strength design method of design, and higher strength concretes and steels, both result in smaller structural members that are less stiff than in the past.

Controlling deflection in concrete structures is important to avoid cracking partitions, glass, and other building components attached to the concrete, to avoid sagging of roofs and subsequent ponding of water, and to prevent noticeable deflection of visible members.

As with other aspects of concrete design, predicting deflection is not as easy as it is with homogeneous materials such as steel and wood. Design is further complicated by the fact that concrete has two phases of deflection: *immediate deflection* caused by normal dead and live loads, and *long-term deflection* caused by shrinkage and creep. Long-term deflection may be two or more times the initial deflection.

There are formulas and procedures that give the approximate initial and long-term deflections. These deflections can then be compared with deflection limitations in the ACI code for various types of members and conditions of deflection. These limitations are expressed in terms of fractions of the total span. See Table 11.3.

Table 11.3
Maximum Computed Deflections

BUILDING CODE REQUIREMENTS 318-35

TABLE 9.5(b) – MAXIMUM PERMISSIBLE COMPUTED DEFLECTIONS

Type of member	Deflection to be considered	Deflection limitation
Flat roofs not supporting or attached to nonstructural elements likely to be damaged by large deflections	Immediate deflection due to live load L	$\dfrac{\ell^*}{180}$
Floors not supporting or attached to nonstructural elements likely to be damaged by large deflections	Immediate deflection due to live load L	$\dfrac{\ell}{360}$
Roof or floor construction supporting or attached to nonstructural elements likely to be damaged by large deflections	That part of the total deflection occurring after attachment of nonstructural elements (sum of the long-time deflection due to all sustained loads and the immediate deflection due to any additional live load)‡	$\dfrac{\ell^\dagger}{480}$
Roof or floor construction supporting or attached to nonstructural elements not likely to be damaged by large deflections		$\dfrac{\ell^\S}{240}$

*Limit not intended to safeguard against ponding. Ponding should be checked by suitable calculations of deflection, including added deflections due to ponded water, and considering long-time effects of all sustained loads, camber, construction tolerances, and reliability of provisions for drainage.

†Limit may be exceeded if adequate measures are taken to prevent damage to supported or attached elements.

‡Long-time deflection shall be determined in accordance with Section 9.5.2.5 or 9.5.4.2 but may be reduced by amount of deflection calculated to occur before attachment of nonstructural elements. This amount shall be determined on basis of accepted engineering data relating to time-deflection characteristics of members similar to those being considered.

§But not greater than tolerance provided for nonstructural elements. Limit may be exceeded if camber is provided so that total deflection minus camber does not exceed limit.

Reprinted from ACI 318-83, American Concrete Institute, 1983

If certain conditions are met, the ACI code gives minimum depths of members in the form of span-to-depth ratios for various conditions. These are shown in Table 11.4.

Table 11.4

Minimum Thickness of Non-Prestressed
Beams or One-Way Slabs Unless Deflections
Are Computed

Member	Minimum thickness, h			
	Simply supported	One end continuous	Both ends continuous	Canti-lever
	Members not supporting or attached to partitions or other construction likely to be damaged by large deflections.			
Solid one-way slabs	$\ell/20$	$\ell/24$	$\ell/28$	$\ell/10$
Beams or ribbed one-way slabs	$\ell/16$	$\ell/18.5$	$\ell/21$	$\ell/8$

*Span length ℓ is in inches.

Values given shall be used directly for members with normal weight concrete (w_c = 145 pcf) and Grade 60 reinforcement. For other conditions, the values shall be modified as follows:

(a) For structural lightweight concrete having unit weights in the range 90–120 lb per cu ft, the values shall be multiplied by (1.65 – 0.005 w_c) but not less than 1.09, where w_c is the unit weight in lb per cu ft.

(b) For f_y other than 60,000 psi, the values shall be multiplied by (0.4 + f_y/100,000).

Reprinted from ACI 318-83, American Concrete Institute, 1983

G. Continuity

Since continuity is such a typical condition in concrete construction, you should be familiar with the basic principles. *Continuity* is an extension of a structural member over one or more supports. An example of a continuous member is placing a 30-foot steel beam over four supports, each 10 feet on center. Since concrete is typically poured in forms extending across several columns (or a slab extending over several beams), concrete structures are inherently continuous. Concrete structures are typically continuous in the vertical direction as well as the horizontal direction.

A portion of an exaggerated concrete structure is shown in Figure 11.5 (a) with deflections due to vertical and lateral loads also shown exaggerated. In the mid-spans of the beams, there is positive moment as discussed in Chapter 3. Over the center column support, however, the loads tend to cause the beam to bend upward with negative moment, while at the outer columns, the beam is fixed.

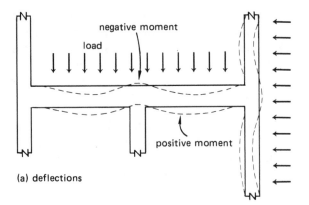

(a) deflections

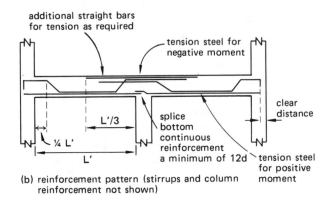

(b) reinforcement pattern (stirrups and column reinforcement not shown)

Figure 11.5   Continuity in Concrete Construction

Continuous beams and columns are statically indeterminate, meaning that they cannot be solved with the principles or equations of equilibrium discussed in Chapter 3. A few of the typical conditions for shear, moment, and deflection for continuous beams are shown in Figure 4.12. Continuous beams are more efficient than simply supported beams because the maximum moment for a given load and span is less than the moment for the corresponding simple beam. This is because the loads in adjacent spans effectively counteract each other to a certain extent.

For concrete structures, the negative moment causes the top of the beam to experience tension rather than the usual compression, so reinforcing steel must be added to counteract the forces just as in the bottom of a simply supported beam. In some cases, straight rebars are added over the supports to act as tension reinforcement. In other cases, some of the bottom tension steel is bent upward at the point of inflection to serve as negative reinforcement. See Figure 11.5 (b).

H. T-Beams

Since floor and roof slabs are always poured with the beams that support them, the two elements act integrally with a portion of the slab acting as the top portion of the beam. In effect, then, what looks like a simple rectangular beam becomes a T-beam with a part of the slab resisting compressive forces. The horizontal portion is called the *flange*, and the vertical portion below the flange is called the *web* or *stem*. For an isolated T-section, the entire top flange acts in compression. However, for stems that are in the middle of slabs or edge beams, the effective flange width is smaller than what is actually available. The various conditions are shown in Figure 11.6. The ACI code limits the effective flange widths as follows.

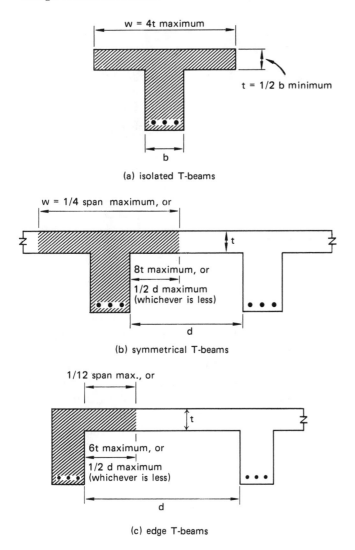

(a) isolated T-beams

(b) symmetrical T-beams

(c) edge T-beams

Figure 11.6 T-Beams

For isolated beams, the flange thickness shall not be less than one-half the width of the web, and the total flange width shall not be more than four times the web width. See Figure 11.6 (a).

For symmetrical T-beams (such as interior beams poured with the slab), the smallest of three conditions determine the effective width. This width shall not exceed one-fourth of the span of the beam, nor shall the over-

hanging slab width on either side of the beam web exceed 8 times the thickness of the slab, nor shall it exceed one-half the clear distance to the next beam. See Figure 11.6 (b).

For edge beams, the effective overhanging slab portion shall not exceed one-twelfth the span of the beam, nor shall the overhanging slab exceed six times the thickness of the slab, nor shall it exceed one-half the clear distance to the next beam. See Figure 11.6 (c).

If the neutral axis is equal to or less than the slab thickness, the section is designed as though it were a solid beam with a width equal to the effective width of the flange. If the neutral axis is in the web, special T-beam analysis is required.

4 CONCRETE SLABS

As part of a structural system of columns and beams, slabs can either span (structurally) in one direction or two directions. The former is called a *one-way slab* and the latter is called a *two-way slab*.

In a one-way slab, reinforcement is run in one direction perpendicular to the beams supporting the slab. Two-way slabs have rebars in both directions and are more efficient because the applied loads are distributed in all directions. However, in order for two-way slabs to work as intended, the column bays supporting them should be square or nearly square. When the ratio of length to width of one slab bay approaches 2:1, the slab begins to act as a one-way slab regardless of the reinforcement or edge supports.

One-way slabs need extra reinforcement to counteract the effects of shrinkage and temperature changes. Often called *temperature steel*, the minimum amount of reinforcement is set by ACI code by percentage as tension steel is, but in no case can the rebars be placed farther apart than five times the slab thickness or more than 18 inches. The minimum steel ratio in any case is 0.0018.

5 CONCRETE COLUMNS

Columns are the most typical of several types of concrete compressive members. In addition to columns, these include arch ribs, compressive members of trusses, and portions of rigid frames. The design of concrete compressive members is complex, especially when eccentric loading is involved or when the member supports both axial and bending stresses. This section will cover the basics of the two most typical types of concrete compressive members: *tied columns* and *spiral columns.* Composite compressive members, which consist of concrete reinforced with structural steel shapes, are sometimes used, but are not included here.

As with other types of columns, one of the primary considerations in design is the effect of buckling of the column caused by the axial load. The overall size of concrete columns usually results in length-to-width ratios of from 8 to 12, so slenderness is often not a critical consideration. However, since the steel reinforcement is very slender, it tends to fail by buckling and pushing out the concrete cover at the faces of the column. To prevent this, lateral ties are required, either as individual tied bars or a continuous spiral as discussed in the next two sections. Ties also hold the longitudinal steel in place before the concrete is poured. If columns are slender, either by design or by using higher strength concretes and reinforcement, then special calculations are required.

The ACI code limits the percentage of longitudinal steel to from 0.01 minimum to 0.08 maximum of the gross concrete cross section. It further requires there be at least four bars for tied columns and six for spiral columns. One reason for a limited percentage of steel is that large numbers of bars create a congested column form and make proper placing of the concrete difficult.

A. Tied Columns

Tied columns consist of vertical steel running parallel to the length of the column near its faces, with lateral reinforcement consisting of individual rebars tied to the vertical reinforcement at regular intervals. See Figure 11.7 (a). The ACI code requires that the lateral ties be at least no. 3 rebars for longitudinal bars up to no. 10 and at least no. 4 rebars for no. 11, no. 14, and no. 18 bars. No. 4 rebars must also be used for bundled reinforcement. Tied columns are most often used for square or rectangular shapes.

The spacing of the ties cannot exceed 16 diameters of vertical bars, 48 diameters of tie bars, nor the least dimension of the column. The ties must be arranged so that every corner and alternate vertical bar has lateral support in both directions. No bar can be more than 6 inches clear from such a laterally supported bar.

The strength reduction factor, ϕ, is 0.70 for tied columns.

B. Spiral Columns

Spiral columns have a continuous spiral of steel in lieu of individual lateral ties as shown in Figure 11.7 (b). The spiral must be at least 3/8 inch in diameter and the clear spacing between turns cannot be less than 1

inch nor more than 3 inches. The distance between the center lines of the turns is called the *pitch of the spiral.* Figure 11.7 shows a square spiral column, but they may also be round.

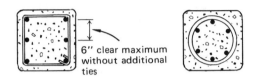

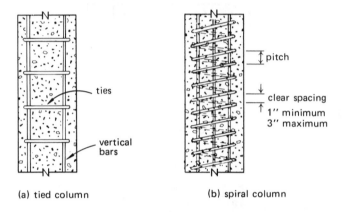

Figure 11.7 Concrete Columns

The strength reduction factor, ϕ, for spiral columns is 0.75, reflecting the fact that spiral columns are slightly stronger than tied columns of the same size and reinforcement. Another important difference to note is that spiral columns are more ductile, meaning that they fail in a gradual manner with the outer covering of concrete spalling before the column fails. Tied columns tend to fail suddenly without warning.

6 PRESTRESSED CONCRETE

Prestressed concrete consists of members that have internal stresses applied to them before they are subjected to service loads. The prestressing consists of compressive forces applied where normally the member would be in tension which effectively eliminates or greatly reduces tensile forces that the member is not capable of carrying. In addition to making a more efficient and economical structural section, prestressing reduces cracking and deflection, increases shear strength, and allows longer spans and greater loads. Prestressing is accomplished in one of two ways: *pretensioning* or *post-tensioning.*

A. Precast, Pretensioned

With this system, concrete members are produced in a precasting plant. High-strength pretensioning stranded cable or wire is draped in forms according to the required stress pattern needed and a tensile force is applied. The concrete is then poured and allowed to cure. Once cured, the cables are cut and the resulting compressive force is transmitted to the concrete through the bond between cable and concrete.

B. Post-Tensioned

For post-tensioning, hollow sleeves or conduit are placed in the forms on the site and concrete poured around them. Within the conduit is the prestressing steel, called *tendons*, which are stressed with hydraulic jacks or other means after the concrete has cured. In some cases, the space between the tendons and the conduit is grouted. The resulting stress is transferred to the concrete through end plates in the concrete member.

SAMPLE QUESTIONS

1. Which of the following admixtures would you recommend to use in a construction project in a northern climate that was built during the summer months if the concrete will be exposed to the weather?

    A. accelerator

    B. plasticizer

    C. air-entraining agent

    D. accelerator and air-entraining agent

2. Which of the following would be the correct placement for primary reinforcing steel for the beam shown below if the spans supported a uniformly distributed load?

A.
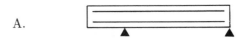

B.
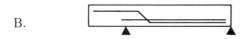

C.
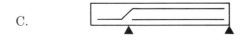

D.

3. The concrete beam shown is proposed to have rebars placed schematically as shown. The strength of the concrete is 4000 psi, and the steel is grade 60. The percentage of steel to achieve a balanced design has been calculated to be 0.0285. What are the minimum and maximum steel areas allowed?

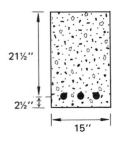

A. minimum = 1.06 in^2; maximum = 9.19 in^2

B. minimum = 1.19 in^2; maximum = 9.19 in^2

C. minimum = 1.06 in^2; maximum = 6.90 in^2

D. minimum = 1.19 in^2; maximum = 7.70 in^2

4. Which of the following are not true about the water-cement ratio:

I. For typical concrete mixes, the minimum water-cement is about 0.50 to 0.65.

II. The water-cement ratio is critical to the concrete strength.

III. Water is only needed for workability and to start the drying process.

IV. Excess water forms small bubbles in the cement paste.

V. The water-cement ratio is sometimes referred to by gallons of water per sack of cement.

    A. II and III

    B. III and IV

    C. I and III

    D. I and IV

5. A number 10 rebar has the following diameter:

    A. 1 1/4 inches

    B. 1 1/8 inches

    C. 4/5 inches

    D. The exact diameter depends on the producing mill.

6. Select the correct statements from the following list.

I. The development length of rebars depends primarily on the strength of the steel and the perimeter length of the bar.

II. Diagonal tension stress can be counteracted by using either stirrups or some of the tension steel bent up at a 45 degree angle.

III. Reducing the percentage of steel to close to minimum can improve the stiffness of the beam.

IV. Compression steel is seldom used unless negative moment is present.

V. Long-term deflection can be two or more times initial deflection.

    A. I, II, and III

    B. I, III, and V

    C. II, IV, and V

    D. II, III, and V

The answers to questions 7 through 10 can be found on the following key list. Select only one answer for each question.

    A0 admixtures
    A1 compaction
    A2 compressive strength
    A3 continuity
    A4 core cylinder test
    A5 curing
    A6 cylinder test
    A7 factored load
    A8 hydration
    A9 load factors

    B0 moisture
    B1 negative moment
    B2 size of aggregate
    B3 slump test
    B4 T-beam action
    B5 temperature
    B6 two-way slab action
    B7 strength reduction factor

7. What should be carefully controlled during placement of concrete?

8. What safety provision accounts for some of the many variables in concrete construction?

9. What usual property of concrete construction improves its structural efficiency?

10. What should you use to judge the quality of concrete being placed at a job site?

12 WALL CONSTRUCTION

Nomenclature

A_g	gross area of concrete wall	in^2
A_s	area of reinforcing	in^2
f_c'	specified compressive strength of concrete	psi
f_m'	compressive strength of masonry at 28 days	psi
F_a	allowable average axial compressive stress for centroidally applied axial load	psi
h	height of wall	inches
k	effective length factor	
l_c	vertical distance between supports	inches
P_n	nominal axial load strength	pounds
t	effective thickness of wythe or wall	inches
ϕ	strength reduction factor (0.70 for concrete bearing walls)	

The two primary classifications of walls are *loadbearing* and *non-loadbearing*. Loadbearing walls support their own weight in addition to vertical and lateral loads. They can be further classified into *vertical loadbearing walls*, *shear walls*, and *retaining walls*. Vertical loadbearing walls support the weight of other walls above, in addition to floor and roof loads. Shear walls are structural walls that resist lateral loads acting in the plane of the wall. Retaining walls, as discussed in Chapter 6, are structural walls that resist the movement of soil.

Non-loadbearing walls support only their own weight, and are used to enclose a building or to divide space within a building. When used for a building enclosure, they do serve to transfer wind forces to the primary structural frame. A non-loadbearing exterior wall is called a *curtain wall*.

Although the primary focus of this chapter is the structural design of walls, there are other considerations in selecting the optimum wall for a particular circumstance. In addition to load-carrying ability, a wall must provide for openings, keep out the weather, be cost effective, satisfy the aesthetic requirement of the job, resist heat loss and gain, and be easy to maintain. The architect must exercise judgment in selecting the wall system to best satisfy all the requirements of a project.

1 MASONRY WALLS

There are many varieties of masonry walls, both non-loadbearing and loadbearing, consisting of single or multiple wythes, either reinforced or unreinforced. A *wythe* is a continuous vertical section of a wall one masonry unit in thickness. For structural purposes, the two primary masonry materials are brick and concrete block.

Masonry walls can be engineered or designed by empirical requirements given in building codes and generally accepted rules of thumb. The model codes differ in some areas concerning requirements for masonry walls; the ones given here are based on the Uniform Building Code. Requirements also vary depending on which seismic zone the building is in. Structures in zones subject to more frequent and severe earthquakes, of course, require additional reinforcement, and there are limitations on the types of mortar and masonry units that can be used.

The specified compressive stress in masonry walls depends on the strength of the masonry unit as well as the strength of the mortar. Because the quality of a masonry wall is highly dependent on the workmanship, the formulas for allowable stress given by the building code assume that special inspection will be made during the construction of the wall. If this inspection is not made, the allowable stresses must be reduced by one-half.

The compressive strength of a masonry wall, f_m', can be based on tests of actual wall samples, field experience based on similar mortar, masonry, and construction combinations, or on assumed values given in the UBC. Table 12.1 gives the assumed designed strength of masonry for three mortar types.

Table 12.1
Masonry Design Strength from the UBC

Compressive Strength of Clay Masonry Units[1] (psi)	Specified Compressive Strength of Masonry, f'_m	
	Type M or S Mortar[3] (psi)	Type N Mortar[3] (psi)
14,000 or more	5,300	4,400
12,000	4,700	3,800
10,000	4,000	3,300
8,000	3,350	2,700
6,000	2,700	2,200
4,000	2,000	1,600
Compressive Strength of Concrete Masonry Units[4] (psi)	Specified Compressive Strength of Masonry, f'_m	
	Type M or S Mortar[3] (psi)	Type N Mortar[3] (psi)
4,800 or more	3,000	2,800
3,750	2,500	2,350
2,800	2,000	1,850
1,900	1,500	1,350
1,250	1.000	950

[1]Compressive strength of solid clay masonry units is based on gross area. Compressive strength of hollow clay masonry units is based on minimum net area. Values may be interpolated. When hollow clay masonry units are grouted, the grout shall conform to the proportions in Table No. 24-B.
[2]Assumed assemblage. The specified compressive strength of masonry f'_m is based on gross area strength when using solid units or solid grouted masonry and net area strength when using ungrouted hollow units.
[3]Mortar for unit masonry, proportion specification, as specified in Table No. 24-A. These values apply to portland cement-lime mortars without added air-entraining materials.
[4]Values may be interpolated. In grouted concrete masonry the compressive strength of grout shall be equal to or greater than the compressive strength of the concrete masonry units.

Reproduced from the 1991 edition of the Uniform Building Code, copyright © 1991, with permission of the publishers, the International Conference of Building Officials.

The allowable axial compressive stress for reinforced and unreinforced walls is determined by the formula:

$$F_a = 0.20 f'_m \left[1 - \left(\frac{h}{42t} \right)^3 \right] \qquad 12.1$$

As indicated in this formula, the allowable stress is determined not only by the masonry strength but also by the slenderness ratio of the wall, just as with column design.

There are five basic types of masonry walls: veneered, single wythe, reinforced hollow unit masonry, cavity, and reinforced grouted masonry. These are illustrated in Figure 12.1.

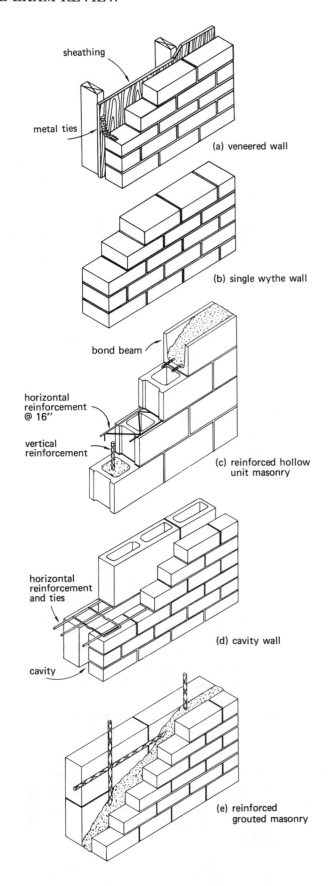

Figure 12.1 Masonry Wall Types

A *veneered wall* is a non-loadbearing wall having a facing of a single wythe of masonry, usually brick, anchored to a backing. The masonry is primarily for decorative and weather-proofing purposes such as a brick veneer wall over a wood stud backing wall.

A. Single Wythe Walls

A *single wythe* consists of a single unit of unreinforced masonry that can act as either a bearing or non-load-bearing wall. Since it is unreinforced vertically, there are limits to the amount of load that can bear on this type of wall, and building codes limit the maximum ratio of unsupported height or length to thickness. For solid masonry walls or bearing partitions designed according to the UBC, the ratio cannot exceed 20. For hollow masonry or cavity walls, the ratio cannot exceed 18.

Example 12.1

What is the maximum unsupported height for a solid brick wall 8 inches thick?

The nominal thickness, t, of the wall is used in the calculation, so the maximum height is $8 \times 20 = 160$ inches, or 13 feet 4 inches.

Even though single wythe walls are not reinforced vertically, they must have a minimum amount of horizontal reinforcement, just as multi-wythe walls must. The most commonly used reinforcement are prefabricated assemblies consisting of minimum 9-gage steel laid every 16 inches. See Figure 12.2.

B. Reinforced Hollow Unit Masonry

This type of wall construction consists of a single wythe of concrete block with vertical reinforcing rods placed in the cells of the block which are filled with grout. See Figure 12.1 (c). Grout may be placed in every cell or just those cells containing the reinforcing. Since concrete block is based on an 8-inch module, the spacing of the vertical reinforcing bars is a multiple of 8 inches.

Horizontal reinforcement is provide by prefabricated units as shown in Figure 12.2. When additional horizontal reinforcement is needed over openings or at the top of the wall, a U-shaped block, called a *bond beam*, is used with rebar placed in the bottom and filled with grout. The minimum nominal thickness of a reinforced masonry bearing wall is 6 inches.

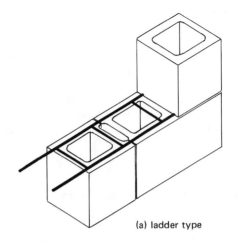

(a) ladder type

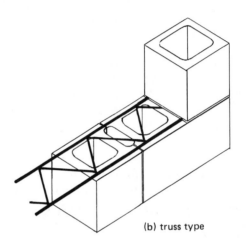

(b) truss type

Figure 12.2   Horizontal Joint Reinforcement

C. Cavity Walls

Cavity walls consist of two wythes of masonry, separated by an air space normally 2 inches wide. See Figure 12.1 (d). Cavity walls have the advantages of providing extra protection against water penetration and additional insulation value because of the air. The cavity is often filled with insulation to enhance the insulation value of the wall. Both wythes may be of the same masonry type, or they may be mixed. A common type of cavity wall is a backing of 4-inch or 8-inch concrete block with an exterior wythe of brick.

The wythes of a cavity wall must be tied together with a corrosion-resistant metal tie at least 3/16 inch in diameter for every 4 1/2 square feet of wall area, or with other approved horizontal joint reinforcement as shown in Figure 12.2. Metal ties are normally spaced every 16 inches vertically.

Example 12.2

What is the maximum unsupported height for a cavity wall consisting of a 4-inch brick facing and an 8-inch concrete block wall separated by a 1-inch space?

In computing the ratio for cavity walls, the thickness is the sum of the nominal thicknesses of the wythes. The maximum height is $(4 + 8) \times 18 = 216$ inches, or 18 feet.

D. Reinforced Grouted Masonry

Reinforced grouted masonry is used where additional load-carrying capacity is required, for lateral loads such as wind or earthquake. Reinforcing bars are installed in the cavity of the wall, and then the cavity is filled with grout. See Figure 12.1 (e).

Reinforcement is usually installed both vertically and horizontally, especially in seismic risk zones 3 and 4 where it is required. For these seismic zones, the code requires that the sum of the areas of horizontal and vertical reinforcement be at least 0.002 times the gross cross-sectional area of the wall, and that the minimum area of reinforcement in either direction be at least 0.0007 times the gross cross-sectional area of the wall. The spacing of the reinforcement cannot exceed 4 feet and must be at least 3/8 inch in diameter.

Example 12.3

What reinforcing should be provided for a masonry cavity wall consisting of an 8-inch concrete block backup wythe separated by a 2-inch space from a 4-inch brick facing wythe?

The UBC defines the gross cross-sectional area as that encompassed by the outer periphery of any section, so the actual width of the above wall assembly is the sum of the actual width of the block (7 5/8 inch) plus the cavity plus the actual width of the brick (3 5/8 inch), or a total of 13.25 inches.

The required horizontal and vertical reinforcing per foot of height or length is:

$$A_s = 0.0007 \times (13.25 \times 12)$$
$$= 0.113 \text{ in}^2$$

The minimum sum of vertical and horizontal reinforcing is:
$$A_s = 0.002 \times (13.25 \times 12)$$
$$= 0.318 \text{ in}^2$$

In deciding on the size and spacing of the reinforcing bars, you need to use standard sizes of bars but you

want to minimize the amount of steel used (and therefore the cost) and the number of bars placed (more bars placed generally increases the labor cost). The area of rebars is given in Table 11.1 in Chapter 11.

Decide on horizontal reinforcing first. 0.113 in² per foot means a minimum steel area of $0.116 \times 4 = 0.45$ in² per 48 inches of height. You could use a #7 bar every 4 feet (area = 0.60 in²), but this size bar would be heavy and awkward to place and make it difficult to grout the cavity. Try a spacing of 16 inches instead or three bars per 4 feet of height:

$$\frac{0.45}{3} = 0.15 \text{ in}^2$$

A #4 bar ($A = 0.20$) spaced every 16 inches would work.

Next, determine the size and spacing of vertical reinforcement. The total area required per 4 foot length is 0.318×4, less the actual area of the horizontal reinforcement:

$$(0.318 \times 4) - (0.20 \times 4) = 0.472 \text{ in}^2$$

Once again, try a spacing of 16 inches. Each bar would need a minimum area of $0.472/3 = 0.157$ in². A #4 bar spaced every 16 inches would be satisfactory.

The grout used for reinforced masonry walls is a mixture of portland cement, hydrated lime, and aggregate. It may either be fine grout or course grout. Course grout has a higher percentage of larger aggregates.

A wall may be grouted in one of two ways. The first is called *low-lift grouting*, which is accomplished by laying up no more than 8 inches of masonry and then placing the grout. The second method is *high-lift grouting*. A larger portion of the wall, no more than 6 feet in height, is laid up and the reinforcing placed. Grout is then pumped into the cavity and mechanically vibrated to ensure that all voids are filled.

The building code specifies the minimum clear dimensions of the cavity less the width of horizontal reinforcing based on the height of the grout pour and whether fine or coarse grout is used. For low-lift grouting with fine grout, the minimum grout space is 3/4 inch plus the width of the reinforcing. For coarse grout, it is 1 1/2 inches. Mortar projections must be kept to a minimum of 1/2 inch and the cavity space must be kept clear of loose mortar and other foreign material.

E. Openings

Regardless of the type of lintel used to span an opening, there is always arch action over an opening. This is shown diagrammatically in Figure 12.3. Unless a concentrated load or a floor load is near the top of the opening, the lintel only carries the weight of the wall above the opening in a triangular area defined by a 60 degree angle from each side of the opening. If a floor line is within a distance equal to the top of this imaginary triangle, the lintel carries the weight of the wall and the weight of the floor load as wide as the opening.

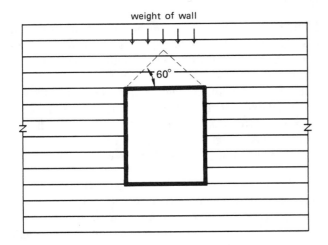

Figure 12.3   Arch Action in a Masonry Wall Over an Opening

Openings in masonry walls may be spanned with masonry arches, steel lintels, precast reinforced concrete lintels, or precast masonry lintels reinforced with rebars and filled with grout. See Figure 12.4.

Steel lintels are often used because they are inexpensive and simple to install and the size and thickness can be varied to suit the span of the opening. Lintels should bear on each end of the supporting masonry such that the bearing capacity is not exceeded, but in no case should the bearing length be less than 6 inches.

2   STUD WALLS

Stud wall systems are one of the most common types of structural systems for residential and light commercial buildings. Stud walls are relatively small members, closely spaced and tied together with exterior and interior sheathing. The sheathing is necessary to brace the small members against buckling and to resist lateral loads.

Stud wall systems have many advantages. They are easy to erect by a small construction crew, relatively

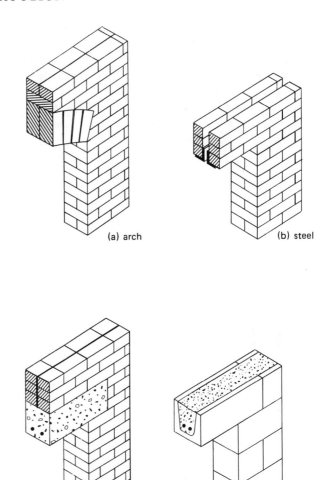

Figure 12.4   Masonry Lintels

inexpensive, lightweight, materials are readily available, they are adaptable to a variety of designs, and the spacebetween the studs can be used for insulation and electrical service.

Stud wall systems allow for many types of exterior finish materials such as wood or aluminum siding, stucco, and brick veneer.

A. Wood Studs

Wood studs are the most common type of material used for stud wall systems. They are typically 2 × 4 members spaced 16 or 24 inches on center, covered with plywood or particle board sheathing on the exterior and gypsum board on the interior. 2 × 4 and 2 × 6 studs can be used for bearing walls up to 10 feet high. If the studs support one floor, roof, and a ceiling, the maximum spacing is 16 inches for 2 × 4s and 24 inches for 2 × 6s.

The most common type of wood stud construction is *platform framing* as illustrated in Figure 12.5. With this method, wood studs one story high are placed on a sole plate at the bottom and spanned with a double top plate at the ceiling level. The second floor joists bear on the top plate, and, when the second floor sheathing is in place, serve as a platform on which to erect the second-story stud walls.

The other method of stud construction is *balloon framing*, in which the studs run the full height from first floor to the top of the second floor. The second floor joists bear on a continuous 1 × 4 ribbon let into the studs, and are also nailed into the sides of the studs. This method of construction is seldom used, although its advantage is that it minimizes the overall shrinkage of the vertical dimension of the wall because the majority of the lumber is oriented parallel to the grain of the wood.

B. Metal Studs

Metal stud systems are similar in concept to wood stud systems except that light-gage C-shaped metal members are used instead of wood. Standard sizes of exterior metal studs are 31/2, 35/8, 4, and 6 inches in depth in thicknesses of 14, 16, and 18 gage. Deeper studs are also available. Metal studs are usually placed 24 inches on center rather than 16 inches. If the entire building is being framed in light-gage metal, floor joists and rafters are constructed of steel members as well.

Metal stud wall systems may be used with other structural framing systems. For example, a building may have a steel or concrete primary structural frame with light-gage steel studs used for nonbearing exterior and interior walls. The exterior stud walls are then faced with brick, siding, tile, or other weatherproof finish material.

C. Openings

Openings in stud walls are framed in the same material as the stud wall itself. Openings in wood stud walls are spanned with headers consisting of nominal 2-inch thick lumber placed on edge as shown in Figure 12.6. The width of the header depends on the width of the opening. Double 2 × 4s can be used on openings up to 3 feet, 2 × 6s up to 4 feet, and 2 × 8s up to 5 feet.

The headers are supported by short studs doubled next to the full height studs and the space above and below the opening framed with cripple studs. Openings in metal stud walls are framed in a similar manner.

3 CONCRETE WALLS

Concrete walls are ideal where high strength, durability, and fire resistance are required. Although concrete walls can be designed just as bearing walls, they usually also act as shear walls and sometimes as deep beams spanning between footings. Having them serve more

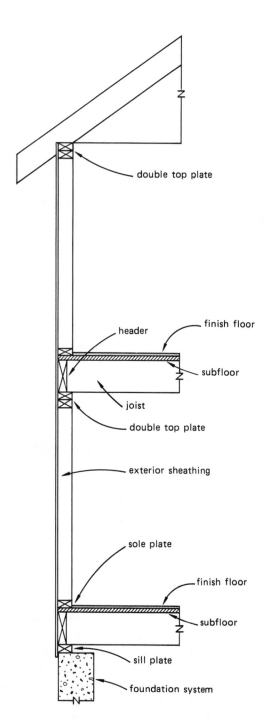

Figure 12.5 Platform Construction

- double top plate
- header
- finish floor
- subfloor
- joist
- double top plate
- exterior sheathing
- sole plate
- finish floor
- subfloor
- sill plate
- foundation system

than one function makes more efficient use of the material and labor required for their construction.

Building codes and the American Concrete Institute detail the many requirements that concrete bearing walls must meet, and like other aspects of concrete construction, they are quite complicated and depend on iterative design processes. However, the following guidelines are a useful summary.

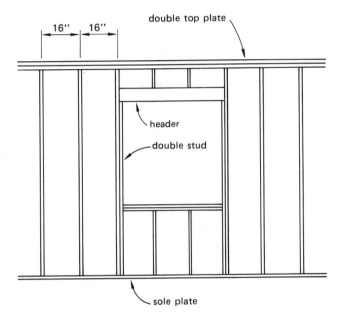

Figure 12.6 Typical Wood Stud Wall Framing

A. Cast-in-Place

When certain conditions are met, the UBC allows an empirical design method to be used. With this method, the design axial load strength can be computed with the formula:

$$\phi P_n = 0.55 \phi f_c' A_g \left[1 - \left(\frac{k l_c}{32t} \right)^2 \right] \qquad 12.2$$

The effective length factor, k, is taken as 0.8 for walls restrained against rotation at the top or bottom or both, and 1.0 for walls unrestrained against rotation at both ends. Additional loads such as seismic and wind loading may require extra reinforcing.

The conditions that must be met in order to use formula 12.2 include the following:

- Walls must be anchored to intersecting elements such as floors, roofs, columns, and intersecting walls and footings.

- The minimum ratio of vertical reinforcement area to gross concrete area must be 0.0012 for deformed bars not larger than #5 with a yield strength of not less than 60 ksi. For other bars, the ratio is 0.0015.

- The minimum ratio of horizontal reinforcement area to gross concrete area must be 0.0020 for deformed bars not larger than #5 with a yield strength of not less than 60 ksi. For other bars, the ratio is 0.0025.

- Walls more than 10 inches thick, except basement walls, must have the reinforcement placed in two layers with the layer next to the exterior face containing not less than one-half and not more than two-thirds of the total reinforcement required.

- Reinforcement cannot be spaced farther apart than three times the wall thickness, or 18 inches.

- Not less than two #5 bars must be provided around all window and door openings, and must be extended past the corners of the openings not less than 24 inches.

- The minimum thickness of bearing walls cannot be less than 1/25 of the unsupported height or length, whichever is shorter, nor less than 4 inches.

- The resultant of the loads must fall within the middle one-third of the wall thickness to avoid eccentricity.

B. Precast Concrete Walls

Precast bearing walls are required to be designed in the same way as cast-in-place walls, including the effects of temperature and shrinkage. Often, extra reinforcing is needed simply to protect the integrity of the panels against the stresses of transportation and erection.

Precast walls are an economical way to enclose a building and provide for bearing if there is sufficient repetition in the panel sizes and configurations to make mass production possible. Rather than serving as a bearing member, precast walls are often nonbearing and attached to a structural framework of steel or precast concrete.

Precast bearing walls are most often connected by field welding steel plates that have been cast into the panel at the precasting plant. Figure 12.7 illustrates some of the typical connections used.

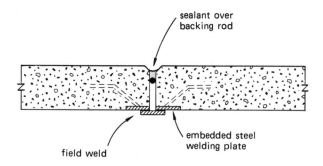

(a) wall panel connection

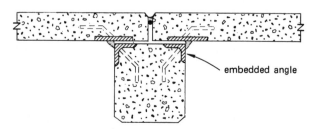

(b) connection to column

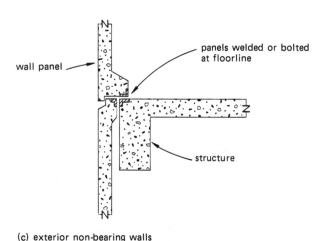

(c) exterior non-bearing walls

Figure 12.7 Precast Concrete Wall Panel Connections

4   BUILDING ENVELOPE

The design of the walls that enclose a building is one of the most difficult detailing problems in building construction because not only does the exterior wall have to be structurally sound, but it must also accommodate

various kinds of movement that occur in all structures. In addition, connections between the cladding and the structure must be designed to allow for on-site adjustments during erection, so the final wall will be within proper tolerances. These requirements exist whether the exterior wall is bearing or nonbearing. However, this section will only discuss the attachment of nonbearing exterior cladding to the primary structural frame.

A. Attachment to Structural Members

Exterior cladding and its attachment to the primary structural frame must resist three basic types of loads: the *dead load* of the wall system itself, *horizontal wind loads*, and *seismic loads*.

The method of providing dead load support depends on the material used and the structural frame. For example, heavy materials, such as brick or concrete block used in one- or two-story buildings usually rest directly on the foundation. In taller buildings, the load must be carried at intermediate floor levels because the strength of a panel or portion of a wall is not sufficient to carry any weight beyond its own dead load.

Figure 12.8 illustrates a typical method of supporting masonry in a multistory building. In this case, the weight of the masonry is carried on a continuous steel angle bolted to the structural frame. Horizontal ties provide for attachment of the exterior wall to the frame and help in the transfer of wind loads as well. The attachment of veneer stone is accomplished in a similar manner, although individual details are somewhat different.

Precast concrete panels are also attached at every floor or every other floor using various combinations of embedded steel angles and plates that are field-welded or bolted together as shown in Figure 12.7.

With metal curtain wall systems, the provision for both dead loads and wind load is made with various types of clip attachment of the curtain wall system to the structural frame. There are many possible ways this can be accomplished depending on the type of curtain wall system, its fabrication, the loads that must be resisted, the type and configuration of the primary structural frame, as well as other variables.

In most cases, some type of steel anchor is firmly attached to the structure at floor and column lines. The support system for the curtain wall is then attached to these anchors using shims and slotted bolt holes to provide for precise alignment of the exterior wall. One system of this type is shown in Figure 12.9.

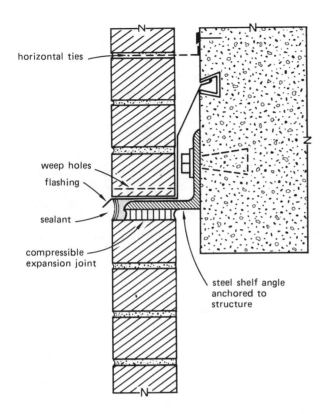

Figure 12.8 Typical Attachment of Brick Facing at
Intermediate Floor

the load is concentrated in the connections to the primary structural system. In severe earthquake zones, additional connections may be required above those needed for gravity and wind loading. Much of the earthquake energy in a curtain wall system can be dissipated by providing joints that can move slightly in several directions with such details as slip joints or flexible bushings between bolts and steel members.

To minimize the possibility of damage to nonbearing panels during an earthquake, they should be anchored vertically at column lines and horizontally at floor lines. It is at these points where the seismic forces are concentrated, so curtain wall panels should not span across these points.

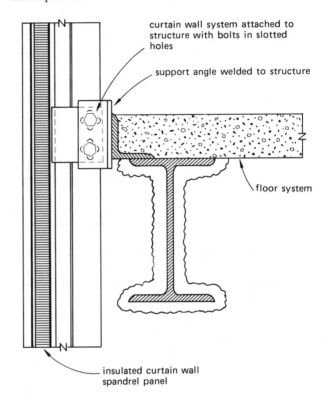

Figure 12.9 Typical Attachment of Curtain Wall

In resisting wind loading, the cladding must maintain its own structural integrity and transfer the wind loads to the structural frame. Wind can either produce a positive or negative load on a component. Quite often, the suction on an exterior wall can be greater than the inward pressure caused by wind. In most cases, however, nonbearing exterior walls are designed to span between supports, so intermediate connections for the transfer of wind loads are not required. One exception is brick masonry, which may require intermittent horizontal ties because of its low flexural strength.

Nonbearing, exterior wall systems in areas of frequent seismic activity must be designed primarily to maintain their integrity and connection to the building to avoid injury caused by falling debris. Although it is desirable to provide for movement and absorption of energy during an earthquake to avoid cracking and damage of the wall material, this is usually not practical for severe earthquakes. Instead, connections and joints should accommodate movement to avoid build up of stresses that could dislocate the wall from the structure.

The design of curtain wall systems is especially important in resisting seismic loads. Of course, the panels must withstand the force of an earthquake, but most of

B. Movement

All buildings move. There are a variety of causes of building movement and the exterior walls must accommodate all of them. Movement can be a result of wind loads, temperature changes, moisture, earthquakes, differential movement of building materials, and deflection of the structure, both immediate and long term.

Building materials expand and contract with changes in temperature as noted in Chapter 2. The amount of movement is dependent on the coefficient of thermal expansion of the material and its length. An aluminum curtain wall system will change dimension to a much greater degree than a masonry wall.

Moisture can cause some material to change size to such an extent that if the change is not accounted for, damage can occur. Wood, of course, swells when wet so siding or structure exposed to the weather must be protected with coatings or allowance made for the amount of movement expected. Even changes in humidity levels can cause wood members to expand and contract.

Differential movement of materials is another important concern. Brick will swell and expand at a different rate than a concrete block backing wall. Metal windows will move in response to wind and temperature changes more than the concrete wall they are anchored to. An aluminum curtain wall will change size much more than the steel frame it is attached to. These examples are just of few of the many situations where differential movement can cause problems.

The deflection of both the structure and the attached exterior wall is something often overlooked. For example, a masonry wall laid up to the underside of a beam or floor can buckle under dead loading or long-term deflection. There should always be some method of providing for this kind of movement. The compressible expansion joint shown in Figure 12.8, for example, allows for minor deflection of the steel angle above as well as provides for expansion of the brick below.

The methods of dealing with all the types of building movement mentioned above are varied, depending on the material and the type and amount of movement expected. A few general guidelines will be mentioned here.

First, there must be *through-building expansion joints* to accommodate large-scale movement of portions of the entire building. These are needed in large buildings where there is a change in height, structural system, major materials, or where differential movement might be expected between various parts of the building. For example, a parking structure connected to an office tower would probably require a building expansion joint between the two structures.

Second, there must be *through-wall expansion joints* to allow for movement in wall sections caused by temperature, moisture, differential movement, and other forces. These are usually made by separating the materials structurally, but providing for weather proofing.

One example of a vertical masonry expansion joint is shown in Figure 12.10. The individual brick walls are securely anchored to the concrete structural frame, but the joint allows each to move independently in the direction parallel to the wall. The dovetail anchors allow for minor movement in the direction perpendicular to the wall. The joint filler and sealant accommodate expansion and contraction while providing a tight seal.

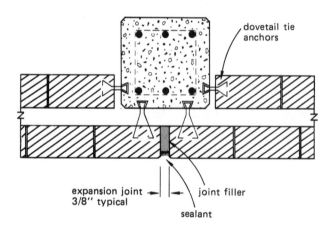

Figure 12.10   Typical Horizontal Attachment of Masonry to Primary Structure

Third, *construction joints* must be used to separate one type of material from another. These joints allow for differential movement as well as providing for clearance when one building component is installed within another. For example, the calked joint between a wood door frame and a brick wall allows the frame to shrink and swell, and allows the brick to move slightly without causing damage to either material.

SAMPLE QUESTIONS

The answers to questions 1 through 3 can be found on the following key list. Select only one answer for each question.

A0 arch action
A2 cavity wall
A3 curtain wall
A4 eccentricity
A5 expansion joint
A6 flexible bushings
A7 high-lift grouting
A8 low-lift grouting
A9 reinforced hollow unit masonry

B0 reinforced grouted masonry
B1 shear wall
B2 slip joint
B3 slotted holes
B4 through wall joint
B5 veneered wall
B6 wythe

1. What should be used to allow for the wetting of an exterior wood panel system?

2. What is a metal stud wall system with decorative concrete block on the exterior known as?

3. The lintels of masonry walls with small openings do not carry as much load as might be expected due to what?

4. In earthquake-resistant structures, metal curtain walls should be attached vertically at the column lines and horizontally at the floor lines because:

A. these points are the strongest possible places for anchoring.
B. building movement during an earthquake is at a minimum at these locations.
C. forces are concentrated at these points and should not be bridged across with panels.
D. it is more likely that the workmanship of connections will be better at these points.

5. Select the correct statements about concrete bearing walls when empirical design methods are used.

I. Reinforcing bars should be placed no more than 1'6" apart.

II. The unsupported height cannot exceed 20 times the thickness.

III. Eccentricity is not critical when the wall is more than 10 inches thick and reinforced with #5 bars or larger.

IV. Openings are reinforced all around with #5 bars or larger extending at least 2'0" beyond the corners.

V. Minimum reinforcing percentages change when bar sizes exceed #6 size.

A. I and IV
B. I, II, and III
C. II, III, and IV
D. IV and V

6. If a client requested you to design a building true to the principles of masonry construction, what type of lintel over openings would you most likely design?

A. concealed steel
B. reinforced masonry units
C. precast concrete sized to fit the masonry module
D. arches of the same material as the walls

7. The exterior finish of a small, two-story building is to be stucco. Which of the following wall systems would be a good choice if cost must be minimized and the labor force is relatively unskilled?

A. masonry cavity
B. steel studs
C. balloon frame wood studs
D. platform frame wood studs

8. Which of the following is not true about masonry reinforcing?

A. The spacing of required reinforcement in grouted masonry walls cannot exceed 3 feet.
B. Joint reinforcement is normally placed 16 inches on center.
C. Ties between wythes of a cavity wall are provided for every 4 1/2 square feet of wall surface regardless of their size or type.

D. In low-lift grouting, the size of the horizontal reinforcing must not be included in the determination of minimum cavity width.

9. A concrete block cavity wall must extend 14 feet from the foundation to a row of joists which will be supported by the wall. What wythe combination must be used for the most economical wall?

    A. two 4-inch blocks separated by a 2-inch space

    B. one 4-inch block and one 6-inch block with a 1-inch space

    C. two 6-inch blocks separated by a 2-inch space

    D. one 4-inch block and one 8-inch block separated with a 1-inch space

10. Which of the following affect the bearing capacity of a masonry wall?

    I.   workmanship

    II.   thickness

    III.   number of wythes

    IV.   mortar type

    V.   unsupported height

    VI.   joint reinforcement

    A. I, II, III, and V

    B. I, II, IV, and V

    C. II, IV, V, and VI

    D. all of the above

13 LATERAL FORCES—WIND

Nomenclature

C	chord force	pounds
C_e	combined height, exposure, and gust factor	
C_q	pressure coefficient for the structure or portion of structure under consideration	
d	depth of building	feet
f	load on individual building element	plf
I_w	importance factor	
L	length of building	feet
M	diaphragm moment	foot-pounds
P	design wind pressure	psf
q	wind pressure	psf
q_s	wind stagnation pressure at standard height of 30 feet as given in the Uniform Building Code	psf
v	diaphragm shear stress	plf
v_s	total shear	pounds
V	wind velocity	mph

1 BASIC PRINCIPLES

Wind is air in motion. The movement of the atmosphere is caused by differences in the temperature of air over various parts of the globe. These temperature differences are produced by the uneven absorption and reradiation of heat from the sun as it strikes the air, water vapor, and different earth surfaces.

As warm air rises near the equator, it forms jet streams that move toward the colder, denser air of the polar regions. Some of the air descends in the temperate regions, forming high pressure systems and then splits, some of it moving north and south closer to the earth. On a global scale, the wind caused by these tempera-ture differences are further affected by the rotation of the earth, resulting in a worldwide wind pattern that is generally predictable from season to season.

On a smaller scale, wind is affected by topography and local climatic conditions. For example, the shores of the Great Lakes have unusual winds unlike the surrounding country, as do the areas along the eastern front range of the Rocky Mountains in Colorado.

A. The Effect of Wind on Buildings

The primary effects of wind on buildings are the lateral forces it places on the exterior cladding and lateral forces on the entire structure. As mentioned in Chapter 2, wind can cause a direct, positive pressure, and a suction, or negative pressure. The exact location of the negative pressure depends on the configuration of the building, but most often occurs on the leeward side and frequently occurs on the sides parallel to the wind direction. See Figure 13.1. It also occurs on the roof, whether flat or sloped.

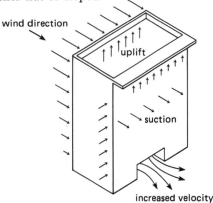

Figure 13.1 Forces on a Building Due to Wind

Smaller, localized areas on a building are also subject to specific pressures that can exceed the pressure on the main body of the structure. This occurs at the building corners, under eaves, on parapets, at the eaves of roofs, and elsewhere.

A building's shape or the location of several buildings in a group can be subject to unusual wind forces that may not affect the structural design as much as the comfort of people and use of the building. Figure 13.1, for example, shows the funneling effect of a small opening. Similar conditions can be produced by two or more buildings placed near one another. The high-speed, localized winds produced can make outdoor plazas and building entries unpleasant at best and unusable at worst. In many cases, wind tunnel testing is required to determine the precise nature of wind around buildings.

Another effect of concern to architects is the drift, or lateral displacement, of a building when subjected to wind forces. Excessive drift can damage brittle or tightly attached exterior materials and can affect the comfort of the occupants near the top of a tall building, and must be minimized. Maximum drift should be limited to 1/500 of the height, and drift between adjacent stories should be limited to 0.0025 times the story height.

Wind can cause a potentially damaging dynamic load on a building. It is called a *resonant*, or *oscillating*, load and can result in the building oscillating side to side perpendicular to the direction of the wind. Dynamic loads can also be induced when repeated gusts of wind strike a building at the same rate as the fundamental period of the building. The fundamental period is the time it takes the structure to complete one full swing from side to side. The Uniform Building Code (UBC) recognizes these potential problems, and requires that structures sensitive to dynamic effects be designed in accordance with approved national standards which usually means wind tunnel testing.

B. Wind Measurement

Wind speed is measured in several different forms. One of the most common methods is called the *fastest-mile wind*. This is the average speed of a column of air one mile long that passes over a given point. Using this method eliminates the effect of sudden, short-term gusts. This type of wind speed is measured with an anemometer.

The value used in designing buildings and other structures is the *extreme fastest-mile wind*. This is the highest fastest-mile wind speed recorded in a certain time period. The UBC uses a 50-year time period in its requirements. The basic wind speeds used for determining wind pressures on buildings are given in Figure 13.2. Because friction against the ground affects wind speed, in order to establish some uniformity in measurement

and reporting, the values shown are taken at 10 meters above the ground. Linear interpolation between wind speed contours is acceptable.

Notice on the map in Figure 13.2 that there are some areas designated special wind regions. These are locales where topography and conditions are so variable that wind speeds are determined by local records and experience, or are individually set by the building official.

C. Variables Affecting Wind Loading

One of the primary factors affecting wind speed is the friction caused by the ground. Since wind acts like water or any other fluid, its speed is reduced when it is in contact with or near other surfaces. There are three basic surface conditions for the purpose of building design: *open country, suburban areas,* and *metropolitan areas*. Open country results in the most severe wind conditions because there is nothing to slow the movement of air.

In each of three cases, wind speed is slowest right at ground level and gradually increases with height until its gradient height is reached. *Gradient height* is that height above which the friction from the ground and other obstructions no longer affects wind speed. For open country, this height is 900 feet; for suburban area, 1200 feet; and for metropolitan areas, 1500 feet. See Figure 13.3.

Below the gradient height, wind speed can be calculated at any given elevation according to a formula that includes the factors of wind pressure at 10 meters, elevation, a velocity pressure coefficient, and a gust response factor. However, for most building design purposes, the UBC simplifies the effects of height and surface exposure into one factor. The use of this factor, C_e, will be discussed in more detail later in this chapter.

Surrounding buildings also affect the wind speed, either by reducing it with shielding effects or increasing it by funneling it between narrow openings. The UBC does not allow for any reduction in wind pressure due to the shielding effect of adjacent structures. However, if wind tunnel tests are conducted on a model of a proposed building, any increases in wind pressure on the building due to adjacent conditions would be taken into account.

2   ANALYSIS OF WIND LOADING

The first step in designing a building to resist wind load is, of course, to determine the forces acting on the structure as a whole and on the individual elements. Then, shear walls, diaphragms, reinforcing, connections, and other components can be selected and sized accordingly.

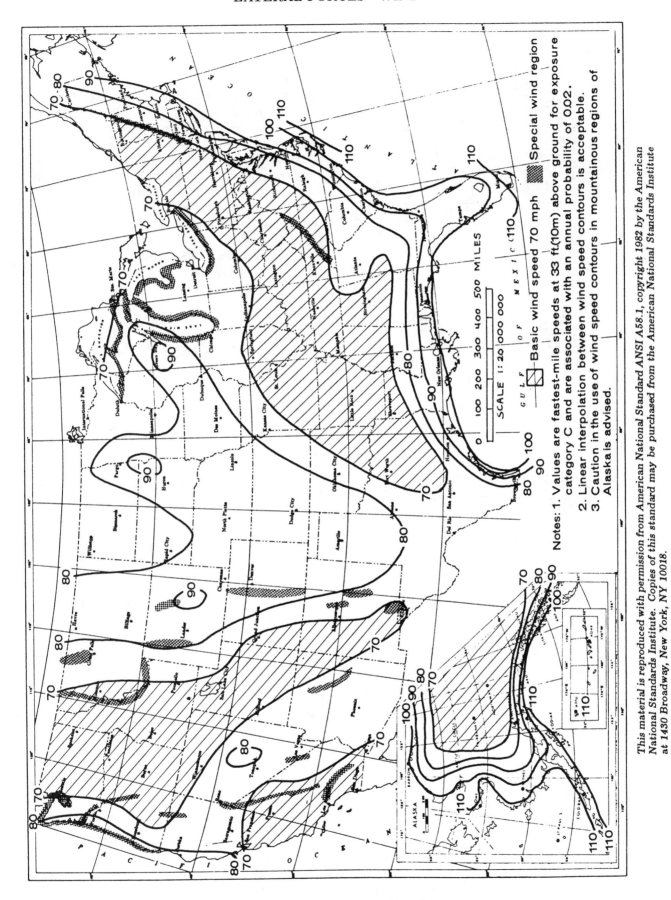

Figure 13.2 Basic Wind Speeds

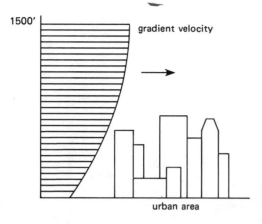

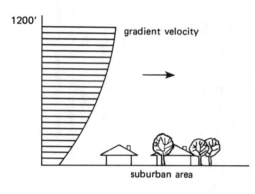

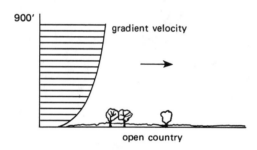

Figure 13.3 Wind Velocity as a Function of Terrain

The pressure acting on the building and individual elements depends on many variables. Complex and lengthy design formulas are available to account for all the variables, and wind tunnel testing may be used to design any building, but the UBC simplifies the procedure somewhat by requiring that the design wind pressure be determined for most buildings by the following formula:

$$P = C_e C_q q_s I_w \qquad\qquad 13.1$$

However, for structures over 400 feet high, buildings subject to dynamic effects, such as those with a height-to-width ratio more than 5 or those sensitive to wind-excited oscillations, must be design in accordance with approved national standards. These involve more complex and lengthy calculations, and, frequently, wind tunnel testing.

A. C_e Factor

The UBC combines the effect of height, exposure, and wind gusting into one factor labeled C_e. Table 13.1 gives these factors and is based on Table 23-G of the UBC. There are three exposure types. Exposure D is the most severe and represents areas with basic wind speeds of 80 miles per hour or greater and terrain that is flat and unobstructed facing large bodies of water more than one mile in width. Exposure D extends inland from the shoreline one-fourth mile or 10 times the building height, whichever is greater. Exposure C has terrain that is flat and generally open, extending one-half mile or more from the site. Exposure B includes areas that have buildings, forests, or surface irregularities covering at least 20 percent of the ground level area extending one mile or more from the site.

Table 13.1

C_e Values

Combined Height, Exposure, and

Gust Coefficient (C_e)

HEIGHT ABOVE AVERAGE LEVEL OF ADJOINING GROUND (feet)	EXPOSURE D	EXPOSURE C	EXPOSURE B
0-15	1.39	1.06	0.62
20	1.45	1.13	0.67
25	1.50	1.19	0.72
30	1.54	1.23	0.76
40	1.62	1.31	0.84
60	1.73	1.43	0.95
80	1.81	1.53	1.04
100	1.88	1.61	1.13
120	1.93	1.67	1.20
160	2.02	1.79	1.31
200	2.10	1.87	1.42
300	2.23	2.05	1.63
400	2.34	2.19	1.80

Values for intermediate heights above 15 feet may be interpolated.

B. C_q Factor

The C_q factor takes into account the differing effect of the wind on various parts of the building. For instance, there is negative pressure on the leeward side, uplift on the roof, and so forth. These factors are shown in Table 13.2. There are two general parts to this table, one for determining loads on the primary frame and wind-resisting systems, and the remainder for calculating pressure on individual elements and special areas.

This table also reflects the two methods by which the UBC requires pressures to be calculated for various types of buildings. Method 1 is called the *normal force method*, which must be used for gabled rigid frames and may be used for any structure. With this method, the wind pressures are assumed to act simultaneously

Table 13.2
C_q Values

PRESSURE COEFFICIENTS (C_q)

STRUCTURE OR PART THEREOF	DESCRIPTION	C_q FACTOR
1. Primary frames and systems	**Method 1 (Normal force method)**	
	Walls:	
	Windward wall	0.8 inward
	Leeward wall	0.5 outward
	Roofs[1]:	
	Wind perpendicular to ridge	
	Leeward roof or flat roof	0.7 outward
	Windward roof	
	less than 2:12	0.7 outward
	Slope 2:12 to less than 9:12	0.9 outward or 0.3 inward
	Slope 9:12 to 12:12	0.4 inward
	Slope > 12:12	0.7 inward
	Wind parallel to ridge and flat roofs	0.7 outward
	Method 2 (Projected area method)	
	On vertical projected area	
	Structures 40 feet or less in height	1.3 horizontal any direction
	Structures over 40 feet in height	1.4 horizontal any direction
	On horizontal projected area[1]	0.7 upward
2. Elements and components not in areas of discontinuity[2]	Wall elements	
	All structures	1.2 inward
	Enclosed and unenclosed structures	1.2 outward
	Open structures	1.6 outward
	Parapets walls	1.3 inward or outward
	Roof elements[3]	
	Enclosed and unenclosed structures	
	Slope < 7:12	1.3 outward
	Slope 7:12 to 12:12	1.3 outward or inward
	Open structures	
	Slope < 2:12	1.7 outward
	Slope 2:12 to 7:12	1.6 outward or 0.8 inward
	Slope > 7:12 to 12:12	1.7 outward or inward
3. Elements and components in areas of discontinuities[2,4,6]	Wall corners[7]	1.5 outward or 1.2 inward
	Roof eaves, rakes or ridges without overhangs[7]	
	Slope < 2:12	2.3 upward
	Slope 2:12 to 7:12	2.6 outward
	Slope > 7:12 to 12:12	1.6 outward
	For slopes less than 2:12	
	Overhangs at roof eaves, rakes or ridges, and canopies	0.5 added to values above
4. Chimneys, tanks and solid towers	Square or rectangular	1.4 any direction
	Hexagonal or octagonal	1.1 any direction
	Round or elliptical	0.8 any direction
5. Open-frame towers[5,8]	Square and rectangular	
	Diagonal	4.0
	Normal	3.6
	Triangular	3.2
6. Tower accessories (such as ladders, conduit, lights and elevators)	Cylindrical members	
	2 inches or less in diameter	1.0
	Over 2 inches in diameter	0.8
	Flat or angular members	1.3
7. Signs, flagpoles, lightpoles, minor structures[8]		1.4 any direction

[1]For one story or the top story of multistory open structures, an additional value of 0.5 shall be added to the outward C_q. The most critical combination shall be used for design. For definition of open structures, see Section 2312.

[2]C_q values listed are for 10-square-foot tributary areas. For tributary areas of 100 square feet, the value of 0.3 may be subtracted from C_q, except for areas at discontinuities with slopes less than 7:12 where the value of 0.8 may be subtracted from C_q. Interpolation may be used for tributary areas between 10 and 100 square feet. For tributary areas greater than 1,000 square feet, use primary frame values.

[3]For slopes greater than 12:12, use wall element values.

[4]Local pressures shall apply over a distance from the discontinuity of 10 feet or 0.1 times the least width of the structure, whichever is smaller.

[5]Wind pressures shall be applied to the total normal projected area of all elements on one face. The forces shall be assumed to act parallel to the wind direction.

[6]Discontinuities at wall corners or roof ridges are defined as discontinuous breaks in the surface where the included interior angle measures 170 degrees or less.

[7]Load is to be applied on either side of discontinuity but not simultaneously on both sides.

[8]Factors for cylindrical elements are two thirds of those for flat or angular elements.

normal to all exterior surfaces. For pressures on the leeward side, the height is taken at the mean roof height and is constant for the full height of the building.

Method 2 is called the *projected area method*, which assumes that horizontal pressures act on the full vertical projected area of the structure, and that vertical pressures act simultaneously on the full horizontal projected area. Figure 13.4 graphically illustrates these two methods for calculating wind pressure.

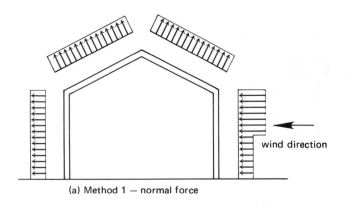

(a) Method 1 — normal force

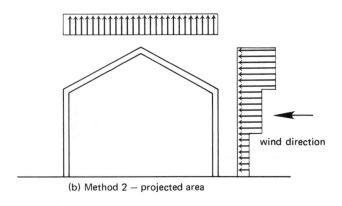

(b) Method 2 — projected area

Figure 13.4   Methods for Calculating Pressures

Method 2 may be used for structures less than 200 feet high, except those using gabled rigid frames, and may be used in determining stability for any structure less than 200 feet high.

C. q_s Factor

The effect of wind speed on pressure is accounted for in the *wind stagnation factor*. The pressures are based on the extreme fastest-mile wind at a standard height of 30 feet, and are calculated with the formula:

$$q = 0.00256V^2 \qquad 13.2$$

The UBC gives the results of the calculation as shown in Table 13.3, which is based on UBC Table 23-F. The wind speeds that must be used are determined from Figure 13.2, from local records, or from local building department requirements if the location is in one of the special wind regions.

Table 13.3

q_s Factor

WIND STAGNATION PRESSURE (q_s) AT STANDARD HEIGHT OF 33 FEET							
Basic wind speed (mph)[1]	70	80	90	100	110	120	130
Pressure q_s (psf)	12.6	16.4	20.8	25.6	31.0	36.9	43.3

[1]Wind speed from Section 2314.

Reproduced from the 1991 edition of the Uniform Building Code, copyright © 1991, with permission of the publishers, the International Conference of Building Officials.

D. Importance Factor

The importance factor, I_w, in Formula 13.1 represents a safety factor for essential facilities which must be safe and usable for emergency purposes during and after a windstorm. The occupancy categories of various facility types are shown in Table 14.4 with earthquake design and the corresponding importance factors are given in Table 14.5.

Example 13.1

A one-story office building 13 feet high is being designed for downtown Rapid City, South Dakota. The building will have a flat roof. Using Method 1, what are the design wind pressures in pounds per square foot for the windward and leeward walls and the roof?

Use formula 13.1. From Table 13.1, the C_e value is 0.62 for a building in a downtown area.

Using Method 1, from Table 13.2, the pressure coefficients, C_q, are 0.8 (inward) for the windward wall, 0.5 (outward) for the leeward wall, and 0.7 (outward) for the roof.

From the map in Figure 13.2, the basic wind speed is nearly 80 miles per hour for Rapid City, and the corresponding pressure, q_s, from Table 13.3, is 16.4 pounds per square foot. Since this is an office building, the importance factor is 1.0.

The various calculations are as follows.

Windward wall:

$$P = (0.62)(0.8)(16.4)(1)$$
$$= 8.13 \text{ psf, inward}$$

Leeward wall:

Because Method 1 is being used, the leeward pressure is considered to be uniform for the full height of the building, and the C_e factor is taken at the mean roof height, which, in the case of this 13-foot building, is 6.5 feet. For exposure B, this is also 0.62.

$$P = (0.62)(0.5)(16.4)(1)$$
$$= 5.08$$

Roof:

$$P = (0.62)(0.7)(16.4)(1)$$
$$= 7.12 \text{ psf, outward}$$

The pressures are summarized in the sketch below.

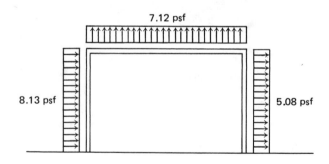

E. Load Combinations Required

As discussed in Chapter 2, the code requires that buildings be designed to resist the most critical effect caused by various combinations of loads. Insofar as wind is concerned, the following combinations must be checked.

- dead plus floor live plus wind

- dead plus floor live plus wind plus one-half snow

- dead plus floor live plus snow plus one-half wind

The one-half factor is included based on the idea that both full snow and wind load are unlikely to occur at the same time.

F. Special Areas and Components

In addition to finding the pressures on the primary structural frame, individual areas need to be analyzed. This is because higher pressures are experienced on elements such as parapets and building corners than on the building as a whole. The pressure coefficients given in Table 13.2 reflect this fact and provide the method by which these greater forces are calculated.

Example 13.2

Find the highest pressure on the corners of the building in Example 13.1.

Looking under the Wall Corners portion of Table 13.2, the C_q factor is 1.5 outward. The other factors are the same.

$$P = (0.62)(1.5)(16.4)(1)$$
$$= 15.2 \text{ psf, outward}$$

Example 13.3

If the building in Example 13.1 had a 2 foot high parapet at the roof, what moment would have to be designed for where the parapet was attached to the roof?

Since a 2-foot parapet would extend to the 15-foot level, the C_e factor would still be 0.62. From Table 13.2, the C_q factor for parapets is 1.3 inward or outward. The design pressure is then:

$$P = (0.62)(1.3)(16.4)(1)$$
$$= 13.22 \text{ psf, inward or outward}$$

The moment is found just as with a beam, with the uniform load of the wind assumed to be acting at the midpoint of the span, or in this case, 1 foot above the roof. The moment is:

$$M = (13.22)(2)(1)$$
$$= 26.44 \text{ foot-pounds per foot of parapet}$$

3 DESIGN OF WIND-RESISTING STRUCTURES

Once the wind forces have been calculated for the various surfaces and components of a building, their distribution to the structural elements must be determined, and then suitable sizes and connections of the structure must be designed to resist them. Before reviewing some of the specific design methods, it is necessary to understand the basics of lateral load distribution and some of the concepts of shape and framing methods used to resist both wind and earthquake forces.

A. Lateral Force Distribution

When wind strikes the sides of a building, the pressures are transferred through the exterior cladding to the points of connection with the floors and roof. The horizontal surfaces of floors and roof act as diaphragms to transfer the forces to the lateral force-resisting elements, which can be the side walls of the building, interior walls, or the structural frame. Walls designed to carry lateral loads are called *shear walls*, because they transfer the horizontal shear to the foundations of the building. Column and beam lines designed to carry wind loads are called *bents*. Figure 13.5 shows a simplified diagram of the transfer of lateral forces using shear walls.

It is helpful to conceptualize the diaphragm as a beam laid on its side, viewing the floor or roof as the web of the beam and the windward and leeward edges as the top and bottom flanges of the beam. The beam spans between the two end walls (or intermediate shear walls) which can be imagined as columns that carry the load to the foundations. Just as with a beam, there is compression in the top, the side facing the wind, and tension in the bottom, or the side away from the wind. These edges are called the *chords*, which will be discussed in more detail in a later section.

When designing a building to resist lateral forces, all of these components must be examined: the shear in the diaphragm, the chord forces, the shear walls, and all of the connections.

Example 13.4

Assume the building used in example 13.1 is 150 feet long and 75 feet wide, and that the two 75-foot end walls will act as shear walls. Assuming the wind force is applied perpendicular to the length of the building, and using Method 1, determine the total force each shear wall must resist and the stress per linear foot along the

shear walls that the roof diaphragm must transfer to the shear walls.

The building and a wall section are shown diagrammatically in the accompanying sketches. The wind load on the roof results from the wind pressure from the midpoint of the wall to the top of the roof.

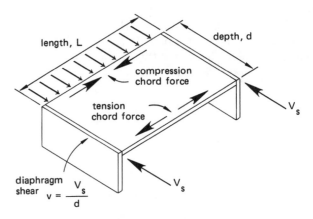

(a) diaphragm loads

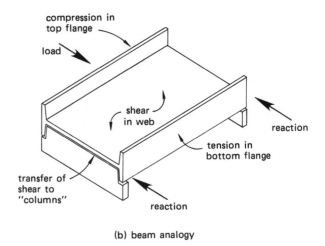

(b) beam analogy

Figure 13.5   Diaphragm Loading

From Example 13.1, the wind pressure was calculated to be 8.13 psf on the windward side of the building. Because Method 1 is used, the negative pressure on the leeward side must be included. This was calculated as 5.08 psf in the previous example problem. These pressures are also shown in the sketch of the wall section. The load per foot of length on the roof is the pressure multiplied by one-half the height of the building.

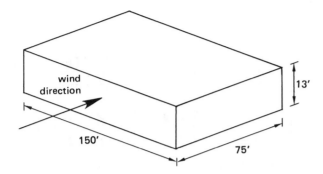

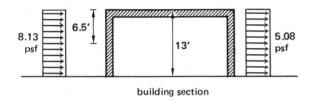

building section

Roof load, windward:

$$(8.13)(6.5) = 52.8 \text{ pounds per linear foot}$$

Roof load, leeward:

$$(5.08)(6.5) = 33.0 \text{ pounds per linear foot}$$

This is a total of 85.8 pounds per linear foot.

The total shear force each wall must resist is found by taking the total load per foot times the length of the building and dividing by two because there are only two walls.

$$V_s = \frac{fL}{2}$$
$$= \frac{(85.8)(150)}{2}$$
$$= 6435 \text{ pounds}$$

The unit shear stress is the total shear distributed along the depth of the building.

$$v = \frac{V_s}{d}$$
$$= \frac{6435}{75}$$
$$= 85.8 \text{ pounds per linear foot}$$

B. Building Shape and Framing Methods

Some building shapes and framing systems are more resistant to wind forces than others. The first consideration in designing a structure to resist wind is the plan shape of the building. Rectangular shapes have a tendency to block more of the wind than round and tapered shapes, but are usually more functional in terms of space planning and are generally less expensive to construct.

(Text continues on next page.)

Rectangular shapes, however, do allow for some adjustment in planning to make them more efficient. Consider the two building shapes shown diagrammatically in Figure 13.6 with the wind coming from an assumed direction. Building A is rectangular in plan, while building B is square in plan. Both buildings have the same height and the same floor area, but building B is more efficient in resisting wind for two reasons.

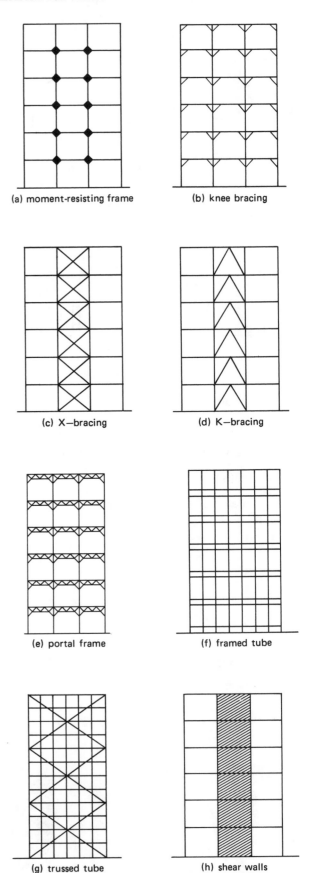

(a) moment-resisting frame

(b) knee bracing

(c) X—bracing

(d) K—bracing

(e) portal frame

(f) framed tube

(g) trussed tube

(h) shear walls

Figure 13.7 Framing Systems to Resist Lateral Loads

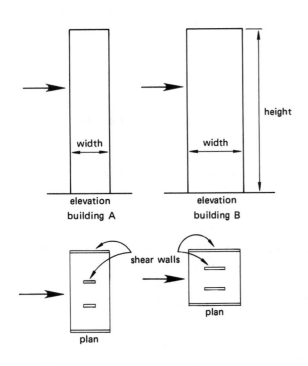

Figure 13.6 Effect of Building Shape on Efficiency

First, the surface area facing the wind is less than building A, so the total force on the structural system will be less. Secondly, the increased width allows for deeper shear walls and a reduction in the height-to-width ratio. Since shear walls act as beams cantilevered out of the ground, the deeper section is more efficient and requires less structural material to resist the forces.

However, if the length-to-width ratio is increased enough, the basic rigidity in the long dimension will distribute the wind forces among the normal structural elements enough so that special wind bracing will not be required; it will only be necessary in the short dimension.

Framing methods are the second consideration that determine a building's inherent resistance to lateral loads. The sketches in Figure 13.7 show some of the basic types of steel framing systems which are used to resist both wind and earthquake loads.

The simplest is the *moment-resisting frame*, figure 13.7 (a). With this system, moment-resisting connections are used between columns and beams as discussed in the section on connections. The connections may consist of simple welded joints or may include small brackets when larger loads are involved. This system is useful for low-rise buildings and high-rise buildings under 30 stories. Above this height, the wind loads cannot be efficiently resisted without additional types of bracing.

Knee bracing, Figure 13.7 (b), is an economical way to provide rigidity to a steel frame whether it is a one-story industrial building or a large high-rise. The bracing struts are usually short enough that they can be concealed above a suspended ceiling if appearance is a concern.

Two of the most common types of lateral bracing for tall structures are the *X-brace* and the *K-brace*, Figures 13.7 (c) and (d). They are usually placed in a central set of bays in a building's structural framework and act as vertical trusses cantilevered out of the ground. The diagonal members can be designed primarily as tension members to minimize their size. With this approach, it is assumed that when the wind loads the building from one side, one of the braces is in tension and the other is not stressed. When the building is loaded from the opposite side, the stresses in the diagonal members reverse. Although both systems are very efficient, the K-bracing system results is less horizontal drift because the diagonal members are shorter, and therefore elongate less under stress.

The portal system illustrated in Figure 13.7 (e) is composed of trusses at each floor level with knee braces connecting the truss to the columns. It is not used very much unless the trusses are also used to support the vertical loads of the floor system or the roof of a one-story building.

As lateral loads increase and buildings become taller, the *framed-tube system* is often used. This system creates a large, hollow tube cantilevered from the ground. It is built of closely spaced exterior columns and beams which are rigidly connected to form a very efficient, stiff structure. See Figure 13.7 (f).

The trussed tube concept shown in Figure 13.7 (g) uses a combination of rigid frame and diagonal braces on the exterior wall. The X-braces span from five to ten floors and result in a structure very resistant to lateral loads. For additional strength and reduced drift, the exterior walls can be sloped slightly like the John Hancock Tower in Chicago.

Finally, a steel frame can be used in conjunction with concrete shear walls as shown in Figure 13.7 (h). The steel frame carries most of the vertical loads while the concrete shear walls transmit the lateral forces to the foundation. This system is frequently used because the concrete shear walls can easily be a part of the core of the building enclosing elevators, stairways, and mechanical duct space. For added efficiency, the shape of the concrete walls can be varied to suit the structural needs of the building, forming H- or T-shaped sections so there is rigidity in both directions.

There are many variations to these basic types of framing systems. The bundled tube concept used for the Sears Tower in Chicago, for example, extends the framed tube idea by grouping nine tubes together. Other systems include belt trusses at intermediate floors and buildings with tapered profiles.

Framing systems for concrete structures follow some of the same approaches as steel with a few variations owing to the nature of the material.

Rigid frame structures can be built out of concrete but moment-resisting connections between columns and beams are not as easy to make, so these building systems are limited to 20 to 30 stories.

For greater resistance, rigid frames are combined with concrete shear walls which are designed to take the majority of the lateral forces. Frame walls can also be used with shear walls so the two act together in resisting wind and earthquake loads.

Framed tubes can be built out of concrete as well as steel. Like steel structures, these are buildings with closely spaced exterior columns rigidly connected with the beams. It also acts as a large tube cantilevered from the ground. When this idea is extended, the system becomes a tube-within-a-tube system where an additional tube of closely spaced interior columns is attached to the exterior grouping with a rigid floor at each level. This is one of the most efficient kinds of high-rise concrete structures exemplified by Water Tower Place in Chicago.

C. Diaphragm Design

A diaphragm must be able to resist the lateral loads placed on it without excessive deformation or failure. It must be designed to act as a unit so the forces can be transferred to the shear walls. Horizontal diaphragms can be constructed of plywood, particle board, concrete, steel decking, and combinations of these materials. Each material or combination has its own load-carrying capacity as a diaphragm member.

For example, allowable shear for horizontal diaphragms of plywood and particle board and allowable shear for

Table 13.4
Allowable Shear for Horizontal Plywood Diaphragms

ALLOWABLE SHEAR IN POUNDS PER FOOT FOR HORIZONTAL PLYWOOD DIAPHRAGMS WITH FRAMING OF DOUGLAS FIR-LARCH OR SOUTHERN PINE¹

PLYWOOD GRADE	Common Nail Size	Minimum Nominal Penetration in Framing (In inches)	Minimum Nominal Plywood Thickness (In inches)	Minimum Nominal Width of Framing Member (In inches)	BLOCKED DIAPHRAGMS — Nail spacing at diaphragm boundaries (all cases), at continous panel edges parallel to load (Cases 3 and 4) and at all panel edges (Cases 5 and 6)				UNBLOCKED DIAPHRAGM — Nails spaced 6" max. at supported end	
					6	4	2½/2⅔	2	Load perpendicular to unblocked edges and continuous panel joints (Case 1)	Other configurations (Cases 2, 3, 4, 5 and 6)
					Nail spacing at other plywood panel edges					
					6	6	4	3		
STRUCTURAL I	6d	1¼	5/16	2 3	185 210	250 280	375 420	420 475	165 185	125 140
	8d	1½	3/8	2 3	270 300	360 400	530 600	600 675	240 265	180 200
	10d³	1⅝	15/32	2 3	320 360	425 480	640 720	730 820	285 320	215 240
C-D, C-C, STRUCTURAL II and other grades covered in U.B.C. Standard No. 25-9	6d	1¼	5/16	2 3	170 190	225 250	335 380	380 430	150 170	110 125
			3/8	2 3	185 210	250 280	375 420	420 475	165 185	125 140
	8d	1½	3/8	2 3	240 270	320 360	480 540	545 610	215 240	160 180
			15/32	2 3	270 300	360 400	530 600	600 675	240 265	180 200
	10d³	1⅝	15/32	2 3	290 325	385 430	575 650	655 735	255 290	190 215
			19/32	2 3	320 360	425 480	640 720	730 820	285 320	215 240

¹These values are for short-time loads due to wind or earthquake and must be reduced 25 percent for normal loading. Space nails 12 inches on center along intermediate framing members.

Allowable shear values for nails in framing members of other species set forth in Table No. 25-17-J of the U.B.C. Standards shall be calculated for all grades by multiplying the values for nails in Structural 1 by the following factors: Group III, 0.82 and Group IV, 0.65.

²Framing at adjoining panel edges shall be 3-inch nominal or wider and nails shall be staggered where nails are spaced 2 inches or 2½ inches on center.

³Framing at adjoining panel edges shall be 3-inch nominal or wider and nails shall be staggered where 10d nails having penetration into framing of more than 1⅝ inches are spaced 3 inches or less on center.

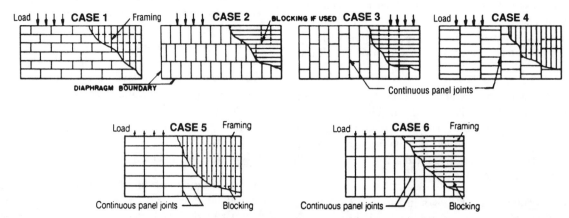

Note: Framing may be oriented in either direction for diaphragms, provided sheathing is properly designed for vertical loading.

Reproduced from the 1991 edition of the Uniform Building Code, copyright © 1991, with permission of the publishers, the International Conference of Building Officials.

plywood and particle board shear walls are given in
Tables 25-J and 25-K of the Uniform Building Code.
The table for horizontal plywood diaphragms is reproduced in Table 13.4. These tables give the allowable
shear in pounds per foot based on the grade of material, material thickness, nail sizes, nail spacing, framing
member size, and whether the material is blocked or
unblocked. Blocked diaphragms are those with solid
framing members at each edge of the plywood or particle board.

Example 13.5

Select a plywood diaphragm system for the loads calculated in Example 13.4.

The unit stress in the roof was found to be 85.8 pounds
per linear foot. Any of the combinations listed in
Table 13.4 will work because the unit stress is so low in
this example. Depending on the spacing of the joists,
a 1/2-inch thickness of plywood would probably be the
minimum thickness for practical use. Any of the combinations using 6d nails at the maximum allowable spacing of 6 inches would work in this instance.

D. Chord Force

As shown in Figure 13.5, wind loading along a floor or
roof of a building produces a compression and tension
force in the diaphragm, just like in the top and bottom
flanges of a beam. This force, distributed along the
depth of the diaphragm, is known as the *chord force*
and is used to determine the kind of connection that is
needed between the diaphragm and the shear walls in
order to transfer the lateral load.

Since the diaphragm acts like a simple, uniformly loaded
beam when it is between two shear walls, the chord
force can be found by first determining the moment at
the edges of the diaphragm using the formula found in
Figure 4.7: $M = wl^2/8$. Then, the chord force is the
moment divided by the depth of the diaphragm:

$$C = \frac{M}{d} \qquad 13.5$$

Example 13.6

Find the chord force for the roof in the problem in
Example 13.4.

As calculated in Example 13.4, the total force on the
roof is 85.8 pounds per linear foot, the length of the
building is 150 feet, and the building depth is 75 feet.

The moment is:

$$M = \frac{(85.8)(150)^2}{8}$$
$$= 241,312 \text{ foot-pounds}$$

The chord force, using formula 13.5, is:

$$C = \frac{241,312}{75}$$
$$= 3217 \text{ pounds}$$

E. Shear Walls and Overturning

Once the wind forces have been transferred through the
diaphragm and chords into the shear wall, the shear wall
must transfer the forces to the foundation. In addition,
the shear walls and the entire building must resist the
tendency for the structure to overturn due to the moment caused by the lateral force. Finally, the shear wall
must be attached to the foundation and footings in such
a way to prevent the entire building from sliding, and
the footings and foundation system must be designed
to resist the additional loads (caused by the overturning moment), which are added to the simple vertical
forces of dead and live loads.

The methods of analysis and design for shear walls are
complex and beyond the scope of this book, but the
following example will illustrate some of the basic principles.

Example 13.7

Considering the same hypothetical building as discussed
in the previous examples, and assuming the shear walls
are constructed of 8-inch lightweight aggregate concrete
block (35 pounds per square foot) with 30 percent open
area for windows, find the total shear forces in one of
the end walls and the overturning moment.

The accompanying sketch summarizes the loads on the
shear wall. The load on the roof is the load per linear
foot times the length divided by 2.

$$\text{load} = \frac{(85.8)(150)}{2} = 6435 \text{ pounds}$$

The loads on the shear wall are shown in the sketch. These are the loads that would be used to design the structure of the shear wall, regardless of what material was used.

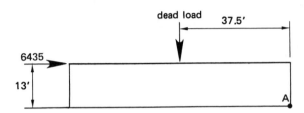

The overturning moment is important to calculate because the building code requires that the resisting moment developed by the dead load on the shear wall be 1.5 times the overturning moment caused by the wind. In this example, the overturning moment is the force at the roof multiplied by the length of the moment arm.

$$M = (6435)(13)$$
$$= 83,655 \text{ foot-pounds}$$

The required dead load moment must be 1.5(83,655), or 125,482 foot-pounds.

The actual weight of the wall allowing for 30 percent void is:

$$(75)(13)(35)(0.7) = 23,887 \text{ pounds}$$

This weight is assumed to act at the midpoint of the wall, so the moment arm is 37.5 feet. The resisting moment is:

$$M = (23,887)(37.5)$$
$$= 895,781 \text{ foot-pounds}$$

This is more than adequate to resist the wind overturning moment without using special anchors attaching the walls to the foundation.

F. Drift

Drift is the lateral displacement of a building caused by a lateral load from a true vertical line. For wind loading, the maximum permissible drift of one story relative to an adjacent story is 0.0025 times the story height. In the example, if the story height is 13 feet, the maximum drift is:

$$(0.0025)(13)(12) = 0.39 \text{ inches}$$

G. Connections

Connections are a critical part of any structural frame that resists lateral loads. These include connections of curtain wall to frame, beams to columns, diaphragm to shear wall, and primary structural frame to the foundation, among others. Moment-resisting connections are fairly common because they occur somewhere in practically any structure designed for lateral forces. Four of the more common types of connections used in steel framed buildings are shown in Figure 13.8. In all connections, the resisting moment increases with increased distance between the centroids of the top and bottom portions of the connection.

One type of connection that has little moment resistance is shown in Figure 13.8 (a). This is a typical steel frame semi-rigid connection. Because the angles are relatively flexible, very little moment can be transferred from beam to column. The connection shown in (b) is sometimes used instead. The increased rigidity of the structural tees can provide a moment-resisting joint.

In order to minimize the number of pieces and assure a good moment-resisting joint, beams and columns are often welded as shown in Figure 13.8 (c). There is usually an angle seat to hold the beam in place during erection and to carry the shear loads, but the welded plates transfer the moment.

For an even more rigid connection, a small stub bracket as shown in Figure 13.8 (d) can be used. The triangular shape is structurally efficient and usually can be concealed by the finish column cover or within a suspended ceiling. There are many variations of this connection detail; usually, it includes a combination of bolted and welded joints.

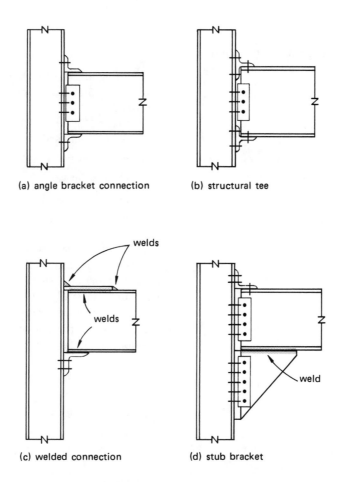

(a) angle bracket connection   (b) structural tee

(c) welded connection   (d) stub bracket

Figure 13.8   Beam-to-Column Connections

SAMPLE QUESTIONS

The answers to questions 1 through 3 can be found on the following key list. Select only one answer for each question.

A0 anemometer
A1 bent
A2 drift
A3 fastest-mile wind
A4 framed tube
A5 importance factor
A6 knee bracing
A7 leeward
A8 moment resisting frame
A9 normal force method

B0 portal frame
B1 projected area method
B2 resonant load
B3 shear wall
B4 trussed tube
B5 X-bracing

1. The John Hancock Building in Chicago is an example of what type of framing system?

2. What must be used for designing gabled rigid frames?

3. A line of columns used to resist wind forces is called what?

4. Select the incorrect statement.

   A. Drift of adjacent floors must be limited to 0.0025 times the floor height.
   B. Overturning is resisted by the dead load moment, which must be 1 1/2 times the overturning moment.
   C. K-bracing provides for a more rigid high-rise structure than X-bracing.
   D. Wind tunnel testing or special calculations are frequently required for buildings over 400 feet high.

5. Using Method 2, what is the design wind pressure on the upper part of a wall of a 40-foot high hospital in downtown Salt Lake City, Utah?

   A. 14.8 psf
   B. 15.8 psf

   C. 17.0 psf
   D. 24.7 psf

6. In designing a sheathing and roofing system for a roof with a 5:12 slope, what pressure coefficient should be used?

   A. 0.7 outward

   B. 0.9 outward

   C. 1.3 outward

   D. 1.7 outward

7. A wood ledger is being used to support and connect a plywood diaphragm floor to a 38-foot long stud wall that is acting as a shear wall. 8d nails, which can hold 82 pounds laterally, are to be used. If the total force on one of the shear walls is calculated as 4600 pounds, what is the minimum nail spacing required to attach the floor to the ledger?

   A. 4 inches

   B. 6 inches

   C. 8 inches

   D. 10 inches

8. Select the correct statements from the following list.

   I. Shear walls are more efficient if they are relatively deep compared with their height.

   II. Trussed-tube construction is often used for both steel and concrete construction.

   III. Wood frame buildings must often be anchored to the foundation to resist uplift as well as shear.

   IV. Welded connections offer an economical way to fabricate moment resisting frames while simplifying erection.

   V. Dividing the total shear on a shear wall by its length gives the value for diaphragm shear.

   A. I, III, IV, and V
   B. II, III, and V
   C. II, IV, and V
   D. all of the above

9. The effect of intermittent wind gusts is taken into account in the UBC with the:

A. C_e factor

B. C_q factor

C. q_s factor

D. I_w factor

10. Which of the following are not true about wind forces on buildings?

I. Wind stagnation pressure is greater in open areas than in urban areas.

II. Corners of buildings require special consideration during the design phase.

III. The negative pressure on the leeward side of a building is taken into consideration in both Method 1 and Method 2 of the UBC design procedure.

IV. Wind velocity increases when the area it moves through is decreased in area.

V. The direction of the prevailing winds at a particular site is used to calculate wind stagnation pressure.

A. I, III, and V

B. I and V

C. II and III

D. III, IV, and V

LATERAL FORCES— EARTHQUAKES

14

Nomenclature

C	numerical coefficient determined by formula 14.2	
C_p	horizontal force factor coefficient for elements of structures	
C_t	numerical coefficient for calculating the period of vibration	
F_p	lateral force on part of a structure	pounds or kips
F_t	the portion of V considered concentrated at the top of the structure in addition to F_x	pounds or kips
F_x	lateral force applied to level x	pounds or kips
h_n	total height of building	feet
h_x	height above base to level x	feet
I	occupancy importance factor	
I_p	importance factor for elements of structures	
R_w	numerical coefficient given in UBC Table 23-O and 23-Q	
S	site coefficient for soil characteristics given in UBC Table 23-J	
T	fundamental period of vibration	seconds
V	total design lateral force or base shear	pounds or kips
w_x	the portion of W that is located at level x	pounds or kips
W	weight	pounds or kips
W_p	weight of a portion of a structure	pounds or kips
Z	seismic zone factor given in UBC Table 23-I	

Although a great deal has been learned about earthquakes and their effects on buildings during the last 50 years, seismic design is still an inexact science. Because seismic design deals with dynamic forces rather than static forces, and, because of the many variables involved, it is often difficult to precisely predict the performance of a building in an earthquake and provide the best possible design to resist the resulting lateral forces.

Another difficulty with seismic design is that the forces produced by an earthquake are so great that no building can economically and reasonably be designed to completely resist all loads in a major earthquake without damage. Building codes and analytical methods of design are, therefore, a compromise between what could resist all earthquakes and what is reasonable. Because of this, the current approach in designing earthquake-resistant structures is that they should first of all not collapse during major seismic activity. Additionally, the components of buildings should not cause other damage or personal injury even though they may be structurally damaged themselves. Finally, structures should be able to withstand minor earthquakes without significant damage.

The analytic methods of analysis and design of earthquake-resistant structures are complex, even with the simplified static analysis method allowed by the Uniform Building Code (UBC). However, a great deal of resistance is provided by the basic configuration and structural system of a building. The design of buildings for earthquake loads requires an early and close collaboration between the architect and engineer to arrive at the optimum structural design while still satisfying the functional and aesthetic needs of the client.

This chapter will discuss some of the basic principles of earthquakes and the primary design and planning guidelines with which you should be familiar. In addition, a basic review of the static analysis method will be presented along with some simplified problems to help explain the design concepts.

1 BASIC PRINCIPLES

The UBC provides for two methods of design for seismic forces: the static lateral force procedure and the dynamic lateral force procedure. The static method treats the seismic loads as equivalent lateral loads acting on the various levels of the building. The total base shear is calculated and then distributed along the height of the building. The dynamic method uses a computer to mathematically model the building so the response of the structure can be studied at each moment in time using an actual or simulated earthquake accelerogram. The dynamic method is very complex and its details are not covered in the A.R.E. The static method is reviewed in section 4.

The UBC is specific about which analysis method may or must be used. In general, any structure may be, and certain structures must be, designed using the dynamic lateral force procedures. The static method may be used for the following types of structures:

- all structures in seismic zone 1 and in zone 2 with occupancy category IV, whether they are regular or irregular

- regular structures using one of the lateral force resistance systems listed in Table 23-O if they are under 240 feet in height (see Table 14.1)

- irregular structures less than five stories or 65 feet high

- structures with a flexible upper portion supported on a rigid lower portion if all of the following conditions are met:

  · when both portions are considered separately, they can both be classified as regular

  · the average story stiffness of the lower portion is at least ten times the average story stiffness of the upper portion

  · the period of the whole structure is no more than 1.1 times the period of the upper portion considered as a separate structure fixed at the base

All other structures must be designed using the dynamic method.

A. Characteristics of Earthquakes

Earthquakes are caused by the slippage of adjacent plates of the earth's crust and the subsequent release of energy in the form of ground waves. Seismology is based on the science of plate tectonics, which proposes that the earth is composed of several very large plates of hard crust many miles thick, riding on a layer of molten rock closer to the earth's core. These plates are slowly moving relative to one another, and over time tremendous stress is built up by friction. Occasionally, the two plates slip, releasing the energy we know as earthquakes. One of the most well known boundaries between two plates occurs between the Pacific plate and the North American plate along the coast of California. Earthquakes also occur in midplates, but the exact mechanism, other than fault slippage, is not fully understood.

The plates slip where the stress is maximum, usually several miles below the surface of the earth. Where this occurs is called the *hypocenter* of the earthquake. The term heard more often is the *epicenter*, which is the point on the earth's surface directly above the hypocenter.

When an earthquake occurs, complex actions are set up. One result is the development of waves which ultimately produce the shaking experienced in a building. There are three types of waves: *P* or *pressure waves*, *S* or *shear waves*, and *surface waves*. Pressure waves cause a relatively small movement in the direction of wave travel. Shear waves produce a sideways or up-and-down motion that shakes the ground in three directions. These are the waves that cause the most damage to buildings. Surface waves travel at or near the surface and can cause both vertical and horizontal earth movement.

The ground movement can be measured in three ways: by acceleration, velocity, and displacement. All three occur over time, with most earthquakes lasting only a few seconds. It is the acceleration of the ground that induces forces on a structure.

The interaction of the various waves and ground movement is complex. Not only does the earth move in three directions, but each direction has a different, random acceleration and amplitude. In addition, the movement reverses, creating a vibrating action. Even though there is vertical movement, this is most often not critical for seismic design. The weight of a structure is usually enough to resist vertical forces. It is the side-to-side movement that causes the most damage.

B. Measurement of Earthquakes

Earthquake strength is commonly measured in two ways: with the *Richter scale* and with the *Modified Mercalli Intensity scale.* The Richter scale measures magnitude as an indirect measure of released energy based on instrument recordings according to certain defined procedures. The scale runs from zero at the low end and is open at the upper end, although the largest earthquake ever recorded had a Richter magnitude of nine.

The scale is logarithmic, each whole number value on the scale represents a ten-fold increase in amplitude. In terms of energy released, each scale number represents about 32 times the amount of energy of the number below it.

The Modified Mercalli Intensity scale is a measure of an earthquake's intensity. It is an entirely subjective rating based on the observed damage to structures and other physical effects. The scale ranges from I to XII with the upper rating being the most severe. Each scale includes a verbal description of the effects and damage of an earthquake.

The Modified Mercalli scale is imprecise because it depends on people's observations, but it does provide information on how an earthquake affects structures and how the same earthquake affects areas at different distances from the epicenter, both of which cannot be accounted for with the Richter scale.

Unfortunately for building design, neither scale is useful. This is because neither provides any information on the acceleration or duration of an earthquake, both of which are critical in the analysis and design of structures. However, they are used for risk analysis and determination of seismic zones.

Objective, quantified data useful for building design is provided by the *strong motion accelerograph.* This machine measures the acceleration of the ground or a building. The UBC requires that in seismic zones 3 and 4 every building over six stories with an aggregate floor area of 60,000 square feet or more, and every building over ten stories regardless of floor area, be provided with not less than three accelerographs. These must be placed in the basement, midportion, and near the top of the building. Some jurisdictions may have additional requirements.

The records obtained by these instruments provide valuable data for research and design of similar buildings in the same geographical area. The acceleration they measure is usually expressed as a fraction of the acceleration of gravity, g, which is 32 feet per second per second. Thus, an earthquake may be recorded as having an acceleration of $0.55g$.

C. Seismic Zones

Based on seismic records, experience, and research, some areas of the United States are determined to have a greater probability of earthquakes than others, and some areas have more severe earthquakes (areas where two major plates abut, for example). This is taken into account by dividing the country into different zones which represent estimates of future earthquake occurrence and strength.

The map used by the UBC is shown in Figure 14.1. The procedure for incorporating the zones will be discussed in a later section.

D. The Effect of Earthquakes on Buildings

When an earthquake occurs, the first response of a building is not to move at all due to the inertia of the structure's mass. Almost instantaneously, however, the acceleration of the ground causes the building to move sideways at the base causing a lateral load on the building and a shear force at the base, as though forces were being applied in the opposite direction. See Figure 14.2 (a). As the direction of the acceleration changes, the building begins to vibrate back and forth.

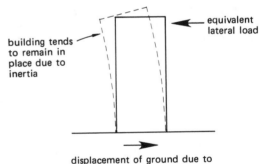

Figure 14.2 Building Motion During an Earthquake

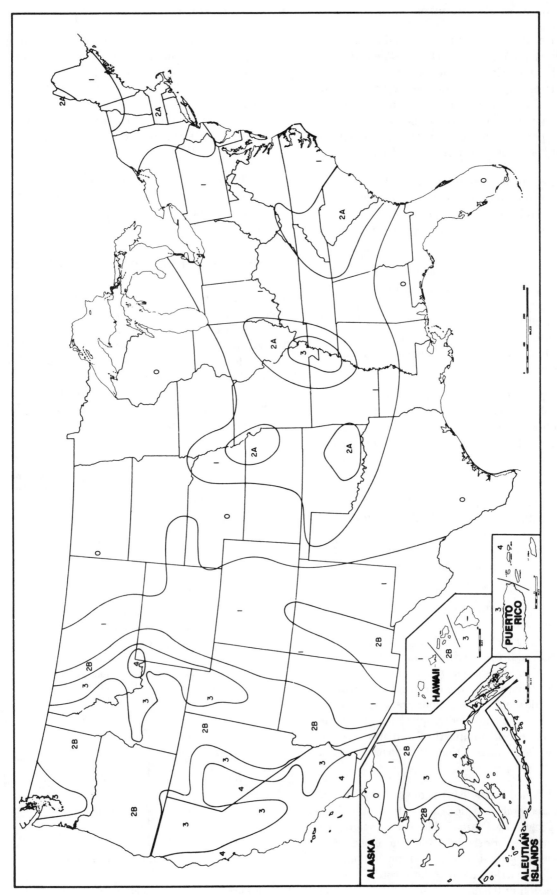

Figure 14.1 Seismic Zone Map of the United States

Reproduced from the 1988 edition of the Uniform Building Code, copyright © 1988, with permission of the publishers, the International Conference of Building Officials.

Theoretically, the force on the building can be found by using Newton's law, which states that force equals mass times acceleration. Since the acceleration is established by the given earthquake, the greater the mass of the building, the greater the force acting on it. However, the acceleration of the building depends on another property of the structure—its natural period.

If a building is deflected by a lateral force such as the wind or an earthquake, it moves from side to side. The period is the time in seconds it takes for a building to complete one full side-to-side oscillation. See Figure 14.2 (b). The period is dependent on the mass and the stiffness of the building.

In a theoretical, completely stiff building, there is no movement, and the natural period is zero. The acceleration of such an infinitely rigid building is the same as the ground. As the building becomes more flexible, its period increases and the corresponding acceleration decreases. As mentioned above, as the acceleration decreases, so does the force on the building. Therefore, flexible, long-period buildings have less lateral force induced, and stiff, short-period buildings have more lateral force induced.

As the building moves, the forces applied to it are either transmitted through the structure to the foundation, absorbed by the building components, or released in other ways such as collapse of structural elements.

The goal of seismic design is to build a structure that can safely transfer the loads to the foundation and back to the ground and absorb some of the energy present rather than suffering damage.

The ability of a structure to absorb some of the energy is known as *ductility*, which occurs when the building deflects in the inelastic range without failing or collapsing. The elastic limit, as discussed in Chapter 3, is the limit beyond which the structure sustains permanent deformation. The greater the ductility of a building, the greater is its capacity to absorb energy.

Ductility varies with the material. Steel is a very ductile material because of its ability to deform under a load above the elastic limit without collapsing. Concrete and masonry, on the other hand, are brittle materials. When they are stressed beyond the elastic limit, they break suddenly and without warning. Concrete can be made more ductile with reinforcement, but at a high cost.

2 STRUCTURAL SYSTEMS TO RESIST LATERAL LOADS

The UBC specifies the types of structural systems used to resist seismic loads. The code requires that structural systems be classified as one of the types listed in Table 23-O. (See Table 14.1.) In addition to outlining the various types of structural systems, Table 23-O gives the R_w factor used in calculations and the maximum height of each type of structural system. There are four broad categories of systems.

A. Bearing Wall Systems

A bearing wall system is a structural system without a complete vertical load-carrying space frame in which the lateral loads are resisted by shear walls or braced frames. Bearing walls or bracing systems provide support for all or most gravity loads. Remember that a space frame is defined as a three-dimensional structural system, without bearing walls, that is comprised

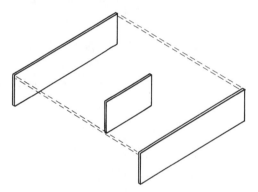

(a) end shear walls and interior shear wall

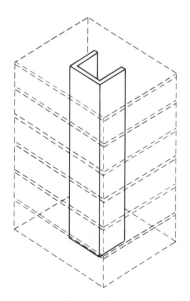

(b) interior shear walls for bracing in two directions

Figure 14.3 Shear Walls

of members interconnected such that it functions as a complete, self-contained unit.

A *shear wall* is a vertical structural element that resists lateral forces in the plane of the wall through shear and bending. Such a wall acts as a beam cantilevered out of the ground or foundation, and, just as with a beam, part of its strength derives from its depth. Figure 14.3 shows two examples of a shear wall, one in a simple one-story building and another in a multistory building.

In Figure 14.3 (a), the shear walls are oriented in one direction, so only lateral forces in this direction can be resisted. The roof serves as the horizontal diaphragm and must also be designed to resist the lateral loads and transfer them to the shear walls.

Figure 14.3 (a) also shows an important aspect of shear walls in particular and vertical elements in general. This is the aspect of symmetry that has a bearing on whether torsional effects will be produced. The shear walls in

Table 14.1
Structural Systems

BASIC STRUCTURAL SYSTEM[1]	LATERAL LOAD-RESISTING SYSTEM—DESCRIPTION	R_w[2]	H[3]
A. Bearing Wall System	1. Light-framed walls with shear panels		
	a. Plywood walls for structures three stories or less	8	65
	b. All other light-framed walls	6	65
	2. Shear walls		
	a. Concrete	6	160
	b. Masonry	6	160
	3. Light steel-framed bearing walls with tension-only bracing	4	65
	4. Braced frames where bracing carries gravity loads		
	a. Steel	6	160
	b. Concrete[4]	4	—
	c. Heavy timber	4	65
B. Building Frame System	1. Steel eccentrically braced frame (EBF)	10	240
	2. Light-framed walls with shear panels		
	a. Plywood walls for structures three stories or less	9	65
	b. All other light-framed walls	7	65
	3. Shear walls		
	a. Concrete	8	240
	b. Masonry	8	160
	4. Concentrically braced frames		
	a. Steel	8	160
	b. Concrete[4]	8	—
	c. Heavy timber	8	65
C. Moment-resisting Frame System	1. Special moment-resisting frames (SMRF)		
	a. Steel	12	N.L.
	b. Concrete	12	N.L.
	2. Concrete intermediate moment-resisting frames (IMRF)[6]	8	—
	3. Ordinary moment-resisting frames (OMRF)		
	a. Steel	6	160
	b. Concrete[7]	5	—
D. Dual Systems	1. Shear walls		
	a. Concrete with SMRF	12	N.L.
	b. Concrete with steel OMRF	6	160
	c. Concrete with concrete IMRF[6]	9	160
	d. Masonry with SMRF	8	160
	e. Masonry with steel OMRF	6	160
	f. Masonry with concrete IMRF[4]	7	—
	2. Steel EBF		
	a. With steel SMRF	12	N.L.
	b. With steel OMRF	6	160
	3. Concentrically braced frames		
	a. Steel with steel SMRF	10	N.L.
	b. Steel with steel OMRF	6	160
	c. Concrete with concrete SMRF[4]	9	—
	d. Concrete with concrete IMRF[4]	6	—
E. Undefined Systems	See Sections 2333 (h) 3 and 2333 (i) 2	—	—

[1]Basic structural systems are defined in Section 2333 (f).
[2]See Section 2334 (c) for combination of structural system.
[3]H—Height limit applicable to Seismic Zones Nos. 3 and 4. See Section 2333 (g).
[4]Prohibited in Seismic Zones Nos. 3 and 4.
[5]N.L.—No limit.
[6]Prohibited in Seismic Zones Nos. 3 and 4, except as permitted in Section 2338 (b).
[7]Prohibited in Seismic Zones Nos. 2, 3 and 4.

Figure 14.3 (a) show the shear walls symmetrical in the plane of loading. Torsion will be discussed in a later section.

Figure 14.3 (b) illustrates a common use of shear walls at the interior of a multistory building. Because walls enclosing stairways, elevator shafts, and mechanical chases are mostly solid and run the entire height of the building, they are often used for shear walls. Although not as efficient from a strictly structural point of view, interior shear walls do leave the exterior of the building open for windows.

Notice that in 14.3 (b) there are shear walls in both directions, which is a more realistic situation because both wind and earthquake forces need to be resisted in both directions. In this diagram, the two shear walls are symmetrical in one direction, but the single shear wall produces a nonsymmetric condition in the other since it is off center. Shear walls do not need to be symmetrical in a building, but symmetry is preferred to avoid torsional effects.

Shear walls can be constructed from a variety of materials, but the most common are plywood on wood framing for residential and small commercial buildings, and concrete for larger buildings. Reinforced masonry walls can also be used. Shear walls may have openings in them but the calculations are more difficult and their ability to resist lateral loads is reduced depending on the percentage of open area.

B. Building Frame Systems

A building frame system is one with an essentially complete space frame that provides support for gravity loads in which the lateral loads are resisted by shear walls or braced frames. A braced frame is a truss system of the concentric or eccentric type in which the lateral forces are resisted through axial stresses in the members. Just as with a truss, the braced frame depends on diagonal members to provide a load path for lateral forces from each building element to the foundation. Figure 14.4 (a) shows a simple one-story braced frame. At one end of the building two bays are braced, and at the other end only one bay is braced. As with Figure 14.3, this building is only braced in one direction and uses compression braces because the diagonal member may be either in tension or compression depending on which way the force is applied.

Figure 14.4 (b) shows two methods of bracing a multistory building. A single diagonal compression member in one bay can be used to brace against lateral loads coming from either direction. Alternately, tension diagonals can be used to accomplish the same result, but they must be run both ways to account for the load coming from either direction.

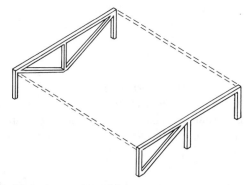

(a) single-story braced frame

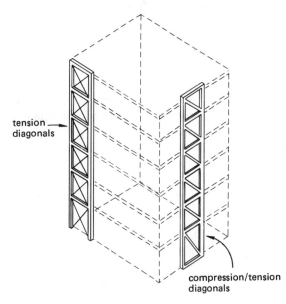

tension diagonals

compression/tension diagonals

(b) multistory braced frame

Figure 14.4 Braced Frames

Braced framing can be placed on the exterior or interior of a building, and may be placed in one structural bay or several. In a trussed tube building, the diagonals span between several floors of the building. Obviously, a braced frame can present design problems for windows and doorways, but it is a very efficient and rigid lateral force resisting system.

C. Moment-Resisting Frame Systems

Moment-resisting frames carry lateral loads primarily by flexure in the members and joints. Joints are designed and constructed so they are theoretically completely rigid, and therefore any lateral deflection of the frame occurs from the bending of columns and beams. The UBC differentiates between three types of moment-resisting frames.

The first type is the special moment-resisting frame which must be specially detailed to provide ductile behavior and comply with the provisions of Chapters 26 and 27 (Concrete and Steel) of the UBC.

The second type is the intermediate moment-resisting frame, which is a concrete frame with less restrictive requirements than special moment-resisting frames. However, intermediate frames cannot be used in seismic zones 3 or 4.

The third type is the ordinary moment-resisting frame. This is a steel or concrete moment-resisting frame that does not meet the special detailing requirements for ductile behavior. Ordinary steel frames may be used in any seismic zone while ordinary concrete frames cannot be used in zones 3 or 4.

Because moment-resisting frames are more flexible than shear wall structures or braced frames, the horizontal deflection, or drift, is greater, so adjacent buildings cannot be located too close to each other, and special attention must be paid to the eccentricity developed in columns, which increases the column bending stresses.

Two types of moment-resisting frames are shown in Figure 14.5.

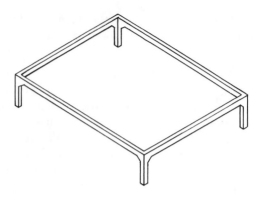

(a) single-story frame

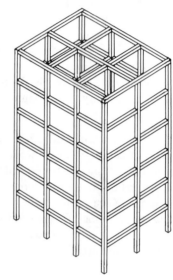

(b) multistory frame

Figure 14.5   Moment-Resisting Frames

D. Dual Systems

A dual system is a structural system in which an essentially complete frame provides support for gravity loads, and resistance to lateral loads is provided by a specially detailed moment-resisting frame and shear walls or braced frames. The moment-resisting frame must be capable of resisting at least 25 percent of the base shear and the two systems must be designed to resist the total lateral load in proportion to their relative rigidities. The moment-resisting frame may be either steel or concrete, but concrete intermediate frames cannot be used in seismic zones 3 or 4.

E. Horizontal Elements

In all lateral force-resisting systems, there must be a way to transmit lateral forces to the vertical resisting elements. This is done with several types of structures, but the most common way used is the *diaphragm*. As discussed in Chapter 13, a diaphragm acts as a horizontal beam resisting forces with shear and bending action. Refer to Figure 13.5.

Other types of horizontal elements include horizontal trussed frames and horizontal moment-resisting frames.

There are two types of diaphragms: flexible and rigid. Although no horizontal element is completely flexible or rigid, distinction is made between the two types because the type affects the way in which lateral forces are distributed.

A flexible diaphragm is one that has a maximum lateral deformation more than two times the average story drift of that story. This deformation can be determined by comparing the midpoint in-plane deflection of the diaphragm with the story drift of the adjoining vertical resisting elements under equivalent tributary load. The lateral load is distributed according to tributary areas as shown in Figure 14.6 (a).

With a *rigid diaphragm*, the shear forces transmitted from the diaphragm to the vertical elements will be in proportion to the relative stiffnesses of the vertical elements (assuming there is no torsion). See Figure 14.6 (b). If the end walls in the diagram are twice as stiff as the interior walls, then one-third of the load is distributed to each end wall and one-third to the two interior walls which is equally divided between these two. The illustration shows symmetrically placed shear walls so the distribution is equal. However, if the vertical resisting elements are asymmetric, the shearing forces are unequal.

Concrete floors are considered rigid diaphragms as are steel and concrete composite deck construction. Steel decks may be either flexible or rigid depending on the details of their construction. Wood decks are considered flexible diaphragms.

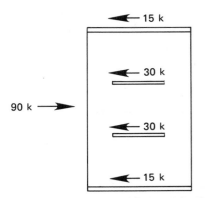

(a) flexible diaphragm load distribution

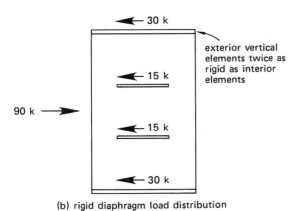

(b) rigid diaphragm load distribution

Figure 14.6 Diaphragm Load Distribution

3 BUILDING CONFIGURATION

In recent years, there has been increased emphasis on the importance of a building's configuration in resisting seismic forces. Early decisions concerning size, shape, arrangement, and location of major elements can have a significant influence on the performance of a structure. Since the design professional plays a large role in these early decisions, it is imperative that the architect thoroughly understand the concepts involved.

Building configuration refers to the overall building size and shape, and the size and arrangement of the primary structural frame, as well as the size and location of the non-structural components of the building that may affect its structural performance. Significant non-structural components include such things as heavy non-bearing partitions, exterior cladding, and large weights like equipment or swimming pools.

In the current UBC, elements that constitute both horizontal and vertical irregularities are specifically defined, so it is clear which structures must be designed with the dynamic method and which structures may be designed using the static analysis method.

The code states that all buildings must be classified as either regular or irregular. Whether a building is regular or not helps determine if the static method may be used. Irregular structures generally require design by the dynamic method (with exceptions mentioned in section 1) and additional detailed design requirements are imposed depending on what type of irregularity exists.

Table 23-M (see Table 14.2) lists and defines five types of vertical structural irregularities along with references to the specific code sections that give specific design requirements. Table 23-N (see Table 14.3) lists and defines five types of plan structural irregularities along with their code references. Note that the definition of torsional irregularity (Plan Structural Irregularity Type A in Table 14.3) mentions diaphragms that are not flexible. Flexible diaphragms are defined in section 2E.

Table 14.2
Vertical Structural Irregularities

IRREGULARITY TYPE AND DEFINITION	REFERENCE SECTION
A. **Stiffness Irregularity—Soft Story** A soft story is one in which the lateral stiffness is less than 70 percent of that in the story above or less than 80 percent of the average stiffness of the three stories above.	2312 (d) 8 C (ii)
B. **Weight (mass) Irregularity** Mass irregularity shall be considered to exist where the effective mass of any story is more than 150 percent of the effective mass of an adjacent story. A roof which is lighter than the floor below need not be considered.	2312 (d) 8 C (ii)
C. **Vertical Geometric Irregularity** Vertical geometric irregularity shall be considered to exist where the horizontal dimension of the lateral force-resisting system in any story is more than 130 percent of that in an adjacent story. One-story penthouses need not be considered.	2312 (d) 8 C (ii)
D. **In-plane Discontinuity in Vertical Lateral Force-resisting Element** An in-plane offset of the lateral load-resisting elements greater than the length of those elements.	2312 (e) 7
E. **Discontinuity in Capacity—Weak Story** A weak story is one in which the story strength is less than 80 percent of that in the story above. The story strength is the total strength of all seismic resisting elements sharing the story shear for the direction under consideration.	2312 (d) 9 A

Table 14.3
Plan Structural Irregularities

IRREGULARITY TYPE AND DEFINITION	REFERENCE SECTION
A. **Torsional Irregularity—to be considered when diaphragms are not flexible.**	
Torsional irregularity shall be considered to exist when the maximum story drift, computed including accidental torsion, at one end of the structure transverse to an axis is more than 1.2 times the average of the story drifts of the two ends of the structure.	2312 (h) 2 I (v)
B. **Reentrant Corners**	
Plan configurations of a structure and its lateral force-resisting system contain reentrant corners, where both projections of the structure beyond a reentrant corner are greater than 15 percent of the plan dimension of the structure in the given direction.	2312 (h) 2 I (v) 2312 (h) 2 I (vi)
C. **Diaphragm Discontinuity**	
Diaphragms with abrupt discontinuities or variations in stiffness, including those having cutout or open areas greater than 50 percent of the gross enclosed area of the diaphragm, or changes in effective diaphragm stiffness of more than 50 percent from one story to the next.	2312 (h) 2 I (v)
D. **Out-of-plane Offsets**	
Discontinuities in a lateral force path, such as out-of-plane offsets of the vertical elements.	2312 (e) 7, 2312 (h) 2 I (v)
E. **Nonparallel Systems**	
The vertical lateral load-resisting elements are not parallel to nor symmetric about the major orthogonal axes of the lateral force-resisting system.	2312 (h) 1

Reproduced from the 1988 edition of the Uniform Building Code, copyright © 1988, with permission of the publishers, the International Conference of Building Officials.

Also note that the definition of nonparallel systems (Plan Structural Irregularity Type E in Table 14.3) includes buildings in which a column forms part of two or more intersecting lateral force-resisting systems, unless the axial load due to seismic forces acting in either direction is less than 20 percent of the column allowable axial load.

The following sections describe some of the important aspects of building configuration.

A. Torsion

Lateral forces on a portion of a building are assumed to be uniformly distributed and can be resolved into a single line of action acting on a building. In a similar way, the shear reaction forces produced by the vertical resisting elements can be resolved into a single line of action. For symmetric buildings with vertical resisting elements of equal rigidity, these lines of action pass through the same point as shown diagrammatically in Figure 14.7 (a).

If the shear walls or other vertical elements are not symmetric or are of unequal rigidity, the resultant of their shear resisting forces, the center of rigidity, does not coincide with the applied lateral force. This is shown in Figure 14.7 (b). Since the forces are acting in opposite directions with an eccentricity, torsion force is developed, which is in addition to the lateral load alone.

When the force on a vertical element caused by the eccentricity acts in the same direction as that caused by the lateral load directly, they must be added. However, when the torsional force acts in the opposite direction, one cannot be subtracted from the other.

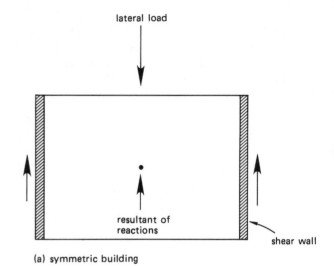

(a) symmetric building

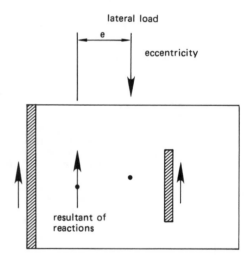

(b) nonsymmetric vertical load–resisting elements

Figure 14.7   Development of Torsion

The UBC requires that even in symmetrical buildings a certain amount of accidental torsion be planned for. This accounts for the fact that the position of loads in an occupied building cannot be known for certain. The code requires that the mass at each level is assumed to be displaced from the calculated center of mass in each direction by a distance equal to five percent of the building dimension at that level perpendicular to the direction of the force under consideration. For example, for a building 50 feet wide and 100 feet long, the center of mass for forces acting perpendicular to the 100-foot dimension is offset 5 feet. For forces acting in the other direction, the center of mass is offset 2 1/2 feet.

The importance of understanding the concept of torsion will become apparent in the following sections.

B. Plan Shape

Irregularities in plan shape can create torsion and concentrations of stress, both of which should be avoided whenever possible. One of the most common and troublesome plan shapes is the re-entrant corner. Figure 14.8 (a) shows some common varieties of this shape. During an earthquake, the ground motion causes the structure to move in such a way that stress concentrations are developed at the inside corners. See Figure 14.8 (b).

shapes are unavoidable, there are ways to minimize the problem. The portions of the building can be separated with a seismic joint, they can be tied together across the connection, or the inside corner can be splayed. These design approaches are shown in Figure 14.9.

A second common problem that arises with building plans is a variation in the stiffness and strength of the perimeter. Even though a building may be symmetric, the distribution of mass and lateral resisting elements may place the centers of mass and rigidity in such a way that torsion is developed. One example of this is shown diagrammatically in Figure 14.10 (a) where a building has rigid shear walls on three sides, but is open in the front.

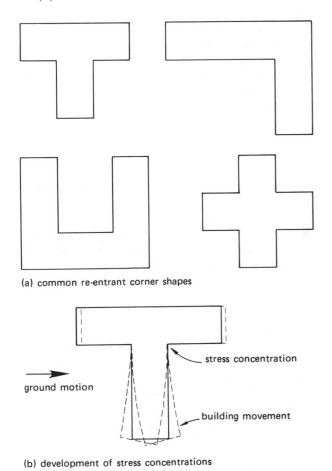

(a) common re-entrant corner shapes

(b) development of stress concentrations

ground motion

stress concentration

building movement

Figure 14.8 Problem Plan Shapes

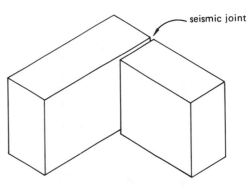

seismic joint

(a) separate wings

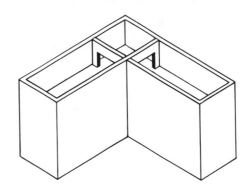

(b) provide strong connection

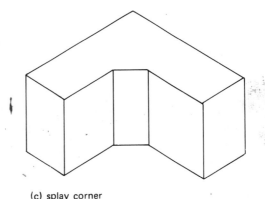

(c) splay corner

Figure 14.9 Solutions to Re-entrant Corners

In addition, since the center of mass and the center of rigidity do not coincide, there is an eccentricity established which results in a twisting of the entire structure as discussed in the previous section and is shown in Figure 14.7 (b).

Of course, building shape is often dictated by the site, the program, or other requirements beyond the control of the architect or engineer. In the cases where such

During an earthquake, the open end of the building acts as a cantilevered beam causing lateral displacement and torsion. There are four possible ways to alleviate the problem. These are shown in Figure 14.10 (b).

In the first instance, a rigid frame can be constructed with symmetric rigidity and then the cladding can be made non-structural. Secondly, a strong, moment-resisting or braced frame can be added which has a stiffness similar to the other walls. Third, shear walls can be added to the front if this does not compromise the function of the building. Finally, for small buildings, the structure can simply be designed to resist the expected torsion forces.

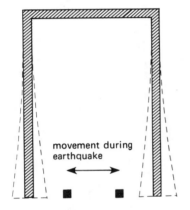

(a) variation in perimeter stiffness—plan

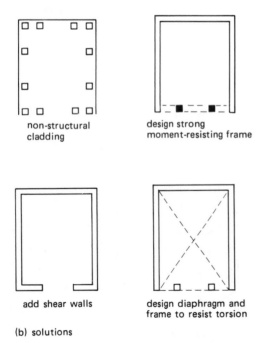

non-structural cladding

design strong moment-resisting frame

add shear walls

design diaphragm and frame to resist torsion

(b) solutions

Figure 14.10 Variation in Perimeter Stiffness

C. Elevation Design

The ideal elevation from a seismic design standpoint is one that is regular, symmetrical, continuous, and that matches the other elevations in configuration and seismic resistance. Setbacks and offsets should be avoided for the same reason as re-entrant corners in plan should be avoided; that is, to avoid areas of stress concentration. Of course, perfect symmetry is not always possible due the the functional and aesthetic requirements of the building, but there are two basic configurations that should (and can) be avoided by the architect early in the design process.

The first problem configuration is a discontinuous shear wall. This is a major mistake and should never happen. Discontinuities can occur when large openings are placed in shear walls, when they are stopped short of the foundation, or altered in some other way. Since the entire purpose of a shear wall is to carry lateral loads to the foundation and act as a beam cantilevered out of the foundation, any interruption of this is counterproductive. Of course, small openings like doors and small windows can be placed in shear walls if proper reinforcement is provided.

Two common examples of discontinuous shear walls are shown in Figure 14.11. In the first, the shear wall is stopped at the second floor level and supported by columns. This is often done to open up the first floor, but creates a situation where stress concentrations are so great that even extra reinforcing cannot always resist the build-up of stress.

The second example, shown in Figure 14.11 (b), is also a common design feature where the second floor and floors above are cantilevered slightly from the first floor shear wall. Even though the shear wall continues, the offset also creates an undesirable situation because the direct load path for the lateral loads is interrupted, and the floor structure has to carry the transfer of forces from one shear wall to the next.

In all cases of discontinuous shear walls, the solution is simple: shear walls should run continuously to the foundation.

Another serious problem with building configuration is the soft story. This occurs when the ground floor is weaker than the floors above. Although a soft story can occur at any floor, it is most serious at grade level because this is where the lateral loads are the greatest. The discontinuous shear wall discussed in the previous section is a special case of the soft story. Others can occur when all columns do not extend to the ground or when the first story is high compared with the other floors of the structure. See Figure 14.12.

columns or lower height. If height is critical, extra columns can be added at the first floor. Another solution is to add extra horizontal and diagonal bracing. Finally, the framing of the upper stories can be made the same as the first story. The entire structure then has a uniform stiffness. Lighter, intermediate floors can be added above the first between the larger bays so they do not affect the behavior of the primary structural system.

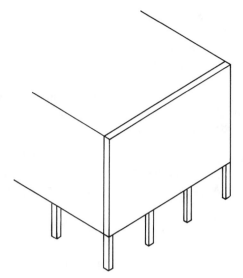

(a) shear wall to column transition

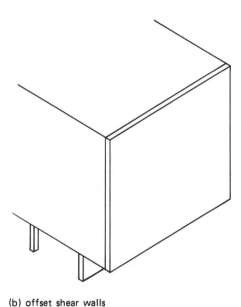

(b) offset shear walls

Figure 14.11 Discontinuous Shear Walls

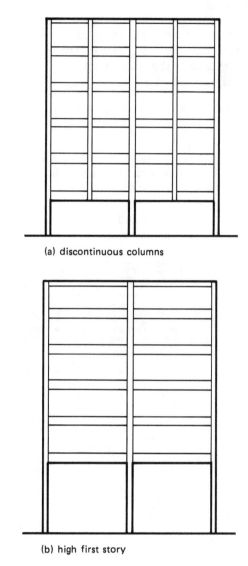

(a) discontinuous columns

(b) high first story

Figure 14.12 Soft First Stories

A soft story can also be created when there is heavy exterior cladding above the first story and the ground level is open. Of course, there are usually valid reasons for all of these situations to occur. For example, a hotel may need a high first story, but shorter floors above for the guest rooms.

When earthquake loads occur, the forces and deformations are concentrated at the weak floor instead of being uniformly distributed among all the floors and structural members.

There are several ways to solve the problem of a soft story. The first, of course, is to eliminate it and try to work the architectural solution around the extra

4   ANALYSIS OF EARTHQUAKE LOADING

This section discusses the equivalent static load method for determining the base shear, or total lateral force, on a building. Except for structures required to be designed according to dynamic analysis as previously mentioned, the UBC allows the total seismic force on the main structural frame to be calculated according to a simplified formula. When using this formula, the base shear in each of the main axes of the building must be determined and the structural system designed to resist the forces.

In addition, the code requires that forces on elements of structures and non-structural components be calculated according to a different formula. This will be reviewed in a later section.

When a structure meets the requirements listed in section 1, the static force procedure may be used. The formula for finding the total lateral force or shear at the base of a structure is

$$V = \frac{ZIC}{R_w}W \qquad 14.1$$

Once the total lateral force is determined, it is used to determine the forces on the various horizontal and vertical structural elements.

Table 14.4
Occupancy Categories

OCCUPANCY CATEGORIES	OCCUPANCY TYPE OR FUNCTIONS OF STRUCTURE
I. Essential Facilities[1]	Hospitals and other medical facilities having surgery and emergency treatment areas.
	Fire and police stations.
	Tanks or other structures containing, housing or supporting water or other fire-suppression materials or equipment required for the protection of essential or hazardous facilities, or special occupancy structures.
	Emergency vehicle shelters and garages.
	Structures and equipment in emergency-preparedness centers.
	Standby power-generating equipment for essential facilities.
	Structures and equipment in government communication centers and other facilities required for emergency response.
II. Hazardous Facilities	Structures housing, supporting or containing sufficient quantities of toxic or explosive substances to be dangerous to the safety of the general public if released.
III. Special Occupancy Structure	Covered structures whose primary occupancy is public assembly–capacity > 300 persons.
	Buildings for schools through secondary or day-care centers–capacity > 250 students.
	Buildings for colleges or adult education schools–capacity > 500 students.
	Medical facilities with 50 or more resident incapacitated patients, but not included above.
	Jails and detention facilities.
	All structures with occupancy > 5,000 persons.
	Structures and equipment in power-generating stations and other public utility facilities not included above, and required for continued operation.
IV. Standard Occupancy Structure	All structures having occupancies or functions not listed above.

[1]Essential facilities are those structures which are necessary for emergency operations subsequent to a natural disaster.

Reproduced from the 1991 edition of the Uniform Building Code, copyright © 1991, with permission of the publishers, the International Conference of Building Officials.

A. Z Factor

The Z factor represents the amount of seismic risk present in any given geographical location. The seismic zone map has six zones with zone 0 being the one of least risk. (See Figure 14.1.) The following list gives the Z factors for each zone as stated in Table 23-I of the 1988 UBC:

Zone 0	$Z = 0$	Zone 2B	$Z = 0.20$
Zone 1	$Z = 0.075$	Zone 3	$Z = 0.30$
Zone 2A	$Z = 0.15$	Zone 4	$Z = 0.40$

B. I Factor

The importance factor, I, is either 1.0 or 1.25, depending on the occupancy categories which are listed in UBC Table 23-K. (See Table 14.4.) The importance factors are itemized in UBC Table 23-L. (See Table 14.5.)

Table 14.5
Occupancy Requirements

OCCUPANCY CATEGORY[1]	IMPORTANCE FACTOR I	
	Earthquake[2]	Wind
I. Essential facilities	1.25	1.15
II. Hazardous facilities	1.25	1.15
III. Special occupancy structures	1.00	1.00
IV. Standard occupancy structures	1.00	1.00

[1]Occupancy types or functions of structures within each category are listed in Table No. 23-K and structural observation requirements are given in Sections 305, 306 and 307.
[2]For life-safety-related equipment, see Section 2336 (a).

Reproduced from the 1991 edition of the Uniform Building Code, copyright © 1991, with permission of the publishers, the International Conference of Building Officials.

C. C Factor

The C factor represents both the period of vibration and the characteristics of the soil. Table 23-J of the 1988 UBC gives the S factors used in formula 14.2 to calculate C. (See Table 14.6.) The S factor must be established from geotechnical investigation, but where soil properties are not known, profile S_3 can be used.

$$C = \frac{1.25S}{T^{2/3}} \qquad 14.2$$

The UBC gives two methods of determining T: an approximate method that can be used for all buildings, and a more complex method based on the deformational characteristics of the resisting elements in the building. The formula for approximating T is

$$T = C_t(h_n)^{3/4} \qquad 14.3$$

Table 14.6
Site Coefficients

SITE COEFFICIENTS[1]

TYPE	DESCRIPTION	S FACTOR
S_1	A soil profile with either: (a) A rock-like material characterized by a shear-wave velocity greater than 2,500 feet per second or by other suitable means of classification, or (b) Stiff or dense soil condition where the soil depth is less than 200 feet.	1.0
S_2	A soil profile with dense or stiff soil conditions, where the soil depth exceeds 200 feet.	1.2
S_3	A soil profile 70 feet or more in depth and containing more than 20 feet of soft to medium stiff clay but not more than 40 feet of soft clay.	1.5
S_4	A soil profile containing more than 40 feet of soft clay characterized by a shear wave velocity less than 500 feet per second.	2.0

[1]The site factor shall be established from properly substantiated geotechnical data. In locations where the soil properties are not known in sufficient detail to determine the soil profile type, soil profile S_3 shall be used. Soil profile S_4 need not be assumed unless the building official determines that soil profile S_4 may be present at the site, or in the event that soil profile S_4 is established by geotechnical data.

In equation 14.3, $C_t = 0.035$ for steel moment-resisting frames, $C_t = 0.030$ for reinforced concrete moment-resisting frames and eccentric braced frames, and $C_t = 0.020$ for all other buildings.

The code also gives another formula for finding the value of C_t for structures with concrete or masonry shear walls. Refer to Sec. 2334(b)2B of the UBC for this formula.

The code states that the value for C does not have to exceed 2.75, and this value may be used for any structure without regard to soil type or the period of the structure. It further states that except for the code provisions that require forces to be scaled up by a factor of 3, the minimum value of the ratio C/R_w shall be 0.075.

D. R_w Factor

The R_w factor is based on the type of structural system used. These factors are given in Table 23-O (see Table 14.1) as previously discussed. For nonbuilding structures, the R_w factor is given in UBC Table 23-Q.

The R_w factor reflects the energy-absorbing capabilities of various types of structural systems. Notice that systems with high ductility, such as steel special moment-resisting space frames, have a higher R_w value than systems with less ductility. Because the R_w value is now placed in the denominator of equation 14.1, a higher value results in a lower value of V, the design seismic force.

E. W Factor

The W factor is the total dead load of the building. Other applicable loads listed here must also be added:

- In warehouses and storage occupancies, a minimum of 25 percent of the floor live load must be added.

- When partition loads are used in the design of the floor, not less than 10 pounds per square foot must be included.

- Where snow load exceeds 30 pounds per square foot, it must also be included except when a reduction of up to 75 percent is approved by the building official.

- The total weight of permanent equipment must be included.

Example 14.1

A small, three-story hospital is being planned for Denver, Colorado. The structure is to be 45 feet high, 80 feet wide, and 170 feet long. Preliminary soil reports indicate 50 feet of soft clay soil. Snow load is 30 psf. If a bearing wall system with concrete shear walls is planned and the estimated weight is 3500 kips, what is the base shear?

From Figure 14.1, Denver is in zone 1, so the Z factor is 0.075.

Because this is a hospital, the importance factor is 1.25.

To find C, first determine the period. Using formula 14.3,

$$T = 0.020(45)^{3/4}$$
$$= 0.35 \text{ seconds}$$

The S factor is 2.0 for soft clay soils (S_4).

Using formula 14.2,

$$C = \frac{(1.25)(2.0)}{(0.35)^{2/3}}$$
$$= 5.03$$

Because this is greater than 2.75, use $C = 2.75$ as allowed by the code.

From Table 14.1, the R_w factor is 6.

Check the ratio of C/R_w:

$$\frac{2.75}{6} = 0.46$$

This is greater than the minimum of 0.075 required by the code so the quantities calculated can be used.

Calculate the base shear:

$$V = \frac{ZIC}{R_w}W$$

$$= \frac{(0.075)(1.25)(2.75)}{6}(3500)$$

$$= 150 \text{ kips}$$

F. Distribution of Base Shear

Once the total base shear is known, it is used to determine the forces on the various building elements. For single-story buildings, this is fairly straightforward. For multistory buildings, the forces must be distributed according to the displacement that occurs during an earthquake. Although structural movement under seismic forces is complex, the static lateral force procedure uses the most pronounced displacement that takes place, which results in an inverted force triangle varying from zero at the base to the maximum at the top. See Figure 14.13 (a).

With this simplified approach, it is assumed that there is uniform mass distribution and equal floor heights, but the code does provide for variations as will be shown in formula 14.4. The sum of the loads at each level equals the total base shear. Also note that while the greatest force is at the top of the building, the shear increases from zero at the top to its maximum at the base. Each floor shear is successively added to the sum from above. This method for the distribution of loads is only for the design of vertical lateral load resisting elements. There is another formula for determining the force on the diaphragm at each level of a multistory building.

To account for tall buildings that do not have a uniform triangular distribution, the UBC requires that an additional force be applied at the top of the building, but only if the period, T, is greater than 0.7 seconds. This force is,

$$F_t = 0.07TV \qquad\qquad 14.4$$

However, this force value does not have to be greater than $0.25V$. The remaining base shear, $(V - F_t)$, is then distributed to the roof and each floor according to the formula:

$$F_x = \frac{(V - F_t)w_x h_x}{\sum\limits_{i=1}^{n} w_i h_i} \qquad\qquad 14.5$$

The value of the denominator is the summation of all the floor weights times their heights at the floor under

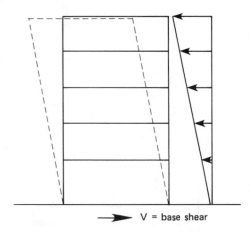

(a) distribution of forces using the equivalent static load method

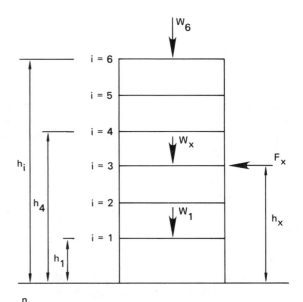

$$\sum_{i=1}^{n} w_i h_i = w_1 h_1 + w_2 h_2 + w_3 h_3 + w_4 h_4 + w_5 h_5 + w_6 h_6$$

Figure 14.13   Distribution of Base Shear

consideration. The formula can be solved easily using a tabular approach as shown in the next example. The values included in formula 14.5 are shown graphically in Figure 14.13 (b).

Example 14.2

A three-story office building located in Gary, Indiana is 40 feet wide and 80 feet long. Each floor is 12 feet high, and the building is wood frame construction with plywood shear walls at each end. Building weights are as follows.

roof	15 psf
floors	20 psf
exterior walls	18 psf
partitions	8 psf

Determine the distribution of shear in the transverse direction.

step 1: Determine the weight of each floor and the total weight. The roof weight is 74 kips, and the second and third floor weights are 142 kips each, for a total weight of 358 kips.

step 2: Determine the seismic factors and calculate the base shear. Gary, Indiana is inside zone 1:

$$Z = 0.075$$
$$I = 1.0$$
$$C = \frac{1.25S}{T^{2/3}} \quad \text{(from formula 14.2)}$$
$$T = C_t(h_n)^{3/4} \quad \text{(from formula 14.3)}$$

Using a value of 0.020 for C_t and a height of 36 feet,

$$T = 0.294 \text{ seconds}$$

Because no soil information is given, use soil type S_3 with a value of 1.5.

Therefore,

$$C = \frac{1.25(1.5)}{(0.294)^{2/3}}$$
$$= 4.241$$

However, because C does not have to exceed 2.75, use this value.

From UBC Table 23-O (Table 14.1), $R_w = 8$ (structure type A1a).

$$W = 358 \text{ kips}$$

The base shear is then

$$V = \frac{(0.075)(1.0)(2.75)}{8} 358$$
$$= 9.23 \text{ kips}$$

Because the period, T, is less than 0.7, $F_t = 0$ so the $(V - F_t)$ value is 9.23 kips.

step 3: Tabulate the values needed for solving formula 14.5, and calculate the results:

1	2	3	4	5	6
level	w_x	h_x	$w_x h_x$		F_x
roof	74	36	2664	0.34	3.14
3	142	24	3408	0.44	4.06
2	142	12	1704	0.22	2.03
			7776	1.00	9.23

The values in column 5 are calculated by taking the value in column 4 and dividing by the summation of column 4, which is 7776. The values in column 5 are then multiplied by the base shear, 9.23 kips, to arrive at the distributed force at each level.

G. Parts of Buildings

The code requires that in addition to the primary structural frame, individual elements of structures, nonstructural components, and their connections be designed to withstand seismic forces. Of particular importance are connections of the floors and roof to the walls and columns, walls to the structural frame, partitions to floors and ceilings, ceilings to boundary walls, millwork to floors and walls, equipment and fixtures to floors, piping and ducts to the structure, and suspended lights to the ceilings.

The force these parts must withstand is determined by:

$$F_p = ZI_pC_pW_p \qquad 14.6$$

The values of C_p are given in UBC Table 23-P. (See Table 14.7.)

Note that the values found in this table are for *rigid* elements. Rigid elements are defined as those having a fixed base period less than or equal to 0.06 second. Nonrigid elements or flexibly supported items have a fixed base period greater than 0.06 second. Unless detailed analysis of a nonrigid element is performed, the value of C_p must be taken as twice the value given in Table 23-P, but it does not have to exceed 2.0.

Example 14.3

It is decided that the building in Example 14.2 is to have an 8-inch masonry exterior and a parapet 3 feet high. Determine the load on the parapet if it weighs 55 psf.

From Example 14.2, $Z = 0.075$ and $I = 1.0$.

From Table 14.7, the C_p value for a parapet is 2.0.

The force on each square foot of parapet is:

$$F_p = (0.075)(1.0)(2.0)(55)$$
$$= 8.25 \text{ psf}$$

This value can be used to determine the moment on the parapet and the subsequent reinforcing required to resist the moment.

Table 14.7
Horizontal Force Factor, C_p

ELEMENTS OF STRUCTURES AND NONSTRUCTURAL COMPONENTS AND EQUIPMENT[1]	VALUE OF C_p	FOOTNOTE
I. Part or Portion of Structure		
1. Walls including the following:		
a. Unbraced (cantilevered) parapets	2.00	
b. Other exterior walls above the ground floor	0.75	2,3
c. All interior bearing and nonbearing walls and partitions	0.75	3
d. Masonry or concrete fences over 6 feet high	0.75	
2. Penthouse (except when framed by an extension of the structural frame)	0.75	
3. Connections for prefabricated structural elements other than walls, with force applied at center of gravity	0.75	4
4. Diaphragms	—	5
II. Nonstructural Components		
1. Exterior and interior ornamentations and appendages	2.00	
2. Chimneys, stacks, trussed towers and tanks on legs:		
a. Supported on or projecting as an unbraced cantilever above the roof more than one half their total height	2.00	
b. All others, including those supported below the roof with unbraced projection above the roof less than one half its height, or braced or guyed to the structural frame at or above their centers of mass	0.75	
3. Signs and billboards	2.00	
4. Storage racks (include contents)	0.75	10
5. Anchorage for permanent floor-supported cabinets and book stacks more than 5 feet in height (include contents)	0.75	
6. Anchorage for suspended ceilings and light fixtures	0.75	4,6,7
7. Access floor systems	0.75	4,9
III. Equipment		
1. Tanks and vessels (include contents), including support systems and anchorage	0.75	
2. Electrical, mechanical and plumbing equipment and associated conduit, ductwork and piping, and machinery	0.75	8

[1]See Section 2336 (b) for items supported at or below grade.

[2]See Section 2337 (b) 4 C and Section 2336 (b).

[3]Where flexible diaphragms, as defined in Section 2334 (f), provide lateral support for walls and partitions, the value of C_p for anchorage shall be increased 50 percent for the center one half of the diaphragm span.

[4]Applies to Seismic Zones Nos. 2, 3 and 4 only.

[5]See Section 2337 (b) 9.

[6]Ceiling weight shall include all light fixtures and other equipment or partitions which are laterally supported by the ceiling. For purposes of determining the seismic force, a ceiling weight of not less than four pounds per square foot shall be used.

[7]Ceilings constructed of lath and plaster or gypsum board screw or nail attached to suspended members that support a ceiling at one level extending from wall to wall need not be analyzed provided the walls are not over 50 feet apart.

[8]Machinery and equipment include, but are not limited to, boilers, chillers, heat exchangers, pumps, air-handling units, cooling towers, control panels, motors, switch gear, transformers and life-safety equipment. It shall include major conduit, ducting and piping serving such machinery and equipment and fire sprinkler systems. See Section 2336 (b) for additional requirements for determining C_p for nonrigid or flexibly mounted equipment.

[9]W_p for access floor systems shall be the dead load of the access floor system plus 25 percent of the floor live load plus a 10 psf partition load allowance.

[10]In lieu of the tabulated values, steel storage racks may be designed in accordance with U.B.C. Standard No. 27-11.

H. Load Combinations Required

As with wind loading, the UBC requires that various combinations of loads on a building be calculated and the most critical one is used to design the structure. For earthquake loading, the following combinations must be reviewed:

- dead load plus floor live load plus seismic

- dead load plus floor live load plus snow plus seismic

Snow loads less than 30 pounds per square foot need not be combined with seismic, and snow loads over 30 pounds per square foot may be reduced 75 percent if approved by the building official.

5   ADDITIONAL CONSIDERATIONS

The complete and detailed design of earthquake-resistant structures is a complex procedure and beyond the scope of this book. However, this section outlines some additional concepts with which you should be familiar.

A. Overturning Moment

Because the inertial force created by an earthquake acts through the center of mass of a building, there is a tendency for the moment created by this force acting above the base to overturn the structure. This overturning force must be counteracted in some way. Normally, the dead weight of the building, also acting through the center of mass, is sufficient to resist the overturning force, but it must always be checked. However, only 85 percent of the dead load may be used to resist uplift. Figure 14.14 shows these two forces and the resulting moments diagrammatically.

B. Drift

Drift is the lateral movement of a building under the influence of earthquake- or wind-induced vibrations. Story drift is the displacement of one level relative to the level above or below. The UBC gives stringent limitations on story drift. For buildings less than 65 feet high, calculated story drift cannot exceed $0.04/R_w$ or 0.005 times the story height. For buildings more than 65 feet high, the calculated story drift cannot exceed $0.03/R_w$ or 0.004 times the story height.

Drift as a limiting factor is important in order to ensure that exterior facades do not break off or crack excessively. When two buildings or portions of buildings are isolated by a seismic joint, they must be separated by at least the sum of the drifts to avoid pounding during an earthquake.

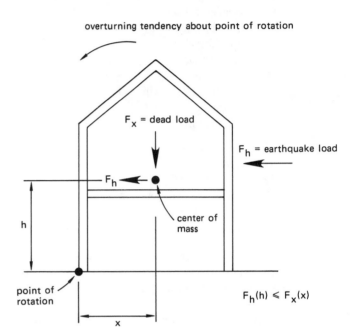

Figure 14.14   Overturning Moment

SAMPLE QUESTIONS

The answers to questions 1 through 3 can be found on the following key list. Select only one answer for each question.

A0	accelerograph
A1	bearing wall system
A2	braced frame
A3	building frame system
A4	ductility
A5	framed tube
A6	irregular
A7	modified Mercalli scale
A8	moment-resisting frame
A9	natural period
B0	reentrant corner
B1	regular
B2	Richter scale
B3	shear wall discontinuity
B4	soft story
B5	symmetric

1. A building is constructed of an ordinary moment-resisting frame and is raised on columns above an open plaza below. What is this an example of?

2. What provides information most useful for seismic design?

3. What describes a building whose lateral force-resisting system consists of members stressed in flexure?

4. A store in Seattle, Washington will have a steel, ordinary moment-resisting frame. It will be 120 feet wide, 180 feet long, 50 feet high, with two stories. Soil reports show stiff soil with the soil depth exceeding 200 feet. The structure has a dead load of 6500 kips, and its period of vibration is 0.19 second in the longitudinal direction. What is the total base shear in the longitudinal direction?

    A.   447 kips
    B.   596 kips
    C.   894 kips
    D.   1475 kips

5. A dynamic analysis method would be required if which of the following conditions existed?

    A. a five-story, square hotel building with a skylight-topped atrium in the middle which comprises 55 percent of the building's area

    B. a 40-story, rectangular office building in seismic zone 3 with an ordinary moment-resisting space frame

    C. a three-story, L-shaped department store

    D. all of the above

6. Select the incorrect statement from the following.

    A. Ductility is important above the elastic limit.

    B. Flexible buildings are good at resisting earthquake and wind loads.

    C. A penthouse swimming pool would not be a good idea in seismic zone 2B.

    D. All other things being equal, reinforced concrete is a poorer choice than steel for a structural system in seismic zone 3.

7. Which of the following are true?

    I. The epicenter is the location of fault slippage.

    II. Vertical ground movement is usually critical when calculating its effect on a building.

    III. A building's fundamental period of vibration is dependent on its mass and stiffness.

    IV. Buildings in seismic zone 1 require some earthquake-resistant design considerations.

    V. Useful information in seismic zones 3 and 4 can be gathered from existing buildings.

    A.   I, II, and III
    B.   II, III, and IV
    C.   II, IV, and V
    D.   III, IV, and V

8. What value of C_p would be used on the first floor in seismic zone 3 to check the stability of a 6-foot-high bookcase?

    A.   0.75
    B.   1.5
    C.   2.0
    D.   4.0

9. The distribution of base shear in a multistory building does not depend on which of the following?

    A.   the height of the building
    B.   the rigidity of the diaphragms
    C.   the distribution of mass
    D.   the height of the floors

10. Select the correct statements about shear walls.

I. The width-to-height ratio should be made as large as possible.

II. The force normal to the shear wall is not critical compared to the shear force in the plane of the wall.

III. Shear walls are best located at the perimeter of the building.

IV. Shear walls should not be offset.

V. Shear walls can be used in a bearing wall system.

    A.   I, III, and IV
    B.   I, II, and IV
    C.   I, III, IV, and V
    D.   all of the above

15 LONG SPAN STRUCTURES— ONE-WAY SYSTEMS

A *long span* is generally considered to be one over 60 feet in length. The study of long spans as distinct structural entities is important because of the unique design problems that arise when structures cover long distances. These problems include such things as temperature expansion and contraction, shipping, and deflection, among others. These will be discussed in detail in later sections.

One of the most important characteristics of long span structures is their lack of redundancy. In structures with many separate, small bays, the collapse of one beam would be damaging, but the majority of the building would remain standing supported by other parts of the framing system. With a long span structure, failure of one portion affects a much greater area, and can even cause collapse of the entire building. The potential for catastrophic loss of life and property is much greater.

Long span structures can be categorized into two broad divisions: one-way and two-way systems. *One-way systems* are characterized by linear members that span in one direction and resist loads primarily by beam action, or bending. A one-way long span generally consists of primary members that bridge the long distance, and a series of secondary members that span between the primary ones, also with simple beam action, and support the floor or roof system. *Two-way systems* distribute loads to supports in both directions and involve complex, three-dimensional methods of resisting loads. Two-way systems will be covered in the next chapter.

1 TYPES OF ONE-WAY SYSTEMS

The following sections outline some of the more typical long span, one-way systems. Most of these use steel or concrete as their primary material because of the high strength-to-weight ratio of steel and concrete. Wood is used for long span construction in trusses and glued-laminated beams.

There are many variables that determine the exact size and configurations of a member to span a particular distance, such as loading and the allowable stress of the material. Table 15.1 summarizes several of the one-way systems along with typical span ranges, depths, and depth-to-span ratios.

A. Steel Girders

Rolled steel members are sometimes used for long spans if the loads are not excessive. The largest rolled section available is 36 inches deep, and its practical span length is about 72 feet. If additional moment-carrying capacity is required, cover plates can be welded to the top or bottom flanges as shown in Figure 15.1 (a).

If longer spans are required for steel sections, they must be fabricated from individual components. The most common type of section is the plate girder, which is composed of sheet steel for the web and either steel bars or angles for the flanges. Figure 15.1 (b) shows a plate girder built up of angles. Figure 10.3 in Chapter 10 illustrates a welded plate girder. Plate girders are efficient long span members because most of the material is in the flanges separated by a large distance, which results in a high moment of inertia.

In order to minimize the amount of steel required (and, therefore, the weight and cost), plate girders used as roof beams can be tapered toward the middle of the span where the moment is the greatest. See Figure 15.1 (c).

Plate girders are often 8 feet deep or more. They are sometimes used to transfer the load of a column to two wider spaced columns to create a clear span below as shown in Figure 15.2. This is often required in buildings

Table 15.1
One-Way Long Span Systems

system	typical spans, feet	typical depths, feet	typical depth-to-span ratios
steel girders	10–72	2/3–3	1/20
steel rigid frames	30–150	2–5	1/20–1/30
glued laminated rigid frames	30–120	1 1/2–4	1/20–1/30
flat wood trusses	40–120	4–12	1/10
pitched wood trusses	40–100	7–17	1/6
flat steel trusses	40–300	4–30	1/10–1/12
pitched steel trusses	40–150	5–20	1/6–1/8
long span joists	25–96	1 1/2–4	1/20–1/24
deep, long span joists	90–144	1 1/3–6	1/20–1/24
joist girders	20–60	2–6	1/10–1/12
glued laminated beams	10–60	1–4	1/24
prestressed single T concrete	20–120	1–4	1/20–1/30
prestressed double T concrete	20–60	1–21/2	1/20–1/30
prestressed concrete girders	40–120	3–6	1/15–1/20
steel arches	50–500	1–5	1/100
concrete arches	40–320	1–7	1/50
wood arches	50–240	1 1/2–6	1/40

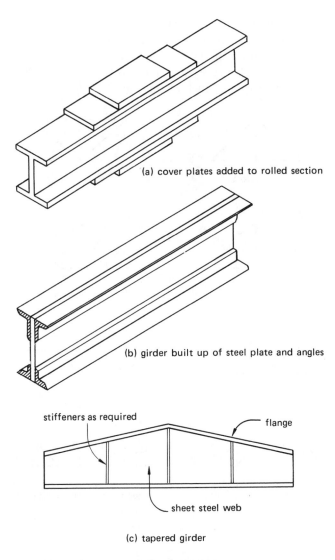

(a) cover plates added to rolled section

(b) girder built up of steel plate and angles

stiffeners as required   flange

sheet steel web

(c) tapered girder

Figure 15.1   Built-Up Steel Sections

such as hotels, where the lobby requires a more open space than the rooms above. In most cases, because the web is relatively thin compared with its length, intermediate stiffeners are required to prevent buckling of the web. These are usually angles welded perpendicular to the length of the web.

B. Rigid Frames

A *rigid frame* is a structural system in which the vertical and horizontal members and joints resist loads primarily by flexure, and in which moments are transferred from beams to columns. When discussing long span structures, a rigid frame has a sloped roof with a rigid, moment-resisting connection between the columns and the roof structure, or the column/roof structure is one continuous member. See Figure 15.3. A rigid frame may have fixed connections between the columns and foundation, and between the two halves, or it may have

pinned connections at these points. With pinned connections, the structure is determinate and does not develop secondary stresses caused by temperature differences. If the entire frame is rigidly connected, it is an indeterminate structure.

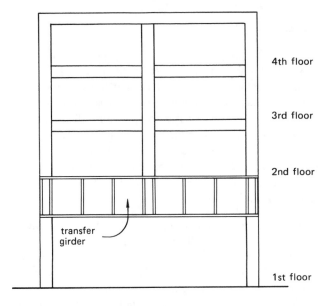

transfer girder

4th floor

3rd floor

2nd floor

1st floor

Figure 15.2   Transfer Girder

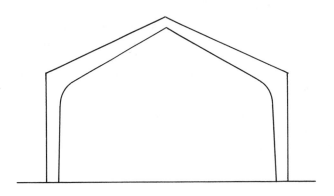

Figure 15.3   Rigid Frame

Part of the spanning capability of a rigid frame comes from the arch action of the sloping beams, through which vertical loads are transferred to the columns through compression as well as bending. In addition, since the two columns are tied together, lateral loads are transferred to both columns, resulting in a more efficient structure. As shown in the illustration, the column and beam are often tapered toward the foundation and ridge. This reflects the fact that the moment is greatest at the junction where more material is needed to resist the forces in the structure.

Rigid frames are used for industrial facilities, warehouses, manufacturing plants, and other instances where a simple, rectangular open space is required. They are primarily constructed of steel, but are also made of glued laminated lumber because each half can be easily fabricated as a single, continuous unit.

C. Trusses

As stated in Chapter 5, a *truss* is a structure comprised of straight members that form a number of triangles, with the connections arranged so that the stresses in the members are either in compression or tension. Trusses are very efficient structures to span long distances because of their primary reliance on compression and tension to resist forces, rather than bending, and their high strength-to-weight ratios. Trusses are usually constructed of steel or wood, and sometimes a combination of materials.

Trusses offer many advantages in bridging large spaces. They are relatively light weight, the space between the members can be used for mechanical services, they can be partially prefabricated for fast erection, they make efficient use of material, and they can theoretically be made as deep and large as needed to span most any distance, although there are practical limits to the span. One disadvantage of a truss, however, is the number of connections, which can increase fabrication or erection time.

Trusses are usually spaced from 10 to 40 feet on center with intermediate purlins spanning between them and bearing on the *panel points*, those points where the web members intersect the top chord. Roof or floor decking then spans between the purlins.

The typical spans and depths of the various types of trusses are shown in Table 15.1. Some of the more common truss configurations are shown in Figure 15.4. Refer to Chapter 5 for more information on truss analysis.

D. Open-Web Steel Joists and Joist Girders

Open-web joists are prefabricated truss members using hot-rolled or cold-formed steel members. These joists have been standardized into three major groups: K-series, LH-series, and DLH-series. The K-series spans up to 60 feet, so the LH- and DLH-series are considered long span. The LH-series is suitable for the direct support of floors and roof decks, and the DLH-series is suitable for direct support of roof decks.

Even though each manufacturer has its own chord and web profiles, the sizes and specifications for manufacturing have been standardized by the Steel Joist Institute.

Long span joists, the LH-series, come in depths from 18 inches to 48 inches and span up to 96 feet. The deep, long span joists, the DLH-series, come in depths from 52 inches to 72 inches and span up to 144 feet. The depths increase in 2-inch increments.

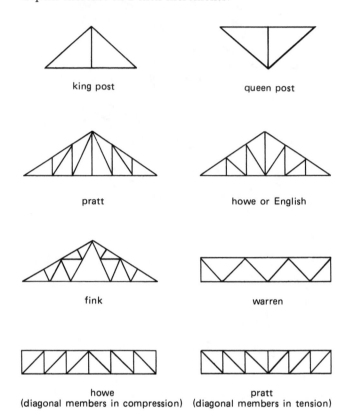

Figure 15.4 Truss Configurations

Open-web joists typically bear on the top chord and have underslung ends. However, square end trusses can be purchased which bear on the bottom chord. The depth of the bearing portion is standardized at 5 inches for the LH-series and for chord sizes through 17 in the DLH-series. For chord sizes of 18 and 19 in the DLH-series, the standard bearing depth is 7 1/2 inches.

There are a number of standard chord configurations. These are illustrated in Figure 15.5. Of course, parallel chord trusses are required for floor systems, but the pitched top chord configuration is useful for roof structures to provide for positive drainage. In addition, there are a number of accessories such as bottom chord ceiling extensions, extended ends for the top chord, and various types of anchoring devices.

Both LH-series and DLH-series joists are manufactured with camber, the amount depending on the length of the top chord. *Camber* is the rise in a beam to compensate for deflection. The cambers range from 1/4 inch for a 20 foot length to 8 1/2 inches for the longest, 144 foot span.

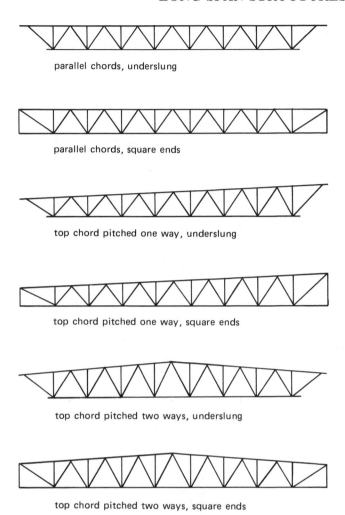

Figure 15.5 Open-Web Steel Joist Configurations

parallel chords, underslung

parallel chords, square ends

top chord pitched one way, underslung

top chord pitched one way, square ends

top chord pitched two ways, underslung

top chord pitched two ways, square ends

Open-web joists are very flexible. By varying the spacing, depth, and chord size, a wide variety of floor and roof loads and spans can be accommodated. They can bear on steel beams, masonry walls, concrete walls, and joist girders. The top chord can likewise support a variety of flooring and roofing systems. Because they are lightweight and prefabricated, erection is quick and simple. For more information, including design methods, refer to the section on open-web joists in Chapter 10.

Joist girders are designed to serve as primary structural members that support evenly spaced open-web joists. Available depths of joist girders range from 20 inches to 72 inches and they can span up to 60 feet. They are manufactured with steel angle sections and although each manufacturer may have its own particular configuration, there is a standard way of designating a joist girder. For example, in the designation 48G8N8.8K, the 48G indicates the depth in inches, the 8N indicates the number of joist spaces, and the 8.8K indicates the required design load in kips at each panel point.

E. Vierendeel Trusses

A *Vierendeel truss* is a structure composed of a series of rigid rectangular frames. However, it is not a true truss because there are no triangles and the members must resist bending as well as tension and compression. See Figure 15.6. It is used when diagonal members are undesirable, and, in many instances, occupies an entire story height when used to transfer loads from closely spaced columns above to column free spaces below.

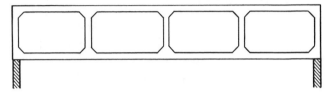

Figure 15.6 Vierendeel Truss

The top and bottom chords of a Vierendeel truss are in compression and tension, respectively, just as with any beam or true truss. However, there is bending moment in the chords as well as in the vertical members. As a result, all portions of a Vierendeel truss must be designed with larger members than would be necessary with a regular truss, and the joints must be capable of resisting moment as well. This is why these trusses often have triangular brackets or short knee braces as shown in Figure 15.6.

F. Glued Laminated Beams

Although glued laminated construction seldom exceeds the 60 foot distance arbitrarily considered long span, it is included because it is used for spans and loads that regular sawn timber is incapable of supporting, and because many of the special considerations of long spans apply to this type of construction. Long distances are spanned by glued laminated members in two primary ways: with straight, rectangular beams and with rigid frame arches.

As mentioned in Chapter 9, glued laminated members consist of a number of individual pieces of lumber, either 3/4 inch or 1 1/2 inch thick, glued together and finished in a factory. See Figure 9.3. Because the individual pieces can be hand-selected free from major defects and the entire member properly seasoned, glue lams, as they are called, have higher stress ratings than standard sawn lumber sections. In addition, much larger sizes are possible, so the span and load-carrying capabilities are much greater for glue lam construction than for standard wood frame buildings.

Glue-lam beams are designed with the same formulas used for other wood construction except a few additional formulas are required to account for modifications in stress ratings when curved members are used. As with sawn members, there are load tables which make selection easier by giving the allowable load per foot based on span and size of beam.

G. Prestressed Concrete

When concrete is used for one-way systems to span long distances, it is nearly always prestressed or post-tensioned. Prestressed concrete consists of a member that has had an internal stress applied before it is subjected to service loads. This stress is applied by stressing high-strength steel strands in a form into which concrete is poured. When the concrete cures, the external stress is removed and it is transferred to the concrete. This process effectively counteracts the tension that concrete is not capable of carrying. The prestressing process also reduces cracking and deflection, and permits concrete to span longer distances with smaller sections than is possible with reinforced, cast-in-place construction.

There are several types of precast sections suitable for long span concrete sections. The three most common ones are shown in Figure 15.7 and include the single tee, the double tee, and the AASHTO (American Associations of State Highway and Transportation Officials) girder.

Single tees are typically 4, 6, or 8 feet wide with an 8 to 12 inch thick web. Depths range from 1 to 4 feet with span capabilities up to about 120 feet.

Double tees are usually 8 or 10 feet wide with a 2 inch flange thickness, and depths ranging from 8 inches to 32 inches. Span distances are less than with single tees; the maximum span is 60 to 80 feet. Double tees typically have a 2 inch thick concrete topping which covers the joints, smooths out any irregularities between adjacent panels, and strengthens the floor or roof assembly.

Double tees are used frequently because of their many advantages. They function both as structure and decking, they are relatively inexpensive to produce, erection is fast, and they can be used either as horizontal or vertical members. In addition, the space between the webs can be used for mechanical and electrical service runs.

AASHTO girders are not used very often in building construction; their use is generally limited to highway

bridges. However, similar rectangular beams can be precast to span long distances with lengths up to 120 feet possible.

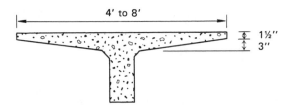

(a) single tee

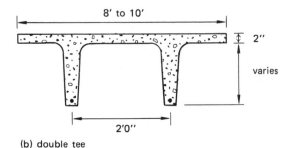

(b) double tee

(c) AASHTO girder

Figure 15.7   Typical Prestressed Concrete Shapes

Other precast shapes include box girders, and channel slabs, but these are not used for building as frequently as the sections shown in Figure 15.7.

H. Post-Tensioned Concrete

With post-tensioned concrete construction, the concrete member is cast with hollow sleeves embedded in it. High-strength steel cables, called *tendons*, are placed in the hollow sleeves, and after the concrete has cured, tension is applied to the tendons by hydraulic jacks. When the design stress is reached, the cables are anchored to the ends of the concrete member with steel plates or by grouting the space between the tendon and sleeve. The post-tensioning equipment is removed, and the resulting member functions in a way similar to pre-stressed concrete.

Post-tensioning can be used in beams, floor slabs, or other sections to increase the load-carrying capacity of the member and to allow for longer spans.

I. Arches

Arches are one of the oldest long span structural systems used by man. This is because an arch depends primarily on compression to resist loads, and ancient materials like stone were very strong in compression. In a true arch, all of the load is carried in compression. For a given set of loads, the shape of an arch that acts in this way is its funicular shape. For an arch supporting a uniform load across its span, this shape is a parabola.

However, in practical terms, there is no such thing as a true arch, because there are always combinations of loads that place both compressive and bending stresses in an arch. For a good working definition, an *arch* is a structure that resists imposed loads primarily by compression with some bending stresses involved.

There are several arch shapes. Some of the more common ones are shown in Figure 15.8. The A-frame and gabled frame are not immediately apparent as arches, but they represent the concept of arch action, in which there is some compression in the spanning member as well as bending. As the slope of the arch approaches vertical, there is more compression and less bending.

As was discussed in Chapter 1, the loads in an arch tend to cause it to spread out unless it is restrained with foundations or a tie rod. For a given span, this tendency to spread, or the *thrust* of the arch, is inversely proportional to the rise, or height, of the arch. As the rise increases, the thrust decreases.

Arches can be constructed with wood, concrete, and steel, and some spans have reached over 1000 feet. For most purposes, however, the typical spans for wood arches range from 50 to 240 feet; for concrete, from 40 to 320 feet; and for steel, from 50 to 500 feet. Typical depth-to-span ratios are about 1:40 for wood arches and up to 1:100 for steel.

Arches can be either fixed or hinged. If the arch is hinged at the supports, it can move slightly under loads caused by temperature, soil settlement, and wind without developing high bending stresses.

When used in one-way structural systems, arches are the primary structural member, and the space between is spanned with secondary members which in turn support the roofing system.

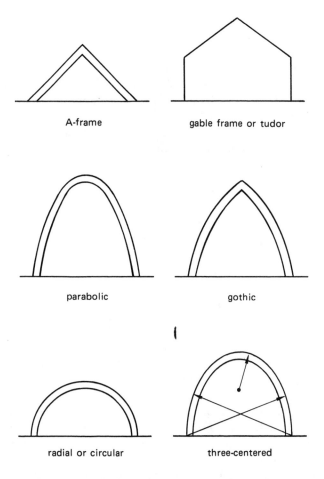

Figure 15.8 Types of Arches

2 DESIGN AND SELECTION CONSIDERATIONS

The selection of the most appropriate long span system for a particular project involves finding a balance between many different factors. This section and the next will outline some of the more important ones for both one-way and two-way systems.

A. Function

All structural systems must meet the functional needs of the building being designed. An auditorium may need a clear span of 150 feet, a sports arena may require an open area large enough for hockey and thousands of spectators, or a manufacturing plant may simply need narrow, but very long, unobstructed bays. A system appropriate for one use may not be the best choice for another use. For example, it would not make sense to use a steel arch capable of spanning 400 feet if long span open-web joists clearing 60 feet would do just as well.

B. Cost and Economy

Selecting and designing an economic long span structural system for a particular project requires that the architect and engineer balance many interrelated factors. There are six general considerations that affect the cost of any structure:

- the structural system

- material

- labor

- equipment

- construction time

- integration with other building systems

Regardless of the relative efficiency of a long span structural system, bridging great lengths always comes at a cost. The first determinant, therefore, is the structural system itself. Generally speaking, it is less costly to build more columns to decrease spans as much as possible than it is to provide deeper and heavier beams or complex two- or three-dimensional systems. All other things being equal, the most economical structure will be the one that spans just the required distance and no farther without stretching the limits of the system.

Since most materials are more efficiently used in compression and tension than bending, a system that reflects this fact will often cost less than one that relies on flexure. X-braced buildings, for example, may use less steel than moment-resisting frames, or trusses may require less weight than comparable solid beams. However, material use may be offset by higher fabricating costs or labor required for assembly.

Finally, deeper bending members are more efficient and require less material than shallow ones. A deep steel beam will weigh less (and cost less), than a shallow one that supports the same load. If other considerations allow it, the architect should provide as much space as possible for structural members.

Material is the second consideration affecting cost. In addition to the size and amount required by the system selected, cost can be affected by the availability of material. For instance, in some parts of the country, steel may be more readily available and at a lower cost than concrete, or a job site may be quite remote from a precasting plant which would rule out prestressed concrete.

The choice of material may also have repercussions for other materials. Steel will require fireproofing while concrete will not, or masonry walls in cold climates may require more complex insulating systems than simple steel stud cavity walls.

One of the major determinates of cost is labor. This is especially true in the United States. Generally, any structural system that minimizes the amount of labor, especially on-site labor, will have an economic advantage. This is why precast concrete is often preferred over cast-in-place concrete.

The other aspect of labor cost is the availability of skilled labor to perform certain building tasks. A brick structure needs skilled masons, and a welded steel frame requires competent welders, for example. In metropolitan areas, this may not be a problem. In more remote areas, the best structural system may be one that is prefabricated and requires simple site assembly.

Equipment required for the erection of long span structures is usually large and expensive. Here, there is a balance between the cost of equipment, and speed and ease of construction. Larger cranes may cost more to rent than smaller ones, but may allow the use of larger, prefabricated members and therefore reduce construction time and the number of connections required.

Construction time has become very important in many building situations due to the high cost of financing. Anything that reduces the building period has the effect of saving money. Therefore, such things as readily available material, prefabrication, simple long span systems, and easy on-site labor can significantly affect the economy of a building.

Finally, any long span structure must be selected so that it integrates with other building systems and components. There must be room for mechanical ductwork without excessive floor-to-floor heights, the exterior configuration must work with the fenestration system, and there must be provisions for easy installation of partitions and finishes.

C. Shipping

Because of their very nature, most long span structures, especially one-way systems, require large components to be shipped to the job site. There are many advantages to prefabricating structural members in sizes as large as possible, but these must be weighed against the practical limits of the transportation system serving the site. For instance, with precast concrete, the largest size possible should be shipped in order to reduce the number of field connections required and to speed erection. However, this goal must be balanced with the practical limits of weight and truck size.

In most cases, the maximum length for truck shipment is 60 feet, and for railroad shipment it is 80 feet. Maximum height for truck shipment is 14 feet. In some special situations, these dimensions are exceeded, but only at greater cost and with unusual provisions for transportation.

Access to the site must also be considered. In constricted urban locations, it may be impossible to maneuver a large truck into proper position for unloading.

D. Acoustics

Acoustics can be a factor in the selection of a long span structural system if the shape is one that concentrates sound reflections. Barrel vaults, domes, and some polygonal shapes can increase the noise level or produce undesirable echos. This can be a critical concern in sports arenas, manufacturing plants, and other buildings where the normal noise level is usually high. Adding a false ceiling or making other provisions for acoustical control can add to the cost of the structure.

E. Assembly and Erection

There are several things to consider about the assembly and erection of long span structures. The first, of course, is the speed and ease of construction, both of which can affect the cost of the building. In addition, the equipment required for erection must be taken into account, as previously mentioned. More importantly, in many instances, are the structural and safety requirements of long span construction. Because long span members are usually large, correspondingly large erection stresses can be developed. Sometimes these stresses are greater than those the member will encounter in use and the piece must be designed and sized accordingly.

Due to the lack of redundant members to support the structure, materials, and workers during erection, it is critical that correct procedures and sequences of construction be followed to avoid instability or overstressing until the entire building is complete and all bracing components are in place.

For example, when open-web steel joists are erected, several procedures must be followed. The hoisting cables must not be removed until bolted diagonal bridging near the midspan is installed. The number of bridging lines that must be installed before the hoisting cables are released depends on the span. If the joist is bottom bearing, the ends must be restrained and bridging installed before the hoisting cables are released. Further, all bridging and bridging anchors must be completely installed before construction loads are placed on the joists.

During erection of joist girders, it is recommended that a loose connection of the lower chord be made to the column, or that some other support is provided to stabilize the lower chord laterally and to help brace the joist girder against possible overturning. For both open-web joists and joist girders, concentrated construction loads must not be placed so as to exceed the load-carrying capacity of any member.

Precast concrete presents special problems with erection because of its weight. While it is desirable to fabricate large members to speed construction and minimize joints and field connections, the practical limits of crane capacities need to be considered, as well as the space available around the building site to maneuver trucks, cranes, and large precast sections. Additionally, each individual member must be properly braced until the complete system is assembled.

F. Fire Protection

As mentioned previously, the requirement for fire protection of structural members may influence the selection of a particular system. In some instances, the cost and difficulty of installing fire-resistant covering may offset the initial economy of an otherwise efficient material. Steel, of course, is especially vulnerable to weakening when exposed to high temperatures.

The Uniform Building Code allows an exception to the fire protection of structural steel in some instances. In Group A (assembly) and E (educational) occupancies, if the structural framework of the roof is more than 25 feet above the floor, fire protection may be omitted. This is why there is no fire protection in many sports stadiums, exhibition halls, and concert halls.

3 TECHNICAL CONSIDERATIONS

Long span structures pose special problems that are not present, or at least not significant, with standard structural systems. For example, a 30 foot long steel beam will expand so slightly with an increase in temperature that it is of little consequence. The expansion of a 120-foot truss, however, can be significant. Because of the non-redundant nature of long span structures and the potential for catastrophic failure, the following considerations are especially important.

A. Connections

Many of the failures of long span structures (as well as standard structures) occur not with the primary spanning members but with the connections. As with other aspects of long span structures, there is less redundancy with connections. If one fails, it can lead to a progressive failure of others when they are overstressed.

In addition to building code requirements, it is often wise to build in extra connections. Shop drawings should also be carefully reviewed to make sure changes were not made by the fabricator and this should be followed up by meticulous field observation to verify that the connections are properly installed and in the proper sequence for the type of material and system being used.

For example, if a rigid connection is made between a joist girder and a column, it must be made only after the application of the dead loads. In such a case, the girder must be investigated for continuous frame action because the girder is no longer a simply supported beam.

B. Envelope Attachment

The connection of roofing and exterior wall materials to long span structures requires special attention. This is due to the larger movements experienced by both the structural system and the building envelope. Expansion and contraction of the primary frame caused by temperature differentials can exert unusual stresses on cladding, so expansion joints need to be designed to accommodate this type of movement.

Deflection of a long span floor or roof is also significant in terms of weatherproof attachment of the roofing material and flooring and ceiling finish.

For simple, one-way structural systems, the end rotation of a beam or girder can be significant for a long span member where it is of little consequence in normal span construction. There must be enough room at the end of the beam to allow for this type of movement without stressing or dislodging the exterior envelope.

C. Ponding

Ponding is potentially one of the most dangerous conditions with long span roofs. It occurs when a roof deflects enough to prevent normal water runoff. Instead, some water collects in the middle of the span. With the added weight, the roof deflects a little more, which allows additional water to collect, which in turn causes the roof to deflect more. The cycle continues until structural damage or collapse occurs.

The UBC specifically requires that all roofs be designed with sufficient slope or camber to assure adequate drainage after long-term deflection, or that roofs be designed to support maximum roof loads, including possible ponding.

For glued laminated construction, the UBC requires that the roof slope provide a positive slope not less than 1/4 inch per foot between the level of the drain and the highest point of the roof. This slope must be in addition to the camber provided by the beams, which must be 1 1/2 times the calculated dead load deflection.

The best design approach is to plan roofs so that there is more than enough slope to provide positive drainage while allowing for the usual construction variances. Instead of 1/4 inch per foot, provide at least 1/2 inch per foot. In addition, pay particular attention to situations that can create ponding. If a roof area depends on drain, some kind of provision must be made for drainage if the primary drain is clogged.

D. Temperature Movement and Stresses

The greater length of long span structures over standard length members means that any movement caused by temperature differentials will be increased in proportion to the length of the member. Where an expansion of one-tenth of an inch in the length of a short steel beam may not pose any particular problem, an increase of three-tenths of an inch may overstress a connection or crack an attached brick wall.

Particular attention needs to be paid to detailing long span structures to account for these kinds of movement. The situation is even more critical if the structure is exposed to the weather where the temperature differentials and movement will be even greater than for interior structural members. Temperature stresses can be avoided by using flexible joints, providing clearance for the anticipated movement, and providing slip joints, among others.

E. Tolerances

Just as with temperature-induced movement, fabrication and erection tolerances are greater for long span structures. Details and connections must be designed to accommodate a member whose length or depth may vary by an inch or more from what is designed and shown on the drawings. Hinged connections, slotted bolt holes, shims, and similar devices are often used to allow for tolerance variations.

F. Stability

Many long span structures depend on secondary framing and horizontal or vertical diaphragms for complete rigidity. During erection, the primary elements, such as arches and rigid frames, need to be braced temporarily until enough of the remainder of the structure can be built to make the entire assembly self-supporting. Although the contractor is responsible for construction methods, the drawings and specifications need to be clear in their instructions. In all cases, industry standards and the recommendations of the manufacturer or fabricator should be followed.

G. Shop Drawing Review

Minor changes in the preparation of shop drawings are a fact of life in the design and construction industry. However, where a slight change from the original details or specifications may be acceptable in a normal struc-ture, such a change can have disastrous consequences in long span construction. The architect should fulfill his or her role in the shop drawing review process and verify that the structural engineer, contractor, and erection subcontractor have thoroughly reviewed the shop drawings, and that any deviation from the original design is completely studied and approved by all parties.

H. Construction Observation

The final step in the correct design and construction of a long span structure is the thorough observation of the erection sequence. Both the architect and structural engineer must be involved in this process to verify that construction is in accordance with the plans and specifications.

SAMPLE QUESTIONS

1. Partitions should not be rigidly attached to the underside of a long span structural member because:

   A. This would decrease the flexibility of future room layouts.
   B. Lateral loads transferred to the partitions would cause them to tip slightly.
   C. Temperature changes would crack the finish material.
   D. Long-term deflection would buckle the partition structure.

The answers to questions 2 through 4 can be found on the following key list. Select only one answer for each question.

   A0 camber
   A1 circular
   A2 deep, long span joists
   A3 funicular
   A4 gothic
   A5 Howe
   A6 parabolic
   A7 plate girder
   A8 ponding
   A9 queen post

   B0 Pratt
   B1 rigid connections
   B2 rigid frame
   B3 tendons
   B4 Vierendeel
   B5 Warren

2. What is common to both deep, long span steel joists and prestressed double tees?

3. What is the ideal shape for an arch?

4. Name the truss that does not have intermediate vertical members.

5. Which of the following is not true about open-web steel joists?

   A. The LH-series and DLH-series are used where open space is needed for floor and roof spans up to 144 feet.
   B. A top chord, single pitched joist can be purchased for either top or bottom chord bearing.
   C. The architect need not specify the required camber.
   D. A 24LH06 joist must always be braced with bridging, regardless of its span.

6. A sports complex is being planned for a large university. One portion will include a 50-meter pool with competition diving boards and areas for spectators. The size of the pool area has been tentatively set at 110 feet wide by 220 feet long by 50 feet high with the spectator area on one side of the long dimension. Glazing is planned along both short dimensions, and the primary exterior finish material is brick.

What structural roof system would probably be best for this situation?

   A. deep, long span joists
   B. glued laminated rigid frames
   C. prestressed, single-T concrete sections
   D. pitched steel trusses

7. Slotted holes are used to:

   I.   provide for erection tolerances
   II. make shop fabrication easier
   III. allow for temperature changes
   IV. let the exterior envelope move to prevent stress build-up
   V.   make precise alignment possible

   A. I, IV, and V
   B. II, III, and IV
   C. I, III, and V
   D. all of the above

8. Select the incorrect statement.

   A. Camber is used to prevent ponding.
   B. Thrust action must be considered when using long span arches.
   C. Glued laminated beams can span farther than sawn timber because the allowable extreme fiber in bending stress is greater.
   D. Special moment connection are required for Vierendeel trusses.

9. Careful construction observation of long span structures is critical for which of the following reasons?

I. to look for overstressing caused by temporary construction loads placed on the structure

II. to check for proper construction sequence

III. to make sure that connections are made according to the shop drawings

IV. to compare on-site materials and components against the drawings and specifications

V. to determine that secondary members are attached to primary members properly

A. I, II, and IV

B. II, III, and IV

C. II, III, IV, and V

D. all of the above

10. What one-way system normally can span the farthest?

A. deep, long span joists

B. flat steel truss

C. wood arch

D. prestressed single-T

LONG SPAN STRUCTURES— TWO-WAY SYSTEMS

16

As the name implies, two-way structural systems distribute loads in two or more directions and consist of members that are all considered to be primary. Because the load is shared by many members in the system and generally distributed to more supports, two-way systems are structurally more efficient than one-way systems. This can be seen by comparing a simple one-way system with a two-way system. See Figure 16.1.

Figure 16.1 (a) shows a single concentrated load on a flexure member. The beam carries the entire load with one-half of the load carried by each support. With a two-way system, as shown in Figure 16.1 (b), the same load is distributed to two flexure members with each support only having to carry one-fourth of the load.

With this type of two-way system, the structure is most efficient if the shape is square so the loads are equally distributed. If the shape becomes rectangular, more and more of the load is carried in the short dimension and less in the long dimension. When the proportion becomes 2:1, nearly all the load is carried in the short dimension. This is why systems such as a waffle slab and flat plate construction are more efficient when the bays are square.

Some two-way systems also offer the advantage of redundancy, which, as noted in Chapter 15, is lacking in most of the one-way systems. For example, the failure of one joint or member of a space frame will not cause the entire structure to collapse.

Two-way systems are more efficient in use of material and can span farther and carry heavier loads than comparable one-way systems. However, one of the disadvantages is that they are more complicated to design and build. The design work is a minor problem today because of computer programs that can calculate highly indeterminant structures. The problem of complex construction still remains, however. Most two-way systems require a large number of pieces and connections, which require a great deal of fabrication time.

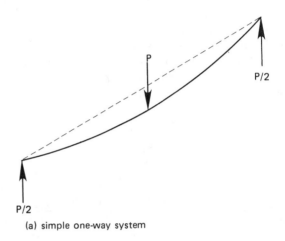

(a) simple one-way system

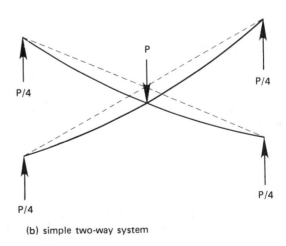

(b) simple two-way system

Figure 16.1   One-Way and Two-Way Systems

An additional limitation of long span, two-way systems is that nearly all of them can only be used for roof structures due to their basic shape. Space frames are the one exception, but even these are almost always used only for roofs and occasionally wall systems. Note that this limitation applies only to long span structures. Other two-way systems, like flat slabs and stressed skin floor panels, do utilize the efficiency of two-way action.

1 TYPES OF TWO-WAY LONG SPAN SYSTEMS

As with one-way systems, there are many types and variations of two-way, long span structural systems. This section discusses the major ones with some of the most-used variations. Table 16.1 summarizes the typical two-way systems, giving typical span ranges, thicknesses, and height-to-span ratios. With the exception of space frames, the height-to-span ratio is not the same as the depth-to-span ratio used with one-way structures. Since all of the systems listed are three-dimensional, they all have an optimum total height that is different from the size or thickness of individual members.

Table 16.1
Two-Way Long Span Systems

system	typical spans (feet)	typical thickness (inches)	typical height-to-span ratios
space frames	80–220	–	1/15–1/25
geodesic domes	50–400	–	1/3–1/5
thin shell domes	40–240	3–6	1/5–1/8
hyperbolic paraboloids	30–160	3–6	1/6–1/10
barrel vaults	30–180	3–5	1/10–1/15
lamella arches	40–150	–	1/4–1/6
folded plates	50–100	3–6	1/6–1/10
suspended cable structures	50–450	–	1/8–1/15

A. Space Frames

A space frame is a three-dimensional structural system that transfers loads through a network of members attached to each other at nodal connection points. Space frames are very efficient structures because of the large number of members and the fact that they resist loads primarily in compression or tension.

One of the unique features of a space frame that is uncharacteristic of many other long span structures is redundancy. Buckling of one member under a concentrated load does not lead to the collapse of the whole structure. This is because the system distributes concentrated loads evenly throughout the entire frame.

There are many configurations for space frames. They all have a top chord grid and a bottom chord grid connected with diagonal bracing. The two grids can be

identical and run in the same direction, or run in different directions while still forming a regular pattern. Grids can be square or triangular, although the square grid is more common.

The simplest type of space frame is a two-way truss system. With this, trusses spanning two directions are interconnected and form a grid of square openings. The diagonal members are vertical and in the plane of each truss, just as with a one-way truss system. See Figure 16.2.

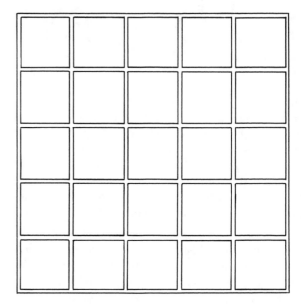

plan

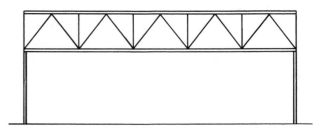

elevation

Figure 16.2   Two-Way Truss Space Frame

A more common type of space frame is the offset grid as illustrated in Figure 16.3. Here, the top and bottom grids consist of identical squares, but the bottom one is offset from the top by one half grid. The two grids are connected with skewed diagonal members.

The module size of a space frame can be varied to suit the functional needs of the building and the structural limitations of the grid members. The depth of the grid can also be varied as necessary, but the most economical depth-to-module ratio is about 0.707. Of course, the larger the module size, the fewer the number of connections, which is desirable in order to save fabrication and erection time and money.

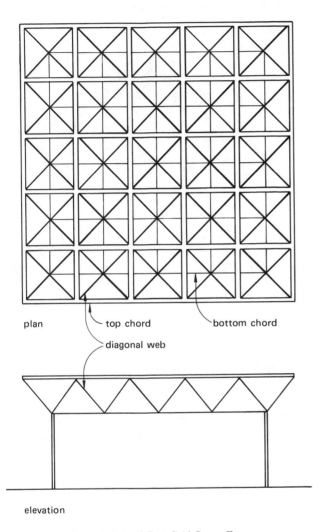

plan   top chord   bottom chord

diagonal web

elevation

Figure 16.3   Offset Grid Space Frame

There are many types of connections. They may be formed of hollow or solid sections with tapped holes for screw attachment of the members. They may be bent plates to which the members are bolted or welded, or prefabricated units that are slipped over the spanning members. Whatever type is used, the connection must provide for attaching the supporting structure, and for attaching the roofing and sidewall system to the primary frame. Some of the typical methods of support are shown in Figure 16.4.

The supports for a space frame can be located at any node but for greatest efficiency they are usually spaced symmetrically. Cantilevers of 15 to 30 percent of the span are possible and even desirable since less chord material is required.

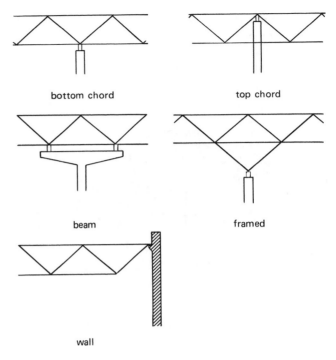

bottom chord   top chord

beam   framed

wall

Figure 16.4   Methods of Space Frame Support

B. Domes

Domes are one of the most efficient structural systems known. This is because the shape of the structure itself helps resist loads placed on it primarily through compression and tension, and, in the case of thin shell structures, shear. There are three basic variations of domes: the *frame dome*, the *geodesic dome*, and the *thin shell dome*.

The forces in all domes can be visualized by viewing a simple circular frame dome as shown in Figure 16.5 (a). The meridian lines act as individual arches, transferring loads to the ground through compression. The meridians are supported laterally by the hoops, those lines running parallel to the horizontal.

For very shallow, or low-rise domes, the entire structure can be placed in compression, without any tensile stresses at all. The vertical load at the bottom of the dome must then be resisted by the ground or a foundation.

For high-rise domes (the most typical situation) when the dome is under a uniform load, such as from its own weight or from a snow load, each meridian tends to compress in the upper part of the dome and expand in the lower part. See Figure 16.5 (b). This deflection is held in check, however, by the hoops. But, because of the deflection, the hoops in the upper part of the dome compress, and the hoops in the lower part are placed in tension. If there is sufficient hoop material at the base of the dome that can resist the tensile forces, the dome is self-supporting without the need for a foundation to carry the thrust. The foundation only needs to carry the vertical component of dead and live loads.

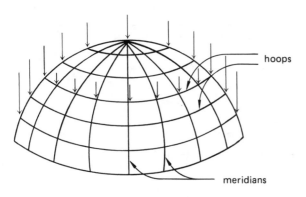

(a) dome action

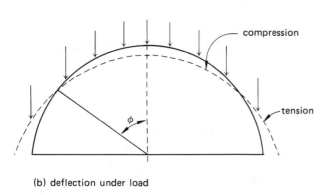

(b) deflection under load

Figure 16.5　Dome Structural Behavior

The point at which the stresses change from compression to tension varies with the load. Under dead load, the angle ϕ, as shown in Figure 16.5 (b), is about 52 degrees; under snow load, the angle is 45 degrees.

As a consequence of all the stresses being in compression or tension, the strains are relatively small. This is why a dome is a very stiff structure with little deflection.

There are several variations of the framed dome. All are approximations of a true dome because only straight members are used. One of the common types of framed dome is the Schwedler dome as shown in Figure 16.6. The areas between the meridians and the hoops are braced with single or double diagonals, and spanned with purlins or directly with the roofing.

C.　Geodesic Domes

Geodesic domes, invented by Buckminster Fuller, are like space frames formed in the shape of a sphere. The grid of a geodesic dome is based on great circle arcs and is composed of spherical polyhedrons, usually formed of equilateral triangles. A geodesic dome can be constructed with a single or double layer of struts.

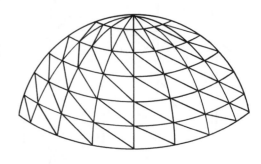

Figure 16.6　Schwedler Dome

Geodesic domes are extremely strong, stiff, lightweight, and enclose the greatest volume with the least surface area. They can easily span 400 feet or more.

D.　Thin Shell Structures

Thin shell structures are a class of form-resistant structures whose strength is a result of their ability to support loads through compression, tension, and shear in the plane of the shell because of their basic shape. The other broad category of form-resistant structure is the membrane which can only support loads through tension. Membranes will be discussed in the next section.

Shells are classified as either singly curved or doubly curved. The most common example of a singly curved thin shell structure is the *barrel vault* as shown in Figure 16.7. Barrel vaults with end frames act as curved beams, with the upper portion in compression and the lower portion in tension. Beam action carries the loads to the two ends where it is transferred by shear action to the end frames.

This structural condition is true only for a long barrel; that is, a barrel whose length is larger than its radius. It is also only true for a barrel supported by end frames and end supports. With such a barrel, there is a tendency for the longitudinal edges of the barrel to deform inward. This is usually counteracted by an adjacent vault or with longitudinal stiffeners. If a barrel vault is only supported by its longitudinal edges, arch action develops along with the corresponding thrust common to arches. If the shape of the barrel is not the funicular shape for the loads, some bending stresses will also be present. Such a barrel vault will have to be thicker than an end-supported vault to account for these additional loads.

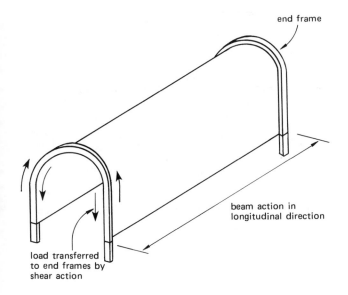

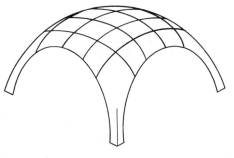

(a) synclastic shell

Figure 16.7 Thin Shell Barrel Vault

A barrel vault shape with rounded hip ends can also be created with a lamella roof. This is a structure formed by two intersecting grids of parallel skewed arches covering a rectangular area. Lamella arches are very efficient because of the interaction between the beams of the two grids and because the short lengths of the beams near the corners have small spans, thus reducing the length of the span of the beams framed into them.

The second class of thin shell structures is the doubly curved shell. There are two types of doubly curved shells. *Synclastic shells* are those with curves on the same side of the surface. *Anticlastic shells* are those with the main curves on opposite sides of the surface. See Figure 16.8. A dome is an example of a synclastic shell, and a hyperbolic paraboloid is an anticlastic shell.

Thin shell domes are very rigid and efficient structures. They are stable for either symmetric or asymmetric loads. In theory, they behave like the frame domes discussed in a previous section, but, because they consist of one continuous surface, each infinitesimal portion is resisting compression, tension, and shear. See Figure 16.9. Compression is acting in the lines of the meridian, and either tension or compression is acting in the hoop direction. Shear is therefore developed in any section to keep the structure in equilibrium.

Another common thin shell is the *hyperbolic paraboloid*. This anticlastic shell is formed by moving a vertical parabola with downward curvature along an upward curving parabola that is perpendicular to it. The resulting form is that shown in Figure 16.8 (b). The shape that a horizontal plane makes with the curve is a hyperbola.

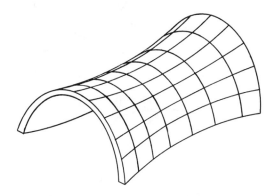

(b) anticlastic shell (hyperbolic paraboloid)

Figure 16.8 Types of Thin Shell Surfaces

Hyperbolic paraboloids can also be formed by straight lines moving along two non-parallel lines. There are many variations of this method of generating these thin shell forms, but one of the most common is shown in Figure 16.10. This form is actually four separate hyperbolic paraboloids arranged to cover a square. In this form, the loads are resisted in the plane of the shell and transferred to the boundaries of the hyperbolic parabolids, where they become compression forces in the edge stiffeners and are transmitted to the foundations. There is an outward thrust caused by this arch action which must be resisted by tie rods or suitable foundations.

In most cases, thin shells can be made only a few inches thick and still be structurally stable, but the minimum thickness is usually determined by the space required for reinforcing steel, minimum cover distances over the steel, and a sufficient thickness to allow for placing the concrete by machine. Building codes also limit the minimum thickness in order to provide for possible bending moments that may be induced in the structure from concentrated loads.

Although thin shells are very efficient in their minimal use of material and have great strength and stiffness, they are often not the structural system of choice in this country because they are labor intensive structures to construct. It is typically less expensive to pay for more, less efficient structural material if it can be erected quickly with as little on-site labor as possible.

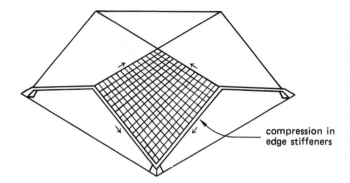

Figure 16.10   Four Section Hyperbolic Paraboloid Roof

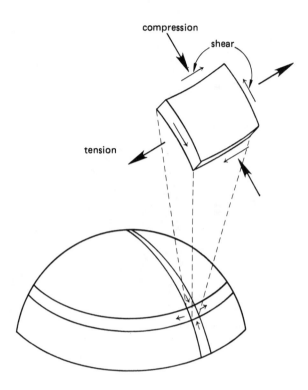

Figure 16.9   Shear Stresses in Domes

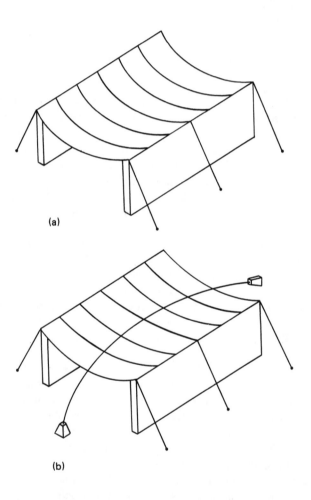

Figure 16.11   Membrane Structures

E. Membrane Structures

Membranes are the second class of form-resistant structures. Unlike shells, membranes can only resist loads in tension. As such, the membrane must be anchored between elements that can be placed in compression like the poles of a tent. Although membranes are very efficient in the amount of material they require, their biggest disadvantage is that they move and change shape in response to varying loads. They also flutter in the wind.

These problems can be counteracted to a great degree by prestressing the membrane with anticlastic shapes. Figure 16.11 (a) shows a simple membrane draped between two horizontal supports. Figure 16.11 (b) shows the same configuration except that a cable perpendicular to the transverse drape has been pulled tightly over the membrane resulting in a doubly curved surface. The resulting shape is much more stable.

F. Air-Supported Structures

Another form of the membrane structure is the air-supported or pneumatic roof. The membrane can still only support loads through tension but the membrane is held in place by air pressure rather than by cables and compression members. The simplest type of air-supported structure is the single membrane inflated like a balloon. Very little air pressure above the atmospheric air pressure is needed to keep a pneumatic structure inflated, but the interior does have to be kept closed to the outside.

Air-supported structures suffer from the same problems as other types of membrane roofs. Specifically, they are unstable under concentrated and varying loads and flutter in the wind. To minimize these problems, they need to be stabilized. One way of doing this is to run cables over the top of the structure so that it is stiffened both from within by the pressure and on the outside by tension in the cables.

Other methods of stabilization include using a double skin structure inflated like a large pillow or with a large number of individual air pockets like an air mattress. These kinds of pneumatic structures also eliminate the need for air lock doors and the continuous pumping of air into the building to maintain the required pressure.

G. Folded Plates

A folded plate structure consists of thin slabs bent to increase the load-carrying capacity. A typical folded plate roof is illustrated in Figure 1.11. Folded plate structures are stronger than simple horizontal flat plates because instead of having a structural depth just the thickness of the slab, the structural depth is as deep as the fold of the plate. Additionally, the span is much less, only the distance from one edge of the slab to the other. See Figure 16.12 (a).

Folded plates resist loads with a combination of slab action in the transverse direction and beam action in the longitudinal direction. However, as shown in Figure 16.12 (a), the slab only has to support loads within the distance from one fold to the next, and the load at the apex of each fold is divided into two components, half transferred to one plate and half to the other. In the longitudinal direction, the entire plate assembly acts as a beam with compressive stresses above the neutral plane and tensile stress below. See Figure 16.12 (b).

Folded plate structures can span up to about 100 feet in the longitudinal direction and about 25 to 35 feet between outer folds of each plate assembly. They are most commonly built of concrete, but can be constructed of plywood, steel, or aluminum as well. One of their primary advantages is that the shapes are simple flat pieces so they can be prefabricated, or, if cast in place, the formwork is easy to build.

Since the exterior slabs of any flat slab construction are more highly stressed than interior slabs, a short stiff-ening slab is usually placed at both edge boundaries to compensate for the additional stress. An example of such a stiffening slab is shown in Figure 1.11.

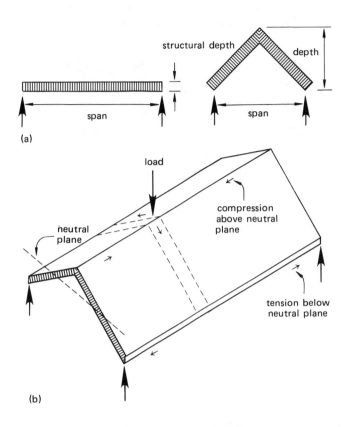

Figure 16.12 Folded Plate Structure

H. Suspension Structures

Suspension structures are similar to membranes in that they can only resist loads by tension. However, this is also one of their great advantages since any given cross section of cable is uniformly stressed because no variable bending stresses can be developed. This results in the material being utilized to its fullest unit stress capability.

Because a cable structure is not inherently rigid, it assumes its funicular shape for any given set of loads. A simple cable supporting one load in mid-span will assume a symmetrical triangular shape. If the load is shifted to one side, the shape of the cable changes.

In cable structures, the amount of tensile force is inversely related to the sag of the cable; the greater the sag, the less the tension in the cable. This can be visualized by examining two cables with different sags supporting the same amount of weight in the middle of the cable. See Figure 16.13 (a). If the load is weight P, each of the vertical components of the reaction must be one-half of the weight as dictated by the laws of equilibrium. However, the resultant of the vertical and horizontal forces acts in the direction opposite from the direction of the cable so a simple force polygon as discussed in Chapter 3 can be constructed.

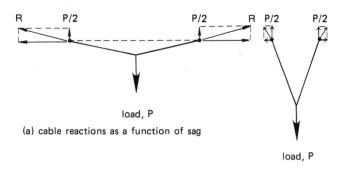

load, P

(a) cable reactions as a function of sag

load, P

compression ring

(b) circular cable suspension structure

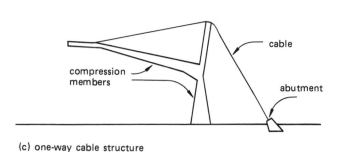

cable

compression members

abutment

(c) one-way cable structure

Figure 16.13 Cable Structures

For a cable with a small sag, the resultant (tension) and corresponding horizontal component are large. For a large sag, the resultant and horizontal component are small. In the extreme case of maximum sag, the cable would hang vertically and there would be no horizontal component.

Of course, as the sag increases, the tensile force, and, hence, the amount of cable cross section area required decreases, but the length of the cable increases. If the efficiency and cost of the structure is dependent on the amount of cable material, then there must be some optimum sag that balances cable length with cable cross section. For a cable supporting a single load in the middle, the ideal proportion is that the sag should be one-half the span so that the cable is at a 45 degree angle.

In building situations, however, single concentrated loads are the exception. A cable structure supports uniform loads. As discussed in Chapter 1, there are two typical uniform loading conditions for cable structures: where the load is uniformly applied on the horizontal projection of the cable and where the load is uniformly applied along the length of the cable. See Figure 1.12 (b) and (c). A uniform horizontal load results in the cable assuming the shape of a parabola, and a uniform load along the length of the cable (such as supporting its own weight) results in a catenary curve.

For these loading conditions, the optimum sag for a parabolic cable is three-tenths of the span, and for a catenary curve the optimum sag is one-third of the span. In practice, however, these sags are not achieved because the low sags would interfere with the function of the building.

For cable-supported structures, there must always be some way of balancing the tensile forces in the cable. This is done with compression members, or by extending the cable across a support to a foundation which holds the cable in place, or with some combination of both.

For circular buildings, the tensile forces can be balanced with a continuous compression ring at the perimeter of the roof as shown in Figure 16.13 (b). If the building is not circular, the cable can be draped over a compression member and anchored to a massive foundation. See Figure 16.13 (c). Circular buildings with cable roofs pose a particular problem, however, because the lowest point of the roof for drainage is in the middle of the span.

Cable-suspended structures have the same problem as membrane structures. Because they can only resist loads in tension, they are inherently unstable in the wind and with concentrated loads or other types of changing loads. Sometimes the flexibility of the cable structure can be stabilized simply with the weight of the roof or other structure. More often, additional cables and a stiffening structure need to be included.

2 DESIGN AND SELECTION CONSIDERATIONS

Many of the design considerations discussed in the last chapter concerning one-way long span systems apply to two-way systems as well. There are, however, a few additional factors that need to be taken into account.

A. Function

As illustrated in the first part of this chapter, most two-way systems are used exclusively for roofs because of their three-dimensional configuration. Two-way, long span systems are also used primarily for enclosing large, open, single-use spaces such as sports arenas and auditoriums. Therefore, the size and use of the building is the first consideration in deciding on the type of two-way system to use.

Additional functional considerations include provisions for drainage, insulation, and waterproofing. Of course, some shapes, such as domes, some thin shell structures, and air-supported roofs, are well suited for positive drainage. Others, such as cable-suspended roofs with their low point in the center, membrane structures that drain toward the interior, and some folded plates that trap water in their folds, present definite problems.

Insulating a long span, two-way structure can be a problem because they are often selected because of their appearance and architectural drama, in addition to their ability to bridge large distances. Adding insulation to the interior may be difficult, impossible, or mar the internal appearance. Placing insulation on the exterior may be equally as difficult, especially if the shape is complex.

Waterproofing presents similar problems for some types of systems. Structures such as space frames, frame domes, and cable-suspended structures have many parts and facets, resulting in a large number of joints which are always difficult to waterproof easily. Other forms, such as domes and folded plates, can easily be covered with liquid-applied waterproofing membranes.

B. Cost and Economy

Most two-way structures are very efficient in their use of material and can easily span long distances. However, other factors mitigate these advantages. The most notable disadvantage with many two-way systems is the increased labor cost required for either their fabrication or erection, or both. A space frame is an example of one such framing type with a great number of connections. The problem can be minimized somewhat by using large module sizes, which reduces the number of connections. This means a lower labor cost and lower material costs for the nodes which are usually the most expensive material part of a space frame.

Likewise, thin shell structures are very efficient in

material use, but are often prohibitively expensive to form because of all the complex curves and careful placement of concrete required.

Occasionally, some prefabrication of shells, folded, and space frames is possible to save money. Shot-concrete can also be used to speed up concrete placement on thin shells.

For some two-way systems, the attachment of roofing and glazing to the structure may be uneconomical. For example, a geodesic dome must have provisions for attaching the non-structural, somewhat flexible skin to the rigid framing members. Then, each joint between the panels must be sealed against the weather. For a large dome, this process can be very expensive.

C. Shipping

Shipping is less of a problem with two-way systems than it is with one-way systems, because most of the assembly is done on site. Components such as connectors and members of a geodesic dome, or the cable for a cable-suspended structure, can easily be shipped to the site.

D. Acoustics

Some shell configurations and membrane structures can focus sounds as discussed in Chapter 15. If the use of the building requires a good acoustical environment, the choice of a two-way system should be carefully evaluated since adding acoustical control can be difficult and expensive to achieve.

E. Assembly and Erection

Since most of the construction of a two-way system is done on site, either by casting concrete or assembling small pieces, shipping large members to a job site or building in remote areas is usually not a problem. However, this advantage is often offset by the higher erection costs due to more labor and components.

3 TECHNICAL CONSIDERATIONS

The technical considerations reviewed in Chapter 15 also apply to two-way systems so they will not be repeated here.

SAMPLE QUESTIONS

1. Select the incorrect statement about spaces frames.

    A. Space frames are different from many long span structures because of their redundancy.

    B. Top and bottom grids of a space frame can run in different directions, but they usually are oriented the same way.

    C. Regularly spaced supports with overhangs are more efficient than supports located at the perimeter of a space frame structure.

    D. Space frames are economical structures because their many connections can be prefabricated.

2. Match the related systems and spans.

    I.   folded plates

    II. hyperbolic parabolids

    III. geodesic domes

    IV. suspended cable structures

    V.   space frames

    1.   30 to 160 feet

    2.   50 to 100 feet

    3.   80 to 220 feet

    4.   50 to 400 feet

    5.   50 to 450 feet

        A. I-1, II-2, III-5, IV-3, V-4
        B. I-2, II-3, III-4, IV-5, V-1
        C. I-2, II-1, III-4, IV-5, V-3
        D. I-3, II-1, III-4, IV-4, V-2

3. A thin shell dome gets its strength and efficiency from which of the following?

    A. meridianal action and hoop tension

    B. compression, shear, and tension in the plane of the dome

    C. distribution of hoop compression in the upper part of the dome and hoop tension in the lower part

    D. arch action in three dimensions

The answers to questions 4 through 7 can be found on the following key list. Select only one answer for each question.

    A0 anticlastic
    A1 barrel vault
    A2 catenary
    A3 frame dome
    A4 geodesic dome
    A5 hoops
    A6 hyperbolic paraboloid
    A7 indeterminant
    A8 lamella
    A9 meridian

    B0 node
    B1 pneumatic
    B3 pretensioned membrane
    B4 redundancy
    B5 Schwedler
    B6 space frame
    B7 synclastic
    B8 thin shell

4. What describes a structure with diagonal bracing and individual arches?

5. Three of the structures listed above share an important property. What is this property?

6. What describes most pretensioned membrane structures?

7. Which of the structures listed above is the least stable under wind loads?

8. A dome is a very stiff structure for which of the following reasons?

    A. Strain is small due to all stresses being in compression or tension.

    B. The boundary of a dome is prevented from moving because of its circular shape.

    C. Lateral loads are evenly distributed throughout the dome.

    D. Tension and compression are balanced.

9. Select the correct statements.

I. Labor is often the primary reason many long span structures are not economical.

II. A high-rise dome in the winter experiences tension above the meridian angle of 45 degrees and compression below this point.

III. Both flat plates and barrel vaults need to have a length greater than transverse span width to be efficient.

IV. The thrust on a cable-suspended structure is directly proportional to its sag.

V. A structure like a suspension bridge makes the cable assume the shape of a parabola.

A. I, III, and V

B. I, II, IV, and V

C. II, III, and IV

D. III and V

10. Membranes are good structures to use because:

A. They are easy to erect.

B. There is always direct, positive drainage.

C. They make very efficient use of material.

D. Their form is one of the most dramatic types of long span structures.

17 SOLUTIONS

1 SELECTION OF STRUCTURAL SYSTEMS

1. B is correct.

I is incorrect because rigid frames may either be hinged or fixed. III is incorrect because the load distribution creates a horizontal thrust as well as vertical loads on the foundations.

2. C is correct.

This question asks you to make a judgment concerning the most important from many considerations. Of course, all factors should be considered, but some are more obvious. Since such a facility would be up a mountain with limited access and a short building season, construction limitations would be of prime importance. This eliminates choices B and D. Resistance to loads and cost are almost always mandatory requirements, so choice A can be eliminated. The selection of choice C is reinforced by the choice of style—an important factor in recreation facility design.

3. D is correct.

There must be continuous sheathing to give the structure rigidity and to provide a solid substrate on which to apply the facing.

4. B5, thin shell, is correct.

5. A8, flat slab, is correct.

Flat slabs have an added thickness around the column which provides extra space for reinforcing bars.

6. A3, cavity, is correct.

A high slenderness ratio indicates that the wall has a high unsupported dimension and would therefore need to be thick to prevent buckling. The two possible choices are cavity and double wythe since both would give a thicker wall than a single wythe. Of the two, a cavity wall has, by definition, a space for reinforcing which would also give added strength to the wall. A double wythe wall may have a similar space for reinforcing, but does not necessarily have one. Cavity is the better answer.

7. B4, space frame, is correct.

From the choices given, there are six two-way systems: flat plate, flat slab, waffle slab, space frame, folded plate, and thin shell. The first three can be eliminated because none of them can span 150 feet. A folded plate can be eliminated because its limit is about 100 feet. From the two remaining choices, the space frame would probably be more economical than a thin shell which requires special forming.

8. C is correct.

Three hinges are required to make an arch statically determinate. Choice D is an incorrect answer because the funicular shape can be found by suspending weights from the arch if the weights correspond proportionally to the anticipated loads.

9. A is correct.

II is incorrect because all three should be square or nearly square. III is incorrect because one-way systems span 20 to 30 feet. V is incorrect because topping is

almost always required to smooth out irregularities and
provide a base for flooring or roofing.

10. B is correct.

Joists can be supported on bearing walls or steel angle
ledges as easily as on steel beams. Various methods of
anchoring and connection are possible, making open-
web joists a very flexible system.

About R_1,

$$3000(8) + 800(14) + 2000(16) - R_2(12) = 0$$
$$R_2 = 5600 \text{ pounds}$$

Since the sum of all the forces in the vertical direction must also equal zero, to find R_1, simply subtract R_2 from the total load of 5800 pounds, which gives 200 pounds. You could also find R_1 (or check your answer) by taking moments about R_2.

10. C is correct.

According to the formula $f = Ea\Delta t$, statements II and IV are not variables.

4   BEAMS AND COLUMNS

1. B4, slenderness ratio, is correct.

From the list presented, several choices are possible, such as end conditions, effective length, and radius of gyration. However, none of these is as important as the slenderness ratio in determining load capacity. The radius of gyration is a geometric property that determines the slenderness ratio.

2. B1, radius of gyration, is correct.

3. A6, horizontal shear, is correct.

4. A4, Euler's equation, is correct.

5. A is correct.

Continuous beams are statically indeterminate, so the three principles of equilibrium cannot be used by themselves to find reactions.

6. C is correct.

III is incorrect because a uniform load produces a variable shear value throughout the length of the beam. IV is incorrect because the modulus of elasticity is an indication of the stiffness of the material—the higher the value, the stiffer the material and the greater the resistance to deflection.

7. B is correct.

First, find the reactions. The weight of the uniform load is assumed to act at its midpoint. Taking moments about R_1,

$$2.3(14)(7) - R_2(18) = 0$$
$$R_2 = 12.52 \text{ kips}$$

The summation of moments about R_2 must also equal zero:
$$-2.3(14)(11) + R_1 = 0$$
$$R_1 = 19.68 \text{ kips}$$

The maximum moment occurs where the shear is zero. Draw the shear diagram.

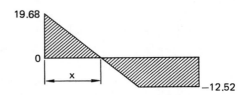

Calculate the distance x, where shear is zero. Since you know the sloped line drops 2.3 kips per foot, it will drop proportionally 19.68 kips in x feet, or:

$$\frac{2.3}{1} = \frac{19.68}{x}$$
$$x = 8.56 \text{ feet}$$

You can find the moment either by calculating the area of the triangle or by calculating the moment of a free-body diagram from reaction R_1 to the point 8.56 feet from R_1.

Area of triangle method:

$$A = \frac{bh}{2}$$
$$= \frac{19.68(8.56)}{2}$$
$$= 84.2 \text{ kip-feet}$$

Free-body diagram method:

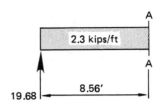

$$M = 19.68(8.56) - 2.3(8.56)(8.56/2)$$
$$= 168.46 - 84.26$$
$$= 84.2 \text{ kip-feet}$$

8. D is correct.

$$S = \frac{M}{f}$$
$$= \frac{3000(12)}{1500}$$
$$= 24 \text{ in}^3$$

Note that foot-pounds must be converted to inch-pounds by multiplying by 12.

9. A is correct.

I is incorrect because the maximum vertical shear is most important. III is incorrect because both positive and negative moments must be known to find the maximum moment.

10. C is correct.

The slenderness ratio is l/r. For wood columns, the least actual dimension is used instead of the radius of gyration so the slenderness ratio is:

$$sl = \frac{8(12)}{5.5}$$
$$= 17.5$$

The other variables in the question are irrelevant to the problem solution.

5 TRUSSES

1. B is correct.

Statement B is incorrect because spacing of trusses depends only partially on the spanning capabilities of the purlins. The other variable is the load that must be supported.

2. A is correct.

The centroidal axes of the web members should intersect at the centroidal axis of the chord member. Answer B can be eliminated because there is not enough information given to know whether or not there are enough bolts. A gusset plate could be used, but the centroidal axes would still need to intersect at a common point.

3. B3, pitched truss, is correct.

4. A7, gage line, is correct.

5. B0, method of joints, is correct.

The method of joints is a convenient method to use when you need to find the forces in the members near a support because there are usually fewer members at this point.

6. B2, panel point, is correct.

Loads are placed on panel points to avoid excessive bending in the members so the truss structure can be used most efficiently.

7. C is correct.

The simplest approach to find the answer is to use the principle that the summation of vertical forces at any point must equal zero. Draw a free-body diagram through member A.

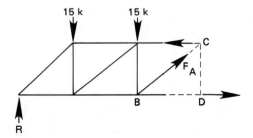

Since the forces in the top and bottom chords have no vertical components, it is clear that only the vertical component of the force in member A is available to balance the two 15 kip loads and the reaction.

First, find the value of the reaction, R:

$$R = 1/2(15 \times 5)$$
$$= 37.5 \text{ kips}$$

Assuming for the moment that the member is in tension (with the arrow pointing away from the joint), the vertical component, F_y, of force A must be:

$$37.5 - 15 - 15 + F_y = 0$$
$$F_y = -7.5 \text{ kips}$$

The number is negative, so the assumption that the member is in tension was wrong. It is in compression. Draw a free-body diagram of member A.

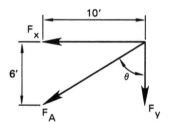

$$\tan \theta = \frac{10}{6}$$
$$\theta = 59 \text{ degrees}$$
$$F_y = F_A \cos \theta$$
$$= \frac{7.5}{\cos 59}$$
$$F_A = 14.56 \text{ kips (compression)}$$

This problem can also be solved using the method of sections, but it is more involved because you first have to find the force in the lower chord using the summation of moments being zero and then find the force in

member A. In addition, extra trigonometry is involved
to find the length of moment arms.

8. D is correct.

9. B is correct.

While any of the methods could be used, the complex
geometry would make the methods of joints or sections
awkward and lengthy.

10. A is correct.

Draw a free-body diagram of the reaction point R_A.

The vertical component of F_{AB} must balance the reaction and the 5 kip load. It must be acting downward
toward the joint so it is in compression.

$$20 - 5 - F_y = 0$$
$$F_y = 15 \text{ kips}$$

$$F_y = F_{AB} \cos \theta$$
$$F_{AB} = \frac{15}{\cos 45}$$
$$= 21.2 \text{ kips}$$

6 SOIL AND FOUNDATIONS

1. B is correct.

Since the choices start with either III or V, you must first decide which of these is the most important. Providing a positive slope away from a building is always the correct thing to do and costs practically nothing if done before the building is constructed. However, since the question stated that groundwater was present, draining surface water away is unlikely to improve that situation. Therefore, the job is to keep the groundwater away from the foundation wall. The probable answer is now either B or D.

You must now choose between either I or IV as the next most important thing to do. Both choices would be good ones and help solve the problem, but since you have already done something to drain water from the walls, the slab can still be a trouble spot. The most likely choice is IV, to use gravel under the basement slab to relieve hydrostatic pressure against the underside of the slab. Since the remaining three steps seem reasonable, this leaves you with choice B as the best choice.

2. D is correct.

If the site is primarily silt and organic silt, none of the other choices is really possible so choice D is the only reasonable answer.

3. B is correct.

Formula 6.8 is used to find the total earth pressure, with the weight of the soil taken to be equivalent to a fluid weighing 30 pounds per cubic foot.

$$P = 1/2Wh^2$$
$$= 0.5(30)(9)^2$$
$$= 1215 \text{ pounds}$$

This pressure acts through the centroid of the pressure triangle or one-third from the base, which in this case coincides with the level of the lower grade.

4. C is correct.

The width of the footing is found by dividing the total load by the soil bearing pressure considering a one foot length of foundation. The loads are:

foundation wall	$4 \times 1 \times 150 = 600$ pounds
footing (assume 3-foot width)	$3 \times 0.67 \times 150 = 300$ pounds
soil (assume 3-foot width)	$3 \times 2 \times 100 = 600$ pounds
dead load	1000 pounds
live load	500 pounds
total	3000 pounds

$$\text{width} = \frac{3000}{1500}$$
$$= 2 \text{ feet}$$

Since a 3-foot width was assumed, the weight of the footing will be less so 2 feet is more than adequate.

5. C is correct.

It is important to remember that soil test logs are not part of the contract documents.

6. A is correct.

III is incorrect because the unified soil classification system is simply a system for designating various types of soils, not their capacities. V is incorrect because the bearing capacity of a particular soil type assumes that it is compacted.

7. A7, Proctor test, is correct.

Specifications refer to the percentage of Proctor density that a fill should be compacted to. This optimum relationship between the density of the fill and its moisture content is determined by the Proctor test.

8. A4, gravels, is correct.

Gravels have the highest bearing capacity.

9. A9, repose, is correct.

You would need to know the angle of repose to determine the maximum slope from one level to the next.

10. A3, grade beam, is correct.

The use of a grade beam with a void under would prevent expansion of the bentonite from causing damage.

7 CONNECTIONS

1. B is correct.

Although it is important that washers be used, the exact type is not as important as the other factors. The length of the bold does affect the allowable strength, as shown in Table 7.1, so the thickness of the members is important.

2. B2, shear plate, is correct.

Both split ring connectors and shear plates would be appropriate for the higher joint loads that would probably be present in a long truss. For a temporary building, however, the shear plate would provide for easier disassembly.

3. A5, Hankinson formula, is correct.

The Hankinson formula gives the designer the method to determine the allowable loads when wood members are not perpendicular or parallel to each other.

4. A4, fillet, is correct.

A fillet weld is the simplest, most commonly used weld for overlapping sections. A plug weld could be used, but it requires punching or drilling the plates in preparation for the weld.

5. A6, headed anchor stud, is correct.

Headed anchor studs are typically used as shear connectors for steel and concrete composite sections.

6. D is correct.

The maximum size of a fillet weld for 1/4-inch thick material is 3/16 inch. From Table 7.6, the allowable load per inch for this size weld made with E70 electrodes is 2.8 kips. The weld is on both sides, so the total capacity is:

$$2.8 \times 6 \times 2 = 33.6 \text{ kips}$$

However, the allowable tensile load on the single bar must be checked. From Formula 7.5, the allowable stress is:

$$0.60 \times 36 = 21.6 \text{ ksi}$$

The area of the bar is:

$$0.25 \times 6 = 1.5 \text{ square inches}$$

The total allowable load is:

$$1.5 \times 21.6 = 32.4 \text{ kips}$$

Since this is less than the allowable load on the welds, this value governs.

7. C is correct.

8. C is correct.

Using Table 7.1, look under the 5/8 column. For single shear joints, the length of the bolt is that in the thinner member so use 1 1/2 inches. The loading is parallel to the grain, so the allowable load on one bolt is 590 pounds. Four bolts makes the allowable load

$$590 \times 4 = 2360 \text{ pounds}$$

9. A is correct.

For any joint subject to vibration or reversal of loads, slip-critical, high-strength bolts must be used. This fact makes the type of hole or direction of load irrelevant to the question.

10. D is correct.

Any nail or screw attachment to the end grain is not allowed by building codes, so II must be avoided. Although attachment to side grain is possible, it is a weak joint and should be avoided. A bolted joint perpendicular to the grain is not as strong as one parallel to grain but need not be avoided. There is nothing wrong with nail penetration over the usual value of 7 diameters, nor is a metal plate detrimental to a bolted connection.

8 BUILDING CODE REQUIREMENTS ON STRUCTURAL DESIGN

1. A is correct.

Choice B is incorrect because wind loads must be used if they result in higher stresses than those from earthquakes regardless of the earthquake zone. Choice C is incorrect because the height is 30 feet. Choice D is incorrect because other design methods can be approved by the local building official if the designer shows that equivalent ductility and energy absorption can be provided.

2. C is correct.

Refer to equations 8.2 through 8.6.

3. B is correct.

I is incorrect because all foundation sills must be treated or made of redwood. II is incorrect because fire stops are required anywhere in vertical openings that could afford passage of fire. IV is incorrect because 1/2 inch is required all around.

4. A3, concrete cover, is correct.

5. A4, deflection criteria, is correct.

6. A7, minimum tensile stress, is correct.

7. B0, size factor, is correct.

Although the beam's allowable stress would also be modified by a duration of load factor, there is not enough information given in the question to tell what that might be. Since the 14-inch depth is over the 12-inch limit, this is a better answer.

8. D is correct.

For snow loading, allowable stresses for wood may be increased by 15 percent.

$$1450 \times 1.15 = 1668 \text{ psi allowable}$$

The section modulus is $S = M/f$.

$$S = \frac{4518(12)}{1668}$$
$$= 32.5 \text{ in}^3$$

The moment must be converted to inch-pounds by multiplying the moment by 12.

9. A is correct.

When seismic loads are calculated, they must always be at full value.

10. C is correct.

II is incorrect because live loads cannot be reduced in places of assembly. IV is incorrect because roofs must be greater than 20 degrees, which is 4.37 in 12.

17-13

9 WOOD CONSTRUCTION

1. C is correct.

2. C is correct.

For snow loading, the allowable stresses may be increased 15 percent. Using the maximum moment, the required section modulus is:

$$S = \frac{1992(12)}{1050(1.15)}$$
$$= 19.80 \text{ in}^3$$

Looking in Table 9.1, a 2 × 10 joist has a section modulus of 21.391 so this will work for bending.

Next, check for horizontal shear. Take the worst case of vertical shear which is the −900 pounds found on the shear diagram. You can neglect the loads within a distance from the support equal to the depth of the member, so the vertical shear to be used in the calculation is:

$$V = 900 - [(9.25/12) \times 173]$$
$$= 767 \text{ pounds}$$

Using formula 9.3 to find the actual horizontal shear,

$$F_v = \frac{3V}{2bd}$$
$$= \frac{3}{2} \times \frac{767}{2(1.5)(9.25)}$$
$$= 82.9 \text{ psi}$$

The allowable horizontal shear of 75 psi can also be increased by 15 percent for snow loading, so the allowable stress is:

$$F_v = 75 \times 1.15 = 86.25 \text{ psi}$$

Since this is more than the actual, a 2 × 10 joist will work.

3. A is correct.

4. A3, compression perpendicular to the grain, is correct.

5. A1, buckling length factor, is correct.

B2, slenderness ratio, would also be used, but the question implies an unusual end condition.

6. B1, size categories, is correct.

7. A is correct.

III is incorrect because multiple member values apply to extreme fiber in bending stresses only. V is incorrect because duration of loading affects the allowable increase in stresses, not the initial selection of values from the tables.

8. B is correct.

If the column has its base fixed in both translation and rotation and the top fixed in translation but free to rotate, the effective buckling length factor, K_e, is 0.80 as shown in Figure 9.2. Multiplying 0.80 by 12 feet gives 9.6 feet.

9. B is correct.

Different values of F_b must be used to find the section modulus depending on whether you use a 4-inch wide beam or a 6-inch wide beam. For a 6-inch wide beam, find the F_v value from Table 9.2 under beams and stringers, and find the section modulus required.

$$S = \frac{8200(12)}{1550}$$
$$= 63.48 \text{ in}^3$$

From Table 9.1, a 6 × 10 has a section modulus of 82.729 with an area of 52.25 square inches.

For a 4-inch wide beam,

$$S = \frac{8200(12)}{1800}$$
$$= 54.67$$

From Table 9.1, a 4 × 12 has a section modulus of 73.828 with an area of 39.373 square inches. Because there is less area in the 4 × 12 beam, it would be more economical.

10. D is the correct answer.

D is incorrect because beams can be notched up to one-fourth of their depth at the ends. The one-sixth limitation is for notches outside the middle third of the span.

10   STEEL CONSTRUCTION

1. B5, wide flanges, is correct.

Wide flanges are used because they have similar moments of inertia about both axes, and are therefore efficient in resisting buckling in both directions.

2. B3, slenderness ratio, is correct.

3. A7, ductility, is correct.

4. D is correct.

First, find the bending moment that must be resisted by the beam. From Table 4.12, the equation is:

$$M = \frac{PL}{4}$$
$$= \frac{12(16)}{4}$$
$$= 48 \text{ kip-feet}$$

Next, find the required section modulus:

$$S = \frac{M}{F_b}$$
$$= \frac{48(12)}{24}$$
$$= 24 \text{ in}^3$$

From Table 10.4, the most economical section is a 12×22 with a section modulus of 25.4 in^3. This does not include the weight of the beam, which would be negligible since it would only add another 0.7 kip-feet of moment.

5. C is correct.

First, convert loads per square foot to loads per linear foot (plf) of joist:

live load	$80 \times 2.5 = 200$
dead load	$40 \times 2.5 = 100$
total load	300 plf

Look in Table 10.9 across the row marked 27-foot span. There is an 18K4 that will support a total load of 303 plf, but only 198 plf of live load at 1/360 deflection. An 18K5 will meet both requirements. There is also a 20K4 that will support 339 plf total load and 247 plf

live load. Although the two are very similar in weight, the 20K4 weighs 0.1 pound less per foot (7.6) than the 18K5 so the 20K4 is the better choice.

6. A is correct.

Look in Table 10.5 to find the total allowable load of 47 kips. The allowable load per foot is:

$$\frac{47}{22} = 2.1 \text{ kips per foot}$$

The maximum unsupported length, L_c, equals 8.5 feet.

7. B is correct.

From Figure 10.2, the k value is 0.80 so the KL value is:

$$KL = 0.80 \times 10$$
$$= 8.0$$

Using the nearest whole number of 8 to enter Table 10.7, read across under the 50 column of a W 12×50 and read a maximum load of 360 kips.

8. B is correct.

Although joists produced by members of the SJI must conform to certain performance specifications, the exact configuration of such things as top and bottom chord shape and web layout may vary slightly from one manufacturer to another.

9. B is correct.

First, find the deflection under maximum load shown in Table 10.5. Looking across the row for a 13-foot span, the deflection is 0.35 inches. The actual deflection is this amount multiplied by the ratio of the design load, 65 kips, to the maximum allowable load of 71 kips shown in Table 10.5 under the W 12×45 column.

$$\Delta = \frac{(0.35)(65)}{71}$$
$$= 0.32 \text{ inches}$$

10. D is correct.

I is incorrect because shear stresses are not distributed evenly and are zero at the extreme fibers. III is incorrect because shear is most significant for short, heavily loaded beams or those with heavy loads near the supports.

11 CONCRETE CONSTRUCTION

1. C is correct.

Air-entraining agents improve concrete's resistance to freezing and thawing cycles, so its use in a cold northern climate would be justified. If the concrete was placed during the winter months, you may want to consider an accelerator so cold-weather protection would be minimized.

2. B is correct.

As an overhanging beam, there is tension (negative moment) in the top portion of the overhang and across the left support, and tension (positive moment) in the bottom portion of the span between the two supports. Therefore, tension reinforcement would be needed in these two locations. Since the span between the supports is longer than the overhang, additional steel would probably also be needed here.

Although the steel placement in choice A would probably work, it shows extra steel not likely required. Since the question asks for primary steel, any compression rebars needed are not included in these diagrams.

The placement shown in choice D is close, but the bottom steel does not extend across the left support.

3. C is correct.

The minimum percentage of steel is found with the formula:

$$p = \frac{200}{f_y} = \frac{200}{60,000} = 0.0033$$

(Grade 60 steel means the yield point is 60,000 psi.)

The maximum percentage by code is 0.75 of the steel required for a balanced design, or $0.75(0.0285) = 0.0214$.

To find the area of the steel, the percentages must be multiplied by the width of the beam by the effective depth of the beam, or 15 inches by 21 1/2 inches = 322.5 in^2

$$A(\text{min.}) = 0.0033(322.5) = 1.06 \text{ in}^2$$
$$A(\text{max.}) = 0.0214(322.5) = 6.90 \text{ in}^2$$

4. C is correct.

The typical water-cement ratio is from 0.35 to 0.40 for concrete mixes without plasticizers or other admixtures.

Water is needed for workability but to allow the concrete to cure by chemical process, not simply by drying.

5. A is correct.

Although actual diameters may vary from one mill to another, the standard designation is the number in eighths of an inch or in this case 10/8 inch or 1 1/4 inch.

6. D is correct.

I is not correct because the development length also depends on the strength of the concrete. IV is not correct because compression steel is often used to provide support for stirrups before the concrete is poured and to decrease the long-term deflection of the beam.

7. A1, compaction, is correct.

Other likely answers for this question are moisture (B0) and temperature (B5). However, these are usually factors that are more important during curing of the concrete rather than placing.

8. B7, strength reduction factor, is correct.

The strength reduction factor accounts for such uncertainties as calculation accuracy, quality control of concrete, the importance of various types of structural members, and other factors. The load factor (a possible answer) accounts for the uncertainty in loads likely to be placed on the concrete member.

9. A3, continuity, is correct.

Since concrete is a plastic material and many members are poured at the same time, continuity is an inherent property of the material. This causes, for example, a decrease in the maximum bending moment in a beam compared with the same span with a simply supported beam. Continuous slabs and beams are also more efficient than a slab resting on a beam.

10. A6, cylinder test, is correct.

The cylinder test measures the strength of the concrete (one of the most important aspects of quality) actually being placed. The slump test, a possible answer, primarily measures the workability of the concrete. The core cylinder test measures the strength of concrete, but only after it is cured.

12 WALL CONSTRUCTION

1. A5, expansion joint, is correct.

Although an exterior wood panel system should be covered with a water-repellent material, there should still be provisions made for the possible swelling and shrinkage of the wood.

2. B5, veneered wall, is correct.

A wythe of masonry attached to a non-masonry wall is called a veneer wall.

3. A0, arch action, is correct.

4. C is correct.

If a weaker construction, such as a metal curtain wall, spanned across a point of maximum concentration, the movement would most likely damage the weaker material.

5. A is correct.

II is incorrect because the limit is 25 times the thickness. III is incorrect because eccentricity is always an important variable. The load must fall within the middle third of the wall. V is incorrect because the percentages change when bar sizes exceed #5s.

6. D is correct.

Masonry is a compression material with very little strength in tension or bending. A pure masonry building would reflect this fact, so openings would be spanned with arches which can carry the load from above without using other, non-masonry materials.

7. C is correct.

While any of these systems would work, the wood systems should be favored due to their ease of construction and the fact that most contractors, skilled or unskilled, can erect a functional wall with a minimum of problems. Of the two, the balloon frame is preferable because it will shrink less than the platform frame. Since stucco is prone to cracking, this is an important concern.

8. A is the correct answer.

The spacing cannot exceed 4 feet.

9. B is correct.

The maximum ratio of unsupported height to thickness of a cavity wall is 18, so the minimum sum of the nominal widths of wythes is:

$$\frac{14 \times 12}{18} = 9.33$$

Rounding up to 10 inches, one 4-inch block and one 6-inch block will be sufficient. The air space is not included in the thickness.

10. B is correct.

III is incorrect because only the net thickness is important, regardless of the number of wythes. VI is incorrect because joint reinforcement is required for flexural strength and resistance to lateral loads.

13   LATERAL FORCES—WIND

1. B4, trussed tube, is correct.

Although the bracing on the exterior of the John Hancock Building is in the shape of an X, it works in conjunction with the remainder of the tube framing and it spans between several floors which is the mark of a trussed tube.

2. A9, normal force method, is correct.

3. A1, bent, is correct.

4. D is correct.

Buildings over 400 feet high always require special design study and wind tunnel testing.

5. B is correct.

From the map in Figure 13.2, the wind speed is 70 mph. From Table 13.3, the corresponding q_s value is 12.6 psf. From Table 13.1, the highest C_e value is 0.84 for that portion at 40 feet using Exposure B. From Table 13.2, the pressure coefficient, C_q, is 1.3 using Method 2 for buildings 40 feet high. The importance factor is 1.15 since this is a hospital (from Table 14.5). Using formula 13.1, the pressure is:

$$P = (0.84)(1.3)(12.6)(1.15)$$
$$= 15.8 \text{ psf}$$

6. C is correct.

Look in Table 13.2. Sheathing and roofing are elements or components, not in areas of discontinuity, so part 2 of the table is used. Roof elements of enclosed structures with slopes less than 9:12 have a pressure coefficient of 1.3 outward.

7. C is correct.

First, divide the total load of 4600 pounds by the allowable load per nail:

$$\frac{4600}{82} = 56.1 \text{ nails (use 57 nails)}$$

The spacing must be the length in inches divided by the number of nails:

$$\frac{38(12)}{57} = 8 \text{ inches}$$

8. A is correct.

II is incorrect because the trussed tube is generally limited to steel because of the difficulty in forming diagonal concrete members and the weak performance of concrete in tension.

9. A is correct.

Table 13.1 (UBC Table 23-G) shows that the C_e factor includes a gust factor.

10. A is correct.

I is incorrect because wind stagnation pressure depends on the basic wind speed, which is the same regardless of the terrain. This is modified by the exposure factor which does change with terrain. III is incorrect because leeward pressure is only taken into account with Method 1. V is incorrect because the wind must be assumed to come from any direction, not just the prevailing direction.

14 LATERAL FORCES—EARTHQUAKES

1. B4, soft story, is correct.

While the framing of the building above would be very rigid, the discontinuity at the first floor would result in concentration of stresses at the second floor line where the columns connect with the rigid frame above.

2. A0, accelerograph, is correct.

Only this machine gives the necessary data for determining quantifiable information that can be used in the design of a structure.

3. A8, moment-resisting space frame, is correct.

4. C is correct.

Seattle is in zone 3, so $Z = 0.30$. The importance factor is 1.0. From Table 14.1 the R_w factor is 6. The S factor is 1.2 because the soil profile is S_2. Knowing the period is 0.19, the C factor can be calculated from

$$C = \frac{1.25S}{T^{2/3}}$$
$$= \frac{1.25(1.2)}{(0.19)^{2/3}}$$
$$= 4.54$$

Because 2.75 is the maximum value required for C, use this.

The shear is therefore

$$V = \frac{ZIC}{R_w}W$$
$$= \frac{(0.30)(1.0)(2.75)}{6}6500$$
$$= 894 \text{ kips}$$

5. D is correct.

All of the choices listed are either irregular buildings or are specifically required to be designed using the dynamic lateral force procedure.

6. B is correct.

Choice B is an incorrect statement because, although flexible buildings have a longer period of vibration and hence less acceleration in earthquakes, a stiff, rigid building is better for resisting lateral forces from wind. Although concrete can be made ductile with proper reinforcing and could be used in seismic zone 3, steel is a more sensible first choice if there are no other mitigating factors to consider. Choice C is a correct statement because a large, concentrated mass near the top of a building is a weight irregularity and should be avoided whenever possible, especially in zones of moderate or high seismic activity.

7. D is correct.

I is incorrect because the hypocenter is the location of the fault. II is incorrect because vertical motion is usually not critical in designing buildings to withstand earthquakes.

8. A is correct.

Table 14.7 gives the C_p values for force factors for non-structural components. A bookcase would qualify as item #5.

9. B is the correct answer.

Choice A is correct because the height of the building affects the calculation of the period, which determines whether or not an extra force must be added to the roof level and therefore be deducted from the total base shear. Both choices C and D are correct because they are parts of the formula used to determine the distribution as given in formula 14.9 in Volume I.

10. C is correct.

II is an incorrect choice because the load created by the mass of the shear wall itself and its connection to the diaphragms must be checked. Bending stresses can be built up in the wall perpendicular to the load which can cause it to fail. III is correct because shear walls located at the perimeter of the building minimize torsion.

15 LONG SPAN STRUCTURES—ONE-WAY SYSTEMS

1. D is correct.

While all of these conditions might occur, the most critical one is deflection from dead loads, live loads, or long-term loads, which would place an excessive stress on the partition. This might cause cracking of finish materials in the best case and buckling of the partition in the worst case.

2. A0, camber, is correct.

3. A3, funicular, is correct.

Theoretically, the ideal is the funicular shape because the arch is only in compression. However, this happens for only one set of loads.

4. B5, Warren, is correct.

Refer to Figure 15.4 for truss types.

5. A is correct.

A is not a correct statement because the DLH series is only used for roof spans up to 144 feet long. Only the LH series is used for both floors and roofs.

6. C is correct.

All of the systems listed could span the 110 foot dimension and provide the required ceiling height. However, two considerations regarding pool areas like this are important: humidity and noise. In all cases, some type of acoustical treatment would be required, but some structural systems would make this easier to accomplish than others. Glue-laminated construction would be eliminated because of the humidity (although water-resistant glue can be used and the members otherwise protected) and because the span distance would require a rigid frame which would stretch the capability of this type of system.

Additionally, a rigid frame shape may not be appropriate for a competition pool. Pitched steel trusses would require a great deal of fabrication and protection from the humidity even though fire protection would not be required. Decking applied to the upper chords of the truss would give an acoustically workable shape, but may create an exterior shape in conflict with the rest of the building.

Deep, long-span joists would easily cover the distance, be quick and easy to erect, and offer a low-profile roof with provisions for drainage. Still, protection from humidity and awkward provisions for acoustical treatment would suggest using precast single T sections instead. The basic shape would create baffles to minimize sound reflections, and the large flat surfaces would accept many kinds of acoustical panels. In addition, humidity would be less of a problem, and precast would still have the advantage of quick erection and simple connections, so it would be an economical choice.

7. C is correct.

I and V are used for similar purposes. There must be some way to account for minor variation in fabrication and erection tolerances. Slotted holes are also sometimes used to allow a construction component to move in one direction while restraining it in the other two directions.

8. A is correct.

Camber is used to counteract the expected dead load of a structural member. Ponding is prevented by providing a positive slope to the roof.

9. D is correct.

The basic responsibility of the architect during construction is to make sure that construction is proceeding in accordance with the plans and specifications. This means that III, IV, and V are correct. In addition, with long-span structures, proper construction sequence is critical. This includes not overstressing entire members until all connections and the entire system is complete.

10. B is correct.

Flat steel trusses can normally span 300 feet. Deep, long-span joists are limited to 144 feet. Wood arches are limited to about 240 feet (although longer spans are possible). Prestressed Ts are good up to about 120 feet.

16   LONG SPAN STRUCTURES—TWO-WAY SYSTEMS

1. D is the correct answer.

D is an incorrect statement because it is the connections that are the most expensive part of a space frame. What makes a space frame economical is its light weight for the span distance and loads that can be carried.

2. C is correct.

Refer to Table 16.1 for the typical spans for these types of structures.

3. B is correct.

4. B5, the Schwedler dome, is correct.

5. B4, redundancy, is correct.

6. A0, anticlastic, is correct.

7. B1, pneumatic, is correct.

8. A is correct.

Stiffness is directly related to the strain, or deflection per unit length. Since there are only compression, tension, and shears in a dome, and since these are of small magnitude, there is little strain and consequently great stiffness.

9. A is correct.

II is incorrect because a dome is in compression above the line and tension below it. IV is incorrect because the tensile stress, or thrust, is inversely proportional to the sag. V is correct because a uniform load on a cable, like that of a roadway suspended from a bridge cable, results in the curve being parabolic. If there were no load, the shape would be a catenary curve.

10. C is correct.

Membranes are efficient structures because all the stress is in tension, so the material is used to its fullest. Although answers B and D are correct, they are not the primary reason why a membrane is a good structure. Answer A may or may not be true, depending on the particular configuration of the membrane layout.

BIBLIOGRAPHY

GENERAL STRUCTURAL TECHNOLOGY

Ambrose, James. *Building Structures Primer.* New York, NY: John Wiley and Sons, Inc., 1981.

Ambrose, James. *Simplified Design of Building Structures*, 2nd ed. New York, NY: John Wiley and Sons, Inc., 1986.

Benjamin, B. S. *Structures for Architects*, 2nd ed. New York, NY: Van Nostrand Reinhold Company, 1984.

Croxton, P. C. L., and Martin, L. H. *Solving Problems in Structures*, Vol. 1, New York, NY: John Wiley and Sons, Inc., 1987.

Engel, I. *Structural Principles.* Englewood Cliffs, NJ: Prentice-Hall, Inc., 1984.

International Conference of Building Officials. *Uniform Building Code.* Whittier, CA: International Conference of Building Officials, 1991.

Parker, Harry. *Simplified Mechanics and Strength of Materials*, 3rd ed. New York, NY: John Wiley and Sons, Inc., 1977.

Parker, Harry, and Ambrose, James. *Simplified Engineering for Architects and Builders*, 6th ed. New York, NY: John Wiley and Sons, Inc., 1984.

Salvadori, Mario, and Heller, Robert. *Structure in Architecture*, 3rd ed. Englewood Cliffs, NJ: Prentice-Hall, Inc., 1986.

Vossoughi, Jafar. *Statistics for Architects.* New York, NY: Van Nostrand Reinhold, 1986.

White, Richard N., and Salmon, Charles G. *Building Structural Design Handbook.* New York, NY: John Wiley and Sons, Inc., 1987.

SOIL AND FOUNDATIONS

Ambrose, James. *Simplified Design of Building Foundations.* New York, NY: John Wiley and Sons, Inc., 1981.

WOOD STRUCTURES

American Institute of Timber Construction. *Timber Construction Manual*, 3rd ed. New York, NY: John Wiley & Sons, Inc., 1986.

Breyer, Donald E. *Design of Wood Structures*, 2nd ed. New York, NY: McGraw-Hill, 1980.

National Forest Products Association. *Wood Structural Design Data: A Manual for Architects, Builders, Engineers, and Others Concerned with Wood Construction.* Washington, DC: National Forest Products Association, 1986.

Parker, Harry. *Simplified Design of Structural Wood*, 3rd ed. New York, NY: John Wiley and Sons, Inc., 1979.

STEEL STRUCTURES

American Institute of Steel Construction. *Manual of Steel Construction*, 9th ed. New York, NY: American Institute of Steel Construction.

Amon, Rene. *Steel Design for Engineers and Architects.* New York, NY: Van Nostrand Reinhold Company, 1982.

Cooper, Sol E. *Designing Steel Structures: Methods and Cases.* Englewood Cliffs, NJ: Prentice-Hall, Inc., 1985.

Crawley, Stanley W. *Steel Buildings: Analysis and Design.* New York, NY: John Wiley and Sons, Inc., 1984.

Parker, Harry. *Simplified Design of Structural Steel*, 5th ed. New York, NY: John Wiley and Sons, Inc., 1983.

CONCRETE AND MASONRY STRUCTURES

Amrhein, J. E. *Reinforced Masonry Engineering Handbook*, 4th ed. Los Angeles, CA: Masonry Institute of America, 1983.

Fling, Russell S. *Practical Design of Reinforced Concrete.* New York, NY: John Wiley and Sons, Inc., 1987.

Nilson, Arthur H., and Winter, George. *Design of Concrete Structures.* New York, NY: McGraw-Hill, 1986.

Parker, Harry. *Simplified Design of Reinforced Concrete*, 5th ed. New York, NY: John Wiley and Sons, Inc., 1984.

LATERAL FORCES

Ambrose, James, and Vergun, Dimitry. *Design for Lateral Forces.* New York, NY. John Wiley and Sons, Inc., 1987.

Arnold, Christopher, and Reitherman, Robert. *Building Configuration and Seismic Design*. New York, NY: John Wiley and Sons, Inc., 1982.

Crawley, Stanley W., Ward, Delbert B., and Arnold, Christopher. *The Architect's Study Guide to Seismic and Lateral Loads in Architectural Design*. Washington, DC: The American Institute of Architects, 1987.

Green, Norman B. *Earthquake Resistant Building Design and Construction*, 3rd ed. New York, NY: Elsevier, 1987.

Melaragno, Michele. *Wind in Architectural and Environmental Design*. New York, NY: Van Nostrand Reinhold Company, 1982.

Stratta, James L. *Manual of Seismic Design*. Englewood Cliffs, NJ: Prentice-Hall, Inc., 1987.

Walabayashi, Minoru. *Design of Earthquake-Resistant Buildings*. New York, NY: McGraw-Hill, 1986.

LONG SPAN

Menzies, John, and Currie, Richard. *Structural Defects in Buildings with Long-span Roofs*. Kensington, MD: Neal Fitz-Simons, n.d.

Schueller, Wolfgang. *Horizontal-span Building Structures*. New York, NY: John Wiley and Sons, Inc., 1982.

Steel Joist Institute. *Standard Specifications, Load, and Weight Tables*. Myrtle Beach, SC: Steel Joist Institute, 1986.

INDEX

hyperbolic paraboloid, 1-10, 16-5
hypocenter, 14-2

I

I-beams, American Standard, 10-3
impact load, 2-5
importance factor, for seismic design, 14-14
inertia, moment of, 3-6, 4-9, 4-10
inflatable structures, 1-11

J

John Hancock Building, 1-11, 13-11
joints:
    construction, 12-10
    method of, 5-3
    through-building expansion, 12-10
    through-wall expansion, 12-10
    types in exterior walls, 12-10
    welded, 7-15
joist, 1-1, 9-10
    concrete, 1-3
    girders, 15-4, 15-5
    open-web steel, 1-2, 1-3, 5-1,
      10-15, 10-17, 15-4
    tables, 9-10

K

K values, of columns, 4-11
keyed sections, 7-17
knee bracing, 13-11

L

lag screws, 7-4
lamella arches, 16-5
laminated beams, 1-2
lateral force distribution, 13-8
lateral force, due to wind, 13-8
lateral loads, 2-4, 8-2
lateral support:
    in wood beams, 9-8
    of open-web steel joists, 10-17
    of steel beams, 10-4
lift slab construction, 1-3
limit, elastic, 14-5
lines, meridian, 16-3
lintel, 12-5
live load reduction, 2-2
live load, 1-11, 2-2, 8-1, 9-7
load combinations
    for design, 8-1
    for seismic design, 14-18
    for wind design, 13-7
loads, 1-11
    combination, 2-4
    concentrated, 4-3, 8-2
    connections for lateral, 13-14
    dead, 1-11, 2-1, 8-2, 9-7
    dynamic, 2-5
    earthquake, 2-5, 8-2

impact, 2-6
    lateral, 2-4, 8-2
    live, 1-11, 2-2, 8-1, 9-7
    method of calculating, 8-1
    on columns, 4-9
    on exterior walls, 12-8
    on truss members, 5-3
    on wood connectors, 7-1
    oscillating, 13-2
    resonant, 2-5, 13-2
    seismic, 8-2, 12-9
    snow, 2-2, 8-2
    soil, 2-6
    symmetry in resisting lateral, 14-7
    temperature-induced, 2-6
    uniformly distributed, 4-3
    wind, 2-4, 8-2, 12-9
loadbearing walls, 12-1
loading, 8-1
log, boring, 6-1, 6-3
long span structures:
    acoustics of, 15-9
    economy of, 15-8
    erection of, 15-9
    exterior walls in, 15-10
    fire protection of, 15-9
long span system selection, 15-7
low-lift grouting, 12-4
lumber (see also wood), 9-1
    design values, 9-3
    grading, 9-1
    sizes, 9-1
    structural, 9-1

M

Manual of Steel Construction, 4-2, 4-9, 5-2, 7-7
masonry walls, 12-1, 12-8
masonry walls, types, 12-2
masonry, grouted, 12-4
masonry, hollow unit, 12-3
masonry, openings in, 12-4
material and labor, 1-13
measurement, wind, 13-2
members, wide flange, 10-3
membranes, 16-6
meridian lines, 16-3
metal studs, 12-6
method:
    dynamic, 14-2
    dynamic analysis, 14-2
    dynamic lateral force procedure, 14-2
    graphic, 5-3
    normal force, 13-4
    of joints, 5-3
    of sections, 5-3, 5-5
    projected area, 13-6
    static, 14-2
    static analysis, 2-6
    static lateral force procedure, 14-2
    strength, 11-7
    strength design, 11-1
    working stress, 11-1
Modified Mercalli Intensity scale, 14-3
modulus of elasticity, 3-4, 4-9
modulus, section, 3-8, 4-2
moisture, 12-10
moisture content, 9-3
moment, 3-4, 4-6
    bending, 4-2, 9-3
    overturning, 13-14, 14-19
    statical, 3-6, 4-2